Roald
Amundsen

Roald Amundsen

TOR BOMANN-LARSEN

FOREWORD BY PEN HADOW

TRANSLATED BY INGRID CHRISTOPHERSEN

The History Press

First published in Norway in 1995 by Cappelen
First published in English in the United Kingdom in 2006 by Sutton Publishing Ltd
This edition published in 2011 by The History Press

The History Press
The Mill, Brimscombe Port
Stroud, Gloucestershire, GL5 2QG
www.thehistorypress.co.uk

This translation was first published with the financial support of NORLA.

British Library Cataloguing in Publication Data
A catalogue record for this book is available from the British Library.

ISBN 978 0 7509 4344 4

Printed in the EU for The History Press.

Contents

List of Illustrations

1. Roald Amundsen's birthplace at the mouth of the River Glomma.
2. The polar explorer's father, Jens Ingebrigt Amundsen (1820–86).
3. The polar explorer's mother, Gustava Amundsen, née Sahlquist (1837–93).
4. The legendary nanny, Betty, with Leon's daughter on her knee, in 1906.
5. Jens Ole Antonius 'Tonni' Amundsen, aged about 15.
6. Gustav Sahlquist 'Busken' Amundsen, aged about 13.
7. Leon Henry Benham Amundsen, aged about 11.
8. Roald Engelbregt Gravning Amundsen, aged about 9.
9. The Greenland explorer Eivind Astrup, who died at a young age.
10. Dr Fridtjof Nansen in his study at Polhøgda.
11. Roald Amundsen and Frederick Cook on a camping trip in the Antarctic.
12. Roald Amundsen and Frederick Cook before going their separate ways.
13. The polar explorer's friends in Tromsø, Gudrun and Fritz Zapffe.
14. Roald, Gustav and Leon Amundsen and Godfred Hansen in *Gjøa*'s cabin.
15. Gjøahavn – Gjøa harbour.
16. 'The first sledge trip'.
17. The first Christmas in a foreign harbour.
18. Gustav J. Wiik (1878–1906) in the 'Magnetic Villa'.
19. The polar explorer in front of the cabin's revised decorations, following their return to civilisation.
20. The *Gjøa* crew await the King after their homecoming.
21. *Fram*, seen in Hvalbukta, Whale Bay, was enlarged and rebuilt many times.
22. Eva and Fridtjof Nansen in front of the fireplace at Polhøgda, Polar Heights.
23. Herman Gade welcomes Roald Amundsen to Christmas celebrations in Chicago, 1907.
24. The Uranienborg villa, with flagpole and bathhouse.

Foreword

As December 2011 is the centenary of him becoming the first person to reach the South Pole, it is perhaps especially timely to reflect upon the character, endeavours and continuing influence of the most successful, though not necessarily the most liked, polar explorer of all time – the Norwegian, Roald Amundsen. Most of us achieve little. A few, by standing on the shoulders of giants, achieve something more. But occasionally a giant roams the Earth, and Roald Amundsen was one such giant.

However, as Tor Bomann-Larsen peels back the layers Amundsen and his supporters deliberately put in place to shield his private life from scrutiny, clues start to surface as to why and how Amundsen took on the most extreme challenges facing polar exploration – and generally succeeded where so many others had failed. More than any other person in polar history, he pushed back the known boundaries of the world's highest latitudes. Bomann-Larsen reveals a troubled, if not tortured, man behind the scenes, both at home and 'at work', which inevitably compromises his heroic reputation. It seems he was all too human.

That he beat Captain Robert Scott to the South Pole is widely known. That he was also the first to reach the North Pole – albeit by air – is not. His complete list of polar achievements never has been, indeed never can be, surpassed.

He served on the ship *Belgica* when it endured the first over-wintering by an expedition in the sea ice off Antarctica (1897–9). He commanded *Gjoa* to make the first single-ship voyage through the North West Passage (1903–6), and established the North Magnetic Pole had a new position since Ross's expedition of 1831 – and in so doing enabled a major scientific discovery about terrestrial magnetism. He led the first team to the South Geographic Pole (1911–12) using dog-teams, arriving just thirty-five days ahead of Scott's man-hauling team. Commanding *Maud*, he made the third voyage in history through the North East Passage, now known as the Northern Sea Route (1918–21), and thereby became the first to have circumnavigated the Arctic Ocean. In an attempt to reach the Pole in 1925, he made the northernmost flight by aircraft to 87°44' North – and then miraculously escaped from an impossible situation 'on the ice'. He was

almost certainly the first to reach the North Geographic Pole in 1926 – with the
Italian Umberto Nobile. Their flight to the Pole from Spitsbergen in the airship
Norge then continued south until the two men reached the Alaskan coast, thereby
also securing the first crossing of the Arctic Ocean – and by its longest axis –
from Europe to America.

Amundsen did it all. He pioneered new routes, made scientific discoveries
and flew flags at both Poles for his country. He travelled on foot, in ships and
by aircraft. He was a pioneering skier, user of dog-teams and ship's Master,
constantly exploiting and combining Inuit craft with emerging new tech-
nologies and knowledge to break new ground. He once described his life as a
'constant journey towards the final destination'. The formidable scale of these
achievements are such that his 1,000-mile plus round-trip with dog-teams over
the Brooks Range mountains to the nearest telegraph station at Fort Egbert near
Eagle City, Alaska, simply to report *Gjoa*'s successful exit from the North West
Passage – while his ship was temporarily locked into the Arctic Ocean sea ice – is
one of many excursions rarely reported or known about.

Following his trans-Arctic Ocean flight he retired from exploration. But while
being flown North as part of a multi-national rescue mission to recover the
crew of Nobile's new airship, *Italia*, which had crashed on its return from the
North Pole, his overloaded plane disappeared without trace on 18 June 1928.
His body was never found. However, Amundsen had already become one of the
world's most famous explorers because he was responsible for 'filling in' the
remaining, and most intriguing and challenging, pieces of the jigsaw – the Poles.
The attainment of the Poles completed the macro-mapping of the world's major
surface geophysical features.

The legacy of Amundsen's prolific endeavours lives on in Norwegian national
culture, and through the activities of the adventurers and explorers, geographers
and earth system scientists now operating in the world's cryospheric regions.
The Amundsen-Scott South Pole Station at 90° South, the Amundsen Sea off
the Antarctic coast, the Amundsen Glacier in the Antarctic interior, and even the
Amundsen Crater (which covers the Moon's South Pole) to name but a few, all
bear witness to the global impact of his achievements.

As the ultimate polar explorer-achiever, perhaps Amundsen should be allowed
the final, if pointed, words on the secret to his success: 'I may say that this is the
greatest factor – the way in which the expedition is equipped – the way in which
every difficulty is foreseen, and precautions taken for meeting or avoiding it.
Victory awaits him who has everything in order – luck people call it. Defeat is
certain for him who has neglected to take the necessary precautions in time; this
is called bad luck.'

Pen Hadow

PREFACE

Roald Amundsen Country

When Fridtjof Nansen inaugurated modern Norwegian polar exploration by stepping ashore on the east coast of Greenland he envisaged the possibility of discovering an ice-free and fertile interior; by the time he unclipped his skis on the west coast he had established with certainty that the continent consisted of ice, ice and nothing but ice. In like manner does the explorer challenge our old charts and received wisdom. He is a seeker after truth much as the writer of history, rather than the unraveller of a biography which moves between the interior and exterior landscape, on the borderline between geography and psychology.

'Feats in the polar regions must be interpreted in the light of the explorer's life,' Roald Amundsen wrote in his memoirs. He acknowledged that polar exploration was also a moral discipline and that human character might be a more important criterion than kilometres and latitudes. It does not follow that he made conditions easy for whoever would come to write his biography.

Roald Amundsen searched after the earth's best kept secrets. But while he uncovered unknown territory, he laid a smokescreen over his own life. Numerous charts can tell us *where* the polar explorer travelled. But the question remains: *Who* was Roald Amundsen?

No one knows the character of an island or a continent before he goes ashore. The following pages will try and uncover, from the haze of oblivion and the fog of myth, the legendary, but until now undiscovered, Roald Amundsen country.

Tor Bomann-Larsen
Drammen

Acknowledgements

I owe a huge debt of gratitude to all the following institutions and individuals for their contributions, and for the trust and generosity they have shown me regarding my work on Roald Amundsen's biography.

Unfortunately, I cannot name everyone who has helped me in this work, but I would like to mention the following: Oddvar Vasstveit and his colleagues at Oslo University Manuscript Collection; the historian Susan Barr at the Norwegian Polar Institute and her colleagues at the Institute's departments in Oslo, Longyearbyen and Ny-Ålesund; Randi Eriksen at Roald Amundsen's home at Svartskog and the chairman of the Supervisory Committee Olav Orheim; Ragnhild Bilet at the Roald Amundsen Centre in Fredrikstad; Arne Pedersen at the Norwegian Film Institute; Gertrude Nobile, Museo Storico-Aeronautica Militare, Rome; Melanie Wisner, Houghton Reading Room, Harvard University, Cambridge, Massachusetts; Didrik Behrens, Tønsberg; Erling Kagge, Oslo; Jean Pierre Peterson, Paris; Rosellen Lillegraven, Juneau; Kathie Harley, Wasilla; Nina Bryn Bieri, the French Chamber of Commerce, Paris; Carsten Carlsen, Buenos Aires; Consul Egill Raae, Rouen; Geir Sørensen, the Ministry of Foreign Affairs, Oslo; Eugene D. Wadsworth, New York.

In addition, my thanks go to Alaska State Library; the Museum on Svalbard; the Royal Automobile Club, London; for access to information from the Public Record Office, including regional state archives in Oslo and Trondheim; to the publishing houses Gyldendal and Aschhoug; and to the Information Service at the American Embassy in Oslo.

During my extensive researches I have relied on the efforts of Åse Ytreland and Hilde Diesen. *Aftenposten* and the journalist Lars-Ludvig Røed generously made my journeys to London and Kings Bay possible.

I would like to thank Stig Andersen, Hilde Diesen and psychiatrist Finn Skårderud for their invaluable advice. In closing I would like to thank my publishers Cappelen for the cooperation that has been necessary with a book which has required input from many sources other than the author. Finally, I would like to thank my editor Anders Heger for his unfailing support.

PHOTOGRAPHS AND PICTURE CREDITS

The photographs have been lent to me by the publishing companies Gyldendal, Aschehoug and Cappelen, by the Roald Amundsen Centre and by the National Library of Norway. In addition the following have kindly contributed photographs: Berit Brynhildsen, Egil Behrens, Patricia Clark, Ole Fladstad, Valerie Farnes, Gunnar A. Lindaas, Alexander Nansen, Gertrude Nobile and Marianne Ræder.

(The numbers refer to pictures in the plate section)

Aschehoug: 1, 9, 16, 21, 26, 29, 69, 71
Cappelen: 10, 22, 32, 36, 79
Gyldendal: 2, 3, 12, 15, 17, 20, 25, 30, 37, 39, 44, 49, 50, 54, 56, 58, 59, 60, 61, 62, 63, 64, 65, 66, 70, 74, 75, 76
Nasjonalbibilioteket (National Library of Norway): 11, 13, 18, 19, 24, 27, 31, 34, 35, 40, 46, 47, 51, 52, 53, 55, 57, 68
Roald Amundsen Centre: 5, 6, 7, 8
Private Collections: 4, 14, 23, 33, 38, 41, 42, 48, 67, 77, 78

Part One: The Dream of the North West Passage

ONE

The Boy from the Sea

Had he caught sight of his own reflection? Or was he trying to swim? A small boy lay in the garden fountain; face down.

His older brothers were busy doing their own thing. It took time before they realised anything was amiss. The small boy was not yet 2 years old and could easily have drowned in a foot of water. At last someone came running. Betty, the nanny, rolled him over onto the grass. Roald Amundsen gurgled and returned to life.

That was the first time.

The scene took place in a large garden. Tall trees surrounded a low-built private house. The boys' home, 19 Uranienborgveien, lay immediately behind Christiania Castle, on the outskirts of Norway's capital. It must have been the spring of 1874. For the most part the castle stood empty. Christiania was a capital city without a regent, a city without power. Norway's territorial identity was somewhat hazy, adjoining as it did the infinite icy wastes and barren lands of the far north. The town was a permanent settlement wedged somewhere between the civilisation of Europe and the forbidding landscapes of primitive nomadic peoples: Lapps, Samoyeds and Eskimos.

Well-informed citizens of the world would have known that Norway was little more than a Swedish province, an untamed and demanding hunting ground for the Swedish kings of the house of Bernadotte. Norway had been passed to its neighbour Sweden during the turbulent reorganisation of the world map following the Napoleonic Wars. It was at this time that the country, sensationally, placed Jean Baptiste Bernadotte, a general in the army of the French emperor, on the ancient throne of Sweden. The general's grandson, Oscar II, now ruled Norway from Stockholm, the way the Danish kings had in their time ruled the country from Copenhagen.

The year that little Roald was fished out of the fountain, a certain tentative political and cultural awakening had taken hold of the inhabitants of this sparsely populated mountain country. On 17 May 1814 Norway had laid down a modern constitution outlining democratic aspirations. In 1884, by parliamentary decree, royal powers were to be reduced even further.

During times of national prosperity it is possible for even small nations to produce important personalities. From this northernmost province there emerged in time the poets Bjørnstjerne Bjørnson, Henrik Ibsen and Knut Hamsun, the composer Edvard Grieg and the painter Edvard Munch. In 1874, however, not one of them had yet made an impact on the international scene. Nor had the man who was destined to make the greatest impact of them all, the polar explorer Fridtjof Nansen.

Once upon a time, over a thousand years ago, the independent Norwegian kingdom had been a proud and flourishing power, its ferocious inhabitants carrying out audacious raids and conquering new land for their Viking warlords. As the nineteenth century unfolded this long dormant self-esteem began to reawaken under the heavy hand of the ruling Bernadottes. The mythical Norway, the native land of giants, was conjured up in the poet's words, the composer's music, and the painter's canvas. A dream of greatness grew in this insignificant nation. It was a dream that might flourish even in the poorest of crofts.

Roald Amundsen did not hail from a family of dreamers.

Like most of his compatriots he could trace his roots back to tiny plots of land and meagre circumstances. His ancestors had eked out a living on the windswept archipelago of Hvaler, towards the Swedish border. The family records go back to the seventeenth century, to the farm Huser on the island of Asmal. Roald Amundsen's great-grandfather, Amund Olsen, improved his lot and bought the old manor house Kåre-Hornes in Skjeberg, on the mainland. His grandfather Ole, who among other things engaged in trade on the Hvaler islands, took the name Amundsen. In 1803 he married Anne Kristine Gravning, who over the ensuing quarter century gave birth to twelve children, of whom Roald's father Jens Ingebrigt, born in 1820, was the fourth in a line of five boys. Honourable, well-built and above all dynamic, the Amundsen brothers all devoted themselves to the sea. As skippers and ship-owners they pooled their resources and their enterprises met with considerable success.

In 1858 the brothers bought a large farm which they divided up. Each of the five built his own home. In Hvidsten in the municipality of Borge, by the mouth of Norway's largest river, the Glomma, inside the Hvaler archipelago, the Amundsen clan established its base.

With time the brothers came to control a significant fleet. It might have numbered some twenty windjammers, both small and large, which traded in every commodity in every corner of the globe. In spite of also acquiring steamships, the ship-owning operations were gradually wound down in the 1890s when the surviving brothers were bearded old men and the era of the sailing ship was inexorably drawing to a close.

Trade has never been viewed as a highly moral occupation, neither then nor today. The captain of his own ship, Roald's father, Jens Amundsen, made good money in the 1850s during the Crimean War. In 1866 he transported 300 Chinese coolies to Havana. The conditions in the hold were such that the voyage narrowly escaped a bloody mutiny – Captain Amundsen himself was attacked with an axe. But not only did he succeed in escaping from the attempt on his life, he also quashed the rebellion. He crowned his triumph by forcing the Chinese to sentence their ringleader to death.

The ship's captain was the absolute ruler of the seas; his life was intertwined equally with those of the lowest ratings and of the powers above. Many were the dramatic seafaring stories brought back to Hvidsten, tales of storms and typhoons, floods and fire-breathing volcanoes. Round the hearth at home talk flowed freely about the sailor's achievements under distant skies and the awesome powers of nature.

In the light of such revelations Jens Amundsen appeared to his sons as a figure truly imposing in stature. His strength of character appears to have been matched only by that of his wife. Gustava Sahlquist was born in 1837 and was seventeen years younger than her husband when they married in 1863. Her grandfather had been a watchmaker in Stavanger; her father, Gustav Sahlquist, took his law degree and became bailiff in the east-coast town of Moss. The bailiff's family had shared aspirations totally unrelated to those of the tough Amundsen clan. Within ten years his wife, if not actually taking command, had certainly taken over the helm of Captain Amundsen's family ship.

In January 1866 Gustava had given birth to the first of her four sons. The event occurred in China during the dramatic voyage on which her husband had acquired the axe-scar and a coolie had gone to his death in a hangman's noose. The others arrived at two-yearly intervals. Roald, the last, saw the light of day on 16 July 1872, at Tomta, the family home at Hvidsten – in a geographical sense peripheral – but nevertheless at the heart of the Amundsen brothers' world-encompassing undertakings.

Just a brisk walk from the house lay the shipping company's tightly packed vessels. A few strokes of the oar, over the sound, on the other side of the River Glomma, stood the Amundsen brothers' shipyard, teeming with life and activity. Roald Amundsen's birthplace, the low, white-painted captain's cottage, commanded a view of it all, and thence to the world beyond.

In October, a few months after the birth of the youngest son, the family's life changed dramatically. Jens and Gustava Amundsen left the Østfold coast, disentangled themselves from family ties, said goodbye to the seafaring environment and moved north to Christiania. The by now grey-haired 52-year-old captain and ship-owner had bought a house in the capital.

One gets the distinct impression that it was Gustava, the ambitious bailiff's daughter, who had steered her family towards the beautiful villa close to the castle. The former captain of the seven seas meekly agreed to live beneath the lofty branches, with no sea view and only a fountain splashing in the garden. He would maintain contact with activities in Hvidsten and continue to command his own ships, but nevertheless, the move would not have taken place without a good deal of soul searching. Such an apparent capitulation must have been motivated by a desire to do the right thing by his sons; however, love for his wife must also have played a part. The new brood of Amundsen brothers would grow up with greater opportunities and be more successful than he and his own brothers had been – the self-taught men from the outermost islands. Jens Amundsen had given them the best possible start in life's voyage. He placed the capital at their feet.

The guardsmen paraded around the out-sized castle where the royal standard was now raised only on the rarest of occasions. The capital's main street, Karl Johan, named after the first Bernadotte, led up to the castle entrance. Further down the road lay the small but august colonnaded university buildings, the Grand Hotel and the Parliament. The National Theatre had yet to be built. Right at the end lay the main station, Østbanen. From there trains departed for the ocean and the world. The ceremonial district of Norway's capital amounted to little more than this one road. Undulating fields and forest-clad hills surrounded the town, which in a European context bears comparison with Cetinje, the capital of Macedonia.

Throughout their adolescence the ship-owner's sons kept in touch with the Østfold coast and their childhood home. Like all the other Hvidsten houses, it remained in the family's possession. Roald Amundsen nurtured his attachment to the sea and yearning for the outside world at the spot where Norway's largest river flowed out into the ocean. His national trait, the core of his being, his affinity to snow and skiing, was developed in the capital, where the Christiana Fjord penetrates deep into the Norwegian bedrock. Ocean and snow, seafaring and skiing, became the backbone of Roald Amundsen's career as a polar explorer.

'Sad times are here,' the 14-year-old Roald Amundsen writes in a letter to his cousin, dated 18 August 1886. 'I have never known sorrow; but now I do.' The body of his tall, white-bearded father had been brought home. Jens Amundsen had fallen ill and died during a voyage, on his way home from England. 'How hard it is to lose a father like ours, but it was the will of God and His will be done above all.'

Roald Amundsen was never able to see his father through the eyes of an adult. By the time his youngest son was born the most exciting episodes of Jens Amundsen's life were already behind him. Travelling continuously, either to Hvidsten or abroad, he must have seemed a remote and heroic figure. The ship's captain who defeated 300 mutineers had become a larger-than-life character in his son's imagination. 'Today we will nail down his coffin in the chapel. No one wants to take the lid off and look at him; our memories of him are so good and there is a danger that he might have changed somewhat between yesterday and today.'

Gustava did not want her sons to follow in their father's footsteps. In her dreams she saw their curly heads crowned with mortarboards, young men striding solemnly towards careers in academia. It was, however, not easy for the Amundsen brothers to fulfil their mother's ambitious aspirations. All four were bright, and financial circumstances had made it possible for them to attend good private schools. But none was particularly academic; rather they were practical; they possessed an urge to travel, a longing for the sea and adventure.

'It makes me content to know that my beloved boys live in loving relationship with one another.' Jens Amundsen wrote home a few weeks before his death. 'God bless you and may it always be so.' Despite his blessing the 'loving relationship' was often put to the test. But the Amundsen brothers, in friendship and enmity alike, exerted a decisive influence on each other's lives. Therefore, before dealing in detail with the youngest, we will cast a quick glance at his three older brothers.

When the ship-owner died the oldest son was already 20 and in the throes of moving away from home. Jens Ole Antonius, or Tonni, was a sportsman, not an intellectual, and like his youngest brother, in possession of a creative mind and the ability to find solutions. He was impatient to succeed as a businessman, preferably in a business based on his own inventions. Tonni became a rolling stone; he moved from place to place and from job to job, most often jobs connected to food production: margarine, crispbread, eggs and, above all, powdered milk. Tonni's biggest gamble was his own-brand powdered milk.

The ambitious businessman married the lawyer's daughter Emma Heffermehl in 1891. The first years of their marriage were spent in Algeria, where their oldest son was born. In all they had four children.

Initially Tonni must have been a merry optimist, full of drive, convinced of a happy future. But his lack of a sense of reality soon hampered him. His career was constantly hitting obstacles, and without learning from the experience he marched towards an ever gloomier future. Without the ability to adjust to economic circumstances he became a burden, not only on his brothers, but above all on his wife's wealthy brother-in-law, the merchant Peter Krag.

Tonni will play merely a peripheral role in the life of Roald Amundsen. It is the two middle brothers who, each in their own way, will influence the polar explorer's career.

Gustav Sahlquist Amundsen was born on 7 June 1868. He earned the much-coveted mortarboard and claimed to be studying medicine. Be that as it may, the colonnaded house on Karl Johan was soon abandoned for a life at sea and a master's certificate. Moreover, he spent time at the military academy and graduated as a lieutenant. He was made a captain in 1902. Gustav was thus, in every sense, a captain; naval and military. But this second oldest brother too was inclined towards business. He started in shipping, but soon spread his net more widely.

Gustav Amundsen married early, the merchant's daughter Malfred Fritzner; as it happens, she was the same age as the youngest brother Roald. A year after the marriage, in 1894, their only son was born, Gustav Sahlquist Amundsen; he too would acquire the title lieutenant and, later, that of captain.

Gustav's nickname was Busken. Like Tonni he was gregarious, entertaining and charming, but he shared his brother's lack of realism. In spite of, or maybe because of, his capacity for brilliant ideas and penchant for taking novel gambles, Busken's business career took a dive.

The once intelligent and resourceful Gustav, like his brother, turned into a heavy burden upon those around him; and not entirely owing to the financial difficulties he got himself into. Gradually a dark side to his character emerged: vacillating, calculating, scheming and aggressive. Using increasingly unscrupulous methods he terrorised his nearest and dearest, and never flinched from dishonesty or downright swindles, threatening time and again to discredit the family name.

Throughout his life Roald Amundsen's allegiance would be torn between his brothers Gustav and Leon, the family's polar extremities.

Leon was born on 4 September 1870. He was closest to Roald in age and appears to have been his younger brother's confidant. Like all the Amundsen brothers he was tall, but of a less assertive and more reserved nature than the two oldest. Leon too became a businessman. He was educated at the commercial college in Christiania and moved to France in 1892 where he was employed in a wine business. He travelled all his life, not for the purpose of discovering unknown wilds but to get to know other countries and develop his linguistic skills.

Leon shared his younger brother's sporting enthusiasm and his older brothers' fianancial aspirations, but nevertheless, there is something thoughtful and inhibited about him. He married late in life and did not throw himself headlong into fanciful enterprises like his brothers. On the other hand, alone among the Amundsen brothers, he possessed a genuine flair for finance. He was trustworthy and conscientious; he had a practical understanding of loss and profit. Leon Amundsen understood that it is often best to keep one's head down. Only once did he gamble, and then with great skill.

Mrs Gustava Amundsen had presented her husband with four sturdy sons. She had manoeuvred them away from windswept islands into polite society – to a fountain behind the castle. But the three oldest showed no inclination towards academic pursuits, let alone an academic career. One by one they abandoned the world of books and embraced a more practical life. Were none of her sons to aim higher than buying and selling, steam and sail? In the end Gustava Amundsen, the bailiff's daughter, was left with one last option. She pinned her faith on Roald.

TWO

The Student of Polar Exploration

Roald Amundsen pulled the wool over his mother's eyes. She was the first person he had ever deceived.

The daydreamer, the youngest son, who wanted nothing more than to hide behind a tall wardrobe, hated to disappoint his mother. He therefore promised, when the time came, that he would honour her dearest wish and take up the study of medicine. But the promise to himself was different. 'In all secrecy – because I have never dared mention this to mother, who I knew would not agree – I have decided to become a polar explorer.'

The quotation is taken from Roald Amundsen's memoirs, *My Life as a Polar Explorer*, a work to which this account must of necessity adhere. It is one of the most impenetrable but at the same time revealing autobiographies ever written. Roald Amundsen wrote it eighteen months before his death, and we will refer to it more fully later in this book. When it comes to the polar explorer's earliest resolves the autobiography is, despite obvious distortion, the most important source we have.

'How did it come about that I became a polar explorer? Well, it didn't really "come about" – as my life has, ever since I was fifteen years old, been a constant journey towards this ultimate goal.' If we are to believe his memoirs, Roald Amundsen took, more or less from the very beginning, charge of his own life – and completed the course from cradle to grave with such consistency that one could be forgiven for believing that it was programmed by divine will: 'What I have achieved as a polar explorer has been the result of a life of systematic, conscientious and painstaking preparation.'

Nevertheless, it all seems to have its basis in a literary stroke of luck. 'When I was fifteen I happened upon the books of the English polar explorer Sir John Franklin. I devoured his books and they became decisive for the direction I chose to take through life.' The year after the coffin lid was nailed down over the ship-owner from Hvaler, the British admiral strode forth from the fabled landscape of the North West Passage and blew new life and direction into the boy.

The dreamer has discovered an authority that leads him to the Promised Land. He describes Sir John thus in his first book: 'His wise face shines forth with strength of character and gentleness; he has a good word for everyone and is loved by all. They trust this old experienced leader from the Polar Regions.' Before at last succumbing in 1847, the British Admiral Franklin made as many heroic as unsuccessful attempts to conquer the North West Passage.

So just why did the Norwegian youngster choose this tragic, long-dead character as his model? Fridtjof Nansen's corresponding choice appears more obvious. His inspiration was the celebrated Swedish polar explorer Adolf Erik Nordenskiöld, who in 1879 had completed the successful voyage through the North East Passage.

Roald Amundsen himself supplies the explanation – it is found in the writings of Sir John:

His description of a return journey from one of the many expeditions thrilled me more than anything I had read before. He wrote how he and some comrades had fought against storms and ice for over three weeks and how they, before reaching the utmost outpost of civilisation, were forced to eat their boots to stay alive. Extraordinarily, it was the suffering that Sir John described he and his men had to endure that most engaged me. Maybe it was the idealism of youth, which, as we know, often yearns for martyrdom, that made me view myself as a sort of crusader of arctic research. I too wanted to suffer for a cause – not in the burning desert en route to Jerusalem – but in the freezing north en route to wider knowledge of the until now unknown wilderness. In every way Sir John's descriptions were of great significance to my future.

Towards the end of his life Roald Amundsen stated unequivocally that his career had been based not on scientific curiosity but on a purely literary experience. It was not the achievements *per se* but 'Sir John's descriptions' which were the deciding factor. Besides, and this was the leitmotif throughout all Roald Amundsen's triumphant expeditions, it was not the victor's laurels but the martyr's glory that called him.

In his book about the conquest of the North West Passage, published twenty years before his autobiography, Roald Amundsen dates his first encounter with Franklin's stories to his eighth or ninth year, not his fifteenth. They are two entirely different periods of a boy's life; the decisive factor, however, is that the British admiral's significance as biographical guide is confirmed in both works.

It is easier to pinpoint the subsequent decisive step in Roald Amundsen's professional development. He writes in *The North West Passage*: 'The 30th May, 1889 was a red-letter day in many a Norwegian boy's life. It certainly was in mine. That was the day Fridtjof Nansen returned from his Greenland journey.' It was in fact an important day for the Norwegian people's mental development; the day the once proud Viking nation regained its self-confidence. Or, to put it crudely: from that day delusions of grandeur were sown in the psyche of the Norwegian people.

In a nutshell: the 27-year-old son of a lawyer and zoologist, Fridtjof Nansen, had been put ashore on the east coast of southern Greenland. From here, as the leader of his five companions and as the first person ever to do so, he had crossed the frozen island's interior with the proud motto: 'Death or the west coast of Greenland'. When triumph was a reality, this campaign 'on the cheap', for initially it had been denied any financial support, was seen as the first major raid by modern-day Vikings. In his vast travelogue *Paa ski over Grønland* (On Skis across Greenland), Fridtjof Nansen took care to emphasise the expedition's national character. In as much as he based the entire journey on the art of skiing, 'the most Norwegian of all sports', he had discovered a Norwegian 'wonder-machine', a new and superior means of arctic transportation. From now on skis were to become the girder that supported the nation's inflated self-esteem.

The Norwegians had understood intuitively what was afoot when the tall, blonde Viking figure of Fridtjof Nansen arrived up the fjord on a sunny day in May. 'Such jubilation and ecstasy have never before been seen in Christiania, as when the Greenland adventurer returned. Nothing bigger seems to have happened in Norway than that Nansen and his comrades really returned. Sixty thousand people welcomed them by the landing stage, fifty thousand accompanied them to the hotel, ten thousand shouted ninety thousand hurrahs; an old retired colonel from Kampen quite simply fell dead on the spot from shouting.' This report, taken from the newspaper *Dagbladet*, was the work of the astonished, and as yet unknown, author Knut Hamsun, the man who would win the Nobel Prize for literature in 1920.

Shortly after Roald Amundsen had scraped through his high school exams, the childhood home in Uranienborgveien was broken up. The young man on whom the family had pinned all their hopes, the future doctor, established his own household at 6 Parkveien, a few yards closer to the castle. Betty, their old nanny, went with him.

For the next three years the young gentleman lived a double life. Officially he was enrolled at the university with a view to studying medicine. 'Like all proud mothers, mine too believed that I was diligent to a point,' Roald

Amundsen writes in his memoirs, 'but to be honest I must admit that I was worse than even the most indifferent of students.' As late as 1893, after two years' delay, the indifferent student just managed to scrape through the compulsory 'Second Exam'. The polar explorer's German biographer insists that Roald Amundsen never got as far as even being registered at the Medical Faculty, let alone actually studying anything even vaguely connected to medicine.

Roald Amundsen's university education was, and remained, a sham, staged for the benefit of his mother. He was loath to disappoint her, and he was too much of a coward to tell her the truth. Above all he badly needed to maintain the appearance of studying medicine so that his mother would continue to put the money at his disposal that would enable him to continue his *real* study, polar exploration.

This first phase of Amundsen's career preparations consisted of physical training and fitness. In the winter he slept by an open window and took every opportunity to ski in the mountains and woods around the capital. He also devoured every book he could lay his hands on about exploration. And he continued to nurture his tobacco-infested daydreams, alone or in the company of other Nansen fans.

In the summer of 1893 Fridtjof Nansen started out from Christiania on board the newly built *Fram*. Five years earlier he had crossed Greenland; now, barely 32 years old, he set out to conquer the entire Polar Sea. The plan was ingenious; within polar research probably the most sensational ever proposed. Nansen would sail a ship of his own design into the pack ice where it would become icebound and drift with the current from east to west across the North Pole. The Royal Geographical Society in London ridiculed the plan but the self-opinionated Norwegian would not be stopped. Besides, this time the people and the government were completely behind him. It was an entirely Norwegian-financed Viking 'raid' which set out to uncover the mysteries of the Polar Sea, to conquer the North Pole and strike a blow for Norway's freedom.

In the autumn of 1893 Roald Amundsen's mother contracted pneumonia. She died on 9 September. Roald was the only son at home in Christiania and her death affected him deeply. Five years later he is reminded of the date in his diary, calling it the saddest day of his life. 'I will remember you, dear Mother, as long as I live.' 'Her death,' Roald Amundsen writes in his memoirs, 'saved her from making the discovery she would inevitably sooner or later have made, that my ambitions and interests pointed in an entirely different direction and that my work to fulfil hers never led me closer to the goal she had chosen. It was thus with great relief that I left university in order to devote all my time to my life's dream.'

Throughout his long career as an explorer Roald Amundsen would have the opportunity to honour the memory of many – not least that of women. He christened ships and planes, named mountains and fjords. Queens and patrons, even Fridtjof Nansen's daughter, were immortalised with a name on a map. Gustava Amundsen, his own mother, had to make do with as few gold letters on a headstone. Her ambitions were never realised.

His mother's death triggered off frantic activity in the flat behind the castle. His first task was to obtain a medical certificate testifying to his superb physique. 'Mr Roald Amundsen has, following lengthy examination, shown himself to be free of bodily defect and in possession of exceptionally good health. He is 180 centimetres tall. His chest, deflated, is 87 centimetres and inflated, 98 centimetres.' In possession of official testimony to these simple facts he could at last sign on to some expedition going north – bound for adventure.

Fram was already en route to its first winter in the ice, but there were other fish in the sea. Roald Amundsen moved heaven and earth, including the Royal Geographical Society in London, to try and obtain a berth with the British Jackson Expedition. This was the expedition which three years later would intercept the skiers Nansen and Johansen on Franz Josef Land. But there was no place for the Norwegian and history was cheated of the symbolic picture of Nansen and Amundsen coming face to face in the far north.

The polar student had to make do with a journey in the Norwegian mountains. Before the advent of the railway between Oslo and Bergen the Hardanger Plateau, in the centre of the kingdom, was in winter considered more or less virgin territory. Fridtjof Nansen's first feat had been to cross this plateau on skis in the winter of 1884. It was therefore perfectly reasonable that the young Amundsen and his two comrades chose to visit a photographer to be immortalised, kitted out in full wilderness gear, before the expedition set out around Christmas time.

This tour was Amundsen's first encounter with a winter landscape comparable to that of arctic regions. The expedition's unchallenged leader was the journalist and ski-philosopher Laurentius Urdahl, who was able to introduce the future polar explorer to the theory and practice of skiing.

At last, in the spring, Roald Amundsen succeeded in travelling north to arctic waters. His immediate plan was to clock up time at sea, enough to enable him to pass the first mate's exam. Nothing suited him better than to sign on to the small sailing vessel *Magdalena* for a journey to the sealing grounds in the north.

At the end of May 1894 Roald posted a letter from Iceland, addressed to his brother in France. 'I am very happy on board; am enjoying the polar sea adventure and the sealing is both interesting and fun, assuming of course that we shoot some.' Thus far they had caught some two thousand seal, but according to Amundsen that was far from enough. The ship had passed 78° North and was en route to the east coast of Greenland. 'Concerning life in the Arctic Ocean, I like it a lot. Its bad reputation is as usual an exaggeration. All the men, from the youngest to the oldest, are my best friends and thus time passes too fast.'

By the autumn Amundsen was back with Nanny Betty in comfortable surroundings in the capital's west end. He could look back on an instructive term. The polar student had ascended mountains in winter; now he could add the title of polar-sea voyager to his credentials.

On 8 November 1894 Roald Amundsen sat down at his desk to write a formal letter, addressed to 'Mr Assistant Secretary, Department of the Interior'. In 'his capacity as polar-sea voyager' the 22-year-old asks the assistant secretary four specific questions: '1) Does the island of Spitsbergen belong to any particular nation? 2) If not, would it be of any consequence to Norway to possess it? 3) How would one go about taking possession of it? 4) Has the government ever considered such an action?'

This is not just any new recruit asking such questions. Young Amundsen's modesty has often been affirmed, but it cannot have been particularly deep-rooted. Spitsbergen, later called Svalbard, was not a piece of land of much consequence, but it was nevertheless considered part of the old Viking empire. And who knew for certain in those far off days how extensive the polar-sea archipelago really was?

The answer arrived one month later, from the assistant secretary in 'the 1st office of the interior'. In other words, even far-flung fishing grounds of unknown ownership were dealt with under internal business. 'I am not in possession of information which would evaluate the importance of Norway's ownership of Spitsbergen,' was the rather vague reply. But a promising invitation followed: 'If you with your experience as a polar-sea voyager can throw some light on the problem, I would be grateful if you could come and see me in the ministry.'

The door to the innermost sanctum is wide open. But Roald Amundsen is not yet ready for his first 'annexation'; he is wise enough to withdraw temporarily, before exposing his young countenance to the ministry's man. 'As far as my experiences as a polar voyager are concerned, they are still reasonably modest. Concerning Spitsbergen I cannot yet commit myself.' However, it is his intention 'to travel to Tromsø in the spring and sail out with one of the vessels which hunt in the waters around Spitsbergen. I will then have the opportunity to discuss this matter with experienced men. In the autumn, on my return, it will be a great

Roald Amundsen

pleasure to visit the assistant secretary and make known to him the experiences I have had.'

This brief exchange of correspondence on territorial matters speaks volumes for the 22-year-old's level of ambition. This is the new recruit poking his nose into the admiral's territory. And it is more than mere fantasy. He has realised that he must keep in with the bigwigs in the ministry as well as with the local experts – 'discussing the matter with experienced men'. Roald Amundsen's goal is already clear: he wants to take possession of new lands.

THREE

The Ice Chest

'The first prerequisite for a polar explorer is to be in possession of a healthy and hardened body.' So Roald Amundsen asserts in his *My Life as a Polar Explorer*. In the same work he describes how he was paraded in front of the military medical board prior to his military service. 'The doctor and two assistants were sitting at a table. The doctor was an elderly chap who, I discover to my great joy and astonishment, was a keen student of the human body. I was naked during the examination. The old doctor inspected me carefully and suddenly erupted in words of praise for my appearance.' The young recruit felt duty bound to explain how he had developed his imposing muscles through 'physical exercise'. 'The old gentleman was so delighted at his discovery, which he considered quite extraordinary, that he called in some officers from the adjoining rooms to come and look at the wonder. Needless to say I was confused and shy about this public exposure and wished the ground would open up and swallow me.'

What is significant about this episode is that in displaying his magnificent physique, Roald Amundsen concealed something else: 'In his delight over my bodily condition the old doctor forgot to examine my eyes.' In his autobiography Roald Amundsen lays bare, for the first time, his impairment: 'I was short-sighted, and not even those closest to me knew about it.'

Roald Amundsen preferred not to see rather than be seen wearing glasses. There is nothing new in the notion that a pair of glasses and pince-nez are incompatible with the idea of a perfect body; it is however somewhat extreme to hide 'even [from] those closest to me' throughout a long life that one cannot see what everyone else sees. Surely this deficiency must have influenced an explorer, for whom good eyesight would appear to be paramount.

However, one person was party to Roald Amundsen's big secret. In December 1896, when Roald was 24, and at sea, he wrote Leon an urgent letter. He enclosed an article bearing the title 'The Healing of Short-sightedness', about a German professor who had presented the medical world with a break-through eye operation. 'I was compelled to cut out the enclosed article. Please investigate *immediately*. Inform them that I am *slightly*, not *very* short-sighted. I am willing to go anywhere to regain my *full* sight. Please make sure *no one* knows about this as it is something I want kept secret. Please do *all* you can.'

In spite of never submitting to an eye operation, Roald Amundsen never wore corrective glasses, other than as a disguise. His impairment and its concealment might have been the cause of the social isolation which would characterise the polar explorer's later life.

In January 1896 Norwegian eyes were turned towards the Arctic Ocean. *Fram* entered her third year in the wilderness. Before long people would expect to hear tidings from the north – if all was well. What no one yet knew was that Fridtjof Nansen, together with the unknown Hjalmar Johansen, had left the ship the year before in a heroic attempt to reach the North Pole. Having been forced to abandon their enterprise, the two compatriots were now, concealed from the world, hibernating like two bears in a lair on Franz Josef Land.

But yet another mystery gripped the Viking population that winter: the young and popular polar explorer Eivind Astrup was reported missing during a ski trip in the Dovre Mountains.

While speculation was rife as to the whereabouts of these skiers, yet another disappearance surfaced in the news columns of the Christiania papers. Two skiers were reported missing on the Hardanger Plateau, two brothers. The family name was Amundsen. Thus is Roald Amundsen's name first brought to the attention of the general public. He appears as he immediately disappears. He starts as he intends to finish – with a disappearance.

Amundsen passed his mate's exams in the spring of 1895 and immediately signed on again with a view to completing his skipper's certificate. At last, on 3 January 1896, he could once again make tracks for the mountains. From time to time Roald's wine-merchant brother visited his native country, where he shared lodgings with Roald in Christiania. This time the brothers set off together; their destination the Hardanger Plateau.

The plan was to cross the plateau from east to west, but they lost their sense of direction and ended up walking in circles. The ski trip turned into a fight for life. Roald Amundsen's battle with death can only be likened to the one which was to end his life in the Arctic Ocean thirty-two years later. 'I woke in the middle of the night. I was lying on my back and my hand was over my eyes – as though it were morning and the light was annoying me. My muscles felt stiff and instinctively I tried to move. I could not move an inch. I was literally frozen inside a block of ice. I tried desperately to free myself, but to no avail. I called on my companion but he of course heard nothing.'

That was how Roald Amundsen described the dramatic climax of the ski trip in his autobiography. Exhausted by hunger and constant exertion he had sought shelter by digging himself into the snow. It was mild, but during the night the temperature dropped. His only hope was his comrade.

I was rigid with fear. I thought, to my horror, that he too would be frozen into the wet snow and would find himself in the same situation as me. If it did not thaw we would both freeze to death, inside our grim coffins.

I soon gave up shouting as it was difficult to breathe properly. I realised that I needed to stay calm or I would suffocate. I do not know if it was lack of oxygen, or whatever, but I fell asleep or lost consciousness quite quickly. But when I came to I heard a faint sound far away. My companion had not been imprisoned. He had not dug himself in; possibly because the previous evening he had been too tired or too exhausted or couldn't really care. Whatever the case, he thereby saved our lives.

In his autobiography Roald Amundsen describes this episode on the Hardanger Plateau as the most dangerous of his entire dramatic career. But it sheds an interesting light on the polar explorer, because Roald Amundsen had recounted the incident once before, immediately after his return in 1896. Bearing the title 'The Amundsen Brothers' Extraordinary Journey across the Hardanger Plateau' he wrote his very first expedition story, serialised in *Fredrikstad Blad*. When he wrote the self-same story about thirty years later much had changed in Roald Amundsen's life, and his recollections were very different.

In the last edition a nameless 'companion' tunnelled in to him; in the first edition it is his brother. And then it was not tiredness or exhaustion that had prevented him from digging himself in, on the contrary: 'On the other hand my brother had been more vigilant. He told me later, many times, that he got up in the night to shake the snow off. I had slept through it all.' In that version it took the brother an hour to force his way into Roald's ice chest, whereas the exhausted and indifferent 'companion' spent three hours to save 'our lives'. Throughout the entire story the 'companion' is not only treated dismissively but is completely dependent upon the ego of the story-teller, Roald Amundsen, who ends up as the expedition's saviour.

The two portrayals of the same journey are characteristic of Roald Amundsen. That night on the Hardanger Plateau it had been Leon who had saved him. But when he wrote his autobiography thirty years later he was in the throes of freezing in once again, this time in a soul-less ice-chest. And this time no one tunnelled in to him. Least of all Leon.

Then one day the papers brought the comforting news that the missing skiers had arrived safely at Bolkesjø. They had been away for three weeks. Roald Amundsen had returned to life for the second time. (One ought to add that a few years later, on his way to visit his fiancée in Bergen, Leon Amundsen re-enacted the 'extraordinary' journey across the Hardanger Plateau.)

Fridtjof Nansen's successor was decided, his election a *fait accompli*, that January in the Norwegian mountains. Roald Amundsen returned. Eivind Astrup did not. One of the stars of polar exploration's firmament was extinguished before it had even started to sparkle. The tragedy hit Roald Amundsen as hard as any. In his later years, Eivind Astrup's portrait was given pride of place on his desk; Fridtjof Nansen was kept at arm's length – on the wall. Astrup, the boy from Christiania, was of his own generation, the same age as Leon. His valiant feats had been an inspiration for the dreamer behind the castle.

The merchant's son Eivind Astrup had left his native country at the age of 19 and set sail for America. Like Leon he had been a student at the commercial college and aspired to a career in business on the other side of the Atlantic. However, the young adventurer soon happened upon far more exciting challenges. As a sportsman and skier he succeeded in securing a place on Robert Peary's first two Greenland expeditions, those of 1891–2 and 1893–4 respectively.

Peary operated in northern Greenland where, from time to time, he made considerable discoveries and garnered dearly bought expertise. However, the ambitious young Norwegian skier found himself in conflict with the American Peary and decided to return to Norway to lay his own plans. At home he solicited support from, among others, the wealthy whale-hunter and pioneer Svend Foyn* and the Swedish balloon expert engineer Andrée. In the premises of Norway's Geographical Society Astrup unveiled plans for a balloon trip to the north. 'It would be possible to fly over arctic regions in a matter of a few hours from Spitsbergen where one could carry out one's studies and, if the wind was favourable, with the help of dogs and sledges, return home.'

Eivind Astrup's interests encompassed both the Arctic and the Antarctic. He had identified more or less the same field of action as Roald Amundsen. Had he not died so young there is every indication that his achievements would have overshadowed Amundsen's. He was only two years older but his head start was considerable. His disposition was attractive and his personality charismatic. In the public imagination he was quickly linked to the fabled grass widow Eva Nansen as well as to Mrs Peary, who, sensationally, took part in one of the north Greenland expeditions.

But fate decreed otherwise. Just as Fridtjof Nansen dreamt about his Eva at home, from a cave on Franz Josef Land, and the Amundsen brothers made preparations for the Hardanger Plateau expedition, Norway's youngest holder

---

* Translator's note: Svend Foyn invented the whaling harpoon.

of the St Olav Order of Chivalry was setting out on his last ski-trip. On 29 December 1895 Eivind Astrup left Hjerkinn on Dovre to walk over the mountain to Utna, where he was to rendezvous with a group of officers, among them Captain Dietrichson who had been a member of Nansen's Greenland expedition.

Eivind Astrup was found lying in the snow three weeks later, not far from where he set off. What had gone wrong? How could Norway's Number Two polar hero drop dead in the snow after a 30-minute ski-trip? Had the 25-year-old been unwell? Was it a stroke, exhaustion, suicide? 'Most probably owing to bad snow conditions Eivind Astrup was carrying his skis, slipped on a patch of ice and hit his right temple on a sharp stone.' was the rather unconvincing report printed in *Aftenposten*. 'There was a lot of blood everywhere.' The bottle of port in his ruck-sack had not been touched.

The arctic explorer's hearse was followed to the capital by staggeringly large crowds. Eivind Astrup was laid to rest at Our Saviour's Cemetery. But the popular charmer from the Arctic lived on in the minds of his fellow countrymen. In the 'hall of fame' Roald Amundsen had created in his mind the young chevalier occupied a position right next to the old martyr, Sir John Franklin.

On 7 August 1896, half a year after his brush with death on the Hardanger Plateau, a happy Roald wrote to his brother Leon in Cognac. 'From June 1st I have been signed on with the Belgian Antarctic Expedition as an able seaman and skier. The trip will last two years and will be most interesting as, of course, it is the first of its kind.'

No sooner had Roald Amundsen posted the letter than the bombshell struck: on 13 August Fridtjof Nansen had reached Vardø, the most northerly point in Norway, accompanied by the 28-year-old Lieutenant Hjalmar Johansen. A week later *Fram*, skippered by Otto Sverdrup, docked in Tromsø. Swedish colony or not, Norway erupted with excitement. A modern Viking raiding party had crossed the Arctic Ocean and completed the task without a hitch. Now, only the North Pole itself remained to be conquered. But in the uproar no one bothered about such petty hair-splitting. Like a royal ship *Fram* sailed south along the length of the Norwegian coast, greeted everywhere by waving banners and an outpouring of nationalist rhetoric, the noble figure of the reincarnated Viking king standing in the stern.

When the ship slipped into the Christiania Fjord on 9 September 1896, the entire capital was on its feet to welcome her. In the castle the ageing Bernadotte king stood ready with medals and ribbons. At the ancient Akershus Fortress the Poet Laureate Bjørnstjerne Bjørnson stood poised to declaim the line from legendary Viking kings to polar explorers' heroic deeds. Every Norwegian breast swelled with pride as never before. In his speech of thanks at the fortress Fridtjof Nansen proclaimed that 'such a daring exploit could have been carried out by but one nation alone, the Norwegian.'

One man was missing in Christiania that day. Roald Amundsen. He and his brother Gustav had signed on the ship *Huldra* and were on their way to Caen where they were hoping to meet Leon. There was, however, no doubt what the topic of conversation would be: *Fram*'s return and the *Belgica*'s departure.

Compared with the Norwegian polar expedition, considerably greater economic worries beset the Belgian Antarctic expedition. The *Belgica* was actually a Norwegian-built barque which the previous winter had been laid up in Sandefjord on Norway's south-east coast for repairs and necessary refitting. Departure had been fixed for the summer of 1897. But even during the planning stages able-seaman Amundsen was promoted to first officer. Few were beating a path to the recruiting office for this cash-strapped and risky voyage.

Roald Amundsen arrived in Antwerp in the winter of 1897 where he would learn some Flemish and complete a course in navigation. He rented a cheap room.

In the spring Leon received a letter in Cognac. It was posted on 24 March 1897. A deeply shaken Roald wrote: 'Last night something so awful happened that I will never forget it. The lady of the house committed suicide by carbon monoxide poisoning.' Roald had been there and it was he who found her the next morning. 'Two zinc buckets were on the kitchen floor and one of them was still burning.' The lady had collapsed on the floor 'stiff and cold'.

Roald Amundsen and the landlady in Antwerp had become lovers. She was married. In his letter to Leon he nevertheless presented himself as merely a witness to the tragedy. 'The lady and I were good friends so I know the circumstances. If I were to start on this story I'm afraid I would never finish.' It was immediately obvious that the landlady's death would affect future plans. That very day he quit the navigation course.

It takes a lot, an awful lot, for Roald Amundsen to abandon his post in the service of polar exploration. 'I'm returning with the first boat as this experience has rendered me unfit to continue here.'

Leon telegraphed his brother and invited him to Cognac. But according to Roald, 'he is fit only to return home as quickly as possible.' The fire in the zinc buckets must have been raging under the feet of this lodger. On 26 March he stood at his landlady's graveside. Early the next morning he left for Christiania. The lady was laid to rest, the husband lived on.

Later Roald told his brother that he had been forced to flee Antwerp. Things were hotting up around him.

The Antarctic beckoned.

FOUR

First Night in the Antarctic

The Arctic had been the real battleground of polar exploration. The *Belgica* expedition sparked off a new and frantic era of exploration, and brought to centre stage virgin territory that had thus far been of only peripheral importance: the Antarctic. Roald Amundsen visited this white continent only twice, the second time to plant the Norwegian flag on the South Pole.

Roald Amundsen served his apprenticeship in the many-faceted art of polar exploration during this first trip to the Antarctic. The expedition was led by Adrien de Gerlache, who, like the ship's captain, was a Belgian. Otherwise the crew was conspicuously international.

This was to be the one and only voyage of discovery in which Roald Amundsen took part as a subordinate – useful experience for a student whose principal career would, arguably, be leadership. Interestingly enough, in *My Life as a Polar Explorer* Amundsen never mentions Baron de Gerlache by name, referring to him only as a 'Belgian sailor'. Discreetly, but unmistakeably, the Belgian national hero is erased from the Norwegian's personal chronicle. Apart from Amundsen himself only the ship's doctor is mentioned by name. These two, the Norwegian first officer and the American ship's doctor, emerge in the memoirs as the Belgian expedition's real leaders.

While the newly fitted-out polar ship lay at anchor in Sandefjord, Fridtjof Nansen paid the expedition a visit. This was the first occasion on which the two Norwegian polar explorers met face to face; Nansen the tall, conquering hero and Roald Amundsen, eleven years his junior, a full 11 centimetres shorter, and as yet untested. But the novice was not the only one to remember the meeting; 'having once seen that face one does not easily forget it,' Nansen pronounced thirty years later.

The *Belgica*'s official departure from Antwerp was postponed by a few weeks in anticipation of further public funds. This was not the last time pecuniary circumstances would delay departures in Roald Amundsen's life. At last, on 16 August the expedition set sail, amid such festivities as usually accompany explorers setting out for the unknown.

On 10 September *Belgica* anchored in Funchal Roads. The crew stepped ashore in Madeira, just like the *Fram*'s crew would twelve years later. Nor was this the only time the *Belgica* expedition would presage later events. The ship crossed the Equator on 6 October, accompanied by celebrations and traditional line-christenings. Roald Amundsen was christened in a tramp's outfit. That, too, an omen.

The journey was intended to introduce the young Norwegian to the common dangers and terrors of polar exploration. It did, however, also reveal it in all its glory. The ship left Rio de Janeiro to a noisy and boisterous farewell; warships from around the world honoured the expedition with a show of flags, brass-bands played and hundreds of sailors added their vigorous 'hurrah!' 'It was a very touching farewell,' the officer notes in the first of what would be a long line of expedition diaries.

The road from the sands of civilisation to the white-out is a long one. In Montevideo once again the crew drank their fill while the more educated on board enjoyed the sights: the elegantly constructed streets, the broad, clean footpaths, the large squares, the electricity everywhere. 'One must not forget the ladies either. Never in my life have I seen so many beautiful women in one place as here.'

The innocent 25-year-old occupying the post of first officer on board the *Belgica* was devoted to his task. Full of hope and confidence he wrote in his diary: 'I wish our commander all well and I will do my duty in order to ensure that his plan will succeed. He has worked incredibly hard on this enterprise and I wish him all well. I will never lose sight of the responsibility I owe, as a Norwegian, to work hard to honour my country.'

There were five Norwegians on board. Roald's status meant that he was billeted with the officers and scientists in the stern; the other four were forward with the 'crew' in the forecastle. Arrangements on the *Fram* had introduced a social revolution; the thirteen-strong crew had all taken their meals around the same table; the *Belgica*'s crew numbered but two more, but kept to the traditional European social divisions.

The expedition left the southern tip of Chile and made for the Graham Land headland on the Antarctic continent. Towards the end of January 1898 the polar vessel entered its true element. 'The fog is like a wall. Icebergs and unknown lands await us.' Gradually it dawned on the first officer that this was no carefully planned scientific journey; rather, the Belgian commandant had set sail on a hazardous, haphazard and random adventure. 'I can only admire his audacity. Onwards or bust. I will follow all the way, cheerful and smiling.'

Just a day after this upbeat entry, on 22 January, stark reality was visited upon the expedition in the form of appalling weather – driving snow, fog and storms, waves that broke over the ship, and the proximity of closely packed icebergs. Four men kept watch, three Norwegians and a Belgian. The first officer was in command. Suddenly a terrible scream rent the air. The young sailor August Wiencke had been washed overboard. In the terrifying battle that followed to save him the other Norwegian sailor, Ludvig Johansen, managed to grab him briefly but could not keep hold. The cold killed the boy and his ashen face disappeared below the waves.

This was Roald Amundsen's first brush with death in polar regions. Fifteen years later the incident resurfaced. On his return from his second Antarctic journey Amundsen received a greeting via the vicar of Moss from the sailor Ludvig Johansen, who was on his deathbed. 'He is touchingly devoted to you. He has animatedly recounted exciting tales from the *Belgica* trip and in them all you are his hero.' A few days later the vicar hands 200 crowns to the dying sailor and his destitute family, accompanied by a greeting from the conqueror of the South Pole.

Though the *Belgica* was hit by disaster in troubled and dangerous waters the ship was touched by luck too, which makes an equally deep impression on the first officer. 'Who could argue, when one experiences things like that, that God does not exist? No one. Coincidence? Coincidences cannot sail a ship. No, no. Your power is great, Oh God, and your mercy infinite. You have guided us like you always have. Hold your hand over us for ever.' Roald Amundsen kept this simple faith throughout his life. Unlike Nansen, he did not look for answers in obscure laws of nature. He found a personal explanation behind the changing landscape and the unfathomable mysteries of the icy wastes.

On 30 January 1898 the untrodden continent is within reach and 'everything ready for the ski-trip'. Together with, among others, the commandant and the ship's doctor Roald Amundsen erected a tent on the south polar land's northerly promontory. 'With the piping hot pea-soup to share, fog and snow and wind were forgotten and the King's very castle could not have been better. Thus we spent our first night on land as yet untouched by humans.' They were soon back on the ship, but Roald Amundsen has taken his first step in the race for the South Pole. He had set foot on the continent and erected his tent before any English naval officer.

But not all the expedition members were in their element. No one had prepared them for an over-wintering and fear spread among the crew. The commander, however, felt it was his duty 'as a Belgian' to continue the journey to the south. So as not to worry the crew they lied about the latitudes. Gerlache confided his real intentions first to the captain and then to his first officer. Roald Amundsen went along with the deception. 'We are thus sailing in a SW direction, with a speed of 3 knots per day. No better.'

On 8 March the *Belgica* was icebound – gripped by both ice and fear. They faced the unknown. No ship had ever before over-wintered in the Antarctic night. All they knew was that their equipment was totally inadequate. The expedition was led by a heroic daredevil trespassing on martyr's territory. The polar student thought it 'is beginning to get interesting'. Whence came his calm? Into whose hands did he so confidently surrender his young destiny?

'You have helped us overcome so much, God, and surely you will still help us. Take us wherever you will and I will fulfil my duty to the last.' Roald Amundsen placed his trust in God, in himself and the ship's doctor, probably in reverse order.

By pure coincidence, or the intervention of a higher power, two men of the calibre to make polar history were on board the *Belgica*, the icebound vessel under the command of a complete amateur: First Officer Roald Amundsen and ship's doctor Frederick Albert Cook. The Norwegian immediately felt drawn to the handsome, likeable American, seven years his senior, who shared his passion for 'the cold climes'.

Dr Cook's name was already known in polar literature. He and Eivind Astrup had been part of Lieutenant Peary's first Greenland expedition. In his only book, *Amongst the Neighbours of the North-Pole*, written in 1895, Astrup describes the doctor as 'a very active and energetic man of about 30, who, during our stay amongst the natives, made a name for himself as the expedition's ethnologist'.

The calm, ever dignified, doctor became Roald Amundsen's true teacher. As soon as they stepped ashore the teacher and his apprentice roped up and crossed crevasses and snow-bridges; 'the experienced polar explorer walking ahead, I follow after.' Together they climbed one of the heights and surveyed the land the apprentice would one day conquer. 'For a short while we view the unknown land, which is soon obscured by fog and driving snow.'

Through Cook, Amundsen is introduced to Peary's methods, but he came to know other things too. 'From time to time the doctor talks to me about Eivind Astrup. What has been said at home, that a relationship existed between him and Mrs. Peary is utter nonsense. In the first place Eivind Astrup couldn't stand Mrs. Peary. Secondly Mrs. Peary was in all respects an honourable woman. And thirdly, the weaker sex was freely available in Greenland. It was impossible to get near an unmarried woman, but so much the easier with married women. One only needed the husband's consent, which was *always* forthcoming. Tungvingva was E.A's chosen one. She was married, 14 years old and childless. Very wise and Greenland's crowned beauty, she was very small. Women are ready for marriage when they are 13.'

Astrup talks about this young Eskimo woman. She was married to Kolotengva, the Norwegian's closest assistant among the natives and his only companion on the lengthy sledge tour to Melville Bay in the spring of 1894. 'No one in the entire tribe could be prouder than Kolotengva, no one more independent or more free-spirited, no one a better friend, more coldly fearless in the face of danger or wiser during the chase. His wife was called Tungvingva, a red-cheeked, smiling child with dark eyes and white teeth.'

Eivind Astrup's liberal attitude to Eskimo marriage was by no means unusual. In fact, this pleasurable side of a tough existence was an important motive for many an expedition member's apparent yearning for the pleasures of nature. The representatives of civilisation found it expedient, in this case, to submit to local custom. Peary himself writes: 'should an explorer consider it his duty to inform a young Eskimo that it is not done to exchange wives with his friend, he must be sure of his arguments, because the young man will most likely open wide his eyes and ask "why not?"'

Roald Amundsen got to hear other unpleasant things about his great idol. 'Dr. Cook, in every way a trustworthy man, informed me, when asked, the following about E. A's much referred-to illness: What I say here is only second-hand, conjecture. On the return of the 2nd Peary expedition the accompanying artist told me that the doctor, Vincent, had used all their available syphilis medicine and had recently been at a loss having run out of all supplies. Typhoid, which it is alleged E.A. suffered from, cannot be contracted in the Polar Regions.'

Having quoted Dr Cook's unconfirmed diagnosis in his diary, Roald Amundsen concluded: 'If it is so, that this brave boy has contracted such an accursed sickness, then I feel doubly for him. His highest and only aspiration was polar exploration. This was denied him in the prime of his life when he was well on the way. Think about this, you, who so easily criticise others, and I think you will modify your judgement. Poor, poor boy.'

The *Belgica*'s odyssey soon developed into a nightmare of epic proportions. The whole affair was a heroic, amateur, improvised flirtation with death. Where life had spent thousands of years in a struggle to adapt and survive merely to exist, now humans, waving national flags, tried to settle in, in the course of one brief polar night.

Scurvy proved to be the *Belgica*'s principal curse. It affected the entire crew and claimed the life of the Belgian Emile Danco. Scurvy preyed on men's fears and, one after the other, members of the crew descended into insanity. Morale was shattered. The bulkheads rang as if to the sounds of emperor penguins' underwater screams: men's incoherent rantings and desperate threats of murder.

Apart from the doctor, whose hands were full, one man adjusted to the frozen hell. It took something like this for him to discover his true vocation in life. The polar night reached its nadir on 30 May and the first officer noted that the sun was on its way back. 'Of course I will be happy to see it again, but I have felt remarkably well all the time and have not missed it for one moment. On the contrary. After all, this is the life I have been yearning for. It was not a childish impulse that caused me to sign on. It was long-term strategy. I regret nothing and hope I have the strength and health to continue what I have started.'

Roald Amundsen got to work. Not, as it happened, as a first officer – the ship was icebound – fate rules – but as an apprentice explorer. He frolicked in the pack ice like a child in a playground. He studied nutrition. He devoured every new dish the Antarctic offered him. Scurvy raged but the first officer put on weight and was the heaviest on board at 87.5kg. To stay healthy it was necessary to eat fresh food, and especially penguins. 'Their meat is excellent, not unlike beef.'

Clothing was a priority. Again, animals, particularly seals, provide the raw material. Night-time too, demanded an outfit. The first officer drew sleeping bags of various designs – Dr Cook's, Astrup's, Peary's. (Peary's patent had sleeves designed for polar bear hunters; if they were attacked at night they could quickly grab a rifle.) Amundsen concluded – for the time being – that Nansen's treble Greenland bag was the most sensible in terms of weight and warmth.

Dr Cook was teacher and fellow student in every sphere of learning. 'As an experienced polar region man I have complete faith in him.' As the commander lost everyone's respect, confidence in the calm, practical and eternally optimistic ship's doctor increased.

Roald Amundsen did not usually dream of his native land, but he never forgot significant dates, neither that of his mother's death, nor Betty's birthday. He imagined her 'plump and pleasant' on an island in the skerries off south-eastern Norway, 'about to pour her guests' coffee'.

On board the *Belgica* each and every national holiday was celebrated with speeches and champagne. On the other hand, 1 May was ignored, certainly 'astern'. Except that the first officer could not refrain from making a few sarcastic comments about 'the socialists' day'. Definitely not *his* day. 'We stay at home and gather strength for the 17th. Now, that's something else. That's the day we'll all shout for joy.'

The first officer was a patriot; he was Norway's man 'astern' on board the prison-ship in the pack-ice. His spirits rose on the national day. 'Light, clear spring morning at home. Jubilant, the flocks of children march through the streets. It is May 17th; it is our day of freedom.'*

* Translator's note: On 17 May, Norway's National Day, schoolchildren march through the streets waving flags and singing patriotic songs.

Six months after the flocks of children were marching in Roald Amundsen's thoughts, on board a conflict was brewing between the Norwegian and the Belgian command. It has come to light that Gerlache had entered into a secret agreement with the Geographical Society in his native Belgium that, whatever happened, the expedition must be led by a Belgian officer. The first officer considered this agreement 'a deliberate offence'. He immediately asked the commander for an 'audience' and made the following announcement: 'For me there no longer exists a Belgian Antarctic expedition.' It has to be said that this was a somewhat strange declaration, made as it was in the commander's cabin on board a Belgian ship icebound in the Antarctic.

The subordinate officer outlined the new situation as he saw it: 'I consider *Belgica* to be a mere ordinary vessel, surrounded by ice. My duty calls on me to help the handful of men gathered here on board. For that reason, Mr. Commander, I will continue my work, and try to exercise my duty as a human being.' Herein lies the reason for the commander's nameless presence in the autobiography Amundsen wrote thirty years later. For Amundsen, Gerlache and his expedition quite simply ceased to exist on 15 November 1898. Roald Amundsen's break with *Belgica*'s ostensible command was a forewarning of similar confrontations towards the end of the polar explorer's life.

Roald Amundsen's single-handed mutiny on board *Belgica* was no rebellion for the cause of truth and justice *per se*. The first officer had not objected when the commander led the crew up the garden path by falsifying the latitudes. When he reacted so uncompromisingly to a hypothetical arrangement, it was solely because he thought the insult was aimed at him personally, and consequently at the country he represented. His behaviour was carefully calculated; 'on the advice of Dr. Cook' he made sure there was written evidence of what had happened. The document would serve as a 'testimony to my actions'.

His new independence enabled the first officer to indulge his national bias. He had no doubt that without the Norwegian contingent the 'expedition would get nowhere.' It does not follow that he was immodest. 'For my part, I have nothing to be proud of, but, as their commanding officer I can testify to these four brave boys' competence. Sad that they get such little praise. Between us and the Belgian nation there exists in thought and deed such a vast difference, that we would never be able to work well together.'

Their first wintering in the Antarctic was on the point of degenerating into permanent torpor and ultimate disaster. It was not a foregone conclusion that the *Belgica* would break loose from the ice at the end of the winter. In his memoirs Roald Amundsen credits Dr Cook with the honour of saving the expedition from its icebound state. Following the doctor's directions the emaciated crew, with yellowish-green faces and clad in pink blankets, set to carving a channel out of the ice. With Dr Cook's ingenuity, experience and indefatigable will, not to mention a certain amount of dynamite, in the end they managed to free the ship from its icy grip. By the end of March 1899 the *Belgica* was back at the southern tip of South America.

Earlier the crew 'aft' had assembled to name the scraps of Antarctic islets near Graham Land which the expedition could justly claim the honour of having discovered. Naturally, the spokesman at the baptismal font was the commander. The expedition's two casualties, the Norwegian August Wiencke and the Belgian Emile Danco, were immortalised on the charts. But towards the end everyone was given the opportunity 'to give a name'. Roald Amundsen would, for the first time in his life, name something upon the earth. 'With great joy I called a beautiful promontory on Wiencke's Island Cape Eivind Astrup.'

At the same time as the *Belgica* turned back for South America a new expedition was on its way into the ice. This too was an international undertaking. The organisation was British, the leadership was Norwegian. Yet another boy from Christiania, Carsten Borchgrevink and the *Southern Cross*, were to acquaint themselves with the Antarctic winter. The expedition left the ship and accomplished the first wintering on the Antarctic mainland. Yet another step had been taken towards the conquest of the South Pole. New expeditions followed in quick succession.

It would be another ten years before Roald Amundsen returned to the Antarctic. But his faith in his choice of mission was total, never stronger than after his experience on the horror-ship, the *Belgica*. During one lonely night-watch on the north coast of Graham Land he summed up his philosophy thus: 'Summer nights and winter nights are both beautiful, but they are not as gripping as this silent, cold, moon-lit polar night. One is gripped by a strange feeling. Did God create this entire, vast area that it should lie forsaken and forgotten by humans? No and no again, surely not. It is our duty to do what we can to discover these God-given riches. Onwards, yes, onwards. Even the ice's impenetrable might must bend to the advance of the God-empowered human spirit.'

FIVE

The Two-pronged Plan

'To my great surprise I see that you are expecting Roald home on Whit Saturday or Whit Sunday and that he probably is now already home.' So wrote Leon Amundsen in a letter to his brother Gustav on 23 May 1899. Confusion reigned about the polar explorer's actual return.

As a logical corollary to his imaginary discharge, the first officer left the *Belgica* to its own devices and returned home from South America on his own; a pattern he would repeat thirteen years later, if under slightly different circumstances. This time, on the whole, only his brothers wondered where he was.

Leon had hoped Roald would travel via France and visit him in Cognac. 'The room, decorated with flags and flowers has been waiting for you,' he wrote home resignedly when he realised that the explorer of the South Pole had turned up in Christiania.

The break with the Belgian kingdom was superficial enough for the first officer to accept the Order of Leopold as the first of his many decorations. That aside, any tribute paid by the regime of a foreign country did not interest him. On his return, apart from Betty and his brothers, he wanted to meet only one man; the giant from Lysaker – Fridtjof Nansen. At last Amundsen had something to offer. He had seen the Antarctic. Nansen had not; only in his dreams, in the cave on Franz Josef Land.

'My most heartfelt congratulations on your successful journey and welcome back from the first human wintering in antarctic regions,' Fridtjof Nansen answered promptly as soon as his compatriot announced his return to his native country. 'It would please me enormously to see you and personally welcome you as it would interest me to learn about your experiences. Whenever it suits you and I am at home you are welcome.'

This unconditional courtesy from the important, normally unapproachable Arctic Ocean explorer must have surprised the returned apprentice. It would take some years before Roald Amundsen understood what was at the bottom of Fridtjof Nansen's palpable interest in his Antarctic experiences.

Unlike Dr Cook, Amundsen did not, on his return, publish a travelogue. It was not the crew's duty to write books. The published word was no private matter, it was official business. It was the job of the boss, however incompetent he might have been. Every expedition leader had the right to compose his own story – undisturbed. It was a principle to which Roald Amundsen stuck throughout his career. History belongs to the leader – the crew are bit players, walk-on parts.

Roald Amundsen had no reason to dwell on the *Belgica* expedition; it had not been his own. Even during the wintering in the Antarctic his thoughts had been focused in a different direction. A main objective of Gerlache's expedition had been the magnetic South Pole. It never got there. In his forthcoming book Roald Amundsen wrote: 'My plans matured during this voyage: I wished to unite my childhood dreams about the North West Passage with the, in itself, far more important objective: *To determine the magnetic North Pole's present position.*'

On 9 September 1899, Roald Amundsen started a new diary. Together with Leon he cycled from Christiania to Paris and from there on to Cognac; Roald continued alone to Cartagena via Madrid. Here he signed on the family-owned barque *Oscar*, which set sail for the United States. The polar explorer needed more time at sea to pass his master's certificate. The paperwork must be in order when one's goal is to conquer one of the world's most dangerous sea routes. He took his bicycle with him. He wrote to Leon that he hoped to 'make use of it in America, as the roads there are, supposedly, so wonderful'.

Roald Amundsen was an inquisitive traveller. He had no need to leave civilisation to make anthropological observations. He wrote to Gustav from Pensacola: 'As far as Pensacola is concerned, it's just rubbish. Nothing to see. On the other hand, there is an abundance of ladies. I have never been to a town with so many brothels, in spite of there only being 20,000 inhabitants. Everything is available. From the sweetest little American lady to a loathsome Negro or Red Indian. There you have it; other amusements there are none.'

Gustav, who a few years earlier had bought his own apartment building at 20 Tidemandsgate, is the brothers' fixed point in Christiania. Every letter received from Roald was accompanied by some instruction, like this one from Pensacola: 'Please enclose 10 kroner in this letter and send it to Betsia.'

In April 1900 the *Oscar* docked in Grimsby. It was in this town that Roald Amundsen managed to secure a complete library of everything that had ever been written about the North West Passage.

At home in Christiania he moved Betty and the remainder of his possessions into 45 Professor Dahlsgate. 'You cannot imagine how cosy we are,' he wrote to Leon, who had just returned from a circumnavigation of the globe. 'No neighbours and a wonderful view over the mountains in Asker and beyond. There are a few children around, but I just barge my way through them.' Roald Amundsen did not linger by the window. Following a summery visit to relatives in Hvidsten and some weeks' military training, he was once again off to sea.

In September 1900 Roald Amundsen enrolled at Deutsche Seewarte in Hamburg to study magnetism. Before travelling to the Emperor's Germany he had applied to study at a British observatory. 'The Director did not accommodate my request.' The rejection by England was not forgotten and was underlined in the autobiography a generation later.

However, from the nearly 80-year-old bachelor Professor George von Neumayer he received only goodwill. He wrote to Leon at the beginning of October: 'Professor Neumayer is considered the absolute authority on the subject of the earth's magnetism. It will thus be very useful to me to have studied with him personally.' A week later the student is pitched headlong into professorial circles: 'Last night, at about 7, as I was about to start work, a messenger arrived with a note from Prof. Neumayer asking me to come to Hotel Streits – one of the large, nice hotels on Jungfernstieg – right next to where I live. Of course I immediately pulled on my tails and rushed over. Prof. N greeted me and introduced me to Prof. Mohn from Christiania – a man of great standing, here and at home. We talked for some time – especially about my planned venture. When Prof. N introduces me he always adds "the young man, who is going to determine the accurate position of the magnetic North Pole".'

Later, Roald Amundsen would take every opportunity to honour the old professor. His student days in Hamburg and later studies at the observatories in Wilhelmshaven and Potsdam form the basis of a positive relationship between the polar explorer and the German Reich.

Roald returned home to Christiania on 20 November 1900, bristling with magnetic knowledge, ready for the next and decisive move en route to the North West Passage. A few weeks before Christmas he called on Fridtjof Nansen to submit his two-pronged plan: the North West Passage and the magnetic North Pole. With its mix of the plain and the popular, and the weighty scientific, the plan was cobbled together in the same way as Nansen's *Fram* expedition and its dual goal: the North Pole and the transpolar current.

No support was more important to Roald Amundsen than the support he might get from Fridtjof Nansen. Following his return from the first *Fram* expedition his position as the world's leading polar scientist was unchallenged.

At the time in question the polar ship was once again to be found in icebound waters. The so-called second *Fram* expedition was being led by Nansen's close colleague from Greenland and the Arctic Ocean, Otto Sverdrup. When the young Amundsen called on Nansen, Sverdrup was sailing among newly discovered islands north of Greenland. He was toying with the idea of the North Pole and was not averse to trying the North West Passage.

According to the captain's confidant on board, Ivar Fosheim, the relationship between the two old friends Sverdrup and Nansen following their return from the Arctic Ocean was not what it had once been. Nansen must probably take the blame for this. His difficult character and dark disposition, especially in these years of conquest, made him an awkward man to deal with.

It has often been claimed that the relationship between Fridtjof Nansen and the eleven-years younger Roald Amundsen was never very warm. However, there is nothing to suggest that Amundsen was received with less enthusiasm at Lysaker than he was in Hamburg. On the contrary, the young man's plans, combining elements of adventure and science, were exactly after Nansen's heart. Roald Amundsen presented himself as a tailor-made successor without – as yet – threatening the professor's own position.

Nansen would recall this meeting with Amundsen in his eulogy many years later: 'He emphasised that this investigation of the magnetic pole was the expedition's mission statement, the scientific core which gave it legitimacy, and that, as they were already there, they might as well include the North West Passage.' This retrospective account shows that Roald Amundsen knew how to play his cards, and in the right order. The outcome was that Fridtjof Nansen backed Roald Amundsen wholeheartedly – both the plan and the man. Subsequently the relationship between these two giants of polar exploration, men from an otherwise insignificant nation, would pass through many phases.

Next move. After the New Year Roald Amundsen made his way to Tromsø, capital of the Arctic Ocean. He was about to conquer the North West Passage and needed a suitable boat. On 14 January 1901, he informed Leon in Christiania that he was in the throes of negotiating the purchase of a ship. Gustav was asked to send 10,000 crowns to Tromsø, 'please note, without causing you any inconvenience'.

It was time for Roald to cash in his inheritance. Nansen is behind him and *Gjøa* is his. After taking possession of the 47-tonne yacht he remained in Tromsø fully occupied refitting the former whaling vessel to his own specifications. 'My social intercourse,' he wrote to Leon, 'is restricted to receiving visitors every Sunday afternoon.' The newly fledged ship-owner had rented a room in the attic with a view of the harbour. 'I invite one or the other of the old Arctic Ocean skippers to coffee and am entertained with lots of stories. Many of these old chaps are interesting and informative.'

In April *Gjøa* set sail for a six-month trial period in northern waters, partly to hunt, partly to carry out research in the name of Professor Nansen. The night before he left Tromsø Roald wrote his brother a farewell letter; the 30-year-old Leon had decided to get married. In Cognac he had become engaged to the Norwegian Consul Marten's not yet 20-year-old daughter Aline. 'Thank you for your brotherly love, which shines through all you do. I hope and am sure, that in Aline you will find the wife you deserve.'

His brother's matrimonial progress, however, did not proceed at the same breakneck speed as Roald's polar preparations. When *Gjøa* returned in September he was in time to contribute to the brothers' joint dispatch of presents – 'cream jug and sugar bowl' – to the wedding in Cognac. 'You know times are difficult, so it's not much,' wrote the polar explorer.

Late in the autumn of 1901 Roald Amundsen made his debut at the Geographical Society in Christiania with a lecture entitled 'My Planned Journey'. In future his life would be more or less equally divided between polar regions and the lecture hall. 'Fortunately I have procured some slides,' he wrote to Leon. 'Without this it would all be too boring.' Their box and the glass-plates became trusted companions for many years to come.

In the New Year of 1902 the polar explorer launched himself into the most difficult stage: the economic. Yet again he took the road to Lysaker. Cognac received the following report: 'In this connection I have approached Professor Nansen and he has promised to investigate how I am to proceed. This is very important for me. I consider the battle half won when that man takes an interest.'

Roald Amundsen, always inclined towards optimistic estimates, believed he could manage with 50,000 crowns, but the money was not easily come by. In the course of two years the impoverished mountain-country had financed the fitting out of two *Fram* expeditions. Rich backers were thin on the ground and their cheque books were rarely in evidence. But Amundsen's confidence in the magician from Lysaker was unshakeable – even a year later: 'I do not know whether the necessary funds have been raised but I feel nonetheless safe as the matter has been entrusted to Professor Nansen.'

The business, practical and scientific preparations for the *Gjøa* voyage spurred Roald Amundsen on to an ever more feverish pace. It was not always easy to chart his movements. 'When I am in Hamburg I will make a detour and come and visit,' he wrote to Leon in April 1902, 'but it will have to be on the quiet as no one must know. It could possibly harm the support I am seeking. So not a word about this to anyone, please.'

In the autumn of 1902 Roald Amundsen first received his master's certificate and then made the unavoidable visit to the powers that be at the Royal

Geographical Society (RGS) in London. Most encouragingly, the Society decided to support the journey, albeit with a nominal sum. Meanwhile, Roald was contemplating another trip to the United States. In this connection he turned for hospitality to his old colleague Frederick Cook, who was keen to receive him. 'By all means, come to N.Y.' The previous year Dr Cook had drummed up some publicity for his friend on the other side of the Atlantic.

In the summer of 1902 Roald Amundsen met up with someone else who was prepared to publicise the *Gjøa* expedition. At the Theatre Café, across the road from the newly constructed National Theatre in Christiania, he was reunited with his old school friend Fredrik Herman Gade. The charming and by now worldly Gade had been brought up on the Frogner country estate outside town but in 1888 he had travelled to his mother's home country and enrolled at the family's alma mater in Boston. Herman Gade was to become his closest friend in a life of many, as yet, unwritten chapters.

Rain falls over the Christiania Fjord during the night of 16 June. Silently, the smallest polar ship of all time, *Gjøa*, is towed down the fjord. The fanfares will have to wait until the ship's return. Only the crew's close families are at the quay to bid farewell.

The expedition's meagre budget had hung like a sword of Damocles over Roald Amundsen right up to the day of departure. In total, not counting the ship and goods, the undertaking would cost 150,000 crowns, three times the original estimate. Loans and guarantees, secured in the days leading up to departure, accounted for 14,000 crowns.

In his memoirs Roald Amundsen compared the night-time departure to some heroic crime, a flight from at least one furious creditor. 'I was desperate and decided to attempt a desperate way out. I sent for my six carefully selected companions, explained my predicament, and asked whether they agreed to my solution. They approved enthusiastically. At midnight on 16 June, we seven left together, in pouring rain, for the quay where *Gjøa* was moored, boarded, cast off and stood out towards the Skagerak and the North Sea. When day dawned on our awful creditor we were safely out in open sea. The Jolly Roger has never seen seven such happy pirates.'

Roald Amundsen's subsequent portrayal of himself as a pirate captain in the service of science, not to mention the Robin Hood of polar exploration, says a lot about the ageing man's self-perception. But as the description of a voyage supported by His Majesty the King and Fridtjof Nansen, it is hardly appropriate.

Three passengers had joined *Gjøa* on its first leg down the Christiania Fjord: Roald's brothers. But now the youngest had become the oldest. Anxiety had worn

Roald down. The 31-year-old left the town of his childhood with the features of an old man.

Gustav and Leon had both been active participants in the expedition's preparations. Gustav had gone begging. His powers of persuasion and charm had helped fleece landowner Anker of 10,000 crowns, merchant Wiel of 5,000. But Busken's own affairs had met with difficulties. He had moved from shipping to trading in coke and wood, and not all his decisions had met with equal success. In reality the second oldest brother's financial circumstances were so wretched that Roald, ere *Gjøa* had left civilisation, found it expedient to insert his nephew, Gustav Jnr, 'as beneficiary of that part which would otherwise under normal conditions fall to my brother G.A'. No one could be sure of returning alive from the North West Passage.

Two days before departure from Christiania Gustav was deprived of his power of attorney which was transferred to Leon, who had moved back home from France that spring to start his own business as a wine-importer. The polar explorer had left his flat to his newly wed brother. He knew that Betty and his affairs were in safe hands as long as Leon was at home.

Gjøa's departure saw the start of a protracted tug-of-war between the brothers. Leon's homecoming pushed Gustav to one side. Who would now be the polar explorer's confidant? Who would bask in reflected glory? Who would stand in the shadows? Who would benefit from any financial gains? So far they had all been equals, nearly. They all represented Roald.

At Færder lighthouse, at the mouth of the Christiania Fjord, the tugboat cast off and returned to Christiania. *Gjøa* continued under her own sails. Goodbye, baby brother.

SIX

The Governor

The single-masted *Gjøa* lay low in the water, laden with provisions, equipment and fuel for an eternity. Courageous seamen had been hunting for the North West Passage for four hundred years; it was vital to prepare for a few more winters.

Squeezed in between the deck cargo were a few ragged huskies, survivors from Sverdrup's second *Fram* expedition which had returned the previous year. The six dogs were kept on a leash until they were well out into the North Sea. The crew, on the other hand, went willingly. They were six in number too, in addition to 'The Governor' as they called him, Roald Amundsen.

No polar ship is without a lieutenant. *Gjøa*'s second-in-command was the 27-year-old Godfred Hansen. Moreover, he was Danish and the son of a former lord mayor of Copenhagen. What was a Danish naval officer doing on board a Norwegian Arctic Ocean vessel? Possibly because *Gjøa* was on its way towards Danish territory – or was it on account of his many pertinent skills? Amundsen describes him as a 'navigator, astrologer, geologist, and photographer'. He was also allegedly familiar with things electrical. *Gjøa*'s first lieutenant was an educated and good-looking man, although maybe a tad effeminate for a polar expedition.

The only person to have sailed with *Gjøa* and Amundsen before was the 30-year-old engineer Peder Ristvedt from Sandsvær. He had met Roald Amundsen three years earlier during their military service and would prove to be the expedition's most trustworthy member.

The first officer was Anton Lund, one of two crew members from Tromsø, at 39 the oldest of them all. He was married and had sailed the Arctic Ocean for over twenty years. Six years younger, the second officer was also a Tromsø man. Helmer Hanssen had left his wife and first-born to sail with Amundsen. He had met the Governor as he was about to depart with the *Belgica* and was the man who would stick by Roald Amundsen through thick and thin and longer than anyone else.

Helmer Hanssen had been recommended for the *Gjøa* trip by the chemist Fritz G. Zapffe, a man after Amundsen's heart. They got to know each other during the polar explorer's long sojourns in Tromsø. The pharmacy, The North Star, would for many years act as Roald Amundsen's private embassy in the Arctic Ocean's capital. The pharmacist's commissions for the polar explorer were countless, the most important of which was to recruit crew straight off the ice. Helmer Hanssen was his greatest find: 'Rather good-looking, unassuming, and seemingly much civilised, average height. Undoubtedly the most worthy of recommendation of them all.' Hanssen's only drawback was that he was married, which added economic strain to the expedition. But Zapffe thought it was worthwhile keeping Mrs Hanssen alive: 'He is so fit and magnificent and neat – I am sure you will find him agreeable.' the pharmacist wrote in his recommendation. It would take nearly twenty years before Roald Amundsen found Helmer Hanssen disagreeable.

Among the six one other would later follow Roald Amundsen to the Antarctic: the legendary polar cook Adolf Henrik Lindstrøm. The stocky gentleman from Hammerfest was born in 1865, on 17 May itself, Norway's National Day. He had no sooner returned from four years as a steward on the second *Fram* journey, than he was yet again heading for the ice. Captain Sverdrup's enthusiasm for the good-natured cook was not entirely undivided. Lindstrøm not only liked food, he was equally partial to a dram or two.

'The last person to join the crew was Gustav Juel Wiik,' Roald Amundsen wrote to Leon in February 1903 from Potsdam, where he was putting the finishing touches to his lightning education in magnetic spheres. 'He is a subaltern in the Navy, has a master's certificate and has been a clerk.' Amundsen saw a budding scientist in the 25-year-old from Horten. 'He will relieve me here now, in order that he, as my assistant, can get used to the instruments.' The youngest and liveliest of the expedition members was, nevertheless, sensitive and philosophical. No one on board the happy vessel suspected that Gustav Wiik would meet his destiny on the far side of the North West Passage.

Godhavn, on Greenland's west coast, was the expedition's last landfall in a civilised location. Here they stocked up on petroleum and increased the number of dogs. In addition the local Eskimos performed a 'gala'. 'They danced particularly well. I have seldom seen better rhythm or surer movement,' Roald Amundsen noted in what until then had been his blank diary. 'The figures come into their own in their tight plus-fours. There are not many pure Eskimo types around. They all have a semi-Danish appearance.'

On the last day of July the expedition set out towards virgin waters. After fourteen days along the west coast *Gjøa* had passed her first obstacle. 'As if by an act of God,' the captain notes, 'the ice opened up and we advanced rapidly towards land without any hindrance.' With Melville Bay, that notorious stretch of water, safely crossed, Amundsen offered 'a heartfelt thanks to God, who led us through'.

Gjøa found herself in picturesque latitudes. 'At the sight of the glacier, where our brave compatriot Eivind Astrup ascended with Peary to start their walk over the inland icecap, I had difficulty in tearing my eyes and my thoughts away,' Roald Amundsen wrote in *The North West Passage*.

On 22 August they came upon the first objects left behind by the ill-fated Franklin expedition and its many rescue missions: graves, marble memorials and ruined depots. 'Empty tins lie scattered around and all one comes across is spoilt,' Amundsen noted following a dejected inspection of holy ground. The only things of value were 'lots of American shoe-leather and a good bit of coal'.

Having left Greenland's coast behind *Gjøa* sailed in a south-westerly direction amid the North Canadian islands. Roald Amundsen's strategy was to search for the North West Passage along a more southerly route than most of his predecessors.

On the morning of 31 August the captain, who had stood watch in the night, was woken in his bunk by a powerful blow to the hull. The second-in-command was at the helm. Amundsen rushed up on deck, followed by Peder Ristvedt: 'At first I saw the Governor in his underpants towering on deck, next I heard a Danish voice, exclaiming triumphantly: "She's holding". In spite of warnings from Wiik and H. Hansen he had run us aground, on shoals that could be seen for at least ¼ mile in every direction.'

Towing the boat off was the least of their problems compared to that of Hansen; Godfred Hansen – first lieutenant in the Danish Navy. It was no longer news to the *Gjøa*'s crew that his navigational skills were non-existent. They had already nicknamed him 'Kjoms' – fool. In his diary Wiik called him a 'mummy's boy, who cannot wash himself, strews his clothes all over deck – and the Governor who is a stickler for order'. Ristvedt described the lieutenant initially as a 'poor thing, very brave when the weather is good, but in bad weather and high seas – then he's timid.'

A few days later *Gjøa* ran aground again. This time several days and nights passed before the storm tore the boat off. Towards the end the situation became critical: 'We bumped over the shallow reef. I was sure our last hour had come. Oh dear, oh dear. Each wave stronger than the last,' Amundsen wrote. 'We quickly threw supply crates into the sea. The ship shuddered violently and slid off. From the bottom of my heart I thanked God for having led us through.'

Having survived storms, fire and grounding, on 9 September 1903, *Gjøa* hove to for her first over-wintering in an inlet on King William Land. The ship was to lie there for nearly two years. Gjøahavn – Gjøa harbour, as the Governor christened the spot, lay south of 70° North, south of what in reality had been the starting point, the harbour of Tromsø – nevertheless, beyond all civilisation and not far from where Sir James Ross had pinpointed the magnetic North Pole in 1831.

Gjøahavn, outermost outpost of civilisation, consisted of two units: the vessel – soon to be snowed under and icebound; and, on a height above the bay, the observatory. This was a house built of crates (only copper nails were used) called The Magnet. Inside this scientific centre Wiik and Ristvedt made their berths. From here the first meeting between Roald Amundsen and the indigenous inhabitants was observed on 29 October 1903.

A handful of Eskimos turned up on the heights above *Gjøa*. Amundsen advanced towards them, followed closely by Lund and Helmer Hanssen, each carrying a rifle. 'It was a most amusing scene and we enjoyed it to the full from our vantage point,' Ristvedt writes. 'The Governor waved his arms around and shouted "Veimi", which is, supposedly, an Eskimo greeting, which it was not. The Eskimos seemed to be on top of the situation, advanced and shouted "Maniktumi".'

Roald Amundsen had himself described this unique meeting of two cultures with considerable irony in *The North West Passage*. On the other hand, in his autobiography – a world war and several decades later – the irony had receded and the Arctic Napoleon had come to the fore: 'They were equipped as for war, but there was nothing to do but meet them face to face. The two units continued, until they were fifteen paces apart, then halted. I turned to my "army" and asked them clearly and with gestures to throw their rifles away. Then I turned to the Eskimos. When their leader saw this manifestation of peace, he repeated it; in as far as he turned to his comrades and gave them an order. They obeyed and threw away their bows and arrows. I was unarmed and drew close to them.'

In all versions the scene ends with applause, hugs and total fraternisation. 'Ristvedt and I lay on the height, held our stomachs and laughed as it was extremely comical,' Wiik ends his tale.

Every polar expedition dreaded the monotony of wintering. Daily magnetic and meteorological measurements were taken; apart from that only the cook was fully employed. Roald Amundsen resorted to Nansen's old trick from *Fram*'s wintering in the Arctic Ocean. He ordered the troops to go skiing. Diary: 'Every morning from 9 to 10.30 we exercised on a hill close by. We called the hill Holmenkollen of course.'*

---

* Translator's note: Holmenkollen is the world famous ski-jump outside Oslo.

One November morning the two occupants of the Magnet were ten minutes
late for breakfast and were reprimanded. 'Thereafter followed the ski-trip,'
Ristvedt noted, not without glee. 'We brought along a shovel. To avenge
ourselves Lund and I built a big jump with a solid lip to it. The Governor was
first to go and I wanted to see him on his back. To be sure, he jumped like a hero
but landed on his back and was hit on the forehead by one of his skis, resulting in
a huge bump. He was followed by the lieutenant who fell on top of the jump and
brought it down with him.'

Peder Ristvedt, possibly *Gjøa*'s most versatile crew member, engineer,
meteorologist, blacksmith, hunter and dog-lover, was becoming increasingly
hostile towards the Governor, not least concerning the treatment of the dogs:
'Today the Governor and I clashed,' he wrote on 20 November. 'Wiik and I had
asked if we could look after "Stilla's" puppies which were expected at the end
of the month. We wanted to have her with us and care for her. The Governor
refused this as he possibly believed, yes, he was positively sure that the puppies,
if they were to grow up as good dogs, had to be hardened from the start.
Consequently "Stilla", who had nowhere to go, gave birth to her puppies today
in minus 30 degrees. I was smithying when she came running with a puppy in
her mouth followed by the entire pack, who took the puppy from her and ate it.
I quickly got "Stilla" inside and she remained there until it was all over.'

The following year 'Silla' (the spelling of the name varies) gave birth to her
puppies, protected by Wiik and Ristvedt. But even then the captain interfered:
'The Governor took Silla's puppies from her today, they are not yet one month
old, now they are on board and howling miserably. That man is ridiculous.'
But next day: 'Silla surprised us today by walking up the ladder from the ice.
It is unbelievable what mother-love can do. She took one of her puppies back,
the others remain in custody with the Governor. He either knows no better, or
he enjoys tormenting animals. Either way, the puppies are not happy, they are
not fed well and they are soaked by excrement and urine.' Two days later: 'The
Governor is bored with his foster children and Silla has got them back. He had
the puppies on board for four days, but when I asked him this morning what he
gave them to drink he said that he had not yet tried to give them anything. What
tenacious little creatures!'

Gustav Wiik, Ristvedt's co-lodger in Villa Magnet, shared his opinion of
the Governor's dog-keeping abilities, but he remained much more open to
the leader's positive attributes. Ristvedt had already made up his mind about the
expedition leadership by the first autumn. It was not the first time he had sailed
with the Governor.

Alongside Roald Amundsen and the lieutenant, young Wiik completed the
educated bloc in the crew. He and the Governor had friends in common in

the capital and shared experiences from Potsdam. Privately Amundsen showed confidence in Wiik, shared his thoughts and discussed his plans with him. On his first birthday on board a present from Captain Amundsen, Hjalmar Johansen's book about his adventures with Nansen, awaited him at the breakfast table. At this stage there seems little doubt: 'The Governor is a brick in every way, easy going and happy-go-lucky.' But Wiik would change his mind, just as Amundsen too had changed his mind about the commander of the *Belgica*. Wiik was young and impressionable. He kept a detailed and frank diary; no other thoughts aboard the *Gjøa* are as easily discernible as those of Wiik.

As time passed relations with the Eskimos developed and the crew came to understand something of their new friends' language. Roald Amundsen learned much more about the fate of the Franklin expedition. The Admiral had died not far from Gjøahavn, on the other side of King William Land. Amundsen continuously kept an eye open for Eskimo handicrafts, for which he would barter, thereby adding to his ethnographical collection. He became particularly excited when some item or other turned up which might hail from the Franklin ships. He picked up information about the bartering methods in use a few generations earlier: 'For an empty crate or something similar the white men get to sleep with an Eskimo woman,' he noted in his diary.

In the spring of 1904 the time had come to track down the magnetic North Pole. Together with the indispensable Peder Ristvedt, Roald Amundsen set out on a northbound sledge journey. The walk to the magnetic point was like wandering around on the drift-ice; the surroundings were in constant motion. 'The Governor contemplated what had become of the Pole,' Ristvedt noted in his sledge-diary.

In the absence of any success in pinpointing the position of the Pole, the national day, 17 May, was celebrated as the high point of the expedition. 'After breakfast we went out, decorated the tent with flags and photographed it all,' Ristvedt recorded. 'Speeches were held for the mother country, the King, Lindstrøm, et al.'

The attraction of magnetism for Roald Amundsen was waning. Six months later Ristvedt noted: 'Wiik works continually on the magnetic north. The Governor and the Lieutenant read novels and smoke and go for walks from time to time. It is unbelievable that a man can change like the Governor has in the course of one year. Last year he worked constantly with his observations. This year he has done nothing and we achieved nothing on our sledge trip this spring that was sufficiently accurate.'

Other things were causing distractions. Roald Amundsen was an untiring observer of Eskimo lifestyle and customs, not to mention the women.

Understandably, the men in Gjøahavn were preoccupied with Eskimo women. 'Some of these women are absolute beauties,' Roald Amundsen recorded in his diary. 'They are rather small but shapely.' Of more than passing interest to him was Eskimo custom on this delicate point. On 26 August he wrote in his diary: 'The men offer their wives for sale very cheaply – yes, for virtually nothing. A wife must obey but I doubt whether she does it of her own free will. I still am not sure about that.' Roald Amundsen noted the prevalence of wife-swapping and bigamy but 'Owing to the preponderance of men among these Eskimos it often happens that a wife has two husbands. Practical people!'

While the Governor and Ristvedt were tracking down the elusive Pole, young Wiik had an innocent rendezvous in the Villa Magnet with Kimaller, 'the most beautiful woman we have seen so far and one would have to look far and wide before one found a more beautiful face.' While her husband was hunting, the young wife, and 'a friend or two', visited the cheery scientist. Cupid's arrow had definitely struck Wiik: 'I am very sad that she left this evening – of course I liked her, very much in fact. And that lout of a husband, he's the biggest layabout I have ever met. She would have starved to death if I had not pinched food for her from the boat. My greatest honour and pleasure would be to put a bullet through his head.'

Roald Amundsen shared Wiik's opinion of Kimaller's husband Angudju: 'That such a woman has fallen into the hands of such a scoundrel, is really too sad,' he wrote in *The North West Passage*. 'Her beautiful eyes and profoundly mournful expression made her very attractive. She possessed what I have not found among the fair sex of the Netchjilli Eskimos – grace.'

Apart from Eskimos and their women, hunting was the expedition's principal leisure pursuit. This particular passion was shared by all but two. Lindstrøm swore by the stuffed variety of game – he was himself an expert taxidermist, and the Governor had no eye for game. He was adamant that polar explorers should not wear glasses. Anyhow, the hunting parties were not all they were cracked up to be.

'Whether they return with reindeer or not, is the question,' Gustav Wiik noted one day in September when the two Tromsø men kitted themselves out to go hunting. 'I smelt a rat when there was a lot of deliberation going on in the Eskimo tent last night. Lund and Hanssen, both old married men, admire these women greatly, but this is going too far.' The Villa Magnet's residents kept the hunting party under binocular surveillance. It was not long before explorer and Eskimo were united and disappeared into the Promised Land.

Four days later Ristvedt and Wiik spied 'two drained and stooping travellers, who on closer inspection turned out to be two married, honourable and indispensable natives of Northern Norway, namely L. and H.H. who had already left their wives and longed for Lindstrøm's fleshpots.' According to Wiik's diary it is not the first time the gentlemen from 'the reindeer town' had resorted to such business. The scientific assistant is plainly indignant, on behalf of himself, marriage and the expedition. The amorous transactions did, after all, require certain 'objects from the expedition's equipment' in exchange for the Eskimo wives.

A generation later Helmer Hanssen wrote in his memoirs that there was 'no demand for Mongol wives, so as a result there was no trade, not even on the part of the four unmarried members of the expedition.' The expedition leader too, in his autobiography, insisted that a highly principled stance had been maintained. He claimed that the Eskimo fundamentally regarded the white man as a divine being, but only up to that moment when he gets involved with native women: 'I therefore grasped the first opportunity to speak seriously with my comrades and warned them against giving in to such temptations.'

This 'first opportunity' is not mentioned in the *Gjøa* journey's diaries. However, there was another episode where the Governor found it necessary to 'speak seriously'. On 3 February 1905, a sick Eskimo boy turned up at Gjøahavn. 'On closer inspection we found that his feet, legs and thighs right up to the small of his back were full of nasty sores, some with a thick scab, others open and seeping. He felt no pain. This was plainly syphilis. He told us that his father, mother and siblings had the same rash. His grandmother had been together with a *kabluna* (white man) in Eivili and probably caught it there. I called all the men together to inform them and added that I assumed the illness was probably rife in the tribe.'

This important event, not mentioned in *The North West Passage*, has been cut out of Gustav Wiik's frank diary, as have many pages of this unique document from Roald Amundsen's first expedition.

A week after Lund and Hanssen's return the Governor himself went camping with the Eskimos. 'This trip is allegedly being called an autumn hunting trip,' Wiik noted in wonderment. 'No instruments are being taken; what an extraordinary affair. The Governor is, from what we have seen and heard, absolutely no shot.'

In the period between the unsuccessful magnetic north sledge trip and the start of the plan's second leg, the quest for the North West Passage, the *Gjøa* expedition found itself in a state of profound malaise. Gustav Wiik noted: 'It is extraordinary to see that already after only one year everyone has lost the desire to work and we all feel the need to get away from the vessel and camp out in the wilderness or even just to go to bed.' The last alludes to the novel-reading lieutenant.

Ristvedt too is bemused: 'The Governor apparently does not like being on board.' Amundsen was no longer the unifying force in Gjøahavn. On the contrary, 'he does his own thing, comes and goes when it suits him.' Ever since the sledge trip Amundsen's leg had pained him. He was taciturn and moody; it was generally assumed that the Governor was suffering from scurvy.

In spite of the suspicious excursions, large parts of the winter were spent on board. They played whist, and brother Leon had not only produced Christmas presents, but cognac too. Despite the Governor at the time being teetotal, it came to pass that one or other of them had a few too many and ended up blind drunk. The lounge was sometimes thick with tobacco smoke. 'When we boarded *Gjøa* neither the Governor nor Hansen G. smoked, now, on the other hand, the Governor is the most energetic smoker of us all, and has to smoke his pipe after meals and many times in between.' Wiik, who is still susceptible to his superior's charms, believed that 'the Governor is a convivial companion and entertaining.'

Lindstrøm became the centre of gravity, the rock on board the ship. No polar night could destroy the cook's sense of humour. 'Saw the first sign of spring today,' Ristvedt confirmed when the second over-wintering drew to a close. 'Lindstrøm has been shooting ptarmigan. It is the first time since we became icebound that he has left the ship. A funny chap. Fat as a pig, but always happy and in a good mood, in spite of having every reason to be bad-tempered.'

The Governor, unpredictable, moody and restless, was the cook's opposite, and studied the steady, if boozy Lindstrøm with a scientist's eyes. 'When he sets his mind on something he never gives up. The others laugh at him, but he just laughs back and continues on his way. He usually succeeds.' The apparently rather simple cook continuously reveals new facets of his character. He is a 'mechanical genius' and a 'competent zoologist'. 'A more able man cannot be found for a polar enterprise.'

The contrast between the broad Lindstrøm and the tall Amundsen was not restricted to temperament. The cook cared nothing for Eskimos, their language or their customs. The Governor on the other hand had discovered a new and fascinating field of research. Trade with the natives became one of his great passions. Officially, only the Governor was permitted to trade with expedition goods. Ristvedt worked at the smithy day and night; he provided knives, axes and other desirable goods for barter. In return the Governor provided valuable handicrafts for the benefit of the expedition and the museums in Norway.

But the scientist in Amundsen was not only interested in material articles and museum pieces. Above all he would have liked to have brought a live Eskimo back to civilisation. 'Our numbers have gone up,' Ristvedt noted close to Christmas 1904. 'The Governor has bought a 10-year-old little orphan boy. We washed him today and cut his hair and gave him new clothes. The

Lieut. has been given the task of educating him.' As the ship's most educated man, the laid-back Godfred Hansen from Copenhagen was delegated the task of educating the savage. 'He's been given a small berth and a sleeping bag and is staying with the Governor.' The experiment did not last long. But it would not be the last time Roald Amundsen tried to recruit primitive people to his family.

Gradually the Governor assembled an Eskimo household that lived and slept on board. He appointed the scoundrel husband Angudju as his private orderly. According to Wiik, 'there were always many of them. I cannot comprehend why on earth he needs them; they eat for three, but he can't afford to feed the dogs.'

Gustav Wiik was employed to be Amundsen's magnetic observations assistant and found it increasingly difficult to accept the leader's new folkloristic bent. On 22 January 1905, he complained: 'For 10 months out of 12 I alone have handled all the magnetic observations. Why the Governor wants to go now when the coldest month is approaching I really do not understand, but after all it is more pleasant to sleep in an igloo than be dependent on everything here.'

On the whole inter-racial peace and tolerance prevailed in Gjøahavn. But from time to time even Amundsen found the presence of the primitive people irritating and tiring. In the middle of February 1905 Ristvedt wrote that the Governor is 'totally belligerent' towards the Eskimos. He had been told that '¼ case of sledge-bread' and 'about 200 portions of pemmican' had been reported stolen from the expedition stores.

Captain Amundsen now displays his resolution, proving himself to be the supreme authority of the wilderness. He sent out a communiqué to all indigenous people present. 'If any of the thieves shows his face again he will be shot mercilessly.' He also let it be known 'that the tent will now be guarded by two men every night and anyone approaching will be shot.' 'I hope this will help,' he confided to his diary, but was not content with that. 'Tomorrow Ristvedt is laying a mine at the entrance to the tent. Should there be a repeat visit I assume it will be the last.'

The expedition leader must uphold his local authority, but this step tended towards over-reaction, considering that for eighteen months the *Gjøa* crew had lived in peaceful co-existence with the easy-going natives. The diaries show that the Governor's nerves were rather ragged this second winter in Gjøahavn.

Apart from never-ending measurements the work on the magnetic pole had ended. But the ship could only tackle the North West Passage in the summer and Roald Amundsen was temporarily hamstrung in sight of his goal. He had staked his all, and a lot of what others had, on this breakthrough. The responsibility was entirely his. The ship, the crew, the creditors at home; the 32-year-old carried the responsibility alone. Behind lay four hundred years of fruitless endeavour, ahead maybe four weeks to success. But he had to bide his time.

The diaries must be read against the backdrop of his fears and the might of the polar night. Nevertheless, the observations of the *Gjøa* crew are of crucial importance to our understanding of the Governor's personality. His name would mean nothing if he did not find the North West Passage. Without it his peers would judge him harshly; they would judge him by standards applied to normal human beings.

'These days one could cut oneself on the Governor,' Wiik noted during this most oppressive period. 'He frets and sulks like a small child and pokes his nose into everything. From now on we can expect sledge-trips and all kinds of things.' The crew never knew where he, or they, stood – literally sometimes, since the Governor could disappear for a couple of days without notice, but in other ways too. Ristvedt wrote that although the Governor can 'fume with anger, he never says anything, just sulks.'

Gustav Wiik noted that the Governor was devious. He gleaned information in his own way. 'He, commonly, would not speak to one directly, but, rather, would get there by speaking to others. He interrogated me last autumn, but won't do it again, because I merely referred him to the person in question.'

Roald Amundsen could be explosive. He could rule with dynamite and rifles. But he preferred to rule by secrecy.

SEVEN

The Flag Triumphs

At three in the morning of 13 August 1905, thick fog lies over Gjøahavn. The Eskimos in attendance see very little. But the sound from the ship's petroleum engine heralds the time of departure.

The seven white men leave the spot on earth they have called their own: Wiik Heights, Ristvedt River, Lindstrøm Valley, Helmer Hanssen Peak, Anton Lund's Isle. Besides they leave a buried tin with a portrait of Professor Neumayer, 'in deep gratitude and respectful remembrance'.

During the spring of 1905 First Lieutenant Hansen, with welcome assistance from Sergeant Ristvedt, undertook a long sledge journey in a north-easterly direction and distributed the names of civilisation along what would later be called King Haakon VII's Coast. Thus the tour of duty is over. The North West Passage beckons.

The major part of the expedition was already behind them. Only two weeks' sailing would remain before the critical straits were conquered. 'The passages were rather narrow and shallow, but we had lovely weather all the way and it was all such a pleasure,' Roald writes in his first letter to Leon after the goal had been reached.

Of course the two weeks presented more than a nerve-racking watch worrying about running aground. But Roald Amundsen was prepared. In spite of no one before him having sailed the entire stretch, he had his predecessors' observations to go by. *Gjøa*'s flexibility and the crew's experience were also decisive factors as they took soundings over unknown shallows. In addition 'lovely weather' and favourable ice conditions played their part. But, as would be demonstrated during Roald Amundsen's next big achievement, his expedition to the South Pole: when the plan is up to standard and the preparations good enough, the actual implementation is the least of the problem.

On 26 August the crew spots a ship. Roald Amundsen, who has had difficulty eating anything during the last few days' nail-biting journey, has described in his autobiography how, at that moment, knife in hand, he threw himself ravenously at a couple of semi-frozen reindeer carcasses, and ate until his stomach could take no more. The pent-up excitement was released.

The boat turns out to be a whaling ship sailing under the American flag. On board this simple vessel the classic scene unfolds between expedition leader and ship's captain, much as it had done between Stanley and Livingstone in the forests of Africa and between Jackson and Nansen on Franz Josef Land: 'Are you Captain Amundsen?'

Later Roald writes to Leon: 'I was most surprised when I stepped on board and was welcomed by name by Captain McKenna, captain of *Charles Hanson* out of S. Frisco.' He welcomed us as the first through the North West Passage and expressed his delight in being the first to do so. He had been ordered to look for us and assist us if necessary – but we had all we needed.'

However, this was only the beginning to the unexpected courtesy: 'On September 26th we stopped at Herschel and were offered assistance from all the whalers there. At the same time I was shown a copy from "The National Soc. of the Pacific" in which I realised the reason for all this goodwill. It was you who had set it all in motion and with the help of Nansen brought it about. May I some day have the opportunity to thank you.'

Leon Amundsen had cleared the first hurdle as his brother's press agent.

On board the *Charles Hanson* Captain Amundsen was handed a pile of old newspapers. It was not the first time during the past two years that the *Gjøa* heard from the outside world. An Eskimo courier had left Gjøahavn and returned on 20 May 1905 with news. The expedition had been informed of the war between Russia and Japan. But on board the *Charles Hanson* acts of war suddenly drew nearer. 'War between Norway and Sweden', hits the polar explorer from one of the old, badly informed American papers.

Gjøa's traverse of the North West Passage happened during a time when her native land found itself in murky constitutional waters. The country was at that moment a kingdom without a king. It had left the union with Sweden but had not yet established its own independent constitution. Relations with the old partner Sweden were so tense that a full mobilisation was ordered. No wonder a paper on the other side of the Atlantic might have drawn rather hasty conclusions.

From Cape Parry, where *Gjøa* encountered her first vessel, to the Bering Strait, where the North West and North East Passages meet, the remainder of the sea route lies open to Alaska. Nevertheless, once again *Gjøa* lies in winter quarters on this stretch of the coast near King's Point. Roald Amundsen justifies the over-wintering by citing the ice conditions; he wishes to safeguard the success against the hazards of an uncertain voyage thorough autumn storms and polar nights. Or did he want the news to reach civilisation before they themselves returned home? Maybe Amundsen thought two years would seem too short a time for such a large undertaking. Nansen had been away for three years, Sverdrup for four. *Gjøa* had enough provisions, what was the hurry?

Gustav Wiik, who no longer thought much of the Captain, was of the opinion that he was losing courage. Not just about sailing, but since the Governor 'heard about the trouble between Norway and Sweden his heart sank and he has since then taken it into his head to spend one more winter on the boat although when we were in Gjøahavn he was sick at heart at the thought of yet one more over-wintering; in truth an indecisive man.'

The prospect of spending a third polar night on board was not embraced with equal enthusiasm by all. But no one was to be forced against their will. On 5 September Wiik noted: 'The Governor was cross with H. Hanssen this morning and on that occasion asked him this afternoon if he wanted to return home over land as he thought one more winter would damage his sense of humour. That is the most despicable offer I have ever heard; is this gratitude for what he has done this trip and after 2½ years?'

But they all stay, and the Norwegian contingent at King's Point is even increased by one man. The expedition stumbles upon the stranded Christian Sten who had already established himself as a paterfamilias among the Eskimos. Mr Sten turns out to be very sociable and is of great help to his compatriots, which Amundsen acknowledges in *The North West Passage*.

Wiik, however, feels that social intercourse with the new Norwegian exposes yet another crack in the Captain's character. Mr Sten is 'torn to bits when he's not present, it is a great shame. The Governor is the boss and it is really extraordinary that they themselves are saints and everyone else evil; well everyone has their faults, but before criticising a man so crushingly one should look into oneself a bit.'

In spite of the local Eskimos being pretty much civilised (i.e. Westernised) and that in addition several whaling ships over-winter at Herschel nearby, *Gjøa* is without direct contact with the outside world. Some more up-to-date newspapers turn up; the war has 'evaporated' and 'the Norwegian Republic' been established. The uncertainty surrounding their native country was nevertheless still palpable. Anyhow, when would the world get to know about *Gjøa*'s great triumph?

The Governor plans a sledge trip to the nearest telegraph station. 'I'll take over everything to do with magnetism here,' Wiik notes in his diary. The expedition had not given up its scientific observations, but Amundsen decides to abandon the local instruments on the boat in order to send a telegraph. He has something important to say: he has sailed through the North West Passage.

On 21 October 1905 Amundsen, an Eskimo couple and a whaling skipper who has run aground, set out towards Alaska's interior. The captain won't return to his ship until five months have passed. This extraordinary sledge trip took them all the way to Eagle City. On his arrival Amundsen wrote the following prosaic résumé in his first letter to Leon. 'We arrived on December 5th, having walked for 1,300 kilometres. I walked every inch of the way so I am quite fit at the moment. The longest day's march was 65 kilometres and took 10 hours.' Eagle City is a tiny dot on the border between Alaska and Canada.

Immediately on arrival the conqueror of the North West Passage sets off for the local fort. He concocts a long-winded telegram in English, stuffed with latitudes and geographic specifications. Then he asks three questions: 'How the political situation? How my family? Would it be possible to get five hundred dollars by telegraph?' The message to the world is addressed: 'Nansen, Christiania'. Half an hour after the telegram has been dispatched the line breaks down.

Five days later the answer from Professor Nansen arrives containing congratulations and reassurances. But Roald Amundsen is obliged to spend a couple of months in Eagle for the post from home to catch up with him. In the meantime he is in good company with the locals and his six dogs. 'They are all very fond of me,' he writes to Leon, 'as I feed them well and thrash them not a lot – which they are not used to. When I'm out walking I'm often surrounded by a pack of baying hounds. They all want to be cuddled so it's hard work. I have also become acquainted with some local dogs and they usually join us for a walk. I am therefore sometimes surrounded by 15 dogs who are vying to see who can jump highest up to me. My present clothing allows me this pleasure.' Roald Amundsen is becoming a fêted man.

On 9 December 1905 Fridtjof Nansen sits by his desk in the newly constructed palatial villa at Lysaker near Christiania and composes a long letter to the conqueror of the North West Passage. In the New Year he will take up his appointment as Norway's Minister in London. His letter is more in the style of a nation-builder than a polar explorer. For the first time Roald Amundsen's remote achievement is expressed within the context of national policy. Fridtjof Nansen congratulates him with all his heart and greets him jubilantly: 'And it all fits in so well, with a splendid chapter in Norway's new history; because since you left the most extraordinary thing has happened that on June 7th this year King Oscar was dethroned and the Union with Sweden dissolved because the King had refused his assent to the unanimously passed law with regard to Norway's consular service. Sweden was furious and we were on the brink of war but now all has been peacefully concluded and Prince Charles of Denmark has been elected as

Norway's King under the name Haakon the Seventh. He made his entry into Christiania two weeks ago.'

Following this history lesson Nansen instructs Amundsen on how to conduct himself with regard to the new constitutional situation. He thought 'it might not be a bad idea' to send a telegram to the new Head of State. H.M. King Haakon, address: Christiania. 'For old time's sake you might telegraph a few words to King Oscar (Stockholm) but I will leave that to you, it is not necessary but might be considerate to the old man.' The superannuated monarch had, after all, sunk 10,000 crowns in the *Gjøa* expedition, a sum King Haakon later felt obliged to equal.

Nansen complains that Amundsen's historic telegram was held back and that parts of it were published in American papers before it reached its intended destination in the newly established kingdom. This was dearly bought experience that would contribute to Amundsen's taste for codes and secretiveness in the future. For exclusive publication rights to the expedition's news on the Norwegian market the newspaper *Morgenbladet* had, before departure, guaranteed 2,000 crowns. Later, in the wake of Roald Amundsen's epic achievement, very different sums would be bandied about.

The polar explorer could heave a sigh of relief. His achievement had not been overshadowed by the acquisition of national independence. On the contrary, it had become part of it. 'Thank God I have not lost Professor Nansen's interest,' he writes to Leon. 'I feared that he might give up on me, after he had been appointed minister in England. But yesterday I got a telegram from Consul Lund in S. Frisco, which shows he has not forgotten the *Gjøa* Expedition. As long as that man is interested in my undertakings I can rest in peace.'

On 3 February 1906 Roald Amundsen leaves Eagle with a stuffed mailbag and heads for *Gjøa* and the whale-hunters at Herschel. 'The trip to the north went well in every way,' he later reports to Leon. 'The 1,300 kilometres took us 30 days marching and that's not bad. The snow was very deep and loose up on the mountains, and difficult to get through. I arrived here on March 12th and found everything in good order.' Amundsen was especially pleased with his second in command during his long absence. 'With his nice, well-bred manners he has won everyone's respect.'

Within a month tragedy would strike *Gjøa*.

At King's Point, in absence of the Governor, they had celebrated HM King Oscar's seventy-seventh birthday and flown the flag in his honour for 30 minutes. But later in the winter this outermost outpost had received information with regard to the new conditions at home. First Lieutenant Godfred Hansen had proposed the old king's birthday toast. He also proposed sending a greetings telegram to the new monarch. 'Had it been sent,' Wiik writes, 'they would have had reason to laugh. It was in rhyme and one whole verse dealt with our magnificence and how honourably we had served the flag and how sad that our voices had not been counted, but that it had all worked out anyhow. I feared that our whole expedition would be made a laughing stock with all the self-praise.'

Gustav Wiik conscientiously continued the scientific work throughout the third over-wintering. This is how he managed to keep things going: 'I look after my magnetic duties, or in other words the whole expedition's duties.' Otherwise the detailed diaries reveal a man fighting with himself to survive in the stifling milieu in which he is imprisoned. Above all, the two complacent and boorish 'northerners' tax his nerves. Gustav Wiik finds it difficult to live in an atmosphere stiff with drink and tobacco fumes, see them chase the Eskimo women and swallow their pig-headed discussions. 'From a distance you are not affected by this and you can live with it, but to get close to them is quite horrible and on a daily basis too.' He has been to sea before, but never 'among such pigs'.

Nevertheless, the Governor is the biggest disappointment. They had both studied instrumentation and surveying at the observatory in Potsdam. They had set out together to find the magnetic North Pole. Only they two were qualified to grasp the expedition's real significance. But after a while the assistant found himself alone with the instruments. From his fixed point he observed that the Pole moved with great speed. It was no simpler to understand the Governor's restless movements. His goal proved to be different from the one his assistant tried to encompass with his routine measurements.

Gustav Wiik gathered a huge amount of scientific material. But his job was not to find the magnetic Pole; it was to legitimise Roald Amundsen's childhood dream – the hunt for the North West Passage. He might possibly have grasped that when he wrote in his diary at Gjøahavn, one year after arrival: 'I anyhow do not work for the Governor but for Science.'

Towards the end of March *Gjøa* received another pile of newspapers and Gustav Wiik's thoughts turned towards another expedition leader and another polar region. 'I see from the papers that Nansen had started to think about a trip to the South Pole before all these political troubles started. I wonder whether he actually means it.' Thus Gustav Wiik documents that Nansen's plans for a South Pole expedition had reached the *Gjøa*. This was one of his last entries.

On 4 March Gustav Wiik wrote home to his mother in Horten that he had been well throughout the expedition. But towards the end of the month he falls ill. Roald Amundsen and his never-attempted medical studies are as close as they come to medical expertise on board. 'The Governor is the doctor, but I do not think he would go far in civilian life,' Ristvedt wrote on an earlier occasion when the patient was the cook. Having analysed the Governor's medical decrees Ristvedt finds it 'extraordinary that Lindstrøm didn't explode'.

Recovery is difficult where there is no diagnosis. The Governor reads off and measures Wiik's fluctuating temperature. He rallies somewhat the last night, then suddenly he suffers a violent shivering attack. Blankets and clothing are useless. Wiik asks Lindstrøm to lie on him. He likes the cook. 'How sad that such a nice man is such a simpleton,' can be read somewhere in his diary. But the next day, 31 March 1906, it is all over. The Governor closes the eyes of his assistant.

Anton Lund knocks a coffin together. But burying a man in those latitudes is no simple matter. At the beginning of May Roald Amundsen writes to Leon: 'Wiik's body is still lying in our old shack. In a few days we'll move him over to the magnetic observatory and bury him there.'

On 6 May Amundsen opens the deceased's diaries, and adds an historic testimonial, addressed to his mother: 'His name is closely associated with the *Gjøa* expedition's scientific results and will ever remain so. His splendid work pays homage to the man.'

Three days later the magnetic observatory is transformed into Gustav Wiik's mausoleum.

Towards the middle of June the time for departure arrives. Roald Amundsen bids farewell to the semi-civilised whaling community north of King's Point. In the diary: 'The Eskimo offspring at Herschel present a sad but at the same time comical appearance. Of course not a single pure-blooded child in sight. Most of them have "*kablunablood*" coursing through their veins, but there are some queer mixtures of mulatto and Eskimo. They are to such a degree comical, that, had it not been for the wretchedness of it all, one would have had to roar with laughter.'

Before *Gjøa* leaves Herschel the expedition is struck by yet another tragedy. Manni, the Eskimo boy who had been attached to the crew for a time, drowns during a fishing trip. 'It was a hard blow for us to lose Manni in this manner,' Amundsen writes. 'We had all become fond of him and wished to introduce him to civilised climes and see how he would fare.'

On 21 August *Gjøa* passes Point Barrow, Alaska's most northerly tip. Point Barrow was later to become a central theme in Roald Amundsen's boldest plans. In the diary: 'It speaks for itself that the Norwegian flag was flying when we circumnavigated this important landmark. Thank God. He has helped us through so much.'

The end was in sight. The time has come for a last scientific survey; the Governor weighs everyone. In the diary: 'I am the heaviest with 90½ kilos. Another record.'

On 30 August the finishing line between Siberia and Alaska is crossed. Unfortunately the weather is appalling. But, according to the diary, the Governor has a last trick up his sleeve. 'I thought to celebrate our passage through the Bering Strait rather formally – but all we managed was to raise a quick glass on deck; a flag up the mast was out of the question.' But the conclusion is unequivocal: 'It was with great joy that we drained our cup. Whatever we might now encounter – we have carried the Norwegian flag through the North West Passage, on *one* boat.'

The next day *Gjøa* reaches Nome, a prospecting town south of the Bering Strait, and inhabited by many Norwegian emigrants. The place is dark and appears deserted when the one-master glides in. But the inhabitants of Nome are prepared. Suddenly a small motor barge appears alongside the ship. Shouts of hurrah break out and 'Norway, Thine is Our Devotion', the national anthem, strikes up. Roald Amundsen is set ashore, his childhood dream achieved.

EIGHT

A Big Man

'Don't forget that from now on you must consider yourself a businessman. Keep quiet, and instruct the crew to remain silent.' This is Leon's urgent message to Roald once the victory is a fact.

The leaking of telegrams had worried the expedition's supporters in Christiania. The time had come to get a grip on the situation. Fortunately, a man by the name of Harry Randall had turned up who was prepared to be Amundsen's agent in the United States. 'He thinks,' wrote Leon, 'that you might make a lot of money on a lecture tour of America, which is of course what you want.' But there was no room for empty talk; every word from the mouth of the lecturer would be worth its weight in gold. 'You, more than any other explorer, can benefit from the business side of it without anyone blaming you. The conditions before your departure were pretty depressing,' Leon wrote, reflecting the sleazy image of even necessary funding.

In Nome Roald Amundsen paid a few visits to the gold mines and, after a couple of days of celebration, bade *Gjøa* farewell. On 5 September 1906, the polar explorer packed his magnetic instruments, stepped aboard the steamer *Victoria* and headed for San Francisco.

Gjøa sailed to San Francisco for her final decommissioning under the command of First Lieutenant Hansen. On 18 April that year the town had been hit by an earthquake and lay in ruins, an event which rather overshadowed his ship's arrival and that of Amundsen himself on the *Victoria*. Gustav Amundsen came to take care of the crew during their stay in America. Roald had already donated the expedition's scientific discoveries 'unconditionally' to the Norwegian government. He left the ship in the stricken town and was thus free of much of his baggage.

On 1 November, he wrote to Leon from Minneapolis: 'I attend one celebration after the other and have no time for much else. I'm tired and exhausted by this indulgence and will be glad when the 8th arrives and we can turn our back on it all and leave with *Hellig Olav*.' As his homecoming draws nearer two things especially concern him ahead of the big day. Leon must make sure that Betty 'is suitably attired for the occasion'. And: 'Please arrange for a magnificent garland of roses – money is no object whatsoever – to be placed on mother's and father's grave the day we return home. You know, nothing is too good.'

The prodigal medical student returns home. The debt he owed his parents was lavishly repaid. The following year he applied to the churchwarden to 'be allowed to place a headstone, about 10 foot high, on my parents' grave'.

Roald Amundsen hastily completed a lecture tour to the largest Norwegian towns and then turned his eyes towards Great Britian. No nation had lost as many people in the quest for the North West Passage as the British. Moreover, the enigmatic Canadian coasts were subject to the Imperial Crown. Amundsen's expedition was of particular interest to the British. In addition, the British Empire of the day took an interest in every sea-going venture. The Royal Geographical Society in London was considered the natural hub of all polar research.

Initially a certain reluctance was detectable in the British perception of a Lilliputian expedition that with seven men and one mast had solved the geographic conundrum with which the Empire had struggled for centuries. Fortunately for the Captain, Fridtjof Nansen was already in London, not just as Norway's ambassador, but as Roald Amundsen's personal spokesman.

Fridtjof Nansen had also had a run-in with the Royal Geographical Society. But his personality and polar triumphs, allied to sound tactics, had earned him a place in the affections of King Edward's subjects. Nansen's combination of boyish candour and aristocratic air made him *primus inter pares* in this sports-fixated, class-dominated society. Such an affinity would never exist between the boy from Borge and his arch-rivals in the British Isles.

The Royal Geographical Society was very keen to welcome the conqueror of the North West Passage as their guest. There was, however, a condition attached: Minister Nansen must be present in London. The date 11 February 1907 was decided upon; Nansen would be present. And if Nansen was there, what need was there for Amundsen?

Three weeks before his arrival in London the lecturer received the following suggestion from the Society's secretary, J. Scott-Keltie, who had no reason to believe 'that your English is not good enough', but still: 'If you think you might have difficulty in making yourself understood, maybe you could read part of the manuscript and allow Dr. Nansen, if he is willing, to read the remainder?'

Roald Amundsen also received an offer from Nansen's English promoter, Gerald Christy, to give a series of further lectures in England. However, large crowds and inflated fees would not be forthcoming. 'Your spectacular expedition attracted attention among the scientific public, but has not caught the imagination of the general public sufficiently to make the lecture tour a financial success.'

Suddenly the North West Passage had little economic significance. It had long been known that as a trade route it had no worth. But it had not always been so. In 1745 a reward of £20,000 had been offered for the discovery of the sea route. Should not that money now fall to Amundsen? The question was raised and the matter investigated 'in the right places' by Minister Nansen. Even before his homecoming he was able to inform Captain Amundsen that 'as was to be expected that prize was now no longer applicable'. It turned out that a long time ago the British government had paid out the reward to a couple of the 'rescuers' who had followed in the wake of Admiral Franklin.

Some twenty years later Roald Amundsen commented on this award in his autobiography: 'It should not be necessary to point out, that however much these competent men deserved a reward for their toil and struggle, *Gjøa*'s journey was the first and only real traverse of the North West Passage.' Roald Amundsen never forgot an injustice. Especially not one that had been committed against him personally. By the British.

The Norwegian's increasingly tense relations with the British Empire were founded on these first negative experiences after his return from the North West Passage. The unquestioning homage he had expected from the country of his hero, Sir John Franklin, had not materialised. Why? Many asked the same question. The Norwegian Consulate informed Amundsen in a letter that 'they are more than surprised by the way in which you and your expedition have been ignored by the British press.' Amundsen's British press agent tentatively suggested that 'the expedition had lacked grandeur despite achieving great things.'

In his initial letter of congratulation the RGS secretary Scott-Keltie gave a clue to the British mind-set. 'There is no doubt that if you had returned home via Cape Horn with your ship, and thus circumnavigated America, before sailing up the Atlantic and along the Thames to London, it would have made a big impression on the British public and thereby you could possibly have got more money from papers and publishers.' The British would have loved that. But that is not what happened. Roald Amundsen arrived in the Empire's capital like any other paying passenger – no ship, no crew, no naval uniforms, no guns booming; in short, no pomp and circumstance. Just Roald and Leon carrying a box of slides.

Two days after the lecture at the Royal Geographical Society Roald's achievements were celebrated, with no strings attached, at the Norwegian Club in London. Gathered for dinner in the grand Hotel Cecil were 152 men and women under the chairmanship of Nansen. In addition the Club had invited a small number of British dignitaries, among them the man who, at that time, had travelled further south than anyone else, the naval officer Robert F. Scott. Unfortunately, Captain Scott would be at sea during Amundsen's stay in London, but in a letter to the Club he expressed his admiration not only for the courageous Captain Amundsen but for an expedition 'that the whole world must applaud'.

In his reply, which according to a journalist was delivered in Norwegian but accompanied by such dramatic gesticulations that even an Englishman would have understood it, Roald Amundsen claimed that the Vikings had been the first polar explorers. Then 'in a flurry of enthusiasm' he pointed to the head of the table, Dr Nansen. He it was whom Norwegians could thank for the return of their glorious past.

Having praised Fridtjof Nansen personally, Roald Amundsen turned his back on England and the series of unprofitable performances and set out on a journey through the rest of Europe, opening to enthusiastic acclaim in Copenhagen, home of the First Lieutenant. Kings were followed in rapid succession by emperors, lecture halls filled in every country. From Rome Roald wrote to Leon, who had returned home to keep an eye on the business, and reported capacity audiences: 'The King very charming, the decoration excellent. This evening a celebration with all the big-wigs. Treatment here better than anywhere.'

In the meantime a highly indignant reminder arrived from the secretary of the Royal Geographical Society. The North West Passage's conqueror had been invited back to the island kingdom to be solemnly awarded King Edward's Gold Medal 'for his work in connection with the magnetic North Pole'. Six weeks had passed since the invitation had first gone out. Roald Amundsen did not even deign to answer the honourable society.

What Messrs Edward and Scott-Keltie in England had overlooked was that Roald Amundsen had become a very busy man. Not only did he travel from city to city, from castle to castle, from slide projector to slide projector, from medal ceremony to medal ceremony; he had turned his hand to writing.

Part Two: The Gamble for the South Pole

NINE

The King's Ship

'The next riddle I set myself to solve was to conquer the North Pole.' These are the opening words in the chapter entitled 'The South Pole' from Roald Amundsen's memoirs of 1927. He continues: 'I also wanted to try and complete the feat Dr Nansen had started a few years earlier, namely to drift across the Arctic Ocean on the polar currents.'

During the preparations for what would be the third *Fram* journey, he consistently emphasised that the goal was *not* the North Pole, but on the contrary the scientific exploration of the 'northern polar basin'. This type of camouflage was necessary with regard to preparation and finances, but when all was said and done and historic milestones were identified the decor was not important; noble motives were unimportant, hard facts were all-important. Who was first through the eye of the needle? Who was first on the tip of the pinhead? Roald Amundsen never held on to a lie longer than necessary, however white and beautiful.

To properly understand the events surrounding the expeditions to the two Poles one needs to forget all that lies between them. The remainder is tactics. It is about the four years from 1908 to 1912. It is above all about four men. The Americans Cook and Peary needed no scientific camouflage; on their continent to hold a record was a good enough reason on its own. The Europeans Scott and Amundsen were dependent on their scientific cover-up. Behind it all a fifth shape loomed large, that of Fridtjof Nansen, the man who gave up the goal of two Poles and sought consolation in the scientist's ivory tower.

Roald Amundsen was a professional polar explorer. That was the work for which he had prepared himself. Throughout the centuries the North Pole had been the pinnacle of all polar research. His 'next task', therefore, was clear for all to see and needed no further argument. But as it was a formidable task it needed another motivating force.

The race for the Poles was not essentially a showdown between nations; it was rivalry between men. The battle for the North Pole would develop into a quarrel between two Americans. The race for the South Pole looked for a long time like being a confrontation between two British naval officers, Robert Scott and Ernest Shackleton. Four years Scott's junior, Shackleton had taken part in Scott's first South Pole expedition from 1901 to 1904; just as Frederick A. Cook had been part of Peary's first Greenland expedition. In both arenas, north and south, related methods and similar routes were used. The younger challenged the older. May the best man win.

Roald Amundsen's position was, seemingly, different. His biggest childhood dream had been to sail with Nansen. He was no rival; on the contrary, he was the master's disciple. But discipleship does not last, not for a man of Roald Amundsen's disposition.

There was one weak point in Fridtjof Nansen's achievements: he had never reached the North Pole. The traverse of the Arctic Ocean was an unquestionable triumph. Amundsen had the ability to make his own plans, but none better than those of Professor Nansen. Besides, this is where he might outdo Nansen. He would set out as a disciple but the very moment he planted the flag on the Pole, Fridtjof Nansen would have found his match, beaten over the same distance.

Fridtjof Nansen was five years younger than the North Pole fanatic Peary, but too old to think of a new traverse of the Arctic Ocean. His last chance to bag a Pole was a lightning offensive to the South Pole, modelled after his Greenland exploits. The plans were ready. Unfortunately, the sportsman was restrained by his intellectual prowess. Like no other polar explorer Fridtjof Nansen acknowledged the division between the forces of vanity and serious research.

Roald Amundsen was not yet so great that he did not need the help of his compatriot. He realised that to succeed the words 'North Pole' could not be mentioned, not even be vaguely alluded to, but so much the more so the scientific intention. When Amundsen proposed to repeat the master's own plan it pandered to Nansen's vanity and to his scientific principles. No one knew better than Nansen the oceanic and meteorological problems that still lay in wait in the polar basin.

It is assumed that Amundsen first aired his plans during a meeting with Nansen in London in February 1907. They were together not only during the banquet in the Norwegian Club and at the Royal Geographical Society; in his capacity as Norwegian Minister Fridtjof Nansen gave a dinner for his compatriot. The salient point during the conversation was *Fram*.

There were two Poles but only one Norwegian polar ship. Were Amundsen to repeat the drift across the Arctic Ocean he would have to requisition the ship for many years. And that unfortunately meant that nothing would become of the Professor's journey to the South Pole.

The master had priority; the disciple could only wait humbly for an answer. While Nansen brooded Amundsen could coolly calculate the outcome. He could handle the alternative; it lay strategically anchored in San Francisco. No one knew Roald Amundsen's intentions for *Gjøa* – why he neither wanted to sail her home nor tried to sell her.

In May 1907 he had received a letter from Helmer Hanssen in Tromsø, who 'is well at all times, only life is too quiet and peaceful, I find it difficult to retire so young.' As a remedy against boredom Helmer Hanssen suggested sailing *Gjøa* back through the North East Passage. 'Not that there is anything to discover or any kind of surprises, but by sailing along Siberia's north coast there might be the opportunity of getting hold of some valuable furs, very cheaply.'

With time Helmer Hanssen would have the opportunity to sail along the North East Passage, but not aboard the *Gjøa*. The Governor had his reasons for leaving the *Gjøa* where she lay, but revealed his secret to no one, not to Nansen, not to Helmer Hanssen. Roald Amundsen's plans were not entirely dependent on the *Fram*. *Gjøa* too had shown she could weather the storm. In fact, Amundsen was not even sure which of the boats he preferred. It depended on so much, not least the Professor's broodings.

In August 1907 Roald Amundsen ended his tour of Europe with a few days in Hamburg before returning to the old country via Baron Wedel Jarlsberg's estate on Jutland. Home in Norway quite sensational rumours about his future plans had been leaked. It was being bandied about that on his next expedition the Captain would be using polar bears as draught animals! And even more sensational: 'I have long considered the idea that polar bears would make excellent draught animals, but I have never believed that it could become a reality. Then I visited Hagenbeck's animal establishment in Hamburg and saw the wonders he had wrought. Hagenbeck is an expert in this field.' Zoologist Carl Hagenbeck had managed to convince Amundsen about the white beast's usefulness to humans: 'Tamed polar bears are the most loyal and domesticated of all four-legged animals. They are better-natured than dogs.'

Roald Amundsen was loath to talk about his plans with regard to polar bears or anything else. But he did confirm that scientific experiments were taking place: 'Next winter Hagenbeck will experiment with a couple and try them in front of the sledge.'

Were it possible to persuade the king of the Arctic Ocean, the polar bear, to accept the harness of civilisation, then dogs, reindeer and ponies would, of course, prove to be draught animals of infinite inferiority. It was an obvious thought and far from original. Julius von Payer, who discovered Franz Josef Land in the 1870s, describes in his travelogue how his men had captured two polar bear cubs. 'The crew, in all earnest, prepared to break them in for the return sledge journey to Europe.'

But was the twentieth century's approach to this problem to be found in the animal kingdom? Immediately after an interview in the newspaper *Aftenposten*, the polar explorer received an approach in strictest confidence from a certain Engineer D.G. Martens, Christiania. He wished to initiate Amundsen into what had been Otto Sverdrup's secret plans for the second *Fram* journey.

'A few months before Sverdrup's departure I constructed some motor sledges. They would travel across the ice, aided by a wheel, in the same way as a polar bear did, or, if you like, an elephant. The gait looked more like an elephant's and was driven by a petroleum engine. No matter that the expedition was fully equipped and the last crown spent, Sverdrup and his friends were so taken by the plan that money was found to construct the sledges and I travelled posthaste to England to have them built.' Martens said that the sledges were never finished on time in spite of postponing the expedition. The decision was taken to forward the sledges north. But after *Fram*'s departure the whole scheme foundered owing to a shortage of funds.

Engineer Martens's solution was no less sensational than that of Hagenbeck. In addition, he uncovered unknown facets of Captain Sverdrup's calm nature. 'You know the journey's official plan, whereas his private plan was, having settled *Fram* in for the winter, to take the sledges and walk to the Pole.'

All his life Roald Amundsen was a soft touch when it came to technical inventions, but it appears that he never went along with Engineer Marten's offer to 'complete the construction of the sledges'. Just a few months before *Fram*'s departure he was offered yet another 'sledge', propelled by a 'comparatively strong gas-engine, furnished with a *double-locomotion action*, invented by yours truly'. The inventor, who demanded 'absolute secrecy' from Amundsen, signed himself Halvor T. Nordbø from Bø in Telemark.

The Christiania engineer estimated the speed of his 'motor-sledge' at 100 kilometres an hour; the village genius from Bø did not hide his achievement under a bushel either: 'Probably the "sledges" might be pushed to cover double or even more of Cook and Peary's presumed times. A piece of cloth against draughts and a small primus would render them sheltered and snug.' Unfortunately Amundsen had to forgo such a motorised idyll. By 1910 the die was cast. It appears he worked only with one alternative to the 'ever footsore' dogs, namely Carl Hagenbeck's 'draught polar bears'.

Fridtjof Nansen had six months in which to decide *Fram*'s destiny. It was no easy question Roald Amundsen had raised, and there was no easy answer.

If any ship had ever deserved the description royal yacht, it was *Fram*. An entire nation had invested its hopes and dreams – and its money – in this vessel.

It had cost this poor, subject country 250,000 crowns to build. *Fram* was the vessel of proud ambitions; she represented a small nation's transformation from dependency to Great Power – the Viking king's ship. It represented strength, courage, enterprise and expansion, glory and pride. But the Viking ship's darker side was to sow fear and destruction, a warship which laid life and land waste.

Fram too had a light and a dark side. The voyage over the Arctic Ocean lent lustre to Norway, had strengthened a feeling of self-esteem and united the people. Fridtjof Nansen became a rallying point and a national leader. But three years in the arctic wastes had been bought at a price; his mind was darkened and his short marriage marred by coldness. In the eyes of Eva Nansen, who had once upon a time christened the ship, *Fram* became a sinister craft. Separation was not the worst part, rather the years of frenzied preparation and above all, marriage to a man who had been profoundly affected by three years in arctic captivity.

Fridtjof Nansen had worked his way through the depressions. His multi-faceted talents were ripe for new challenges of a scientific, and soon also political, nature.

Norway's independence had rounded off Nansen's national ambitions. The South Pole would crown his exploits as a skier and polar explorer. For someone who had roamed the northern pack ice on skis and with dogs, Antarctica's solid ice cap would be more like an Easter stroll on the Hardanger Plateau, or a ski trek across Greenland. His skis were waxed, the ship waiting. He merely needed to tear himself away from the tyranny of diplomacy – and from the woman who had devoted her life to him and borne his children.

No, Nansen was not on the threshold of freedom, rather deeply imprisoned by a moral conflict – between consideration for Eva and consideration for himself. Eva and Fridtjof Nansen were married on 6 September 1889, soon after his return from Greenland. Plans had already been made for *Fram*'s traverse across the Arctic Ocean, the Viking raid which robbed their marriage of its foundation. Hustle and bustle ensued – lecture tours, books, a life in the public eye, and then, the battle for independence and the winters in London. Always true to himself and his ideals, to Eva alone was Nansen disloyal. Other women had enticed him into adventures which demanded neither courage nor stamina, just a tiny flaw in the big man's character.

Fridtjof Nansen had no national and scientific reason for conquering the South Pole. He had a plan which he knew would succeed, a position which would render the plan possible and he had, like all polar explorers, a large portion of vanity. Fridtjof Nansen never reached the northernmost point. There was one chance left; the South Pole, the tabula rasa, an empty page in the chronicle of mankind, waiting for his signature.

The door-bell sounded at Polhøgda, Polar Heights.

It was late September; the Minister had returned from his holiday in the country, the suitcases were packed ready for London. Then Roald Amundsen stepped into the large, dark hall at Polhøgda. The younger man announced his arrival; the Minister is called for.

Nansen entered his wife's bedroom. Here the first line of the drama was played out. She said: 'I know what you have decided.' She had found him out. He stood for a moment, squeezed between his wife's gaze and his own conscience. Somewhere on his way down the stairs he made the final decision. The last line of the drama: 'You can have *Fram*.'

The drama reached its own conclusion without Amundsen having uttered one word. He felt infinitely relieved when he left the scene at Polhøgda. Later the weight of an entire continent would rest on his shoulders.

TEN

Polar Bears as Draught Animals

Minister Nansen returned to London. At the same time Roald and Leon Amundsen set out for America where promoter Randall had organised a lecture tour to many parts of the United States.

Carnegie Hall in the metropolis of New York was the setting for the first talk, in October 1907. 'To enable us to fill an assembly room which holds 2,500 people,' the promoter had written, 'in such a way that it will appear a success, we are to a certain extent dependent on your compatriots.' That type of heady national triumph was supported primarily by large colonies of Norwegian immigrants. This was not unique to the conqueror of the North West Passage, the promoter hastened to explain – even Nansen's lecture had been unsuccessful in its time 'financially, nearly everywhere where the Norwegians failed to turn up'. What a relief.

Roald Amundsen had hoped to make good money during a winter in America. Besides, he had hoped to meet his old friend and mentor from the *Belgica*, Dr Frederick A. Cook in New York. But already in July Randall had reported that 'Dr. Fred. Cook was out of town, no one knew where.' Extraordinary. Only after Amundsen had left the metropolis did a note turn up containing warmest congratulations.

The letter was a mystery. It was written on headed notepaper from a New York hotel and dated 7 November 1907. The choice of notepaper might have been a deliberate element of the doctor's disappearing act. At the time in question he had long since set sail for the north – although it would be another four months before Dr Cook started his march towards the North Pole. 'I am sorry not to be present during your visit. I have been told that you will be over in April and if so, write to me, beforehand.'

The letter indicated that Dr Cook was loath to unveil his plans to his old confidant. Was it competition he feared, or had he something to hide? If there was one month Frederick Cook would *not* be in New York it was April 1908. Precisely then he would be right at that unmentionable spot to which Roald Amundsen's thoughts were always turned. Probably – or not at all.

Leon was back in Christiania on 18 November and soon received reports from a moderately happy lecturer: 'On this side of Christmas I will have pocketed 1,000 dollars and that is at least something.' After Christmas came the turn of the west coast. 'I intend to give *Gjøa* a thorough inspection to see if she might survive another trip.'

Did Amundsen mistrust Nansen's promise to surrender *Fram* for the North Pole journey? Did he want to save money by using the smaller *Gjøa*, or did he want greater independence from the Professor? The *Gjøa* was still lying in San Francisco, a convenient point of departure for the Bering Strait and the Arctic Ocean. Whatever his motives, he saw no reason to show his hand. 'Please keep quiet about all this.'

On 14 December (for the time being an incidental date) Roald Amundsen was fêted in the capital of the United States. 'The celebrations yesterday were a high point in every way. The world and his wife were present – ambassadors, ministers, etc. The President was suppose to have attended but was prevented owing to his daughter's illness. Vice President Fairbanks presented me with a gold medal. The medal is huge, 250 dollars worth of gold. On the front is depicted the whole American Continent and the magnetic North Pole is set with a star of blue sapphire. On the back is a dedication to me. It towers above all my other medals.' Roald wrote proudly to Leon: 'The evening was not just a celebration of me – no, a celebration of Norway from first to last.'

But on the other side of the Atlantic Amundsen's native country was stricken with grief. Just before Christmas the curtain came down over Polhøgda. 'A sad message about Mrs. Nansen's death. I immediately telegraphed the Minister,' Roald wrote to Leon. Nansen entered another polar night. The cremation took place quietly, the ashes scattered to the four winds. Somehow Leon managed to deliver a wreath.

Roald Amundsen celebrated Christmas with his friend Fredrik Herman Gade in Lake Forest outside Chicago. The head of the Gade dynasty, Gerhard Gade from Frogner Manor outside Oslo, had been present at the big reception in Christiania. His three sons had all studied at Harvard and chose to establish themselves on the other side of the Atlantic: John in New York, Horace in Boston and Herman in Chicago. As they had all married into influential and exceedingly rich American families, their contacts were invaluable to their childhood friend.

Herman Gade played an important role in Roald Amundsen's life. A mere one year his senior, his was a different character from that of his friend: extrovert, courteous, typically gregarious. Man-of-the-world Gade was round and lithe. His desire was to achieve something outside the wallet's easy anonymity; in that he was indomitable. The ambitious lawyer and businessman was as dependent on

Roald Amundsen's brilliant celebrity status as the polar explorer was dependent on the capitalist's connections and good offices. Against the backdrop of the camaraderie of their schooldays a friendship developed based on mutual cooperation and characterised by a certain intimacy which was rare among Roald Amundsen's friendships.

All his life the polar explorer was drawn towards idyllic family life and its snug comforts. Herman Gade's comfortable retreat in Lake Forest was called after Frogner, his childhood home outside Christiania. The lawyer, his three sons and wife Alice lived here in generous abundance, the arctic traveller's ever longed-for resting place. Roald Amundsen used every opportunity to visit Chicago but his overnight stays were not, however, always at Frogner.

The deft Herman's contacts included the town's well-healed purveyors of tinned foodstuffs. Sometimes it was necessary to direct his talents for organisation, in consultation with the motherly 'hostess' Carrey, to enquire whether, under cover of her discreet wings, one or other 'little girl-friend' might be available.

The polar explorer disliked idleness. 'What on earth shall I do Saturday night?' he asked Herman, and without waiting for an answer: 'My old friend Carrey might have a solution. Ask her whether the little French one, the "lively" one, is free and get her to meet me at her house at 9 this evening. As I trust implicitly in your never-failing organisational skills, I'll go there directly.'

In his memoirs Roald Amundsen insists that he had lived his life 'according to the strictest notions of honour'. According to the moral standards of the day, however, that might not have stopped him from entering into paid liaisons with women of easy virtue. The notions of honour in any case did not bar him from trading for Eskimo women. It was purely a question of satisfying a basic need, little different from that for food and shelter. The urge was the same in Pensacola and on Greenland, in Chicago and in Gjøahavn. Only the price varied; what in one place was paid for in dollars was in another place offered in exchange for empty crates or a sewing needle.

The polar explorer's relationship to his surroundings, human and animal, animal and human, was functional. He could eat a dog or love a woman, love a woman or eat a dog. Men hunt; they will give their all for a gun. Women sew; they will give their all for a needle. Everything is on the move for someone in a hurry. The carcasses await new depots; depots for hunger, depots for love. He was a man en route – towards his goal.

Christmas was a time for reflection. 'How is Nansen?' Roald asked in a letter to Leon some time in the New Year. 'Will he stay at home or resume his post?' Is he off to London or maybe thinking about a trip to the South Pole? Now that he no longer has anyone to consider – now that he is free to travel to the world's whitest extremity in order to forget his black moods.

In the course of February 1908 Amundsen must have received information from Hagenbeck in Hamburg in which he reported that the polar bears were making strides as 'draught animals'. He wrote to Leon: 'Have read the Hagenbeck affair with interest but if I take *Gjøa* there won't be room for the bears.' Only the *Fram* was large enough to accommodate Hagenbeck's polar bears.

Such was the life of a polar explorer. While travelling the world lecturing about his last journey, the next voyage was already being planned. Soon the plans would have to be made public. The title had been decided upon: 'An intended exp. to research the northernmost polar basin.' That sounded serious enough. Not a word about the North Pole, not a word about the polar bears.

In March he was able to inform Leon from San Francisco that *Gjøa* was wearing well. Nevertheless, 'I will try and get rid of her somehow.' Roald Amundsen had decided upon *Fram*; and on the polar bears as 'draught animals'.

At the end of April the lecturer was back in Europe. He had earned a few bucks, but his greatest asset was nevertheless the glory surrounding his name. In a letter from London he asked Gade to look after the box of slides he had forgotten in the Chicago Club; the same place where he at one time walked away from his galoshes. All details a polar explorer should not forget!

During the summer of 1908 Roald Amundsen set off for Bergen 'after consultation with Nansen', to study oceanography, just as at one time he had studied magnetism in Hamburg. Science takes its toll! For the first time the prospective oceanographer crossed the Hardanger Plateau by train. 'The journey over the mountains was wonderful,' he wrote to Leon on 24 July 1908. It was here on the plateau that the two brothers had wandered around aimlessly twelve years earlier. Now the railway lines were *in situ*. 'In a short time we are transported from a beautiful summer landscape up into ice and snow – wilder than anything I have ever seen from a railway. It is a work of genius.' Science was defeating winter. In San Francisco he had already experienced 'a technified summer'. He had visited 'paradise; motorcar roads through roses and oranges'. Technical developments fascinated the polar explorer, but he nevertheless held on to the polar bear.

On his return from the States Roald Amundsen had made an important decision. He had bought a house. Just as Fridtjof Nansen had built his castle at Lysaker after the *Fram* journey, he too sunk the profits from his own expedition into his own house. Not exactly a castle, but a spacious bachelor pad along Swiss lines, in a sense a summer cottage. The house lay by the sea at the head of the

Bunnefjord, south-east of Christiania – accessible from the water, a steep and rugged approach from any other direction.

Ever since he moved away from home, Roald Amundsen had wandered from one address to another in Christiania. The cottage was situated near the Bålerud quay at Svartskog, 15 kilometres closer to his birthplace in Borge. Leon had already spent a couple of summers by the Bunnefjord, and of course it was he who took care of the transfer and the necessary alterations. Roald called the place Uranienborg, rather as his friend Gade had christened his home Frogner. Thou shalt honour thy father and thy mother. The nanny Betty moved into the servants' quarters. He called that Little Uranienborg. It was all very idyllic.

Roald Amundsen prided himself on providing for anyone who had stood by him, whether lodgings for old Betty or work for his *Gjøa* men. In America he had heard that Peder Ristvedt was out of work. Captain Amundsen was of the opinion that the state should provide for a crew who had given 'their all for Norway'. He asked Leon to give his old engineer a call. 'At the same time I'll write to Løvland [the Prime Minister] and give him a piece of my mind.'

But not every situation could be resolved by writing to Løvland. A rather delicate personal storm was brewing – delicate and private. It concerned Gustav. His brother had landed himself in an economic mess. At the same time Gustav bore his brother a grudge. Was it not he who had provided the means when the foundations were laid for the *Gjøa* journey? But to whom did all the kudos go?

'I appealed on behalf of an unknown person who was setting out on a fabulous journey, which might possibly succeed or most probably fail. The Collection Committee worked for the Knight of the Grand Cross of St Olav whose journey succeeded and whose name is known, not only in our country, but all over the world. According to the Book the Collection Committee has absolutely nothing to do with the expedition.' This is Gustav Amundsen's undated summing up of the *Gjøa* expedition's finances. The so-called Collection Committee, represented by the capitalist Axel Heiberg and Alexander Nansen,* was 'warmly thanked' in the preface to *The North West Passage*. Had the time not come for the Knight of the Grand Cross to repay Busken in recognition of his services?

From Bergen Roald wrote to Leon: 'G. sent me a telegram in which he asked me to send him 1,000 crowns without delay – for the time being.' In reality the need was for 3,000 crowns, a year's salary. Roald was of course very keen to help, with a job, house, money, or whatever. But nothing to do with Busken was simple.

'It's the same old story all over again.' There was a pressing need for 1,000 crowns, or maybe 2,000, and then the worst debts could be settled, his honour

---

* Translator's note: Fridtjof Nansen's brother, a lawyer.

restored, his wife's health improve, and his son get by. Busken knew how to touch the Knight of the Grand Cross's sore point. But Roald soon realised that his brother's finances were a black hole. He tried to push the problem onto someone else; Leon would have to put things straight, or Lawyer Nansen. He had the Arctic Ocean to worry about. That too was a black hole.

On 10 November 1908, to great excitement and in the presence of Professor Nansen, Roald Amundsen submitted his expedition plans to the Geographical Society in Copenhagen. 'The next day the King and Queen subscribed to the charity and things have been going so well that ⅔ is already secured,' Roald Amundsen reported, enclosing one of his characteristic financial calculations to Herman in Chicago. 'Offers for goods are pouring in: toothpaste, shoe polish, and the most extraordinary articles in a motley mess. Not to forget mouth organs and remedies against hair loss.'

Gade's services were not to be sneezed at, however; seven years require an awful lot of tinned food. Without entertaining too many illusions regarding the pemmican producers' scientific interests, nevertheless the polar explorer sent his latest lecture over to the meat town. 'If you see Armouer then show it to him and tell him that his chances of sending goods to the Pole are now greater than ever.' He was alluding to advertising, for shoe polish, tinned food and the Kingdom of Norway.

Applications to join the expedition started to arrive. One was dated Skien, 24 November 1908: 'I have studied your plan with the greatest interest, which I in some ways am already familiar with as I took part in the first *Fram* expedition with Nansen.' It was signed F. Hjalmar Johansen. The name was still well known, although only twelve years had passed since he returned home from Franz Josef Land with Fridtjof Nansen. He had spent the previous winter on Spitsbergen and 'realised that I am still not altogether unqualified for such work'. The applicant then gave an account of his wider qualifications and ended by saying 'in other respects I refer you to Professor Nansen.'

Fredrik Hjalmar Johansen had never really got a grip on civilised life. As Nansen's companion on the matchless ski tour towards the North Pole, on his return he was immediately promoted, from an unknown lieutenant to a polar hero by the grace of Nansen. But when the festivities came to an end and the decorations were taken down Johansen found himself a captain in the Army with a permanent posting to Tromsø. Soon a thousand men were under his command, plus a wife and four children. The monotonous round of everyday life had arrived somewhat suddenly. He was a humble and loyal man, but the stark contrasts of existence had shaken him. The skier from Skien never really got his life back on track again. He was unable to hold the family together, retired from the Army, but immediately regretted it. Yesterday's hero sought refuge in alcohol. Time and again he asked Nansen for money, pleas the big man could only decline with great difficulty. It was not much easier for *Fram*'s new leader to turn down Johansen's request to return to his old ship. References from Nansen decided the matter. The application was granted.

Of course, Hjalmar Johansen represented a valuable contribution to what was now called the third *Fram* expedition. And it was not the first time that Amundsen engaged a man who was more experienced than himself. Lindstrøm had sailed with Sverdrup before he joined *Gjøa*. He too, like Johansen, had the reputation of liking a drink. Several of the new crew had sailed on the second *Fram* expedition. But Hjalmar Johansen alone had sailed with Nansen. Hjalmar alone had walked towards the North Pole on skis and with sledges like Amundsen himself envisaged. Hjalmar alone had saved Nansen's life and hibernated with him in a cave on Franz Josef Land. And only Hjalmar had shared a sleeping bag with Fridtjof Nansen. Hjalmar Johansen was used to being Number Two; it was not so easy to be Number One.

By the time *Fram* left the Norwegian coast, Leon, the expedition manager, had on several occasions been confronted by Johansen's hopeless financial position. In Tromsø Johansen pawned a ruby-encrusted silver salver and several other trophies from his glory days. A friend asked for help to save the valuables as Johansen himself 'has no energy and can do nothing on his own'.

The brothers Amundsen also heard from the captain's sister in Skien. She wanted to be reassured that wages could be drawn for the family's keep. In addition, she thanked the expedition management for 'what you have done for Hjalmar. I am the only one of those closest to him with whom he can correspond and I know that he is very grateful.' Of course, Amundsen could assure her that 'Capt. Johansen would have 50 crowns docked off his wages for his wife.' And he added reassuringly: 'I hope Captain Johansen will be very satisfied with life on board to which he is so suited.' So far, so good.

Towards the end of 1909 Roald Amundsen made an obligatory trip to London to present his plans to the Royal Geographical Society. What could the British authorities say? This was Nansen's old plan. It was bold but well tried. One could only applaud. Even the Society's authoritative secretary showed his best side. 'Keltie is completely changed. He is the nicest, friendliest person you can imagine,' Roald reported back to Leon. 'His first question was whether you were here, how you were, etc.' Scott-Keltie had even promised to support the trip with a couple of hundred pounds. 'And that's something.'

In February the Norwegian government agreed to grant 75,000 crowns for the refurbishment and modernisation of the national Viking ship, to prepare it for a new journey into Arctic waters. That was quite something too.

During the summer Leon could inform the faithful supporters, the newspapers *Aftenposten* and *Morgenbladet*, that 'the ladies in Bergen are sewing silk burgees.' Oh yes, the whole country was involved. Next stop North Pole.

On 20 March the polar explorer travels to Gjøvik. The next day Solicitor Castberg and wife and Amundsen set off on a Sunday outing. They travel in two sleighs, the solicitor in one, his wife and Roald Amundsen in the other. The snow is metres high, but the sleighs are warm, one of them at least.

Leif Castberg was a tall and elegant man – cheerful, sociable and liberal in outlook. At only 32 years of age he had already served one term as mayor of the town where he had succeeded to his brother's law firm. His brother was the current Minister for Justice in the Gunnar Knudsen government; Johan Castberg, one of the country's most controversial and radical politicians.

The solicitor had a wife who suited him, Sigrid Castberg, called 'Siggen' or just 'Sigg'. She was beautiful, independent and much fêted. Like her husband she had been born in Skien, but grew up with broader horizons, in America. They married at the turn of the century. She bore her husband three daughters, of whom two survived.

But Gjøvik was no longer the place for Sigrid Castberg's dreams, except, maybe, during this one weekend in March. She had met the polar explorer some time ago; it might have been during the festivities for *Gjøa*'s homecoming. When in September 1907 he made a note of who was to receive a copy of his debut book *The North West Passage*, 'Mrs. Solicitor Castberg, Gjøvik', was high on the list.

There is something very generous, even magnanimous, in the gesture when a husband, virtually *à la* Eskimo, stands to one side and allows his tall guest to climb into the sleigh with his wife. The solicitor's winter chalet lay snowed under in a small valley. The polar explorer cleared a way to the door. The married couple followed. The timbered 'Furuheim' Pine Cottage was freezing cold, every reason to keep their overcoats on; the host lit the stove and made a fire in the open hearth. Sigrid improvised a meal, while the polar explorer glanced at the visitors' book. His host had a way with words, was good at jingles. The guest noted the motto of the place: 'Love and let live.' They partook of a meal; the polar explorer wanted to brew coffee. He grabbed a fist of embers, held them down in the kettle. The coffee boils. The host is impressed. Bring out the punch!

It was getting dark. The wife was impatient. They had a long sleigh ride ahead.

The polar explorer and the solicitor's wife met again at the Grand Hotel in Christiania on 8 April. Midnight arrived. It was a public place; he was a well-known personage. 'Love and let live.'

A few weeks later 'Siggen' celebrated her thirty-second birthday. 'The guest of honour is our captain. Away from the sun, up to the Pole.' The husband had composed a song; he had a way with words, was good at jingles.

Sooner or later the boiling point would be reached – like putting embers in a kettle.

ELEVEN

Pulling the Wool over the World's Eyes

A stomach full of ice and a cool head. These were the prerequisites for a polar explorer in 1909 – the year of great confusions in the history of polar exploration.

During the summer of 1909 Ernest Shackleton made his entry into London. He had beaten his rival Scott's record. The British naval officer had reached 88° 23' South and could, from henceforth, call himself Sir Ernest. A mere 180 untrodden kilometres remained to the Pole.

Let us imagine ourselves at the head of the Bunnefjord. In a backwater south of Christiania two brothers are busy organising an expedition to the North Pole. Fourteen men for seven years. There are numerous things to think of. Roald dictates. Leon writes. Only four months till departure – 1 January 1910.

'Did you remember polar bear feed?'

On 1 September Roald opened the newspaper. Finally there is news of his good friend Dr Cook. He is en route from Greenland to Copenhagen after spending the winter in northern Canada. The doctor dropped in on the North Pole.

'When?'

'April 1908.'

'Wasn't that when he wanted to meet you in New York?'

'Funny.'

'You must send him a telegram.'

'Take a note: "Warmest congratulations on your brilliant deed. . . ." Where do you say he'd been?'

Frederick Cook was keen to meet his old friend in Copenhagen. But Amundsen could not spare the time. He was thinking of setting off to the north. '. . . Hope to see you in the States,' he concluded his telegram of congratulations.

What were the polar explorer's thoughts, one has to ask oneself? On 6 September Roald Amundsen sent the following letter to a dear cousin in Pensacola: 'You might have expected a telegram in answer to your questions but as I have nothing definite to say about Cook's journey I have this to say. Cook is my old friend form the *Belgica* expedition and he is in every way a fine man whose statements must be considered to be completely dependable. Scientists will now examine his observations which I hope will bear out the correctness of his claim.'

In the evening telephone number Svartskog 805 rang on the second floor at Uranienborg, at the head of the Bunnefjord.

'Had Captain Amundsen heard the news that Peary had been to the North Pole?'

'When?'

'In April 1909.'

'Where?'

'The North Pole.'

Fourteen men. Seven years. Icebound. Roald sank slowly down into a chair.

'Did you remember the polar bear feed?'

Nevertheless, on the morning of Wednesday 8 September Roald travelled to Copenhagen. In the office on the second floor a message was waiting for Leon: a list of the *Fram* crew. The Captain topped the list. 'Write to Thv. Nilsen (. . .) and tell him the exp. is postponed and will get under way in a few months. He is considered the second-in-command. Give the same reason to all the others. Possible departure July 1910.' The decision had been made. When? On 7 September, possibly the night before. Where? In Roald Amundsen's mind. Such a decision could only be made there.

On 9 September *Morgenbladet* confirmed the departure. 'Roald Amundsen left for Copenhagen yesterday where he will meet with Dr. Cook and confer with the Inspector for Northern Greenland with regard to dogs for the *Fram* journey. The Captain will return on Friday.' Not a word about polar bears. Of course the expedition would use dogs, but they would not first be transported from Greenland to Norway. The four-legged creatures would be taken on board in the north, as Nansen had done in his time. Amundsen formulated his orders in Copenhagen and rearranged the dogs' route, in accordance with the new plan.

What was going through Roald Amundsen's mind? He was intent on equipping a scientific expedition to the northerly polar basin. Equipment had been ordered from every part of the world, money collected, the ship built and financed according to government decree, the scientific preparations were far advanced, the crew hired. . . . But they were still short of money. And who would want to invest in a North Pole expedition when the North Pole had already been conquered? Had he not asked Gade to tell his American pemmican suppliers that this would be their only chance to 'see their wares photographed on the North Pole'? Did he think about all that? Yes, but they were not his first thoughts.

Roald Amundsen thought about himself. 'If I wanted to retain my name as an explorer, sooner rather than later I needed to win a sensational victory in one way or another,' he later wrote in his memoirs. 'I decided on a coup.' There were only two alternatives. One of those evaporated in April. Was it in 1908 or 1909?

The second one, had that one too not disappeared from the map – wiped off by Shackleton? No, 180 kilometres remained. That meant another two days' march, maybe three, in a headwind. One hundred and eighty kilometres, to become part of history, to be immortalised.

All was ready – ship, provisions, crew. But was there not someone else wanting to go to the South Pole? Someone? Everyone wanted to go to the South Pole. The Pole was after all history's full stop. What was he waiting for?

The Bunnefjord was a backwater. Roald Amundsen wanted to be off to Copenhagen to talk to his old teacher Dr Cook, the man who had been to the North Pole and who would like to go further – to the South Pole. On 4 September there had been a notice to the effect that Dr Cook's South Pole plans were ready; child's play for a man who had walked to the North Pole on his own two feet. The time had come to constrain the doctor, to get the dogs south. Polar bears are not suited to the Antarctic. Did Cook encounter tame penguins at the North Pole? After all, everything went round in circles, from north to south, from south to north. The ice in the stomach had melted; the head was still cool.

He needed to get away from Bunnefjord, away from the northerly polar basin. Only 18 kilometres to the main railway station, 180 kilometres to the South Pole. Leon would have to manage the rest.

There was jubilation and hullabaloo in the Danish capital. Roald Amundsen checked in to the same hotel as the North Pole traveller. Later a newspaper reported that 'what brought Amundsen to Copenhagen in the first place were all the attacks on his friend Dr. Cook. Roald Amundsen wanted to demonstrate his friendship and moral support. The two were continually seen together.' Yes, but that was not the reason for his journey to Copenhagen. The Norwegian's journey had been planned before the world woke up to the news of Engineer Peary's attempt to discredit Dr Cook with the allegation that Dr Cook had never set foot on the North Pole.

The polar battle of all time was brewing between the two Americans. Peary started it all. He had everything to win, nothing to lose. Number Two on the Pole was no honorary title, just a memo to a wasted life. Death to Dr Cook.

The old seadog Otto Sverdrup was also in Copenhagen on 'business matters'. Dr Cook's point of departure had been precisely those areas mapped by the Captain during the second *Fram* journey. In the newspaper columns of *Danebrog*, Sverdrup gave his full support to the 'Norwegian route' and Dr Cook's efforts. 'As for Peary,' the captain answered coldly, 'all I know is that he has been trying in vain for twenty-six years to find the North Pole.' Colleague Amundsen was not afraid to take a stand either. 'Peary's behaviour fills me with the deepest anger and I want to proclaim publicly that Dr Cook is the most reliable Arctic traveller I know and it is simply unreasonable to doubt him and believe Peary.'

On 10 September Dr Cook left the enthusiastic town. The handsome, blue-eyed American arrived at the quay in an automobile, accompanied by the stocky, reserved Captain Sverdrup. On board MS *Melchior* he was met by another Norwegian, Roald Amundsen, who was to accompany him on board to Kristiansand. Amundsen had already telegraphed ahead and warned the town of the hero's arrival: 'Consider his North Pole journey completely reliable.' Sverdrup and Amundsen both decided to believe the doctor. They trusted Cook but, equally, disliked Peary. The dislike had its roots in old wounds connected to Eivind Astrup but also in the American's inclination to claim ownership over charted as well as uncharted land.

In Kristiansand Dr Cook was hailed for the last time as the North Pole's undisputed conqueror before boarding the American boat *Oscar II*. In his speech of thanks he praised Norwegian polar explorers and wished colleague Amundsen good fortune and success on his journey north. Only one could win the race but science needed all the men it could get.

On 13 September Roald Amundsen was back at his desk in his study in Bunnefjord. That same day London announced that Captain Scott intended to go south.

'Where?'

'To the South Pole.'

'When?'

'In August 1910.'

A stomach full of ice, Roald. Keep your head cool, Leon. 'Everything was prepared quietly and calmly,' Roald Amundsen wrote later in *The South Pole*. 'My brother, whose silence I could rely on implicitly, was the only one I took into my confidence. He rendered me much and important assistance during that time.' What on earth did Leon say when his brother confided in him that north had become south?

It was not something he would have done on his own. Leon never took the plunge. He was business-like, conscientious, precise and measured in all his movements. On the other hand, he was no narrow-minded backwoodsman. Leon had crossed the Hardanger Plateau on skis and sailed around the world. He spoke fluent French, English and German. He possessed a diplomat's discretion and an economist's respect for numbers. As a breadwinner he was securely rooted in a bourgeois lifestyle.

The polar explorer Tryggve Gran was one of a handful of contemporaries who described the reserved brother's role in the South Pole expedition. 'Leon is a very shrewd gentleman, and if some delicate situation arose, which it frequently did, he was left to pick up the pieces. Double-dealing like that needed a smart and resourceful head.' Leon was tailor-made for the job of Roald's secretary and manager. Not only did he complement Roald, but as his brother he could advise and, if necessary, contradict.

From a business point of view, the decision was bold but correct. Science was not Leon's strong point. The South Pole was a gold mine. Anyhow, the orders had been issued; the attack postponed, the troops moved, the strategy changed.

Roald 'trusted Leon implicitly', but he never talked to anyone else. He discussed tactics, but his morals were his own, and no worse than those of any other Napoleon. Was it not the general's prerogative to feign an attack from the north but plan an offensive from the south?

There was but one crack in Roald Amundsen's new plan. However, it was deep and its character was moral. Someone else was supposed to have sailed *Fram* to the Antarctic. True, he led the public and his rivals up the garden path, but he had no right to deceive Fridtjof Nansen. The third *Fram* journey was based on Nansen's plans, grounded on his prestige and his scientific preparations. Moreover, it was founded on his surrender of his own intention of conquering the South Pole.

Why did Roald Amundsen not come clean about his new strategy to the man in the tower? Fridtjof Nansen possessed every qualification for understanding his colleague's predicament – that the loss of the North Pole as an object of advertising constituted an economic threat to the expedition's scientific plans. With the help of Nansen the South Pole journey could be launched in the full glare of publicity, maybe even before Captain Scott had announced his intentions.

But what if Nansen rejected the idea, or if he demanded his moral right to be in command? Strictly speaking Amundsen would have to run the risk. But when he chose to keep silent, it was because he never considered his compatriot a partner or a colleague. On the contrary. Fridtjof Nansen was his most dangerous rival in the battle for the South Pole.

In October Sir Ernest Shackleton arrived in Christiania, where he was fêted by jubilant crowds. Roald Amundsen gave a speech praising his heroic trek over the South Pole plateau. The remaining 180 kilometres he hugged close to his own chest.

In the meantime the Cook–Peary battle raged on. The doctor had some difficulty presenting credible evidence and the American establishment was starting to side with his rival. Amundsen got embroiled in it again when he travelled to America to arrange deliveries for *Fram*.

Letter from Roald to Leon, dated 17 November, New York: 'Some way from land I received a wireless [message] warning me to look out for reporters, who will accost me by the score to gauge my opinion about the Cook–Peary fight. At the quarantine point *N.Y. Herald* arrived in a yacht and dozens of newspaper people and photographers had hitched a lift on the customs tug. Thank God Gade was there too.' It was necessary for him to behave diplomatically. 'Cook lives just outside town and I will pay him a visit. His stock is low at the moment – *no one* is siding with him.'

Fifteen years later Gade suggested in a letter that his friend's knowledge of human nature was not always spot on, that from time to time he needed to be protected from himself. 'Of course it is natural that as far as possible you trust in those whose good nature you have learnt to respect; as I had every opportunity to remember the time I travelled from Chicago all the way to New York harbour to warn you about your erstwhile friend and colleague from the *Belgica* expedition.'

In a hotel room in New York Roald Amundsen confided in his childhood friend Herman Gade that he was about to lead the world up the garden path. In time two other colleagues were let in on the secret: the oceanographer Bjørn Helland-Hansen, who, from his base in Bergen, would prepare the expedition's oceanographic programme, and Thorvald Nilsen, *Fram*'s ship's captain. They were both confronted with a *fait accompli*. Both accepted. During the spring of 1910, in private, he confided the change of course to his most faithful supporter, Fritz G. Zapffe. (The Tromsø chemist was to have taken part in the expedition but had had to withdraw for personal reasons.) Face to face, Roald Amundsen was a man who could change north into south without losing credibility.

The polar explorer kept a low profile that tricky winter of 1910. Some things were no longer very important, like Hagenbeck's polar bear experiments or even Sem-Jacobsen's dragon trials. To enable him to scout for open leads and new land in the Arctic Ocean, Amundsen had started to develop man-bearing kites. During the experiments in the summer of 1909 the expedition's second-in-command, Captain Engelstad, lost his life when he was struck by lightning.

Lieutenant Sem-Jacobsen continued to work throughout the winter, but for some reason the polar traveller had lost some of his enthusiasm.

Instead of building kites he built a house – a prefabricated house that could be assembled on the South Pole land. Otherwise the most pressing job was the procurement of huskies, '90 dogs at 12 crowns and 10 bitches at 10 crowns' delivered to Christiania at the right time and with the correct paraphernalia. Roald Amundsen wrote to the Danish Inspector in Northern Greenland: 'I understand that it would be of immense value to me if I could get hold of two, in your opinion experienced, Eskimos of the right age, to look after the dogs.'

However, getting hold of natives was surrounded by infinite royal bureaucracy. In spite of Cook and Peary's reliance on Eskimos, in the end, *Fram* sailed south without Greenlanders in her hold. After all, Eskimos no more belonged in the Antarctic than polar bears did in the land of the penguin.

It was necessary to increase the number of crew in keeping with the new plans. The last two to be signed on were a Russian oceanographer, hand-picked by Helland-Hansen, and a Swedish engineer, supplied by the Diesel factory. Otherwise Amundsen succeeded in putting together a national crew whose centres of gravity lay in the naval bastion of Horten and the Arctic Ocean town of Tromsø. Joining him from the *Gjøa* expedition were the polar geniuses Lindstrøm and the restless paterfamilias Helmer Hanssen.

Uranienborg was excellently situated for anyone who liked keeping himself to himself – squeezed between the hill and the fjord. A stranger would need to confront the dogs. A maid opened the door and closed it. Leon answered the phone: 'The Captain is not at home.'

At Easter Robert Scott came to Norway to try out his new wonder-machine, the motorised sledge. Before the party left for Norway's own home-grown Antarctica at Fefor, on the railway line between Christiania and Bergen, he had a meeting with Nansen. He also made a phone-call to Svartskog. Captain Scott had already written to Amundsen regarding a conference of scientific collaboration between the Norwegian North Pole expedition and the British South Pole enterprise. Unfortunately, Mr Amundsen was not at home.

However, Captain Scott did not give up. A man who could sail twice to the Antarctic was capable of twice giving Svartskog a tinkle. Before the motor sledges were transported back to the British Isles the Englishman dialled again: Svartskog 805. Mr Amundsen was still away. Where was he?

Well, where was Dr Cook?

TWELVE

The Coup

Leon Amundsen travelled alone to Madeira. He took passage on a steamer from Hamburg and arrived at the exotic island in the Atlantic on one of the last days of August 1909.

The tall, distinguished-looking Norwegian put up at the Bellavista Hotel in Funchal. His first duty in the sun-drenched town was to collect post from the Norwegian consulate. There he received a parcel containing the latest letters from his native country, addressed to Captain Amundsen and his crew. Next he inspected the provisions which had been ordered. Thereafter, all he had to do was wait. On 4 September, he quietly celebrated his fortieth birthday, with a glass of Madeira and a view of the sea.

Every one of ship-owner Jens Amundsen's sons was a gambler. The second youngest son was not the worst, for he played for lower stakes and with more realism than the others. He was the only one of the four who had not at one time or another run through all his money. Leon was a professional. He had kept a straight face for an entire year – in a game of poker about glory and about money, the gamble for the remaining Pole. Leon took part without risking anything material; he only bore the strain.

On the morning of 6 September *Fram* dropped anchor in Funchal Roads. That day was the first anniversary of the announcement of Robert E. Peary's conquest of the North Pole. The broad-beamed, heavily laden ship arrived, wrapped in a haze of secrecy. It had left Norway on 7 June, on the fifth anniversary of the realm's independence. In the intervening time the ship had undertaken oceanographic trials in northern waters. The draught animals had been taken on board in Kristiansand.

The dogs represent one hundred question marks. Was it necessary that they should suffer this heat, around Cape Horn, around the world? Could they not have jumped aboard somewhere near the entrance to the Bering Strait? And anyhow, what was a house doing in the hold? A hundred questions and one house for an answer.

While the *Fram* still lay at anchor in Kristiansand Roald Amundsen drafted the following document: 'We hereby declare, on our honour, not to divulge, either in writing or orally or by signs, what is being discussed at this meeting.' The document was dated 30 July, and signed by the ship's three officers: the skipper Thv. Nilsen, K. Prestrud and Hj. Fr. Gjertsen. This 'meeting' let all the ship's officers in on the big secret. Well over a month later, before arrival in Madeira, Sverre Hassel signed a similar promise of secrecy. Hassel was an experienced man; he had sailed alongside Sverdrup. Besides which, it was he who took delivery of the dogs when they arrived from Greenland. Hassel was closest of all to the hundred question marks. The Captain deemed it wise to give him an answer.

During the afternoon Leon Amundsen climbed aboard. He carried with him the last letters the crew would receive for a year and a half. The ship rode at anchor for three days, repairs were undertaken and cargo loaded. The crew went ashore to stretch their legs. One man was paid off and sent home following a decision by the officers. 'Having listened to advice from our crew we declare that steward Anders Terkelsen Sandvik has told lies and tried to sow discord and quarrels amongst his comrades.'

The hour of truth had arrived.

On 9 September the ship was ready to depart. The brothers Amundsen arrived at 4.30. Like his brother the expedition leader had also taken the opportunity to spend a few days in a comfortable hotel during his stay in Madeira. Apart from the crew Leon Amundsen was the only outsider on board. He would carry the ship's letters back to Norway.

Below deck Hjalmar Johansen was busy writing a farewell letter to his wife Hilde at home in Skien. 'Many thanks for the letters. I will study them carefully once we are out at sea; at the moment there are a hundred and one things to do before a ship can leave port, all the men are on deck, I'm sitting here scribbling in my shirt-sleeves, the sweat is pouring down my face. Anyhow, that apart, the heat is not affecting me; I thought it was going to be a lot worse. (I must go now.)

'But, good heavens – what a surprise! It was all over in just 15 minutes! We're not going to the North Pole – we're going to the South Pole. Amundsen called everyone together and announced that, since September last year, plans had changed considerably. In the light of the contest between Peary and Cook, one at least of whom might have reached it [the North Pole], we have, secretly, changed our plans. We will now partake of supper and thereafter make straight for the South Pole where 10 men will be put ashore on the ice and take up winter quarters. *Fram* will continue to Buenos Aires with the remaining 10. Additional crew will be taken on board in Buenos Aires and a period of oceanographic research will ensue, after which the *Fram* will pick us up in 1912. Talk about surprise. And Amundsen himself is exceedingly surprised that nothing has leaked out for, after all, the revised plan was put in place already a year ago. He said he could not force us to join him but he wanted to ask each and every one of us if we wanted to come. The answer was a unanimous yes!'

Like the rest of the crew Johansen had prepared himself for between three and seven winters in the Arctic Ocean. In that respect the considerably shorter South Pole expedition was a relief. In spite of it allegedly being an extension of the third *Fram* expedition the gloomy voyage to the North Pole was now pushed aside. Roald Amundsen was wise enough not to intimate at this juncture who would be picked for the polar trip and who would have to devote their time to marine research. Personally, Hjalmar Johansen had no doubt.

'Now many questions have been answered, with regards to equipment and things, as I was of the opinion they were to be used on the pack ice, and A obviously realised that I was confused about a lot of things, especially the house, which we were supposed to erect on the pack ice, and other things too. He laughed with me this evening and said he knew my wishes had come true – viz. going south to the ice there. He knew about that.' The last bit alludes to Nansen. It was during the wintering on Franz Josef Land, in the lair, that Fridtjof Nansen had developed his plan to conquer the South Pole.

The moment twenty men crowded around the maps of the South Pole on the decks of *Fram*, was the moment eclipsed only by one other single event – when five pairs of hands planted Norway's flag on the South Pole.

When the commotion had subsided, and everyone, like Johansen, had added the sensational postscript to their letter, the entire expedition sat down to dinner. At 9 o'clock Leon Amundsen stepped ashore carrying the letters. With him in his mail bag was his brother's announcement to the King, to Nansen and the nation in general. These letters had been composed in the Captain's cabin during the month-long voyage down to Madeira.

Each and every crew member shook the hand of the manager. When Leon Amundsen was rowed ashore all connection to the outside world was severed. 'My brother has taken it upon himself to convey the news as to where we are headed,' Roald Amundsen wrote in a later account. 'I do not envy him the task.'

Thirty minutes later the diesel engines were running. The polar ship moved off. All was quiet; the night was starry. Roald Amundsen was relieved – 'a wonderful night.'

The tactics at home in Norway were the same as the ones used by Roald Amundsen on board the *Fram*. It was important to seek support from the most influential protagonists before informing the masses.

It really all depended on one man. In addition the King would be advised before the general announcement.

It is noteworthy that Amundsen, sailing on a ship which after all belonged to the Norwegian state, saw no reason to specifically notify the government or Parliament. At the turn of the year Gunnar Knudsen's benevolent government had stepped down. The new powers that be would have to make do with information from the newspapers.

The letters to the palace in Christiania and to Lysaker were to be delivered by courier on the morning of 1 October. Leon himself marched straight up Karl Johans Gate, while oceanographer Bjørn Helland-Hansen had been allocated the considerably longer and more difficult leg out to Polhøgda. This assignment demanded a specialist who could immediately assure the Professor that the expedition's scientific purpose had taken precedence over all other decisions.

In the accompanying letter to Helland-Hansen the polar explorer emphasised how important it was that the King and Nansen 'receive the communication at *the same time*'. Roald Amundsen was right when he later characterised the South Pole operation as a coup. It was stage-managed like a *coup d'état*, like a palace revolution. The rebellion struck simultaneously at strategic points. The opposition was given no time to give the alert, to consult between themselves or to consolidate their position.

Amundsen prostrated himself in writing before Fridtjof Nansen. The letter opened by alluding to the fall of the North Pole: 'this was the deathblow to my enterprise. I realised immediately that I could no longer anticipate the monetary support that I needed. That I was right is confirmed by Parliament's resolve of March–April 1910, whereby they rejected my plea for additional funds of 25,000 crowns.' The deputies' refusal arrived at a convenient time; Professor Nansen's scepticism of parliamentary majority decisions was well known and of long standing.

Consequently, in his lonely battle for science Amundsen has been forced to woo 'the masses' by conquering the South Pole. Only thus could the forthcoming oceanographic voyage to the north be economically secured. It was difficult for Nansen to contradict this line of reasoning without weakening their common cause – science. But now to the crux of the matter. 'I have time and again been on the verge of confessing to you, but always turned away, fearful that you would stop me.' Stop him from what? From saving the voyage to the north or from sailing to the south? As already mentioned, only one man existed who could stop Roald Amundsen. And only one motive existed for trying to stop him; the motive that Fridtjof Nansen wanted to conquer the South Pole himself.

The letter-writer apologised for not having informed Scott. 'I will in the meantime do all I can to meet him down there and inform him of my resolve and he will have to act accordingly.' This is quite sensational information as Amundsen knew full well where the English were in the habit of establishing their base. On the other hand, this new-found candour towards Nansen did not stretch as far as to reveal his own plan of putting ashore in Hvalbukta (Bay of Whales).

'Where we will put ashore down there I have not yet decided, but it is my intention not to get in the way of the English. They, of course, have priority. We will have to make do with what they discard.' This was very noble. Amundsen had already calculated that the Norwegian base would lie one whole degree of latitude closer to the Pole than Scott's base in McMurdo Sound.

Roald Amundsen initially stands forth as a humble dog before his master, as Dostoevsky's Raskolnikov before God. 'Do not judge me too harshly. I am no humbug, I was forced by necessity. And then I ask your forgiveness for what I have done. May my future work atone for my offence?' Fridtjof Nansen would use these words, for what they were worth. Certainly, Roald Amundsen would atone – in the name of science.

The actual answer to the letter was composed by Fridtjof Nansen two and a half years later. By then, whatever his thoughts it was important immediately to assume the correct position. The South Pole had already been lost. The issue now was to save the journey to the north. In his letter Amundsen wrote that if he had 'such means as were necessary for my originally planned voyage – about 150,000 crowns, then I would gladly have dropped this additional voyage.' It was the word 'additional' that stopped Nansen in his tracks; the *main expedition* was still intending to explore the northern polar basin.

That same evening the capital's press was summoned to a conference at the Hotel Continental. Before Leon Amundsen read out his brother's declaration he must have met Helland-Hansen for a last thorough review of the situation. In a letter to Leon a few days later, the oceanographer wrote from Bergen: 'The original to Roald's message needs to be well hidden as the change to the text on one point might be construed as a "falsification".'

Roald Amundsen's proclamation to the people of Norway was front-page news in Christiania's press on 2 October 1910. The sensational headlines read that the *Fram* 'steers a course to the Antarctic regions, there to take part in the battle for the South Pole'. It is not as dramatic as that, however: 'It is merely an extension of the expedition plans – no change.'

Now to the one point mentioned by Helland-Hansen. It dealt with concealment. 'I have earlier not mentioned this to any of those who assisted me in the task of preparing this expedition, as I initially wanted to wait and see if it would be possible.' This is Leon's diplomatic wording, handwritten and inserted in his brother's typewritten declaration. It replaced a paragraph which from Roald's side had been unashamedly frank. 'By making this decision, and without having informed those who have stood by me in my work and who have helped me, I know I will hurt many. But it was not possible. So many difficulties would have piled up even to the point where if the plan had been known I might have had to give it up. For it to succeed I had to work in secrecy.'

Why shout your guilty conscience from the roof-tops if Nansen had already accepted the situation? Thus Leon must have reasoned when he replaced his brother's admission with a phrase along the lines of 'wait and see'.

Thus the statement to the people appeared more coolly calculated than the letter to Nansen with all its sincere denunciations and obvious excuses. A skilled gambler does not expose his worst cards without a purpose.

The sensational front-page notice closed with the following sober information: 'You can count on hearing from us again in February–March 1912. We will then continue to San Francisco, where the last preparations for the drift across the Polar Basin will be made.'

Leon Amundsen conducted his brother's correspondence. To him it was nothing new that two personalities lurked in Roald Amundsen's ego. In his alter ego was hidden something of the polar explorer's strength. His talents became many-sided, his capacity enlarged – he could even be in two places at once. That last point Captain Scott would learn to his cost.

On 3 October Leon Amundsen posted the letters he had brought with him from Madeira from the expedition members to their relatives. At the same time he dispatched the following telegram: 'Captain Scott Terra Nova Christ church (New Zealand) Beg inform you Fram proceeding antarctic'. Signed: Amundsen. Sent from: Christiania. Even Captain Scott knew that Amundsen had left Christiania months ago.

'It appears that it's all blowing over, there won't be any major difficulties,' Helland-Hansen wrote to Leon three days after the bomb-shell. The oceanographer and the manager both heaved sighs of relief. No one had publicly opposed Amundsen's proclamation. In view of Parliament's refusal of support the whole nation was to a certain extent responsible for the *Fram* expedition's dramatic U-turn; and there existed no tradition in Norway of criticising the country's flag-ship.

Carsten Borchgrevink was one of the many authorities whose opinion was sought; the Norwegian had led an English expedition during the first over-wintering of the Antarctic continent. His criticism was that Amundsen had not put his trust in 'reindeer' as a source of locomotion: 'I advised Scott to use reindeer.' On the other hand Borchgrevink informed the newspaper *Tidens Tegn* that he had all along known where Amundsen was headed. 'Otherwise why did he take 90 huskies with him?'

Hjalmar Johansen wrote in his diary from on board *Fram* that 'Amundsen is very astonished that Nansen did not suspect the journey's goal, in spite of having pronounced his surprise at the dogs.' The Professor's attitude said a lot about his unshakeable belief in his polar heir. But this relationship of trust had now been lost. Fridtjof Nansen no longer supported his younger colleague out of enthusiasm but rather from a sense of duty, a stance that also reflected the attitude among the people. Under the surface opinion was smouldering.

'Now we must just hope that all goes well with the dogs and the disembarkation,' Helland-Hansen concluded his summing-up letter to Leon, 'then everything will be fine, in spite of reindeer, ponies and automobiles.' Not a word about polar bears.

THIRTEEN

A Business Trip

The South Pole expedition was to consist of three sections. First of all, the land party: nine men under the leadership of Roald Amundsen, based at Framheim on the Antarctic mainland. Second the sea party, which would engage in oceanographic research in the Atlantic from *Fram*. It consisted of ten men, led by the ship's captain, Naval Lieutenant Thorvald Nilsen. Third was the expedition's business concerns, with offices in Christiania and its environs. It consisted of one man, the expedition's twentieth member, Leon Amundsen. While the government ship *Fram* transported the modern Vikings over the world's oceans, the manager travelled free on Norway's state railways 'in his capacity as the *Fram* expedition's representative'.

Postal services between the expedition's three sections were, to put it mildly, thin on the ground. They were limited to *Fram*'s departure and arrival at Hvalbukta and a few other ports of call. Nevertheless, the brothers Amundsen, and especially Leon, wrote copiously during the entire two-year separation. Delivery was rare but the pile of letters was all the bigger when it arrived. Lieutenant Nilsen was answerable to Christiania too. All three section leaders had to be prepared to make independent decisions.

'Hope you have had a happy yuletide – here everything passed in Peace and Quiet without any visits or our visiting anyone,' Leon wrote to Roald in the New Year of 1911. Of course Christmas on board *Fram* had been very special.

'Lieut Nilsen and I had decorated the salon on the occasion and it looked excellent. We covered everything with signalling flags and under the ceiling hung thick garlands of tissue paper – a present from Mrs. Schroer. 16 pretty little coloured lanterns – they were a present too – were hung up and we removed the other lamps. Everyone was invited to dinner at 5 p.m. Without the knowledge of any of the guests I had hung the phonograph up in my cabin. The mugs with the King and Queen were put out and made it all look a lot more festive. We shut out the day light so it was completely dark. With the coloured lanterns lit it made our good salon look like a fairy castle. It was a solemn occasion.'

This was his theatrical side emerging: Roald Amundsen, the director and producer. His understanding of light as a special effect was particularly developed. During parties at Uranienborg he would give the serving girl precise instructions on how and when discreetly to turn down the lamps. Not to forget the sound: 'When everyone had sat down I turned the volume up. "Silent Night, Holy Night," surged towards us, sung by the famous Danish opera singer Herold. Not a single dry eye.'

The spectacle possessed every dramatic element: atmosphere and surprise, a religious aura, carried on the wings of technology. And it was all seemingly inexplicable – for all bar the man who had staged it. Perfect! 'I have never experienced such a moving and solemn Christmas Eve.'

There was not quite the same ambience over things at home, in the winter landscape. 'The atmosphere is not exactly what we had expected. There is not much sympathy with regards to the difficulties you have encountered, let alone enthusiasm in connection with the change of course. On the contrary, and in spite of your reasons having been reproduced clearly in the newspapers, the general feeling everywhere is rather acid. Of course there are exceptions. I must mention first of all the King and thereafter Fridtjof Nansen who both see things clearly.'

Leon could confirm that 'the majority of the press' had been enthusiastic. Nevertheless, there was cause for concern. 'There are anyhow murmurings among the backers and in all probability there will be murmurings in Parliament when the case is debated. I must therefore today absolutely advise you that even if the result is the very best, you must not return expecting to be fêted, as no one thinks that is deserved. But one thing is certain; should the result be good, then the mood will rocket sky high; but in my opinion it is too late then. I think you must complete the journey to the North [Pole] before you allow yourself to be officially received at home.'

Of course it was above all the finances that worried the manager at home in Christiania. 'The position is no better and maybe even worse, than when *Gjøa* sailed.'

One of the few attempts to try and explain the lack of enthusiasm was printed in the newspaper *Kysten* (*Coast*), a precursor to Norway's *Trade and Shipping Times*. The article was front-page news on the day following the South Pole declaration, and was entitled 'Roald Amundsen – a victim of his friends'.

Nowhere did the article attack the man who 'is the object of undivided admiration'. Instead its author took up arms against the polar explorer's new 'friends', those who, after his return from the North West Passage 'took possession of him, enclosed and isolated him, heaped praise on him and confined him to their narrow circle.'

The innocent polar explorer could not be blamed for the expedition's straitened financial circumstances and the consequent unhappy arrangement regarding the South Pole. He was a helpless victim of bad influence: 'consequently Mr Amundsen was made the scapegoat for his new "friends"' behaviour. A tacit opinion spread that he had become a victim of polar snobbery. Interest among the general public diminished and his popularity fell. When the case came up in Parliament the atmosphere there too had turned rather cool.'

The well-informed author maintained that the polar explorer's only true friends were those who had supported him before he became a fêted man. Then, too, he had been burdened by financial difficulties. 'Difficulties that during his absence weighed heavily on those nearest to him.'

Anyone who knew that Roald Amundsen's own brother Gustav was connected to *The Coast* realised who was behind the unsigned article. Gustav Amundsen now made a frontal attack on the leading 'friend', namely his brother Leon – the man who had pushed him away from Roald's immediate presence.

During the winter a bitter struggle ensued between Gustav and Leon, who was given leave to live at Uranienborg during Roald's absence. The conflict was put into the hands of lawyers, but not before Busken had broken with his younger brother Leon in a sixteen-page letter filled to the brim with pent-up frustration and hatred.

Leon's eternal headache was Busken: 'Sad that the man cannot pull himself together and behave seriously so we could be together like other families, but his money matters go from bad to worse and he gives not a toss if he is guilty of culpable behaviour.'

The oldest brother Tonni was also problematic. The ever-optimistic inventor had developed a method of producing dry milk and had established himself on the west coast. Soon, however, he lost the position of manager and Leon could only conclude that 'Tonni's affairs in Jæderen are not going well.'

Betty alone was no trouble. But even the nanny's well-being stood or fell in the game for the South Pole.

Framheim, 7 February 1911. Roald Amundsen made the last adjustments to the letter which was to travel north on *Fram*. 'On 11 January, without any difficulties, we reached the large ice-barrier. You cannot imagine what a powerful sight it was. As far as the eye could see east–west the 100 foot ice-wall rose into the air. The next day we encountered the large bay in the ice waste where I had decided to seek winter quarters. On the 14th we moored alongside the ice's edge to investigate the conditions. Found immediately a suitable place for our station.'

Here the Norwegians erected their winter quarters, surrounded by fourteen tents: 'And as solid as our building are the men who occupy it. A more stalwart and agreeable group of comrades than the 8 who have followed me so far it would be impossible to find. Everywhere is singing and laughter and jubilation.' Portions of the letters to Leon were written with a view to publication in the newspapers, 'but don't do it in my name'.

Further: '4 February was a day full of surprises. When in the morning we went to fetch supplies 2 boats were moored by the ice's edge, instead of one. We all of course immediately knew whose it was – *Terra Nova*. Scott was not on board.' During that chance meeting between the two polar ships by the edge of the enormous Antarctic continent, a third party was for the first time able to look behind the scenes: 'they were extremely impressed by what they saw. If they hinted that our quarters lie on unsafe ground, please do not concern yourself. We are safe where we are.' The British exposure of the Norwegian base was a setback for Leon. He had hoped to parcel out Roald Amundsen's strategy on the open newspaper market. Now *Terra Nova* would be the first to report the news.

But that disappointment was not the only strain for an expedition that was already showing a heavy deficit. 'It is true,' the explorer wrote to his manager, 'I have raised wages by 50% for everyone who will remain aboard the ship.' From time to time a man with ambitions must rise above financial realities. 'I do not know whether the expedition coffers can stand this but it will have to stand the test.' The division of labour between the two brothers was clear: the South Pole was up to Roald, the rest to Leon. 'You best understand what must be done and just arrange everything in the way you think best.'

Before concluding his letter from Framheim the polar explorer touched on his plans regarding the positioning of depots, and finally the sore point: 'Assuming Nansen is interested, then let him know this. I thought I might write to him from here, but I am so uncertain what he makes of it all that I have refrained. Send him my regards.' Should the Professor have lost enthusiasm, the polar explorer pinned his faith on the rest of humanity: 'It seems to me, as things now stand, that this contest might interest the world.'

No doubt, news from the Antarctic ice field about the creation of two expeditions raised the temperature in more civilised regions. Leon reported that the 'announcement in England was received with mixed feelings, whereas the atmosphere at home changed completely.' The national competitive spirit was at last stirring. On your marks, get set – in the Antarctic and the press. It was a war on two fronts: in the field and in the media, on own territory and behind enemy lines. 'I dare say that the campaign, from our point of view, has been run with much diplomatic insight in as much as the entire English press are of the understanding that it is out of the question that this is some disloyal competition; this is not least owing to Nansen's pronouncements and especially his articles in *The Times*.'

Leon could report that the mood had changed: 'each country now sides with their man.' At last the hard cash started to move too. 'The initial news stimulated the English who immediately started a collection for Scott's deficit, and that has rubbed off on us, so now the same thing is going on here for *Fram*; in other words we are making sure that there will be sufficient means to complete the North Pole journey.'

Leon tested the waters to gauge whether there might be a possibility of a national collection. He was in constant contact with important people like the brothers Nansen, the polar sponsor Axel Heiberg and Herman Gade 'of whom the last-mentioned is keen to take up the case'.

While Roald Amundsen was tackling the Antarctic his best friend Herman Gade made equally heroic attempts at gaining a foothold in his former native land, Norway. Right up until *Fram*'s departure from Norway Amundsen had lobbied Foreign Minister Irgens to admit Gade to the Foreign Service. He also made sure that the Minister nominated John Gade, Herman's brother, and one of the expedition's large donors, for a Knight of St Olav.

It proved problematic to place the free-thinking businessman from the States in the Norwegian diplomatic service. Herman Gade's differences with Parliament and government soon developed into an affair of staggering dimensions. Leon wrote to his brother that 'his planned diplomatic career has been provisionally broken off and he and Irgens have fallen out with each other.'

However, Leon's paramount task was to exchange the detour to the south for hard cash. 'It is not all that easy to get anything out of such an extraordinary business but I will do my best in the hope that you bring back the victory.' Rates for telegrams, articles, books and lectures were dependent upon the expedition results, dependent upon Amundsen reaching the South Pole. On Whit Saturday, 5 June 1911, Leon set out for London. This was where the battle for the hearts and minds of world opinion would be fought; this was where contracts would be signed and income secured. In the capital of Empire an ally joined himself to the brothers Amundsen, from behind enemy lines.

Leon called on Fridtjof Nansen's old promoter Christy to talk about his brother's affairs. After a while another polar explorer's name cropped up. 'We spoke about Shackleton and he advised me to look him up, which I was not keen to do. He then phoned S. and he straight away said he wanted to talk to me. I went to see him immediately and met him with Captain Davies who will now lead Dr. Mawson's Australian expedition to Cape Adare – later Dr. Mawson arrived too. They had been quite critical of you to begin with but to my great surprise the tone had now changed completely and everyone present took your side against Scott. As far as Shackleton is concerned it must be jealousy or irritation about Scott's journey to the South. Apparently, immediately Shackleton returned home and before he had had time to settle, Scott made the decision to go south so that under the circumstances Shackleton himself had no chance to even think of it. (Although Christy is of the opinion that Sh. had decided not to go south again.) Whatever the truth of the matter, Shackleton is furious and has placed himself at my disposal for all information and arrangements (this is, of course, completely confidential as officially he can do nothing other than take Scott's side). Captain Davies went so far as to pronounce that he hoped you would beat Scott; the reason being that Scott, in spite of having an agreement with Dr. Mawson, that he, Mawson, alone would use Cape Adare as an operations base, has himself set a party ashore there, forcing Mawson to disembark elsewhere. There are some very favourable circumstances for you in England as Shackleton is now a very powerful man; through the *Daily Mail* he managed to raise £12,000 for the Mawson expedition in four days and he has a large following on his side and against Scott.'

Back in Norway Leon immediately contacted Foreign Minister Johannes Irgens: 'He was very pleased with what I could tell him about Sh. He, I., is going to England to represent the King at the Coronation and will invite Sh. for lunch and talk to him.' Leon had thus managed to establish a pretty delicate connection between Norway's Foreign Minister and the British national hero Sir Ernest Shackleton. To be on the safe side a knighthood might not be out of place – 'to ensure support from Sh'.

Roald Amundsen had paid little attention to the foreign policy consequences of challenging a British naval captain. It was up to the politicians to make sure that the battle did not sour relations with the Great Power. After all, it was all about the conquest of an entire continent – the sixth continent.

The remaining members of the Royal Geographical Society in London had rather more mixed feelings about Amundsen's detour: 'Markham is very anti (but he is considered a jabbering idiot), Scott-Keltie is actually nervous (Sh. advised me not to look him up), on the other hand the President is all right and says "let the best man win".' All in all, the journey to London had given Leon an even deeper understanding of how 'extraordinary' the South Pole expedition was, from a financial point of view. 'There are so many alternatives in that there are two expeditions and one will beat the other or one gets through and the other not, or neither of them, that I have to say the business has become so complicated that no one can really unravel it all.'

FOURTEEN

The Capitalist

During the spring of 1911 the manager's most pressing problem bore the name *Fram*. Having left Hvalbukta the ship arrived in the Argentine capital where preparations were made, according to plan, to set out on an oceanographic journey to the South Atlantic. This scientific exploitation of the polar vessel had no real connection to the South Pole venture. The Atlantic Ocean journey was above all a sop to the man in the turreted room.

That the mission was not accorded top priority was demonstrated by the skipper, Lieutenant Nilsen, in his letter to the manager, dated 9 May. 'When I left the Governor he said that everything would be arranged by the time we arrived in Buenos Aires. Hundreds of things needed to be done, with the ship and other things. On our arrival here I immediately made my way to the Norwegian Minister and Don Pedro Christophersen, who asked me whether I had a letter from the Governor, which I did not. None of them as much as gave me a single penny and I had to borrow money from a Norwegian ships' chandler to pay for the hotel.' The situation was precarious, the lieutenant could pay neither salaries nor harbour duties and on board there remained only ten cases of provisions.

A week before departure from Kristiansand Roald Amundsen had received a telegram from the Foreign Minister concerning a hugely rich estate owner by the name of Don Pedro Christophersen. The ageing Norwegian-Argentinian had declared himself willing to provision the ship when it called at Montevideo. But this time there would be no South American port of call and it was an open question as to how Don Pedro would react to the change of course. Not only the oceanographic journey but *Fram* too, the South Pole expedition's mother-ship, was in danger of total ruin.

There was no hope of being saved by officialdom. In January Leon had been informed, via the Foreign Minister, that one dared not push for any more funds. If the case were to be heard in Parliament, Leon advised, 'Criticism from many quarters would be strong and harm the cause as I fear that the money could possibly be used to bring *Fram* home and lay her up.'

Don Pedro Christophersen had never met Roald Amundsen; neither would there be many opportunities for the two to spend time together. Nevertheless, by virtue of his fortune and his overwhelming generosity Don Pedro became one of the polar explorer's most important mainstays during the remainder of his career.

Peter Christophersen – such was his original name – was born in 1845 and emigrated to Argentina at an early age. He worked in shipping and, as a consequence of his two marriages, came into possession of enormous estates. Roald Amundsen's relationship to the distinguished landowner developed into something resembling an impoverished artist's dependence on his royal patron.

In his many letters to the supreme steward of earthly goods Roald Amundsen lauded his benefactor like a court poet from a bygone age: 'In daily life one so often meets wickedness and malice so that even the small goodness that exists often disappears.' Thus does the polar explorer begin a eulogy, written during the winter of 1913, directed at his patron. 'I am sometimes tempted to believe that mankind consists of an infinite number of bad, unreliable beings who want nothing good. But thank God, when I think I have reached the stage where everything is wrapped in a cold, indifferent fog then the sun breaks through and you are there, always the same fine, noble character, whom I praise God I encountered along the way.'

As in most such cases this too was in exchange for something: gold for glitter; ready cash for the gloss of Roald Amundsen's name and achievements – paid out in decorations and mountain tops named after the donor. But that in no way ruled out noble feelings, least of all from Amundsen's side. 'You talk about writing off debt with friendship. I beg and implore you, never take your friendship away from me, always allow me to keep that, even when there is no debt to write off.' Tied to an obvious element of practical calculations, the sun king Don Pedro exerts a positively medieval pull on the polar explorer: the need to subordinate oneself to someone, to serve and suffer under the powerful, noble ruler: 'I thank you and will continue to show you the deepest gratitude, as long as I have a drop of blood in my veins – I can never thank you enough.' His childish subservience is reminiscent of the young Amundsen's affections for Fridtjof Nansen. But whereas that relationship came increasingly to be characterised by a battle of wills, over the years the link between Don Pedro and Amundsen was established along straight lines: the one stood for gold, the other for the splendour of the deed.

Like the much younger Herman Gade, Don Pedro had two brothers both of whom became involved in Amundsen's affairs. The white-bearded Christophersen brothers would represent the polar voyager in South America in the same way as the Gade brothers did in the north. Both dynasties were rooted in finances and diplomacy.

After a few painful weeks on dry land, on the roadstead outside Buenos Aires Don Pedro at last decided to dip into his pockets, and the expedition could get on with its oceanographic research. Lieutenant Nilsen heaved a sigh of relief but did not chance any more calls en route. 'One does not happen upon a Don Pedro in every port.'

If Thorvald Nilsen had felt himself abandoned when he arrived penniless in South America there was at least one man who had kept him and the oceanographic research in mind. It was a relief for the young skipper to receive a letter from Fridtjof Nansen. 'It would be wonderful if we Norwegians also in this field could prove ourselves superior. The world will look upon the *Fram* expedition as not merely a sporting expedition, etc., as some people are saying, but as a serious scientific undertaking, one which will command respect.'

Professor Nansen later proved to be extremely satisfied with the oceanographic work undertaken in the South Atlantic. The scientist on board was not in fact a 'Norwegian' but the talented young Russian Alexander Kutchin. It says a lot about the scientist's place in the pecking order that he received 60 crowns per month, the lowest pay of all the *Fram* crew.

During the summer, after the oceanographic voyage had started, Leon received a letter from Don Pedro giving the reasons for this shoddy generosity. Apparently the landowner had interpreted the change of course quite differently from the narrow-minded local Norwegian patrons. To him the plan was 'the most excellent inspiration by this extraordinary, ingenious man'.

Don Pedro was, quite simply, a find; a gold mine from the Argentinian pampas. In Leon's rapid calculator of a brain a long-term strategy started to take shape. He advised his brother 'to make his acquaintance as soon as possible – apparently he has a charming family (grown-up son and daughter) and believes he can help you in the future if needs be.' To this half-pecuniary, half-private request he adds a warning: 'Remember one thing, to keep an accurate account of any money you might receive from him – he is a businessman and would appreciate such things.' For one moment he visualises his brother and adds: 'You can always get Nilsen to do it, he is practised in such work.' How large the sums actually were that Don Pedro paid out was not easy to ascertain as he merely agreed to cover all *Fram*'s expenses.

Returned from the Atlantic foray it is exactly Thorvald Nilsen who continues to liaise with the Christophersen family. The lieutenant is in no doubt that Don Pedro is keen to finance both the South and North Pole ventures. 'He is anyway one of the nicest men I have met; but anyhow I think that the Grand Cross has made an impact. It might not have titillated his vanity much but it certainly has his wife's. I have heard that Argentinians are rather receptive to flattery in the shape of decorations, etc., and as you know Don Pedro's wife is the daughter of a president and belongs to one of the "best families" in the Argentine. Both she and her daughter were anyhow very amiable. I might be kidding myself of course and this between you and me only.' The lieutenant might be kidding himself about a lot, with regards to mother and daughter.

Argentinian money notwithstanding, the polar voyager had supporters in northerly latitudes too. On 28 June Leon could report that, albeit unofficially for the time being, King Haakon was willing to contribute 5,000 crowns for every year *Fram* was delayed by the additional manoeuvre to the south. 'This gift has been such a delight to receive, not only the sum of money but because the King therein stamps the detour with his approval thus causing his example to catch on.'

A week later Leon was granted an audience at the palace. 'The King was very nice and kept me for 45 minutes.' In spite of the fact that between them the two gentlemen had no arctic experience, they both took a lively interest in the icy wastes. During the audience His Majesty gave expression to his belief that Peary, in spite of his new title of Admiral, could not possibly have reached the most northerly point. Moreover, he is also of the opinion that the South Pole voyager should not return home 'until after the North Pole trip'.

As a dealer in anticipated South Pole telegrams it was useful for Leon to chat to the Head of State. Such extraordinary business necessarily unfolds at a certain level: 'The English are of course jealous and the French are siding with them (owing to politics) and the Germans are preoccupied with Filchner [Wilhelm Filchner travelled to the Antarctic in 1911 on the polar ship *Deutschland*]. I had hoped to interest the Americans and of course that is still possible.'

Around 1 September Leon finished the letter to his brother which would sail with *Fram* from Buenos Aires: 'Autumn is on its way but for you that means spring and therefore the transition it is not as sad as usual. I know that you will now start the march southwards in earnest and I am with you in thought every day on the long and dangerous journey.'

FIFTEEN

A Heroic Deed

Of all the temporary settlements that Amundsen was to erect in the world's inhospitable regions, Framheim was the most elaborate. Like Gjøahavn, the outpost bore the name of the ship which had brought them there, an outpost beyond the reach of all and every normal form of communication.

If one excluded the ingenious prefabricated house, which soon disappeared under mounds of snow, the pointed tents for the provisions and dogs gave the settlement the look of a camp for exiled Native Americans. Dug out under the snow cover, however, were workshops, a sick-bay and storerooms which afforded the inhabitants a safe haven against the exigencies of the polar night.

On the entire continent there existed not one single native to provide variety or create distraction, merely a handful of British. From time to time they came to visit; more and more often, but mostly in the Norwegians' dreams.

There were nine Norwegians, handpicked by Amundsen. It did not follow, however, that they were all men after his own heart. The lieutenant's name was Kristian Prestrud; technically he was a sort of second-in-command, though without any form of polar experience. On the other hand, like most lieutenants in the Navy, he was presentable and good at writing poetry. But Prestrud was not the only one who lacked a snow and ice track-record. From his home town of Svartskog Amundsen had picked Jørgen Stubberud, a handyman and a simple soul whose carpentry skills Amundsen had often used. Stubberud was the colony's most accomplished darts thrower.

Neither had the 40-year-old Oscar Wisting been able to parade his talents as a polar explorer. He had been recruited from the naval shipyard in Horten. Amundsen soon took to the shy, stocky gunner. Although neither of them subscribed to the double sleeping bag the man from Horten soon turned out to be tailor-made for Amundsen's needs. Wisting was a man of few words and few thoughts; he was no visionary out to grab the Pole, but a practical, dogged all-rounder and loyal like a deck full of tail-wagging huskies.

With time Wisting became the epitome of how a colleague, man and human being should behave. The relationship was mutual: 'I stayed with Captain

Amundsen throughout all these years because I was so fond of him. I could never imagine myself leaving him for another man.' This admission was made by Wisting when death parted them. Only then was the partnership over.

The only one who could compete with Wisting for the position of the Governor's closest subject was Helmer Hanssen. Following the *Gjøa* expedition Hanssen's appetite for polar life has been whetted – a life of prodigious sweat and dazzling glory. Captain Amundsen knew his worth. On the other hand, Hanssen knew what the Governor wanted. He was able to surpass even Wisting in the zeal of his loyalty. But the man from Tromsø was less sober-minded. While Wisting hailed from the well-regulated naval town of Horten, in Hanssen's veins flowed the icy waters of the Arctic. He could lapse into wilfulness and was sometimes unable to keep his mouth shut.

This was Adolf Henrik Lindstrøm's third great polar expedition. (Or rather: he was and he was not part of it all.) The cook and the clown, Lindstrøm was simultaneously in the centre and on the side-lines. He was indispensable, but lived an isolated life of practical intelligence and mental simplicity. Without his moustache he might have looked like a genial market-woman. The *Gjøa* men called him 'Madame Larsen'. He was the expedition's soothsayer and preferred solitaire to darts. 'Just so,' was the Lindstrømian motto. A man after the Governor's heart, 'naïve, plump, happy and willing' is how Amundsen summed him up in his diary. 'No better man ever trod the polar regions.'

Roald Amundsen knew how to appreciate men like Lindstrøm – conscientious, simple-minded men. 'He has rendered Norwegian polar expeditions greater and more valuable service than any other. May the Norwegian peasants, my God, why are we dependent on such riff-raff, once understand this,' he wrote in his diary. When Amundsen mentioned the Norwegian peasants he was usually alluding to the majority in Parliament, a reactionary nameless mob deaf to each and every petition. Lindstrøm had a loyal heart, worth more than all the world's treacherous minds put together.

The three remaining inhabitants of Framheim had, individually, a more independent relationship to Amundsen. Theirs was a position outside Amundsen's autocratic rule. Olav Bjaaland from Morgedal* made just one guest performance as a polar explorer. Amundsen met him on a train and invited the ski-racer to join the expedition. That was a Nansenesque move. Ever since the farmers' sons from Telemark started exporting ski-techniques to Christiania in 1868, Telemark in general and Morgedal in particular were held in high esteem. Nansen had hoped to entice Bjaaland's fellow villagers, the brothers Hemmestveit, to join him on his Greenland crossing, and thus draw national comparisons.

---

* Translator's note: The cradle of skiing stood in Morgedal.

Roald Amundsen was less impressed with such ingenuity. But as this peasant from Telemark crossed his path, why not? Not only was Bjaaland a medal winner from Holmenkollen, he was also a brilliant maker of skis. And Amundsen got him cheaply. 'The lad' from Morgedal had accepted a wage of 70 crowns per month. Later Amundsen was to pay dearly for the man from Morgedal, literally a heavier price than for anyone else.

The other man from Telemark, Hjalmar Johansen, was an outstanding skier too, and, in contrast to Bjaaland, very experienced with dogs. Johansen's ice and snow experience was fully equal to that of the Governor, and his forbearing nature did not prevent him from making important decisions. Johansen had already burnt many bridges. He had left both the armed forces and his wife. To all intents and purposes he regretted both; Hjalmar Johansen was on his way out. The South Pole might prove a turning point for him – or the end of the line.

To judge from the wages, Hassel was by far the land party's most valuable member. While Lieutenant Prestrud and Captain Johansen received 100 crowns per month, Hassel, in his position as skipper, was paid 150 crowns. Not only had Sverre Hassel sailed four years with Captain Sverdrup, he had served two years in the Navy and was a fully qualified officer and captain. Moreover, next to Johansen he was the expedition's foremost dog expert.

Sverre Hassel was looking forward to a career as a customs officer. For sure, he enjoyed adventure, but no reckless polar explorer would blow the sober-minded civil servant off his course. He had not been scheduled to take part in the North Pole expedition, just to join in for part of the way to take charge of the dogs. When, before arrival in Madeira, Amundsen had had to inform Hassel, as the only civilian participant, about the change of direction, the customs officer had requested twenty-four hours to consider the proposition before giving his consent. Next to the Governor Sverre Hassel was the strongest and most reflective character at Framheim. He kept a diary.

Before *Fram* had reached her new destination Hassel had made up his mind about the leader of the third *Fram* expedition: 'Mr. A. is not in possession of the consideration and self-control which were, exceptionally, two of Sverdrup's best qualities.' Hassel soon felt Amundsen's disapproval and assumed it was owing to the exorbitant sum Amundsen was forced to pay in order to entice the dog expert to take part in the expedition. He was all the more surprised when his expertise as dog handler was completely overlooked.

Hjalmar Johansen, too, made his observations, not about the Governor but about the dogs. 'If one is dealing with draught animals and wants the best out of them one is obliged to treat them as if they were at least as intelligent as one self.

That will be an advantage when the pulling and life on the ice begins. If one has treated them badly by beating them unreasonably, so that they do not understand why they are being beaten, one can be certain that such a dog will kick up a row when pulling in a team. When such a dog sees a chance to run off it is not easy to catch it. I think they possess a marked sense of justice.'

Further on Johansen notes that the Governor's team 'was scattered to the four winds on account of reckless, unreasonable and foolish treatment.' If not to the same extent as during the *Gjøa* expedition, the treatment of the four-legged expedition members would play an important role in the relationship between the Captain and some of his men.

In contrast to Johansen, Sverre Hassel assumed a cool, distant and very conscious attitude to his new Governor. Early on he dispensed with any hope of being selected for the South Pole party. The dejected civil servant approached the expedition in his own way; his purpose went beyond the South Pole. 'For that matter, I will, to the best of my humble ability, try to be patient and behave in such a manner that I will regret nothing.' Even before they reached the Antarctic Sverre Hassel was aware that a confrontation with Roald Amundsen was unavoidable. He knew he had everything to lose. Consequently, he decided to steer clear of Amundsen. Not an easy task.

The 7 June 1911 was celebrated in Hvalbukta. Norway's National Day, 17 May, had been more modestly celebrated as Lindstrøm's birthday. Hassel wrote in his diary: 'Amundsen did not bother to observe the national festival – in his opinion 7 June was the day.'* It was also the anniversary of *Fram*'s departure from Bunnefjord in Oslo.

Framheim was decorated with bunting and portraits of royalty. Dinner consisted of four courses. The Governor gave a speech. Hjalmar Johansen got up during the coffee; he proposed a toast to the Captain. 'There would be no problem in assuming the correct attitude if the leadership were true, real and straightforward,' Hassel wrote. 'Prestrud toasted the sea-going party.'

Summer and winter are topsy-turvy in the Antarctic. On 23 June, Midsummer Night's Eve, Christmas presents were opened. The Governor humours the seasons; he is lord of the festivals.

Harmony reigns. It is unbelievable. 'Not a single misunderstanding, no sour looks, nothing, nothing, just comradeship.' Roald Amundsen hinted at a blissful state of affairs. 'Continuous cooperation in friendly company characterised by earnest and unqualified confidence in the success of our goal.'

---

* On 7 June 1905 King Oscar of Norway and Sweden abdicated and the union between the two countries was dissolved. Prince Charles of Denmark, via a national referendum, became King of Norway and took the name Haakon VII. Constitution Day, 17 May, is now Norway's recognised national day.

Everything was under control. Everything, bar the British and the passing days. When would Scott move? Move? Scott won't move, he'll get in behind the wheel of his motorised caterpillar and roar across the icecap. It's more like taking the train from Oslo to Bergen over the mountain plateau. He won't even have to wait for a rise in temperature. What had that fellow from Bø said about motorised sledges with electric heaters? Technology is progressing by leaps and bounds. Who really knows how far the British have got? Didn't that engineer Martens have to go to England to develop his motor-sledge?

The Norwegians were on time. The depots were in position before the long winter nights set in. True, the Governor was ill for a period; he suffered badly from a bleeding rectum in the Antarctic winter – an old wound from the *Gjøa* expedition – and he chose to abstain from the last depot-tour. He handed the leadership over to Johansen. 'He is the oldest and most experienced.'

He recovered; the dogs were well fed; all the equipment ready. Everything was on schedule, according to Amundsen's timetable. But what about the British? Which timetable is Captain Scott using?

Roald Amundsen decided to break camp early. Everything was ready, everything except the weather. Spring was long overdue. But on 8 September the Governor could wait no longer. They set off, eight men, two tent teams, countless numbers of dogs. The temperature was about –30°C. Amundsen imagined the sledges with the black supply cases looked like coffins. It would soon turn considerably colder.

On 12 September they were in need of some warm sustenance. A bottle of gin had burst in the cold, so the chaps pinned their faith on some aquavit. It was cold work crowding around a solidly frozen bottle of aquavit in order to thaw out somewhat. The Governor was expecting a temperature of –60° that night.

At the depot, 80° South, they unloaded the 'coffins' and turned for home. Amundsen had to choose between temporary defeat and complete collapse. On the morning of 16 September they set out on the last 75 kilometres back to Framheim. Hanssen and Stubberud were suffering from frostbite; Prestrud was in an even worse condition. The lieutenant shared a sleeping bag with Johansen. At night Prestrud gave off as much heat as Nansen but was not much good during the day. His dog team had disintegrated and he too was suffering from frostbite. Johansen let him ride with his emaciated dog team the last lap of the journey.

First to reach Framheim at four in the afternoon were Hanssen, Wisting and the Governor himself. Roald Amundsen hitched a ride with Wisting. If one were to view the aborted expedition as a shipwreck, it did not look good that the Captain saved his own skin. Seen from a cynical point of view the mission's three most important protagonists had returned home safely. With Wisting and Hanssen safe and sound, Amundsen could always have made another attempt. The expedition was saved.

Bjaaland arrived two hours later, safe and sound, with a frost-bitten Stubberud. Next in was Hassel – he too was frost-bitten. At half past midnight the last sledge with Johansen and Prestrud arrived. 'God knows what it had been doing en route,' Amundsen later wrote in his book *The South Pole*. However, he knew all too well how Johansen and Prestrud had been occupied en route. Behind the sigh lurked the most dramatic incident of the whole expedition. The one and only heroic deed.

The dogs had been unable to pull Prestrud. The lieutenant lagged behind. But Johansen had waited, for hours on the icy cold plateau. Initially he had overtaken Hassel. (That was important as he thereby had a witness to the incident.) Hassel gave Johansen a tent but there was no primus and virtually no food. Still, Johansen had braved the cold, hunger and dark, waited and helped the lieutenant home. Hjalmar Johansen had saved Prestrud.

Roald Amundsen had saved himself.

When the two tumbled in from the dark the Governor asked them what the hell they had been doing. Hjalmar Johansen might at that moment have saved his life. But he did not condescend to answer; he went straight to bed. He was raging inside.

At the breakfast table next morning Hjalmar Johansen burnt his last bridge. In the presence of everyone he read Roald Amundsen the riot act.

Captain Amundsen's position at the breakfast table was precarious. Johansen spoke with the authority of experience, from the cave on Franz Josef Land and filled with holy wrath from the preceding day. The Captain's 'leadership qualities had been shipwrecked'; he later summed up the situation. The lieutenant backed him. They are nearly all in accord. From whom does Amundsen seek support? From Helmer Hanssen, from Lindstrøm? From the cabinet and the government? He has nothing with which to shore himself up either inside or outside the walls of Framheim. For all he knows the King, Nansen, the entire population have turned their backs on him. *Fram* might have been towed home and confiscated. And now his own men are in revolt.

In the hours that followed Roald Amundsen demonstrated the force of his leadership. And in the days that followed: his human frailty. The short period of open debate was soon replaced by a brutal power struggle. The Captain confronted each and every man individually. He knew that they had everything to lose, nothing to gain, by siding with Johansen. As the last man, at midday, the lieutenant partook of humble pie. Thus Johansen had lost his most important supporter. 'The Mutineer' had been isolated. 'It goes without saying that he is, by his behaviour, excluded from the 3rd *Fram* expedition, Amundsen concluded in his diary.

Hjalmar Johansen's situation was now akin to the one in which Amundsen had found himself when he broke away from the leadership of the *Belgica* expedition. But whereas Amundsen's withdrawal had been accompanied by calculated pride, Johansen's internal exile soon took on an unhappy and helpless aspect. The confrontation with Amundsen had set him back yet again. He eventually agreed to take part in an alternative expedition eastwards to King Edward VII Land as 'a private person' under the command of Prestrud and with Stubberud as a third member.

As a rebel Hjalmar Johansen never represented an alternative; he was a professional and he was strong, but he lacked the will and the energy to challenge Amundsen. An expedition to the South Pole, under Johansen's command, while Amundsen remained behind playing solitaire with Lindstrøm in Framheim, was out of the question. The energy was Amundsen's, his the will to lead, the will to reach the Pole at all costs. In truth, Johansen could never have threatened him, just diminished his authority. That was bad enough.

The period between 17 September and the departure for the South Pole on 21 October was the coldest of the whole expedition, in spite of spring having arrived in earnest. 'A. has not spoken a word to Johansen since the big Day of Judgement, with exception of the man-to-man talks regarding the subject', Hassel wrote in his diary, in mid-October. Frost-bitten feet heal but the internal frostbites are many and deep.

It was the Governor's responsibility to make peace; that would have cost him an admission and an effort; nevertheless for the sake of Johansen, for Nansen and for himself and the expedition – he should have made the effort. But Amundsen frankly feared Johansen. 'There must be no dissenting voices on our expedition,' he wrote in his diary. 'When they come from an old polar hand like him they can be especially harmful.'

One day Hjalmar Johansen felt the house literally vibrating. Was it the sea ice packing up against the barrier? Amundsen cared little for Johansen's theories. He noted that Prestrud 'felt nothing at all. H H likewise felt nothing.' His is the majority. Might it be that the vibrating was inside Johansen?

Roald Amundsen had decided to divide the expedition in two, a southern party and an eastern party. That was a fortunate decision, a fortunate consequence of an unfortunate situation. By limiting the South Pole party to five, at the eleventh hour, he had arrived at a correct solution.

The Governor had appointed Kristian Prestrud, the repentant lieutenant, to lead the so-called East Party to King Edward VII Land. The obvious solution would have been to appoint Captain Johansen to this commission. That would have been seen as an honourable climb-down and at the same time would have relieved the lieutenant of having to partake in Johansen's humiliation. Prestrud owed him his life. But the Governor too was in debt to Johansen for having saved the expedition and him personally from the scandal the lieutenant's death would have caused. Johansen quivered with anger. There were no cracks in the Governor's expressionless mask, however.

Roald Amundsen's ability to interpret the drama from more than one angle was non-existent. His eyes were focused on the South Pole.

SIXTEEN

The Dance round the South Pole

Roald Amundsen's 'lack of self-dramatisation, his gift for making things seem easier than they were', are the words of Roland Huntford towards the end of his major work about the race for the South Pole. But this was precisely part of the equation. The achievement appeared out of nowhere, effortlessly, perfect. It would speak for itself.

Roald Amundsen had a flair for scenic effects, but not for the drama's core structure. In spite of having personally experienced Admiral Franklin's suffering, he did not properly grasp the general craving for the human dimension; that the underlying trials were what gripped the public imagination and gave the feat magnitude. He wished to rise above both the difficulties en route and the subsequent ovation. All must appear easy and simple, but at the same time incomprehensible and conventionally grand.

It was a piece of cake, was the first thing Amundsen said when the polar party returned to Framheim; 'we cannot report privation or danger or major hardship'. Of course, the more than three-month-long voyage through unknown and exposed terrain included all of that. But, as long as they reached their goal it amounted to nothing much.

Five men, four sledges and fifty-two dogs, set off towards the south on 20 October 1911. Only a small number of dogs would make it all the way to the Pole. But what about the men? Johansen believed there were too few draught animals for such a large party and predicted that Hanssen would be the sole member to accompany the Governor all the way. 'I won't be surprised if we see Hassel and Bjaaland here in a couple of months. Maybe Wisting too,' he wrote when they left.

The route to the South Pole can be divided into three phases. Initially there is the relatively flat barrier, from about 79° to 85° South. The critical phase follows next: the ascent and crossing of what Amundsen would call Queen Maud's Mountain Range with subsequent difficult glacier sections from 85° to 87° South. Finally, all the way to 90° South, lies the South Pole plateau, flat but at extreme altitude. Roald Amundsen's only fixed point for the voyage into the unknown were his studies of Shackleton's journey through similar terrain further to the west, the route of which Captain Scott would make use.

Roald Amundsen's forte, compared with the English expedition, was that he knew his metier through and through. Dogs, skis, sledges – all of them tried and tested by Nansen, Sverdrup and himself. The same applied to the problems of cold and nutrition. Peary, Cook and Astrup; their experiences were solid weight at Amundsen's disposal. Only two things could prevent him from reaching the South Pole: the unpredictability of the terrain and the human factor.

As Johansen had from the very start, Bjaaland and Hassel came to entertain deep scepticism about Amundsen's leadership. They were critical of many of his decisions, among others of his estimates of rations for dogs as well as humans. But above all it is the Governor's personality which they disliked.

On 19 November, in the middle of the difficult ascent, some sort of discussion developed into bickering between Amundsen and the stubborn farmer from Telemark. Hassel in his diary described this second rupture as 'a small settling of accounts'. Just like Johansen a month earlier, Bjaaland was asked to leave. But as the man from Morgedal was no navigator Sverre Hassel was directed to accompany his comrade back to Framheim; they were to return as soon as they had reached the summit. Johansen's predictions were about to come true.

The medal winner from Morgedal and Holmenkollen then made the only move which could possibly have persuaded Amundsen to change his mind. He 'ate humble pie and pleaded with the Captain to reverse his decision, which Amundsen then did. However, he reiterated that he would not stand being contradicted.'

The microscopic drama – the man from Morgedal on his knees in front of the almighty Governor – was played out against a backdrop of enormous, as yet undiscovered, mountain formations. In his diary Roald Amundsen was content to commit the scenery to paper. Humans dwindled and became unimportant among these unseen mountain tops and dizzy peaks. The journey continued the next day.

Once they reached the top, twenty-four dogs were slaughtered. Amundsen himself did not partake of the bloodbath. Wisting was cook. Animals and humans gorged themselves on dog cutlets and a large depot was laid out. The place was christened 'The Butcher'.

About ten days later the expedition found itself in difficult crevasse-ridden terrain, 'The Devil's Ballroom'. The Governor was irritable in the extreme. Crampons had been left behind at 'The Butcher' and Amundsen feared they might have had to retrace their steps and retrieve them. 'A thousand thoughts rushed through my mind,' he wrote in his diary. 'The Pole lost maybe for such a trifle.'

The two weeks it would have taken to recover the crampons might decide the race in favour of the British. That explained some of the Governor's stand-offish behaviour, his sudden fits of aggression and bad moods. What to the others were practical details were to the Governor the be all and end all. The South Pole plateau lies between 2,000 to 3,000 metres above sea level; Roald Amundsen's drop would not have been much less. From the very moment he altered course from north to south the expedition had been without a line of retreat. However well it was all planned, only the South Pole could save Roald Amundsen, and he knew it.

Sverre Hassel portrayed the Governor as 'distant and cantankerous'; Hanssen and Wisting were 'his two buddy-boys'. Time and again clashes were followed by sulking. 'One would think the man has a screw loose. He has many times in the last few days actually initiated quarrels, an extraordinary stand to take for a Governor and leader for whom peace and good camaraderie should be the main target.' Thus wrote Hassel two days before they reached the Pole. Amundsen's nerves were stretched to breaking point. At any time they might see signs of the British.

On 14 December they reach the point, in Amundsen's words: 'An extremely flat snow plateau.' It was not easy to find the invisible place on which to plant the flag. Roald Amundsen christened the area Haakon VII Plateau and sent up a prayer to heaven: 'Thanks be to God!'

He called the camp Polheim – Polar Home – a misnomer for he had found a home where it would be impossible to live. For the first time during the journey they smoked. To everyone's astonishment Amundsen brought out a pipe. The others whittled bamboo smoking gadgets by cutting tips off their ski-poles. The man from Morgedal alone was equal to the historic occasion; he fished out a silver case and proffered cigars all around.

When all five had helped themselves three cigars remained – one for Stubberud, one for Prestrud and one for Johansen. They gazed at them before handing the matches round. The man from Telemark uttered a few well-chosen words in his beautiful, regional lilt, and presented Amundsen with the case. Johansen too had once held a speech for the Governor. It does not go without saying that the tip of Olav Bjaaland's cigar glowed here at the uttermost point of the world.

The Norwegians spent several days taking observations. They took bearings to establish the exact 90th degree and kept an eye open for the British. 'We have all made diligent use of the field glasses to see if there is sign of life in any direction, but in vain. We must be the first here.' First again; Roald Amundsen had beaten the British for the second time.

They abandoned the place on 18 December. The Captain left behind a letter addressed to King Haakon. It would most probably never drop through His Majesty's letter box. Hassel's thoughts were with their rivals. 'It won't be nice for Scott, if he gets here now, to arrive and see the tent with the Norwegian flag and the burgee with *Fram* on it.'

The mission is accomplished, the Pole conquered and land discovered. Rations can be increased. 'During the sledging today Amundsen announced that from now on we could use 4 pieces of pemmican in the soup.' Hassel was clearly not of the opinion that the success had made the autocrat less exalted. One morning Bjaaland and Hassel were taken to task for having snored in the tent. 'That's OK by me but things can be said in several ways. Mr. A always chooses the nastiest and most *haughty* one.'

According to Hassel, Helmer Hanssen is the only one who absolutely knew how to play the role as the Governor's permanently fawning subject. He kept that position until a week before arrival at Framheim. But then 'Hanssen has fallen into disgrace. He allowed himself to disagree with His Majesty Amundsen regarding Else [one of the dogs] which Hanssen insisted smelt, but Amundsen could not smell anything. For the time being they are not talking.'

At the crack of dawn on 26 January 1912, the polar party consisting of five men, two sledges and eleven dogs were back at Framheim. It had taken them ninety-nine days to cover approximately 3,000 kilometres. Having chosen the right moment to start, the expedition was on the whole brilliantly planned and carried though. But was it in itself the goal or just a commercial 'detour'?

This question was answered in an amazingly frank manner in Hassel's return-journey diary. Lieutenant Prestrud had pronounced before departure that it really did not matter whether the Norwegians got to the Pole before or after Scott. 'Amundsen has taken Prestrud to task several times and reproached him severely. He was at it again this evening. He would not have wanted to be Number Two for all the tea in China.'

For all the tea in China he could have equipped a scientific expedition to the northerly polar regions not once but two or three times. Amundsen could not have expressed it more clearly. The journey to the South Pole had been no enforced 'detour'. The Pole was the goal. The detour lay ahead, to the north.

When the Pole party returned to Framheim, *Fram* was already at the ice barrier with news from home. Roald Amundsen was told that not everyone was equally enthusiastic about the race to the south. 'Is the Polar question one to be solved by Scott alone? I couldn't care less about these idiots. Nansen has, as always, with his cold, clear common sense had to calm things down. There's no accounting for some people.' In his diary it was imperative that Amundsen drew a line between the confused masses and those individuals who supported him. 'I admire the King for his manly behaviour.'

In Amundsen's eyes, these three – Nansen, the King and Don Pedro Christophersen – had saved the enterprise. They had trusted him. 'When all turned their backs on me – they offered me their hand. May God bless them.'

Now the party needed to be off as quickly as possible. The race had not been won until the telegrams had been dispatched; the last stage had not been completed until the ship had reached civilisation. Ice and weather conditions might still decide the whole outcome. Roald Amundsen did not know that Captain Scott was already a defeated man. The English had reached the polar point one whole month after their competitors. As *Fram* sailed away from the ice barrier, heading north, the five valiant pedestrians were still on the South Pole plateau. Let down by their motor-sledges, dogs and ponies, they were forced to man-handle the huge loads themselves. And the heaviest load of all was the letter to King Haakon, signed by the man who had got there first. Captain Scott and Roald Amundsen had one thing in common: both had resorted to underhand tactics. Before challenging each other they had had to outmanoeuvre their own compatriots, Ernest Shackleton and Fridtjof Nansen respectively. For both there was but one way to return – triumphant; neither could afford to return home defeated.

As *Gjøa* once left Gjøahavn in a mist, so Framheim lay enshrouded in fog as *Fram* headed away. Hassel wrote on 31 January: 'The place that had been our residence for a year we left without a backwards glance. The fog was too dense. But I doubt if any of us regretted that.'

The crew on board for the third *Fram* journey was fed up to the teeth with polar research and all its tribulations. And this was just the start. After three weeks at sea Hassel wrote: 'A. today dispatched a list aft in which he asks every individual whether they want to go north, yes or no. Everyone except Beck said no.' The result must no doubt have been depressing for the Captain. He fell back on his old tactics, however, and sounded out each man individually. Three days later the answer had changed. 'A. has now spoken to everyone aft about going north, except L. Hansen. All have agreed (!) except Bjaaland.'

On 7 March 1912 *Fram* dropped anchor outside Hobart, Tasmania. Representatives of the port authorities stepped on board. Nothing had been heard of the *Terra Nova*. They were first again. No one was allowed ashore bar one. Hassel wrote: 'A. went ashore in the doctor's boat at 12.15. He was carrying his telegram briefcase. I bet he won't let go of it.' A few hours later a cargo of fresh fruit and vegetables arrived on board. 'Some reporters have been lurking alongside in a boat. They leave empty-handed. No one is allowed aboard yet.'

Dressed like a modest sailor Amundsen holes up in a – according to his diary – 'miserable little room' at the Hotel Orient in the idyllic port. Next he dispatched three coded telegrams, to the King, to Nansen and to Leon. He added one to each of the venture's most important sponsors, Axel Heiberg and Don Pedro Christophersen. Then he settled down to await instructions from his brother in Christiania.

'Received this morning telegram from L. who advises me to send main telegram to *Daily Chronicle*, London. This I did immediately.' Latterly, and on behalf of his brother, Leon had signed a five-page contract with the British newspaper the *Daily Chronicle* for exclusive rights to the South Pole story outside Scandinavia. The agreement contained several hypothetical sums of money, depending on the outcome of the race. The final result proved a profitable £2,000. In practice the agreement had been brokered by Scott's arch-rival Sir Ernest Shackleton, who had always been convinced that the Norwegian would win the battle. Since Leon's visit to London he had sounded out the possibilities of obtaining the best deal from his contacts among British publicists. Using his own experiences, he also planned how to handle the news to best advantage. In the final contract between Amundsen and the *Daily Chronicle* Sir Ernest Shackleton is named as arbitrator.

On 7 March Leon Amundsen was met by representatives of several newspapers at the East Station. Via a telegram from Reuters news agency the rumours were circulating that *Fram* had that morning arrived in Tasmania. It was now only a matter of hours before messages from Roald Amundsen would start coming in. The first telegram would be addressed to the King but sent to Leon. All the telegrams would be in code. The only man in the world able to decode the South Pole telegrams was Leon Amundsen.

At 11 o'clock he was informed, via telephone, that a telegram awaited him with the telegraph inspector. He sat down to decipher it. 'It was as you can imagine,' he later wrote to his brother, 'no one could ever have had such exciting work.'

Having decoded the core words 'Pole reached', we might assume that even a level-headed man such as Leon Amundsen would have heaved a sigh of relief before stuffing the piece of paper into his pocket and leaving the building. Before departing he first sent a return message to Hobart and received the telegram addressed to him, signed 'zhmbw' – Roald. It was now of paramount importance that nothing leaked out until the *Daily Chronicle* had received its gilt-edged telegram from Hobart.

'All day I carried the news around alone – I dared not confide in the papers or the King who luckily was not at the Castle but out on field manoeuvre in Sandvika.' Leon remained quietly in the little office he had fitted out in a relative's house in town. Towards evening 'the old geezer' phoned – that was the brothers' nickname for Fridtjof Nansen. He had received an unintelligible telegram. They agreed to meet outside the National Theatre, 'where I at 10 o'clock in the evening confided the news to him.' Nansen's telegram was worded: 'Thank you for everything. Problem solved. All well.'

Together they walked up to Akersgaten and informed *Tidens Tegn* and *Aftenposten*, who had signed contracts worth 4,000 crowns for the Scandinavian rights. 'Everywhere there was rejoicing.'

At midnight Leon arrived in Sandvika, west of Christiania, by car. He located the operation's headquarters and asked for an audience with His Majesty King Haakon. 'The King had in the meantime wisely ordered his adjutant not to allow me entry as he thought this would attract attention. He asked me to trust his adjutant with the contents of the telegram, which I refused, but borrowed an envelope in which I placed the news and then left.'

When he returned to Christiania Leon decided to inform one more person this last night; tomorrow news would erupt that the world had been conquered from Pole to Pole. He stopped by the masonic lodge. The tall windows were lit up; the strains of music were carried towards him when he opened the doors. It was the freemasons' annual ball. Leon had rendezvoused with Professor Nansen in the dusk by the National Theatre and with the King's adjutant in a dingy hallway. Now at last he was standing at the entrance to a banqueting hall. The ladies' dresses sparkled, the men's medals twinkled. Leon glanced at his own pedestrian outfit. He did not step inside but sent for the man presiding over the night's festivities, high court judge Alexander Nansen, the Professor's brother.

They faced each other: Amundsen, unassuming, showing signs of the day's excitement; Nansen, wide-eyed, enthusiastic, intoxicated, in full evening dress. Formally, but with an undercurrent of exultation and relief the following words were spoken: 'The Pole is conquered, fourteen to eighteen December last year, all is well.' 'He was beside himself, stretched both arms in the air and grabbed my shoulders and looked me straight in the eye'. The two – Leon Amundsen and Alexander Nansen – each the brother of a famous brother. They had made it, at last, the Pole!

Behind them the penguins kept on dancing.

SEVENTEEN

Fridtjof Nansen has his Say

The world had received the news. On the evening of 11 March the *Fram*'s crew stepped ashore in the enticing port of Hobart. Every man received £1 pocket money.

Sverre Hassel was in no hurry; he waited until the following day. On shore he happened upon one of his shipmates, already the worse for drink. 'Johansen has been boozing,' Hassel noted in his diary. Hjalmar Johansen had swallowed his disappointment and kept his cool throughout the journey. He wrote home that he was 'well and quick as ever'. But his courage failed him when he came face to face with civilisation. Of all the crew, his experience was of defeat. He, who should first have been Nansen's and secondly Amundsen's closest companion at the two Poles, returned as a subordinate of Lieutenant Prestrud's expedition to the long-since named King Edward VII's Land. It was liberating to get away from the *Fram*; it was good to drown one's sorrows. 'Now he wants to leave for home from here,' Hassel wrote. 'He spoke to A. this morning. It appears that he will be allowed to leave.'

The monthly wage transfers to Hjalmar Johansen's family in Skien suddenly ceased. They were given no explanation. In a letter to the manager Amundsen wrote a short and brutal note: 'Johansen shown the door. A rascal.' The diary entry of 15 March: 'Paid off Johansen today who could not possibly remain on board any longer.' It appears from this that Amundsen was the initiator and shut Johansen out. Hassel's diary, however, interprets it differently; Johansen himself wanted to withdraw.

On 15 March 1912, in Hobart, a document was concocted, written by Roald Amundsen, signed by F. Hjalmar Johansen: 'I declare that on signing off I have received 600 crowns, sufficient means to get me home. At the same time I promise, on my honour, to abide by the contract signed between the *Fram* expedition's leadership, Roald Amundsen, and myself in Christiania.' The last bit refers to the promise of secrecy. In cases of dismissal Amundsen applied a certain procedure whereby two expedition officers were required to confirm irregular behaviour. This was used in Madeira when the steward was dismissed, but not in Tasmania for Johansen.

Strictly speaking, the South Pole conqueror had things to think about other than the 'rascal' Johansen. He had moved himself into a hotel and would not be joining *Fram* on its onward journey. His contact with the crew was sporadic. Hassel bumped into Johansen once again in Hobart: 'He had been given sufficient travel money he said.'

The messages sent home, among others to Nansen, only served to confirm the impression that Johansen had been mercilessly kicked out. It was in Amundsen's interests, and best fitted the picture, to paint Johansen as the rebellious 'rascal' and himself as the authoritative, principled Governor. In the light of Johansen's later fate Amundsen thus took on a far larger responsibility than was his due.

On 20 March the Governor paid *Fram* a visit and took a hasty farewell of his crew. The polar ship set sail straight for Don Pedro's Argentinian coast while Amundsen made a brief detour to Australia and New Zealand for his first lectures. The important lecture tours would follow. The time had come to convert the South Pole triumph into ready cash.

At home in Norway Leon had managed to negotiate a contract with a publisher worth 111,000 crowns, beating all previous records. Jacob Dybwad in collaboration with Danish publishers Gyldendal were to bring out the book in Norway and Denmark. It would be an ongoing production to be produced in pamphlet form. Publishers from several countries were queuing up to secure the rights. Professor Nansen had promised to write the introduction.

The poet's battle with words commenced. Roald wrote to Leon from Sydney on 17 April: 'Herewith the first 4,200 words. Please arrange with Vilhelm Krag to go through the manuscript. If there are not enough words he can add some. There cannot be too many. Let me know how many Nansen delivers. I hope 20 thousand.' This was to be a monumental work – worthy of the conquest of the South Pole. Unfortunately, the word-adder, the poet Vilhelm Krag, was attached to the publisher Aschehoug who had withdrawn from the battle for the book's rights.

To enable him, continuously and without interruption, to produce tens of thousands of words, Roald Amundsen went to South America with the SS *Remuera*, travelling incognito as Engelbregt Gravning, sporting a fake beard and dark glasses. On 21 May he was welcomed with open arms in Montevideo by the wealthy Don Pedro. The not very speedy polar ship arrived in Buenos Aires five days later, on Argentina's day of independence, and to great jubilation.

On 30 May the Norwegian La Plata Association held a grand banquet for Roald Amundsen and his men. The speeches kicked off with a toast to the King and ended with the polar explorer's expression of thanks. According to Hassel, Amundsen had a lot of people to thank. Apart, of course, from Don Pedro, he emphasised Lieutenant Nilsen and the sea-party, 'then he very hastily named his comrades from the wintering. He said he knew he was an unpleasant man to work with. And he is right. However, it is extraordinary how an honest admission of one's faults can help alleviate the dislike they create.' For once Sverre Hassel praised his Governor: 'A. spoke well.'

While *Fram* lay at anchor in Buenos Aires the crew, paid for by Don Pedro, were sent home on a passenger ship. The two officers and Hassel travelled first class, the others went steerage. The South Pole conquerors Wisting and Hanssen felt badly degraded. The Governor had appointed Sverre Hassel as the bearer of valuable materials and documents to be given to Leon. Roald Amundsen trusted the distant but self-opinionated man. Throughout all the hardships he had maintained the correct attitude to his superior. In itself a full-time job.

The expedition's two leaders remained in Argentina. Lieutenant Nilsen stayed in town to oversee *Fram*'s repairs and further preparation for the North Pole journey. Rumours circulated that Nilsen might have nurtured private ambitions connected to Buenos Aires. During his last visit idle gossip had reached the manager to the effect that 'the Lieutenant stands a chance of becoming a son-in-law,' to Don Pedro himself.

Roald Amundsen resided at the Majestic Hotel until the most pressing celebrations were over. On 11 June he allowed himself to be transported out into the provinces to lodge at Don Pedro's exceedingly comfortable country house Carmen, called after the landowner's daughter and wife. Here the polar voyager was to complete his work about the conquest of the South Pole.

Leon sent Roald Amundsen belated but updated news about the celebrations and enthusiasm in his native country. On 8 March, when the news had been released, all flags flew and steamships hooted in Christiania harbour. All businesses of importance held celebration parties. Of course Nansen had had his say: 'Immediately the news was known Nansen gave a long talk about you in the Geographical Society in the old hall with the King and Queen present.'

On this occasion Leon could report an embarrassing intermezzo in connection with the many personal names with which the South Pole map was now adorned. *Inter alia*, a glacier which cut down through Queen Maud's Mountain Range was called after Axel Heiberg. 'Heiberg too took the floor but his turn of phrase was rather unfortunate. He mentioned he was in superior company with Queen Alexandra and Queen Maud, but that this neighbourliness posed no danger as the temperatures down there were too low. The Queen was appalled and left the hall pretty indignant, without speaking to anyone, as soon as the talk was over.'

The Norwegian King had not only supported the South Pole journey financially, but he had also used every, albeit rare, occasion to communicate personally with his Antarctic commander. Unfortunately, his native country had been struck by a 'very sad strike and a subsequent lock-out', but His Majesty's thoughts had nevertheless been with his subjects on their trek to the South Pole.

Fridtjof Nansen, with his 'cold, clear understanding', maintained a deliberately cool attitude towards Amundsen during this period. His trust in the unpredictable South Pole voyager had been severely undermined. In December Alexander Nansen had expressed to Leon 'very serious' doubts as to 'whether the North Pole expedition might now take place'. If the lawyer was that sceptical, someone else must have prompted him.

If his brother aired doubts the Professor expressed unshakeable trust in Roald Amundsen on all public occasions. In his introduction to *The South Pole* the journey is placed in a national context as only Nansen himself could do. However, the Professor laid particular stress on the leader's personal qualities. 'It all depends on the *man*; here as everywhere else.' This was a deed executed by a man with the minimum of fuss, a man who said no more than he could do. 'How true to form is his telegram home. So sincere and straightforward, as if it were an Easter stroll in the mountains. It talks about what has been gained, not about how they toiled. Every word is manly. The right person was bound to be so; unassuming and strong.'

With all this homage Fridtjof Nansen laid the foundations for a further relentless demand. In his conclusion he nailed Amundsen to the cross like a helpless Jesus to his inevitable fate: 'Next year he heads towards the Bering Strait, into the ice and cold and dark of the north, to drift across the North Pole Sea for at least five years. As an undertaking it appears virtually superhuman; but he is the man for that too. *Forwards* is the name of the ship, *forwards* is his motto. [Norwegians thought 'Forwards' was Nansen's motto.] And forwards is where he is going. The important journey, which will now commence, he will execute as doggedly as the one he has just completed.'

The polar explorer had received his first private letter from Professor Nansen when *Fram* returned to Hvalbukta. In this letter he made clear his fellow feeling and faith in his compatriot – that he would cope with the situation – 'assuming it is at all possible within human endeavour'. He also referred to an article from *The Times*: 'It has been told to me that the mood has changed in England.' As always the Professor emphasised the scientific results: 'As you know for me it is irrelevant whether you reach the South Pole or not, although undeniably, it would be splendid to include it if at all possible.'

In his first letter, addressed to the Argentine after the outcome was known, Fridtjof Nansen's personal remarks were more sparing. 'It [the deed] is of course in every respect great,' he wrote and referred to the preface and other official comments. On the other hand the letter was crammed with oceanographic discussions with an eye to the forthcoming 'main journey'. The Professor made every effort to kindle the polar hero's enthusiasm for 'wave-movements', 'salt-content measurements', 'nitrogen links' and other strange scientific phenomena in the, as yet, unconquered scientific world.

Before leaving for 'Carmen', Roald Amundsen received yet another letter, one which caused him embarrassment. It was from Gjøvik, from Sigrid Castberg. Among the enormous pile of congratulations telegrams in Hobart had been a jolly and, in itself, non-committal word: 'Skaal' – cheers!

Having given the letter some thought he decided not to answer.

During the polar explorer's absence private relations between Mr and Mrs Castberg had been through a crisis. The whispers of malicious tongues might soon turn it into a public scandal. The conqueror of the South Pole could ill afford to be implicated, now that the whole of Norway and half the world followed his every move.

EIGHTEEN

History is being Written

In the shadow of 'Carmen's' shady pavilions Roald Amundsen tore to the South Pole and back, for the second time. He wrote at breakneck speed. He spared his hand by shrinking the letters to make them near impossible to read with the naked eye. The publisher in Christiania regarded the pencil-written filigree manuscripts as the purest handicraft; no hesitation, no correction. Every letter was equivalent to one, or ten, metres covered over the ice, transcribed on to paper; each daily stage amounted to 4,000 words.

The chapters regarding the sea journey, 'To the South' and 'To the North', he left to Kristian Prestrud. But as both chapters would appear under his name he asked Leon to go through them carefully: 'If "I" has been used then change it everywhere to "we".' But what was there to write about when so much could not be mentioned and everything else was a piece of cake? 'In chapter II, I need an accurate description of the diesel engine,' the poet told Leon. 'If the description can be made to last 5,000 words so much the better. The best solution would be to get it direct from Diesel with permission to reproduce it in the book.'

Unfortunately, there was little scientific padding. Could Nansen possibly conjure up 15,000 words about oceanography? 'If not I'm not sure what to think up.' The work proceeded apace, although it was not easy to write a two-volume creation about a three-month ski tour for a man for whom words were to be treated with scepticism. The telegram was the only literary genre which he fully mastered. What had his colleague Nansen not said? 'Every word is manly.' The more words the more womanlike, the further diminished the deed. The feat was the work of men. 'I think I'll scrap chapter VII: Home again. As you no doubt will realise it's not possible to make much of it.'

In one area Roald Amundsen really could maintain his word-production ad infinitum without resorting to watering down his tremendous achievement. He could write the conquered continent's history. This was material the author had studied, as at one time he had worked his way through the chronicles of the North West Passage.

But a problem lurked in the material – a problem by the name of Frederick A. Cook. For many Dr Cook would appear a minor character in the history of the South Pole, but not for Roald Amundsen. He was the man who did not forget his teachers. A huge monument had been raised over the grave of his parents; in the Antarctic an even larger memorial to his nanny – Betty's Top. The frail 'Geheimrat', the professor by whose table and desk he studied in Hamburg, was portrayed in the South Pole history. 'As long as Antarctica stands the name Neumayer will be intrinsically bound to it,' he wrote. Precisely. All names bound to his, en route to his destination, had to be mentioned and remembered. Dr Cook's too.

To Roald Amundsen such acknowledgement was a matter of course, but not so for Leon. The showdown regarding the North Pole represented a latent threat to the South Pole voyager's credibility. The public had got used to thinking of polar explorers as cheats, and Roald Amundsen had led the world up the garden path. Observations and calculations notwithstanding, the only real evidence that the Norwegian had reached the South Pole was Captain Scott's testimony and the letter to King Haakon. That it was actually en route, no one knew, no one dared hope.

When Leon read his brother's exuberant praise of Dr Cook he smelt a rat. Quickly he took advice from Professor Nansen as well as the American ambassador and the brothers Gade. The recommendations were unanimous. On 7 June the author received by telegram the following diplomatic appeal: 'Omit Cook book advisable.' A few days later the South Pole historian had subjected his opinion to a tactical revision. The subsequent telegram was thus worded: 'Drop Cook'.

Meanwhile, the American was not entirely erased from the history of the South Pole. The positive report about Dr Cook's efforts during the *Belgica* expedition still stood. To balance the picture he added a postscript which did not exactly support the doctor in the ongoing battle about the North Pole. The conqueror of the South Pole washed his hands of the matter: 'Little did his comrades realise that a few years later he would be considered one of the world's worst humbugs; a psychological enigma, only worth studying for those who can be bothered.'

Leon's battle against 'the North Pole swindler' Dr Cook needed to be fought on two fronts. The manager had ascertained that the American was touring Germany that summer and intended to visit Norway in September. Dr Cook was making a desperate attempt to regain his lost position. The meeting between the discoverers of the two Poles would form the very climax of his tour. Leon realised that a hostile world press might well characterise this as a meeting of criminals by two like-minded polar cheats.

As always Leon left no stone unturned and put out diplomatic feelers. His brother's American promoter strongly advised him against any association with Dr Cook, while the Norwegian ambassador in Berlin reported a continuous boycott. Leon decided to do all he could to 'frustrate the doctor's journey' to Norway. 'I will have him understand,' he wrote to his brother, 'that he will be received with displeasure by you and the press.'

Leon's glacial attitude to Roald's old friend, the absolute demarcation between the two Poles, was probably necessary, if only to avoid a new, undignified phase, a repetition of the one which had been played out in connection with the North Pole. Large sums were at stake: in reality it was about Roald Amundsen's position as the South Pole's unchallenged conqueror. Luckily Leon could seek support from contemporary professional authorities. As opposed to Otto Sverdrup and Roald Amundsen, Fridtjof Nansen had never unreservedly hailed Frederick Cook as the North Pole's discoverer. Now he was able to back Leon Amundsen in his businesslike manoeuvres.

The pressing situation caused Roald Amundsen to turn on himself. As the saviour of the *Belgica* expedition he owed Dr Cook his life. Now, in the decisive moment, he was forced to betray his friend. He would go far, but not as far as forfeiting his own South Pole to save Dr Cook's North Pole.

Leon Amundsen needed all his energy and all his diplomatic nous during this frantic phase, while his brother was hidden away somewhere in the Argentine and the fruits of his triumph were being safeguarded in every quarter. Not least was the relationship with England delicate and demanding. So far there had been no sign of Captain Scott. Obviously not everyone shared Sir Ernest Shackleton's undivided enthusiasm. Lord Curzon, President of the Royal Geographical Society, let drop a remark about the Norwegian's 'changed plans' which smacked of criticism. In addition, the Society had forthwith invited the polar voyager to an open lecture in the Queen's Hall, rather than in the more prestigious Albert Hall, where personalities like Nansen, Shackleton and Peary had performed. Sensitive, bordering on the obsessive, to anything that could be construed as remotely denigrating, Roald Amundsen responded by cancelling all planned engagements in England.

The decision not to visit the heart of Empire and the subsequent loss of face might have proved extremely expensive. Leon asked the Society's secretary to make direct contact with his brother in the Argentine. Scott-Keltie protested that the noblest sentiments for the Norwegian's great achievement prevailed in all quarters. However, it would take more than a secretary to move Roald Amundsen to change his mind. King Haakon and Queen Maud would both have to be involved.

Only following the audience on his return to Christiania did the matter appear to have been resolved. The polar voyager wrote to Don Pedro: 'According to the wishes of the King, I have consented to go ahead with the scheduled lectures in England. Personally I would have preferred to abstain, but when the King wishes it what else can I do?' Such was a subject's heavy lot.

In addition to Dr Cook and Lord Curzon a new threat appeared on the horizon. Hjalmar Johansen arrived by steamship in Sandefjord on 11 June 1912. Rather than travel on to his family in Skien he took the train to Christiania. From there he dispatched the following telegram home: 'Long, tiring voyage. All well!'

The circumnavigation had not been without its hiccups for the semi-ostracised, deeply disappointed Hjalmar Johansen. His travel money ran out in Melbourne. Via the local consul and the Foreign Office the problem landed on Alexander Nansen's desk. In consultation with Axel Heiberg the expedition lawyer decided to bring Johansen home 'to avoid scandal'. Reporting to Captain Amundsen, Alexander Nansen wrote, 'he will be sent home in the least expensive way without any cash in hand, in so far as the ticket will be bought for the entire distance. This was done and unfortunately the affair has cost the expedition 505 crowns.' What a homecoming! The man who fifteen years earlier arrived in Norway at Nansen's side, and was hailed along the entire length of the country's coast, arrived home like so much general cargo.

In Sandefjord the first man to return from the third *Fram* expedition was interviewed by a *Morgenbladet* correspondent. He spoke loyally about the Governor but could not refrain from mentioning that the ski trip with Nansen had been considerably more demanding. Otherwise he said little. How far would the man's loyalty stretch? Lawyer Nansen sensed the conflict that lay behind his return and disliked the free-ranging Johansen, all alone on the scene. 'As I was fearful that too much fuss might be made of Johansen, and that this might lead to a scandal, that same day I telephoned all editorial offices in Christiania and confidentially explained the position and asked them not to interview Johansen. And they did not,' the lawyer reported.

Telephone in hand, Lawyer Nansen pursued the politics of isolation. Moreover, he was used to loyal editors. 'The newspapers have behaved impeccably,' was the lawyer's verdict. They had behaved correctly during the entire South Pole journey and when the triumph was an established fact newspapers country-wide placed column inches and premises at the disposal of a large national subscription. Many years would pass ere Roald Amundsen met with criticism from the home-grown press.

One week after arriving home the stocky figure of Hjalmar Johansen surfaced in High Court Advocate Nansen's offices. He was broke and demanded

300 crowns which he said was owing to him from the expedition's coffers. But money was difficult to coax out of the Nansen brothers now. Johansen presented his version of events but the lawyer had already made up his mind. 'This affair with Johansen is a great pity,' he wrote to the polar voyager; 'I also hear from my brother that he was rude and insubordinate to you. How unfortunate to have this unpleasantness on your expedition.' Fridtjof Nansen had shown renewed confidence in his old companion when he recommended Johansen to his younger colleague. Now it had all developed into a financial strain and an 'unpleasantness'. The High Court Advocate slipped the fallen hero 10 crowns; a loan without guarantee.

There were few places left for Hjalmar Johansen. Polhøgda was empty. The Professor had left on an oceanographic journey, off to Spitsbergen in his private yacht *Veslemøy*. One day he walked into Leon Amundsen in the street. He did not have the authority to pay signed-off members of the expedition either.

On 1 July the *Fram* crew was welcomed with pomp and circumstance in Bergen. The next day the celebrated company boarded the train for the capital, arriving in the evening. Although the leading protagonists were missing, a full programme had been arranged. Amundsen and Nansen were both present at one remove during a dinner at the Grand Hotel, represented by their brothers. Second-in-command Nilsen was remembered during the speeches. Only Johansen was kept out, literally.

The celebration of the crew members culminated in a national festival on a summer's day in St Hanshaugen, the large park in the centre of the capital. Hjalmar Johansen was pushed in from the side-lines. But unlike his fellow South Pole voyagers he had other things on his mind than applause. He wanted to have his say. Did he want to give his own version of events? Or did he simply want to join in the general tribute to the Governor, to *Fram*, to Norway? Possibly he regretted signing off in Hobart, as he regretted so much in his life. But a close eye was being kept on the broad-shouldered, slightly rough, figure.

Alexander Nansen reported to Roald Amundsen: 'When during the celebrations on St. Hanshaugen Hjalmar Johansen pushed forwards to give a speech I stopped him, and when he insisted I told him straight out that I had a strong hand against him, that he better remain in the background, as otherwise he would suffer. He abandoned the speech. Of course he was drunk.' The wheel had turned full circle. Fridtjof Nansen arrived home with Hjalmar Johansen, to jubilation from the entire people. Fifteen years later another and more pedestrian Nansen held him back when he once again wanted to receive the people's jubilation.

But the problem did not disappear with a firm hand to his shoulder. 'Hjalmar Johansen lurks in every corner,' wrote Lawyer Nansen. In spite of the pledges to secrecy and press boycotts, an interview appeared in *Aftenposten*. Johansen lifted the veil somewhat. Perhaps all was not well after all. Earlier Johansen's wife had asked Leon whether she might publish extracts from her husband's *Fram* letters. However, with reference to crew contracts and publishing rights Leon declined, but he had read the letters and realised that they did not always coincide with his brother's interpretation of events.

With the logic of a businessman Leon sees that Hjalmar Johansen is in possession of one chapter, namely the *history* which could undermine the shining heroic deed. Johansen was a loyal soul, but the man found himself in desperate straits. Leon wrote to his brother: 'He is penniless and I am rather worried that he might start producing articles and books – that will shake all the arrangements. I do not know whether I'll be forced to act.' Later the Governor actually put aside 300 crowns, to support Hjalmar Johansen when needed.

However, a considerably larger threat to the South Pole voyager's newly found cash flow was one of his other brothers. No sooner was the triumph a fact, than Gustav announced his arrival with the demand for a payback of an old 'debt of honour'. Leon's advice was to leave 'all such business to Alex otherwise you'll just pay out for nothing.' As a lawyer, and of the hard-hearted kind, Alexander Nansen was the only person able to handle Gustav.

Busken was in the throes of damaging the family's honourable reputation. Using his name and with 'collateral' in Roald's funds he had persuaded the cashier of the newspaper *Kysten* to lend him 1,600 crowns out of the company's funds. When no money was available at the agreed time, the loan suddenly takes on the character of embezzlement. Only their wish not to blacken the name of the South Pole explorer during the nation's proud hour prevented the lawyers from immediately taking the matter to court.

One more question had to be settled between the two hemispheres that summer, the Polar Hero's return. Roald Amundsen had felt it necessary to send the crew home. The expedition was thus dissolved in as much as *Fram* would not immediately sail on to San Francisco and hence north to continue the 'main journey'.

A certain period of rest would in any case have been necessary, to restock the ship and harvest the financial fruits of the 'detour'. The Governor had not really visualised any celebration of the crew in Norway. After all, the expedition had not yet been completed. But the victory telegram from Hobart had turned everything on its head. No one doubted that the conquering hero would return to Norway. Only Roald Amundsen himself wanted to remain abroad. Before accounts had been settled regarding the trip to the north, the celebrations were side-tracking him.

However, on this point the manager is unwavering. 'Your wishes can in no way be accommodated as it would be a huge disappointment to everyone and besides the bookshops will lose out on much advertising for the book.' The bookshops would anyhow be cheated out of the really big homecoming.

Roald Amundsen boarded *Highland Warrior* unnoticed and left Buenos Aires one day in July, just before his fortieth birthday. Everyone, bar Lieutenant Nilsen and Don Pedro's family, thought he was still at 'Carmen', writing. They were sworn to secrecy.

The upright, old gentleman particularly abhorred the deception. 'Your secret disappearance, naturally enough, gave rise to surprise, discussion and regret and I have personally experienced a measure of self-reproach.' This was the only expression of disapproval Don Pedro voiced, having been Amundsen's generous host during the last months. 'Acquaintance with you – dare I say the warm friendship which developed between us – belongs to the most pleasant periods of my life, and I am proud and happy to be associated with the great adventure whose creator and hero you have been.'

On 31 July a clean-shaven man wearing large horn-rimmed spectacles stepped off the Copenhagen train in Christiania. He went under the name of Engelbregt Gravning. Unobserved, he boarded a tram, got off at Drammensveien and walked the remaining metres through the park up to the castle. The general had returned to his monarch and could at last, in his own voice, report: The South Pole is conquered.

One man who put Amundsen's global cavorting into perspective was the poetic chemist Fritz G. Zapffe. 'You are fabulous!' he wrote in a letter from Tromsø. 'Surprise us and the world time and again. You are the great hero of the imagination – disappear, flap your wings all over the world so all its inhabitants stop and listen – quietly disappear again, unobtrusively, only to reappear and hit us with another surprise. Ask nothing for yourself, just give, large gifts with an extravagant hand to all mankind. I understand the *Fram* men when they say: Amundsen is the best man in the whole world.'

NINETEEN

The Road to London

On 20 August 1912 an important dinner party was being held at the palace in the mountain-country's capital. The *Fram* boys had been rounded up from far and wide, dressed in tail coats, to take part in the first celebration with the Governor since the banquet in Buenos Aires six months earlier. The South Pole's conqueror had on the whole stayed quietly at Svartskog. The book needed completing, there were lecture tours to be planned.

On 9 September Roald Amundsen lectured to the Norwegian Geographical Society and gave the first account of how the southernmost regions of the earth were conquered by Norwegian skis. The preceding evening he had invited all the crew members to celebrations in the Grand Hotel. Everyone was presented with an inscribed gold watch on a chain. Once again the captain had arranged a surreal performance – like the one staged during those Christmas celebrations on *Fram*, such a long time ago, when the South Pole was still virgin territory.

The capital's reporters described the scene: 'A true-to-nature South Pole had been set up in the Red Hall. The lamps threw a red glow over the snow-covered plateau in the centre of the table, where the Norwegian flag was planted in the sparkling snow. Marzipan figures on skis surrounded Polheim. *Fram* lay icy white, ringed around by seals. On loan from the Oslo Zoological Museum, Antarctic animals and birds were grouped in picturesque formations. No speeches were held and the dinner lasted until well after midnight in high spirits.' In such moments, surrounded by marzipan figures and stuffed animals, did Roald Amundsen bind the men closer to himself. The brutal decisions, the crude remarks, evaporated in the red glow of history. No speeches, but for each man a gold watch and chain.

The lecture in the Circus the following evening was the largest public performance ever staged by the Geographical Society during its 25-year history. The entire diplomatic corps was present. In the royal box Their Majesties were accompanied by an emperor president, Prince Roland Bonaparte, President of the French Geographical Society. In addition the world and his wife were in attendance; everyone bar Nansen.

The Professor was still dawdling home from his oceanographic tour to the waters around Spitsbergen, although in truth he was a good way down the Norwegian coast. Perhaps there was no need to hurry back to see another man hailed for what had once been his dream role. Perhaps he wanted to proclaim to the people that all and every water sample pulled on board the research ship *Veslemøy* was of greater importance to the life and work of mankind than this triumphal banner planted in the navel of vanity.

'Roars of applause engulfed him as he walked up the aisle wearing the Grand Cross of Saint Olav and the Fram Medal,' wrote one reporter. 'Captain Amundsen stood on the platform, erect and motionless, kind as always, and waited for the resounding Bravo's and shouts of Hurrah and rounds of applause to die down at long last to allow him to speak. Then he launched himself into the lecture, no sophistry, with a voice which might easily have reached [to the corners of] a larger hall than this.'

After the talk a couple of hundred guests assembled for a dinner and dance in the Grand Hotel's Rococo Hall. Unfortunately, the star of the occasion was in a hurry. In his last manuscript he wrote: 'A rich and varied menu is for people who have nothing better to do.' Roald Amundsen left before the dessert; he needed to catch the Bergen train. The guests rose and applauded; the orchestra played the national anthem. Escorted by Helland-Hansen he stepped into a waiting car and set out for the railway station. The tour had started.

From Bergen the tour was to continue to the larger Norwegian towns, then over the border to Sweden, on to Copenhagen, Berlin, and so on – to England, France, Italy. After a quick Christmas celebration at Svartskog he would leave Europe and at the turn of the year tour North America until the summer. The plan was to board the polar ship in San Francisco and continue the journey north through the Bering Strait. However, this plan had changed already during his stay in Norway.

Roald Amundsen wrote to Don Pedro that 'it has been necessary to postpone the expedition's departure by one year. I cannot find anyone to take over the oceanographic investigation and must therefore educate myself.' The polar hero was forced to return to school – not the most exciting prospect, but a pupil must obey his master. 'This postponement is unfortunate, but – as Nansen says – absolutely necessary.'

The third *Fram* expedition found itself in murky waters. The expedition still consisted of three elements. The actual ship was laid up in the Argentine under the command of Thorvald Nilsen and the financial supervision of Don Pedro. *Fram* was to be overhauled and re-equipped before the journey to the north.

The expedition's active component, the lecture party, consisted of Captain Amundsen, and Amundsen alone. He would now visit, not the world's most godforsaken parts, but, in as short a time as possible and taking in as many as possible, the Western world's assembly rooms. He had already skimmed over Australia, Asia and South America.

The third element held his ground in Christiania. In addition to his administrative tasks the land-based crew was now under Leon Amundsen's command. Some of them still drew wages from the expedition coffers. In one way or another they needed to be kept occupied. It wasn't really fair that the Governor alone was returning to school. Adult education was the thing. The expedition's finest craftsman, sail-maker Rønne from Horten, was put to learning book-binding. The other man from Horten also showed a certain and marked manual dexterity. After a short period Leon reported: 'Wisting will most probably not spend all day on dentist and doctor training so I suggest he starts on a tinsmithing apprenticeship.' Soon the newly qualified doctor and dentist Oscar Wisting, the universal genius from Horten, sat his apprentice exams as a tinsmith. The once so unpolished rough diamond Helmer Hanssen gambled on the development of personality and joined the freemasons.

But they were not all equally willing to learn. Jørgen Stubberud's personal recommendations were not of the highest. He was also in the habit of cavorting around with the expelled Hjalmar Johansen: 'one gets the feeling that he cannot tolerate the laurels.' Jørgen was only at home when he got away from town and could carry on his own trade with hammer and nail. There was such work aplenty as Roald gave Leon leave to extend 'Little Uranienborg' in old farmhouse style.

Someone who had been struggling since his return was the signed-off member Olav Bjaaland. Already in August he wrote to his old Governor 'that I have been so penniless since returning home that I feel like turning to blowing up safes.' But rather than holding up a bank the man from Morgedal landed a deft punch on Roald Amundsen's vulnerable spot: 'I want to remind you of our conversation in Kristiansand before we set off south, when I asked to be released from the trip, and you said: "I care the devil for money, you'll get all the help you need, and you won't regret the trip."'

Time would show that Olav Bjaaland needed a lot of help. And since the day when he had eaten humble pie in the Antarctic mountains he knew how to put pressure on the Governor: 'I have lived in hope and trust to you, that you would do something for me, otherwise I would not have accompanied you, so I hope you will answer my prayer.' Nothing was more important to Roald Amundsen than never to fail the men who in their childlike confidence had entrusted their lives to the master.

Olav Bjaaland had suddenly decided that he wanted to take the step from ski-maker to ski-factory owner. He built himself a whole little factory and the Governor allowed him to use Polheim as the brand name.

At the close of October the brothers were nearing the end of the South Pole magnum opus. Roald wrote to Leon from Königsberg: 'Insert a thank-you like the one about the *Gjøa* trip, please. You'll know yourself whom to thank. I would like to include your name too. Do not leave it out.' Leon dealt with the thank-yous but would rather not mention himself as 'you have already mentioned me in the text and as I am an employee further mention would not look good.' It is the nature of the beast to lie low. Later others would contribute towards further erasing Leon's name from the story.

Alexander Nansen and Axel Heiberg led the fund-raising campaign. They were hoping that Roald Amundsen's South Pole triumph would create a financial base on a par with the one Nansen had established after the first *Fram* expedition. 'We would very much like to see you secure a fortune, large enough to make you independent in the future,' the lawyer wrote in a report in 1912. The combined public and private contributions to the third *Fram* expedition at that time amounted to 330,000 crowns. The short-fall would have to be made up by proceeds from the book and the lecture tours.

The brothers Amundsen conducted their literary and rhetorical activities from a financial standpoint. They were sensitive to ethnic peculiarities. In the book's German version they consented to tone down the glorification of King Haakon VII with his Plateau in order not to offend the social democratic portion of the Kaiser's readers. And they willingly negotiated with the Americans how best to adapt the lecture to the New World's demanding public.

In fact, Roald Amundsen's American promoter Lee Keedick had received alarming signals from Australia that the Norwegian cut a poor figure on the rostrum. Keedick immediately wrote to Leon and suggested that the lecturer take English lessons. Moreover, he advised against too much science and asked the polar voyager to go in for a bit of humour: 'Shackleton did this with excellent results.'

Roald Amundsen was not very keen on English lessons, but otherwise he had few objections. 'If anything humorous can be made of the lecture, that's OK by me. Fire away.' According to Leon, all the American requirements were 'in the interest of the tour – it has nothing to do with hair-splitting or jealousy like in England.'

There were other worries concerning Britain. They were prepared for the worst, among other things that they would refuse to acknowledge the South Pole region under the name of Haakon VII Land, as it was supposed to be only a corner of Shackleton's King Edward VII Land. But Roald Amundsen had the support of the Germans. They had already inscribed their maps with Haakon VII Plateau. 'The English will probably avoid it – like they do most things. Let them. We cannot find *Gjøa*'s journey on any English chart either.'

Anyhow, in the polar voyager's mind a territorial conflict is brewing – between the windswept plateau Haakon VII and the equally uninhabitable land, named after the King's dead father-in-law Edward VII. As usual Leon sounds out the experts. Herman Gade had already agreed to check Roald's English diction. It now appeared that the out-of-work diplomat had something to say about high-level political conflict. 'Gade thinks that you must stick to your guns in England which he is sure in America will make a good impression, and should the press find it expedient to open up a campaign it can only serve as good publicity.'

To this the roaming commander answered – from St Gallen in Switzerland – with one of his distinctive aphorisms. 'I am determined to demand my right in England. A man who relinquishes his rights, loses himself and loses respect and sympathy everywhere.' The Norwegian knew his own strength and added: 'After all, England is not the whole world. In this instance it will find itself isolated.'

Leon had yet a third matter to discuss with Herman Gade. It was known that the former Foreign Minister Christophersen was to celebrate his eightieth birthday in Nice on the French Riviera. His brother Don Pedro and family would attend the celebrations and for several reasons Roald Amundsen really should be there too.

On 2 October Leon submitted a new, bold and long-term plan. 'It appears that nothing will develop between Miss Carmenzia and Nilsen or anyone else, and Gade and I have come to the conclusion that she is in every way most suitable for you. Would it not be a good idea to start working on it now? You really should not let such a nice family and good catch slip through your fingers, and if it works out your own happy family will be there waiting on your return.' A smart move and entirely in Leon Amundsen's spirit. A move that would solve, for ever, Roald's private and pecuniary circumstances. It could all be arranged in the course of a few sunny days on the French Riviera.

Roald Amundsen got the message; he must turn up at the eightieth anniversary. It always paid to flatter Don Pedro. Perhaps he was not entirely opposed to Leon's reasoning. 'Well, I'm not absolutely sure how long I can stay in Nice,' he wrote from Bremen on 12 November. It was obvious that Leon would like to have seen a bit more enthusiasm. 'I think you are silly not to make hay while the sun shines. You know the family and the time is right and I don't think you could do better.' These were strong words from someone who was usually very discreet where his brother's private affairs were concerned. This was the businessman speaking.

There was nothing wrong in marrying for money. The brothers Gade had made good matches; Don Pedro himself had married money twice. A good match need not mean the end of a good life. On the contrary. After all, these were the days of double standards. His tendencies were markedly double – two names, two existences. The earth had two Poles. Roald Amundsen was able to conquer them both.

And yet, this strategy was not in keeping with the polar explorer's inclinations. He might be scheming, brutal, insensitive, cynical. But at heart Roald Amundsen was a romantic – a man of romantic acts.

Certainly, he had had a divided relationship with the female sex. On the one hand he might have been the victim of buy and sell, a physical businesslike affair. But on the other hand, she needed to epitomise his most beautiful and uncompromising dream. After months and years in the most godforsaken regions of the world Roald Amundsen still believed in God and his belief in the grand passion was equally firmly entrenched.

Prior to Nice London was next in line. London had two sides also. On one hand, it was the battlefield where he fought for his honour and rights, on the other, it was the town of pleasure. He dreaded the one, looked forward to the other. Herman Gade had announced his presence. That augured well – for the other!

TWENTY

The Goddess of Bliss

' Dear Mr. Amundsen. May I be allowed to welcome you to London in the autumn? The Norwegians here would be so happy if you could meet with us one day, preferably an evening for dinner. Would you be kind enough and give me a date?'

This invitation, in a pile of others, dated 2 August and signed by Norway's Minister in London, Benjamin Vogt, was to have far-reaching consequences for Roald Amundsen. The date was fixed at Saturday 16 November 1912. That was the day the Norwegian colony would hold its gala dinner at the Hotel Cecil in London to celebrate Roald Amundsen.

'The god of bliss is a woman. If you desire her you must grab her and abduct her. It is no good playing a mandolin under her window.' Roald Amundsen chose this quotation, from the author Rex Beach, for his book *The South Pole*. In only one other place did he touch on the feminine aspect in an otherwise masculine book; just before the assault on the South Pole: 'The road to our goal opens up ever wider. We start to glimpse the castle in the distance. A while yet she sleeps, but the time approaches, when she will be woken by a kiss.'

Roald Amundsen stepped ashore onto English soil in Dover on Thursday 14 November 1912. That same evening, according to his promoter, he was 'magnificently received' in London.

On the European continent the South Pole conqueror left behind a successful tour and packed halls. Before the last receipts had been counted Leon received 40,000 Deutschmarks from the German promoter. The previous twenty-four hours had seen him hailed by King Albert at the head of the Belgian people. Now he had reached the expedition's critical point. As a guest of the Royal Geographical Society he put up at the Royal Society Club of which he had recently been made an honorary member. Let battle commence.

On Friday the 15th he lunched with the Norwegian Minister, Benjamin Vogt. The Minister was a sober-minded lawyer in his late forties. During the Swedish settlement his role was one of importance and as Norway's First Minister in

Stockholm he was used to handling delicate matters. He was a good friend of Fridtjof Nansen whose position he now occupied. Nansen had been minister five years ago, when the conqueror of the North West Passage came to town carrying a projector under his arm. Then Leon too had been present. This time the brother wrote from Kristiansand: 'Hope the evening in the Geographic goes OK.'

The evening goes OK. No geographic clashes between Haakon VII and blessed father-in-law Edward VII. According to the *Daily Chronicle*: 'The South Pole Hero, by his fearlessness, his unassuming attitude, and his scientific knowledge, is as extraordinary as Fridtjof Nansen.' The pinnacle had been sealed.

'I see from the papers,' wrote a relieved Leon, 'that the London lecture went smoothly, which was nice and also economically advantageous.' But something *had* taken place. Not during the lecture but during the subsequent dinner. It came to light fifteen years later in *My Life as a Polar Explorer*.

During the dinner, George Nathanial Curzon, 1st Marquess of Kedleston and the Society's President, gave the speech. It was he whose remark six months earlier had triggered so many diplomatic complications as to make the visit to London virtually impossible. Curzon was one of the British Empire's greatest characters. As Viceroy of India he had ruled with great and assured power. Under his stage management Edward VII was proclaimed emperor of all the Hindus. Lord Curzon was a defender of the right to rule and had distinguished himself as a steadfast advocate of the House of Lords' legitimate rights. Curzon was, even in England, notorious for his eloquent arrogance. So: 'After a few well-chosen words, having given the reason for my lecture, and having stressed the importance I put on the dogs, who had contributed so much to our luck, Lord Curzon ended his speech with the following: "I therefore take the liberty to propose three cheers for the dogs", while he very clearly emphasised his sarcastic and disparaging meaning by turning to me with a soothing gesture, in spite of my not having moved an inch, and urgently asking me not to answer this very transparent insult.'

Such is the detail in which Roald Amundsen reproduced this abhorrent episode half a generation later. Certainly, the Royal Geographical Society immediately challenged the accuracy of this interpretation, and one should not trust entirely in Roald Amundsen's autobiographical references. Nevertheless, one must assume that his description of the episode contains a kernel of truth.

British understatement was not for Roald Amundsen. He did not understand that Lord Curzon had felt the need to save just a small bit of Empire honour with the help of an underhand joke. Of course, the Lord's understanding of the Norwegian's inner thoughts can hardly be said to be impressive. The dog-cheers prioritised the glory of Empire before the feelings of the guest, whom he now insulted for a second time. It is tempting to speculate that the great nation and the great man were equally petty.

However, initially unnoticed and later, when the memoirs were published, the most conspicuous thing about this explosive exchange is nevertheless what it tells us about Roald Amundsen's bottomless sense of inferiority. He had been fêted in country after country; he had charmed the capital of Empire. After all, Lord Curzon, the sovereign ruler of a vast empire, represented with his after-dinner speech the losing party. The victor was Roald Amundsen, the Norwegian skipper and skier. He had outsmarted the Empire's lions, its tigers and elephants; Lord Curzon grudgingly gave him his dogs.

The day after the lecture at the Royal Geographical Society, 16 November 1912, Roald Amundsen would later come to consider a red-letter day. It never made it into his autobiography, however. It belonged to the secret part of the polar explorer's life, a part which, from that day forth, would assume increasing importance and, in time, determine ever more of his actions.

As it had done in 1907, the Norwegian colony arranged its celebration of Captain Amundsen at the Hotel Cecil. Decorated in the sumptuous style of the 1890s, and, with its 800 rooms, the hotel was in its heyday Europe's largest. For this occasion the large banqueting hall was adorned with real Norwegian flags surrounded by artificial snow and ice. In addition there was, according to the newspaper report, 'a beautifully sculptured work of art, representing the *Fram* men at the very moment they planted the Norwegian flag on the South Pole'.

Minister Vogt gave the after-dinner speech. He praised the polar explorer for having shown his fellow patriots 'that action, not words, gave worth to life's aims'. Roald Amundsen, 'deeply touched', thanked him. Three times three hurrahs. Not a single bark or yap was heard. The singer Gina Oselio, Bjørnstjerne Bjørnson's ex-daughter-in-law, slightly past her prime, led the company in 'Norway, Thine is Our Devotion', the national anthem. 'The party continued in the most pleasant atmosphere,' the report concluded.

The god of bliss was a woman. But what was the colour of her dress? Many women swarmed around the South Pole conqueror. It never dawned on him that he met her on that evening.

Sunday evening, the 17th, Roald Amundsen gave a private lecture in the grand premises of the Royal Automobile Club. 'An exceptional number of members and guests had gathered in the Club House, and so unexpected was the rush that at the last moment improvised solutions had to be found to accommodate everyone.' Thus reports the Club journal. On the Monday the polar explorer gave a lecture in an overflowing Queen's Hall. Roald Amundsen was gaining in popularity in the British Isles.

The polar explorer set off on a month's tour of the Kingdom. On 28 November he wrote to his friend Herman Gade from Sheffield, 'So nice to see you again. I'll miss you terribly when I return to London.' Gade had accompanied his friend throughout all the celebrations in London, and not only the official ones either. 'I see your smiles, you swine. And I am sure wicked thoughts are running through your mind, like – he'll find a bit of fluff somewhere. Well, as you know, I'm not going to lie about. Life is short and won't repeat itself – not in this shape or form.' Presumably he is praising the female shape, or excusing male vice – or both.

He was back in London on 6 December. 'Your brother appears to be on excellent form and in good humour,' the promoter reported to the manager Leon, not without admiration, considering the crowded programme. The same evening Roald Amundsen wrote to Gade that he had 'lunched at the RAC, where a greater part of the Norwegian colony was present'. In the evening he gave a lecture in the assembly hall of London University. 'On Sunday I am having lunch with Bennett and his wife here at the Savoy.'

Roald Amundsen rarely accepted this type of, strictly speaking, unnecessary invitation. There were enough compulsory, unavoidable parties and responsibilities of an official nature. Anyhow, he had lectured every evening except, when possible, on Sundays. When he now accepted Mr and Mrs Bennett's invitation we must speculate that he was pursuing a goal, something that had caught his eye at the Norwegian party. Something wearing red.

The Savoy and Cecil Hotels stood side by side on the Strand. The Savoy was no less fashionable than the Cecil. The Savoy too was an architectural gem; a product of the lavish Edwardian period. Here the Empire's most distinguished representatives dined, with their wives, or other women, to the music of Strauss, in mirrored halls and among ostentatiously ornate stucco. The polar explorer had a weakness for grand, luxurious hotels. He knew how to cultivate the best life had to offer.

Charles Peto Bennett, his host, was a solid and courteous gentleman in his late fifties. Not only had he travelled extensively throughout the British Empire, but he had also been all over the world bar Russia and Chile. He was a rich businessman and could afford to enjoy life's bounty. He appreciated a good menu, a first-class port, a game of whist or the vista of a rural idyll from the back of his Rolls-Royce.

Charles Peto Bennett was a timber merchant, son of a timber merchant with storehouses on the Thames. He imported exotic timber, such as teak and mahogany, from the Far East. But he traded with Norway too and had often visited the forest-clad country, sometimes as far north as Trondheim, 63° North.

It was in the cathedral city, a few years before the last coronation, that the soon to be 50-year-old met his wife. She was not yet eighteen.

In contrast with the Norwegian colony's party on 16 November, this feast was an intimate, family gathering. Fifteen sat down to dinner; the menu, decorated in honour of the guest, with its numerous courses and fine wines, was printed in French. Apart from the hostess and the guest of honour there was one other Norwegian present, a young man with the pleasing name of Astrup – Arvid Astrup. He was a cousin of the timber merchant's young wife, the beautiful lady in red – the guest of honour's dinner partner. She was quite tall, dark blonde, sparklingly merry, radiantly self-confident – the focus of everyone's attention.

It was immediately obvious to all the guests what was happening when the polar explorer's eyes met Mrs Bennett's deep, emerald green glance. He had met his goddess of bliss, he was filled with an irresistible urge to 'grab her and carry her off'.

Christmas was drawing near. The Governor ordered wine and cigars for his men. 'Send Wisting and Helmer 500 crowns each,' he wrote to Leon, 'but tell them to keep their traps shut, or it might cause a lot of trouble.' Some presents were covert bribes, others the world could know about. The old, famous nanny, Betty, was ill. 'Take her fresh flowers and goodies every day she's in hospital, please.'

But not everything could be put right with banknotes and fresh flowers. In Christiania Lawyer Nansen was called upon by High Court Lawyer Bugge regarding Gustav Amundsen's financial affairs. 'They are, as usual, in a bad state,' Nansen reported and enclosed a list containing more than thirty defaults on loans. In addition the famous brother received a medical certificate with regards to Captain Amundsen's state of mind. (Gustav Amundsen used the title Captain too.)

A very 'distressed and tortured' brother had sought out 'Dr Dedichen's spa for the mentally ill' and related his tragic tale to the medical professionals. Apparently, everything could be traced back to his self-sacrificing behaviour during the *Gjøa* expedition. 'When Roald returned home the brother never received the support he expected and this affected him deeply. He has suffered deprivation as, owing to his brother, he was forced to declare himself bankrupt, and that essentially because he paid his debts out of pride and dignity, debts that were not his responsibility.' So, Busken's misfortunes had their origin in his brother's success. Gustav Amundsen had not lost faith in his famous brother, but he was deeply disappointed 'as the financial support which he had expected or the reflected glory in which he had looked forward to bask never materialised.'

Via Leon and monthly payments Roald supported his sister-in-law Malfred who was forced to suffer this difficult and unstable brother. In addition, he asked Leon and Lawyer Nansen to arrange matters as best they could. 'I am not involved.'

Busken had turned into a threatening shadow which menaced the polar explorer along the pinnacles of success. Earlier in the autumn Leon had written: 'The condition for your continued support must be that they move away from the Bunnefjord for good – we need peace and quiet and not a Captain Amundsen number 2.' But Roald found it difficult to tear himself away from the other Captain Amundsen. Busken knew how to manipulate Roald: the beggar did not want money; it was the 'debt of honour' that he wanted repaid. Besides, he needed a job and a house.

The polar explorer pinned his faith on Gade, who had just been made a member of the board of directors of the newly established Norwegian America Line. 'Just two words. My brother Gustav is applying for a job in the America Line – I do not know what sort of job. Please do something for him if you can. It would take five years off my age to place him in a permanent job.'

On 11 December Leon received a disappointing Christmas message from Belfast. Roald wrote: 'I'm not coming home. It is too much just for a couple of days.' The polar explorer had made other plans. Meanwhile the lecture tour of the British Isles was nearing its end. In spite of its apparent success, the profits were considerably less than expected. And there was worse; the English promoter hinted that Roald Amundsen should renounce a full fee in those cases where idealistic societies had lost money on the lecture – 'like other great explorers have done.'

To the polar explorer this was a huge provocation. In a letter from Dublin, he wrote to Leon: 'I won't let these damned English off one single penny. Tell him that in so many words. I do not know the contract but I will not yield a single point to this "plum pudding nation". Tell him that I do not toil for the benefit of the English but so that I can finance my life and raise the necessary means for another expedition.' His indignation is not directed solely at the promoter, Gerald Christy; it includes the entire nation. 'After my travels in this country I couldn't care less for other people's wishes.'

Loyally Leon fulfilled his brother's wishes, albeit with a more diplomatic turn of phrase. Nevertheless he was surprised at the force of his brother's reaction. In his answer he tried gently to correct the impression with a reference to Lieutenant Nilsen – *Fram*'s skipper had returned to Europe and was spending a few days with the Governor in England. 'Nilsen appears not to share your views about the English, who he feels welcomed you sympathetically. I hope you both arrive at a compromise.'

Neither Leon nor Lieutenant Nilsen could prevent the dogs' bark, which had already been planted in the polar explorer's inner being, from growing into a chorus of contemptuous cheering Englishmen.

On 16 December the South Pole's conqueror left the empire of plum pudding eaters and made his entry into Paris. 'Amundsen was received like a king and appointed a Grand Officer of the Légion d'Honneur, a distinction not awarded to any other explorer,' the Norwegian Minister Wedel Jarlsberg wrote in his memoirs. The French knew how to appreciate a Napoleon of the ice wastes. Three days later he was received by King Victor Emmanuel in Rome.

When Foreign Minister Christophersen fell seriously ill the South Pole explorer was excused from going to Nice to take part in the planned celebrations. After the visit to Italy he hastened back to Paris to present Don Pedro and his daughter with a de luxe edition of *The South Pole*. A not too lengthy gathering with the family Christophersen on the banks of the River Seine had been arranged.

Leon was under the illusion that, having cancelled his trip home, his brother would spend all of Christmas in Paris. Now however, via circuitous routes, he was 'informed that you are intending to spend Christmas in London – I knew nothing about this – I thought you wanted to be with the Christophersens; you might as well come home as I know you find London boring and obviously it will not be cheap.'

Nor would Paris have been a cheap affair, but a prolonged Christmas gathering with Don Pedro's family might have led to a very lucrative investment. The manager would have to wave goodbye to Don Pedro's gilded daughter. But he nevertheless found that the time had come to instruct the polar explorer in the rudiments of economics. 'As you continue your journey you must remember that what you now make is not profit but capital and it is important to consume as little of your capital as possible. If you do, then when you return home from the North, you can procure such a capital that the interest therefrom will secure you a comfortable living. But the opposite will result in the yields scarcely covering demand, and to be forced to eat into the capital is in the long run sad. I have not yet given up hope of seeing you at Christmas,' Leon concluded his urgent Advent message. He knew his brother's soft spot. But had he known what forces drew Roald back to London he would have given up all hope of a joint Christmas by the banks of the Bunnefjord.

Christmas Eve the polar explorer celebrated in Wedel Jarlsberg's Paris mansion. Christmas Day he took breakfast with the Christophersens. And then: goodbye Carmenzia.

This is not to say that Don Pedro's daughter was not worthy of the South Pole conqueror's admiration; on the contrary. Thirteen years later the capitalist described, not without pride, how Carmenzia had been waited on by the Prince of Wales, heir to the imperial throne, during a visit to Buenos Aires. The polar explorer answered gallantly, poetically. 'He could hardly have found a finer or more exalted object for his respect and admiration than your daughter. I hope that you do not take offence at my remarks when I say that all these years she has appeared to me as the highest ideal of womanhood.'

Roald Amundsen checked in to the Carlton Hotel in London. At the turn of the year he would board the steamship *St Paul* and sail for the New World. But the last days of this triumphant year were be spent in the boring capital, the hateful Empire. We do not know exactly *what* he was doing. But we know *why* he was there.

Her name was Kiss. Everyone called her that. But she was christened Kristine Elisabeth Gudde, born 10 February 1886 in Trondheim. The family belonged to the solid middle classes but had to make do with one maid and were in no way wealthy. The youngest daughter was the apple of the family's eye. When the oldest daughter was given a new frock the mother would say that, 'Kiss only needs a simple frock and a blue Alice band in her hair to make her beautiful.' There was no lack of boys who wanted to carry Miss Gudde's violin home from music lessons.

The family's life took a new direction the day a wealthy British businessman came to town. Charles Peto Bennett was nearly as old as Kiss's father, but that did not stop him from marrying the youngest daughter. Before Norway became an independent country Kiss had left the old cathedral city of Trondheim. With her worldly husband the young girl set out on a long journey. Before she had reached 21 she had given birth to two sons, the younger one in Australia.

Later the couple settled in London, in Stamford Hill, in a large flat which they shared with the timber merchant's old mother. The marriage between Charles Peto Bennett and his young wife must have resembled the relationship of a protective father and his not yet grown-up daughter. Not only was she young, but she came from a small country and was not used to the overwhelming surroundings of a metropolis. Her husband kept her on a tight rein; he suffered from the older man's jealousy of a young wife.

But Kiss was a strong personality – intelligent and quick to learn and with a talent for the dramatic. She was bound to her husband by an indissoluble pact, but within this framework she became an equal. Their needs were fundamentally different, but they lived in a marriage where mutual respect and, above all, their two sons bound them together.

Of course, some things were missing. Kiss Bennett was 26 in 1912, gregarious, with a zest for life, realistic but also romantic. She lived on the sunny side of the world's sumptuous centre of activity. Following pregnancies and births she was keen to make up for some of her lost youth. She might have had a few affairs. Frivolity was permitted in King Edward's England. A lot was tolerated, except scandal. That was not tolerated.

Then the South Pole's proud conqueror arrived in town, a fellow countryman. She brushed down her red dress and played her feminine cards as only she knew how. Mr Bennett actually had nothing against the polar explorer. He knew how to appreciate a race between men, preferably a motorised race – but dogs? Never mind; the timber merchant had nothing against dogs. This polar explorer was supposedly an important man, highly esteemed in automobile circles and, if it pleased his wife, well then, the Savoy.

When Roald Amundsen, on the threshold of New Year 1913, boarded *St Paul*, he had entered into a love-pact with Kiss Bennett which he thought would prove stronger than marriage.

From now on all other women were out of the question. He continued to receive letters from Sigrid Castberg; and he decided to tell Herman Gade to deal with the 'Gjøvik Affair'. In January he wrote from America that all must end. 'I, for my part am now bound, absolutely and completely, so that I cannot make a stride in either direction – which I might otherwise have been able to do.' The polar explorer gave up Sigg Castberg for Kiss Bennett.

There are several similarities between Sigg and the nine years younger Kiss. They were both strong personalities, with an ability to take the initiative, also towards men. Their complex national backgrounds – Sigg was half-American – gave them a freer position in relation to their surroundings. They were fêted, extrovert and good-looking – obvious targets for a man's admiration. They were women of high status, and they both belonged to another man.

Following that Christmas in London, Roald Amundsen considered himself a married man. Even the happy bachelor existence with his best friend Gade seems to have entered a new phase. 'As I have already told you, I am now completely and utterly bound – and for ever a "good boy" as far as that is concerned.'

The polar explorer would soon learn to play the mandolin.

TWENTY-ONE

An Ultimatum

A shot went off in Christiania. The luxury steamship with Roald Amundsen on board was making a winter-crossing of the Atlantic. 'Hjalmar Johansen shot himself in Oslo,' Leon wrote on 4 January 1913, 'which I imagine you are already aware of, via telegrams.'

Hjalmar Johansen had left a few toiletries and an unpaid bill at Mrs Bye's Hotel and made his way up Karl Johansgate and Drammensveien. In Solli Park he took out a six-shooter military revolver and pointed it at his forehead. Presumably the bullet was aimed just at him. But it struck at least two other men: Fridtjof Nansen and Roald Amundsen. It also struck at the heart of the nation.

Two days later Leon Amundsen and Jørgen Stubberud, with two of the deceased's relations, accompanied the coffin from the hospital to the West Station. Leon had reserved the railway carriage that would carry Hjalmar Johansen's body from the capital to his home town of Skien. On the coffin lay a huge wreath with a small visiting-card bearing the name of Roald Amundsen. 'Convey my warmest sympathy to Johansen's relatives. As I know neither them nor the circumstances it is not possible for me to do it myself,' the polar explorer wrote to Leon, from across the ocean.

The funeral, on 9 January, they decided between them, was paid for by his two employers, Nansen and Amundsen. Leon did his best to guide his brother through this tragic affair, without appearing too hypocritical. 'Owing to the relationship between you and him I did not feel I could do much more. To lay a wreath with a ribbon and hold a speech thanking him for everything, by the grave-side, I thought inappropriate. However, Nilsen, Prestrud and Hassel travelled down from Christiania and obviously did not think I had done enough as I read from the papers that Prestrud lay down a wreath on your behalf and said a few nice words. I think it should have been from his comrades. Nansen sent a most wonderful wreath with an inscription and got a Skien man to put it on the grave, but he himself did not turn up owing to "family illness" (that was unfortunate and I think the people from Skien thought so too).'

It appears that neither Leon nor Johansen's fellow citizens were fully aware of the tragedy that had struck Polhøgda, Nansen's home, that winter. If they had been, they might have understood that Fridtjof Nansen remained by his youngest son's bedside as he lay dying rather than give a speech at the grave of his companion. He wrote an obituary which ended: 'Hjalmar Johansen's soul was entirely without treachery.'

If that was the case, who betrayed Johansen? Fridtjof Nansen himself? His army superiors? Roald Amundsen? His comrades in Framheim? Did the entire nation betray the simple athlete who became a fêted polar hero? Maybe he was betrayed by many and it is certain that many failed him. But ultimately, it is difficult to deprive a person of the responsibility for his own life.

'However sad it was,' Leon wrote the day after the shooting, 'it was for the best as there was no improvement in sight.' This was the general opinion. *Morgenbladet* wrote: 'Death must have seemed a release.' But Roald Amundsen's triumph would be forever associated with Hjalmar Johansen's tragedy. The shot in Solli Park reveberated like an echo from the start gun for the sledging expedition; when Roald Amundsen could not wait to reach the Pole or return to Framheim, Hjalmar Johansen had saved Prestrud's life and with that the expedition's reputation. Roald Amundsen's South Pole journey had, in the end, acquired its first victim.

In the Geographical Society journal's review of *The South Pole* a few weeks on, the sensitive question was raised as to whether Johansen's exclusion from the polar party had contributed to his death.

'Carnegie Hall was crammed to overflowing and bursting with enthusiasm. As in Washington I was awarded a large gold medal.' On 15 January Leon was informed about the reception in the United States. 'Following this excellent start I have every reason to believe we will do good business.' The American promoter Lee Keedick endorsed the polar explorer's excitement. 'Captain Amundsen's first lecture in New York put more dollars in the kitty than any lecture given by any other explorer in this town.' Yet another record.

Roald Amundsen was invited to lunch with President Teddy Roosevelt and, together with the official discoverer of the North Pole Admiral Peary, was congratulated on his deed. Snap-shots of the two, plus a third, Ernest Shackleton, travelled around the world. Leon was delighted: 'Surely, Keedick will use this for advertising,' but also vigilant: 'You must not enter into business with the gentlemen, especially Shackleton, who allegedly has gambled away what he has earned (300,000 to 400,000 crowns).'

Not long ago Leon had reported that Sir Ernest's brother had been arrested in South Africa on charges of embezzlement – an obvious parallel with Roald

Amundsen's brother Gustav who had now been reported to the police for his involvement in the newspaper *Kysten*'s cash reserves. In consultation with Lawyer Nansen and having assessed the evidence, Leon thought it wise to pay the disputed 1,600 crowns out of the polar explorer's account. It was expensive to keep the family name untarnished.

On 11 February 1913 came the bombshell: *Terra Nova* had reached civilisation the previous night. The telegram containing Captain Scott's tragedy hit the world. The entire British polar party had died on the return journey. Three of them had been found in a tent about 80° South. 'It is sad but not unexpected,' Leon wrote the same day. 'I have instructed Lt Nilsen on behalf of the Expedition to deliver a card to the Eng. Minister.' It was a good thing Leon knew how to take care of etiquette. Roald wrote from Chicago: 'I sent Evans [the second-in-command] a telegram and the two Mrs. Scott and Wilson. Nothing to England of course.' In war one does not offer one's condolences to the enemy.

A few days later Leon expanded on his reflections concerning the tragedy: 'This awful tragedy is of course here too the topic of the day. Many had expected this as the entire expedition was organised in such a way as to invite disaster. I consider now that for all parties it is an advantage that you were at the South Pole otherwise one can be certain that a new British expedition would be organised without delay and probably without changing anything of the old style. And the result could be catastrophe upon catastrophe like in its time the North West Passage was.' This is a point of view which Leon believed the British would eventually come to share. 'If there should be any inclination towards bitterness Scott would be the one who should have felt it. But it does not appear that he has said anything as such and one must say of him that he was as much a gentleman as a hero.'

Neither bitterness nor reflection characterised the mood of the American public, but rather the sensational nature of the event. 'Scott's sad death has given my lectures added force,' the polar explorer wrote from Chicago. 'The numbers, which had stated to drop, have picked up.' The show must go on.

'My brother must be the one who most keenly feels Scott's tragic death,' Leon wrote to the *Gjøa* lieutenant Godfred Hansen; 'it cannot be much fun to lecture about his own triumph while his thoughts involuntarily dwell on the sad catastrophe.' There must be no external sign of a connection between triumph and tragedy. 'Your feelings,' Leon wrote to his brother, 'are restricted to heartfelt sympathy. And that must be one's point of view however the drama develops in the future.' Once again Leon stood forth as the level-headed strategist whose future plans far exceed that evening's takings.

The loser's tragedy affected the winner Amundsen in two ways. Criticism was voiced, above all in the British press. But Norwegian Foreign Service personnel could report increased appreciation of the Norwegians' achievement, among other places in Germany. The Norwegian vice consul in Melbourne sent this reflection back to the Foreign Office: 'It is extraordinary how the report of Scott's expedition has indirectly increased Amundsen's popularity here. First of all, the fact that Scott found Amundsen's tent has cleared away any doubt the general public might have had, in spite of all observations, as to whether Amundsen had in reality reached the Pole. Next, Scott's unhappy fate has contributed towards the Australian public's appreciation of the magnitude of Amundsen's deed.'

During the winter the air was thick with newspaper rumours that Amundsen wanted to equip his forthcoming expedition with something as outrageously modern as an aeroplane. If that were the case, who would fly it? The first person to volunteer was the dogsledge-driver Helmer Hanssen. 'I must be allowed to tell you,' he wrote to Leon, 'that I have an overpowering urge to acquaint myself with the use of that sort of conveyance.'

The manager is more reserved: 'Surely it is not your intention to use this for your push [to the North Pole]. I trust more in dogs, skis and sledges and do not think you should abandon that system. But a good pilot to reconnoitre would of course be a bonus.'

The reports from the polar explorer himself were, to put it mildly, contradictory. On 20 March it is 'possible' to 'include something like that'. A week later he wrote to Leon that 'the aeroplane is just American nonsense'. Later in the spring, however: 'Helmer and Wisting must both learn to fly – but we have time enough in San Francisco.'

Don Pedro received his briefing in a letter dated 19 April. By then it all appears to have been decided: 'I have ordered 2 hydroplanes for the journey. During a flight I made in San Francisco it dawned on me what use I could make of this means of transport. The danger of falling down is less than I thought.' The winged vehicle spoke to the explorer's imagination. He was reluctant to return to Nansen and start the oceanographic studies. He was searching for something new and motivating; something that would make the 'main journey' exciting and enticing.

The burden sat heavily on Roald Amundsen that winter and spring in America. First the shot in Christiania, then the telegram from *Terra Nova*, both threatening the conqueror's standing; in addition, so many expectations on so many fronts. It all had to do with give and take. The businessman John Gade, who had contributed 20,000 crowns to the South Pole journey, worked ceaselessly for Roald Amundsen during the tour of the States. He hoped his efforts would benefit his brother.

Herman Gade's more-or-less undeserved misfortune in the Norwegian Foreign Service worried the polar explorer. At the end of February he sat down and wrote to the newly appointed Prime Minister Gunnar Knudsen ('I must congratulate you on the brilliant liberal victory') about the brothers Gade and their contribution to the fatherland and about 'Herman Gade's future in Norway'. The polar explorer invested the missive with his entire prestige: 'As my dearest childhood friend and a man whom I have always cherished for his noble, wise and cultured manner, I would personally be exceedingly grateful to you if you would grant him this satisfaction and give him the opportunity to sacrifice himself for work in service of the country, [something] which he has so long desired.'

The brothers Amundsen had more unresolved and pressing matters to negotiate with the Norwegian government. Earlier in the year Leon had received an audience with Prime Minister Knudsen where he had been given alarming signals. The new government was not willing to grant more money. Anyhow: 'He was planning the abolition of the system of orders and he mentioned that the last government should have made sure that, as promised, Don Pedro's son, Lieutenant Nilsen and Gade had been decorated. I will now call on Bratli [the former Prime Minister] and if it is not OK apply for an audience – this thing must be resolved, especially for young Christophersen, otherwise a scandal will ensue. You know we telegraphed Don Pedro last autumn: "Perutcho to be knighted". The manager can also report that the *Fram* skipper as well as crew are "expecting big things from you and the state".'

Several expedition members applied personally to the Governor. The difficult case remained that of Bjaaland, to whom Amundsen had already promised money to set up a ski factory; in the end the sum rose as high as 20,000 crowns. Leon predicted that the money would be lost. 'Bjaaland is a wonderful companion and good at different things, but he is no businessman.' Many thousands of crowns from the expedition coffers disappeared into the bottomless ski-making pit. The Governor had promised; the Governor kept his word.

Reports about the treacherous politicians made a big impression on the man to whom honesty was paramount. His reactions were stronger than the manager had predicted. In February the polar explorer wrote from Ottawa in Canada: 'Have just sent Nansen a long letter and told him I will halt all work regarding the expedition until *all* promises have been met. In other words, I present my fatherland with an ultimatum and ask you to deliver this to whom it may concern, whoever that is, probably Gunnar Knudsen. Tell him, that until all promises – given to me by the previous ministry – are honoured, the expedition will be postponed, or, possibly, cancelled. The previous ministry promised: Nilsen promoted to Captain or Knight of the Order of St Olav. Sums of money or positions to my comrades as suggested to me in a communication to Bratli. Perutcho's and Gade's decorations. Without total and complete compliance – reiterate to G.K. – I will halt all work.' The polar explorer had made his stand as a strong, unyielding man: 'It's either or. I am getting bored with all this prevaricating.'

At the same time Roald Amundsen informed Don Pedro that he had dispatched his last 'ultimatum'. The most sensitive of the 'breaches of promise' affected the sun-king's son. One's word is one's word, a decoration a decoration; not on any account must the patron's confidence be jeopardised. 'I have just written to Fridtjof Nansen and informed him that a broken promise is too frail a basis on which to begin the long drift across the ice. I have ordered my brother to act on my behalf – and unless all promises are met, I will down tools.' All for Don Perutcho!

By 12 March both Fridtjof Nansen at Polhøgda and Leon Amundsen at Svartskog had received their letter bombs. None of them expressed themselves particularly enamoured of the polar explorer's attitude. Leon writes: 'Talked to the old man who was quite surprised and thought it would be a sorry affair if the expedition's continuation came to nothing. All in all a sad affair, for you too, as it would not look good if it came to light that the South Pole journey was for the purpose of making money for the North. However, we decided that I would ask for an audience with the Prime Minister and inform him of the contents of your letter as you have asked me, but that I continue here as before – anything else would not be possible as if we stop now we risk missing the departure next year.'

While the Professor sat in his tower and thought it all through yet again, the manager appeared in the Prime Minister's office the very next day. However, the matter was not solved with a stroke of the pen. 'I do think you must calm down and not push this,' he wrote to his brother. 'The point is that only the decorations could already have been awarded. Positions can only be considered for those of the crew who remain at home. They will be taken into consideration when they *apply* for something vacant and one cannot expect anything else. The time will be ripe to protest if there is a refusal or promises are not kept – that is a different matter.'

But the polar explorer would not be restrained. In his answer he insisted that in particular the crew who were to accompany him to the north must first be guaranteed permanent state employment on their return. 'This is what Bratli promised and what I must demand be carried out, in that I have told the boys.' So: 'Yet again, I *demand* the promises be honoured. Helmer will be informed that he will have the custom's office post when he returns, and likewise the others – in the respective positions I have mentioned. Do not be put off with "it can't be done". Not only can it be done – it must and will be done.'

As the prospect of new government grants appeared unlikely, Leon resurrected an old idea: 'The question of expedition stamps, which Knudsen did not think impossible; we might now secure a whole series of stamps and I consider this more advantageous than the grants.' This scheme, as part of the brothers' money-making plans, would rear its head in many guises. The idea of a polar stamp and polar post-cards had its roots in Leon's enthusiastic pursuit of philately. But nor could one hurry along the stamp politics of a nation. In order to stave off a new outburst from the other side of the Atlantic, Leon adds: 'There's no need to hurry until we see how things turn out. I consider it impossible to speed things up.' The polar explorer's answer was nevertheless a command: 'See that the stamp business is sorted out.'

At last, on 2 April, the giant at Polhøgda sat down to answer. The letter reached Roald Amundsen twenty days later in North Dakota. 'Have just received 7 pages from the old man,' he reported home, rather dejected. 'He feels personally responsible for my anger, which of course was not intended.'

Following Leon's conference with the Prime Minister the transatlantic traveller received a letter from Prime Minister Knudsen reassuring him of the government's best intentions. Roald Amundsen, in spite of maintaining his totalling unyielding attitude, was reasonably confident that his demands would be met. However, his letter to Nansen had triggered off an avalanche from the past which would weigh him down with all its might.

TWENTY-TWO

The Big Promise

The seven-page letter from Polhøgda was actually the answer to the letter Leon Amundsen had brought from Madeira two and a half years earlier. For the first time ever Fridtjof Nansen laid bare his thoughts and feelings to the compatriot who became his rival in the battle for the South Pole.

A mere two weeks before the Professor received Roald Amundsen's ultimatum, his youngest son Åsmund had died following a long illness. The letter caught Nansen in a period of meditation, when fate was not an easy thing to accept.

Having written seven pages to Amundsen he wrote an even more comprehensive letter to Captain Scott's backer, the former Royal Geographical Society President Sir Clements Markham. The Professor threw all his weight behind the defence of his younger compatriot. By portraying Amundsen as the executor of his, Nansen's, own work, he placed Amundsen beyond reproach. The letter took the form of a speech for national defence, but is at the same time more intimate and detailed than the letter to Roald Amundsen. He started the letter by describing his own grief: 'It is now not always necessary to journey to the polar regions to seek suffering and pain.'

In his letter to Roald Amundsen Nansen did not once mention his personal suffering. He concentrated on the receiver's situation. The letter to the British admiral was directed at an equal; Amundsen he treated as an indulgent teacher would chasten his star pupil. 'I imagine that all these long lectures in such a hectic country must have taken it out of you and made you nervous and out of balance.'

Fridtjof Nansen could not understand why Amundsen would possibly consider jeopardising the expedition for the sake of some 'broken promises' with regard to government posts, promotions and decorations – awful rubbish and bureaucratic nit-picking when viewed from the larger perspective. Unless, of course, he was fed up with the whole thing, 'but then I imagine you would tell me straight.' The pupil was depicted in the eyes of the master as 'someone who will break his big promise' for the sake of mere trifles.

Nansen grabbed the opportunity to spell it out. 'You might not have realised it, but for your sake I have made a bigger sacrifice than for any other living being, in that I abandoned my trip to the South Pole, the keystone of my life as a polar explorer, and gave up the *Fram* in order that you could drift across the Arctic Ocean.'

What did Nansen mean by 'any other living being'? The Professor chose his words with the same disingenuousness as Amundsen would when he is being economical with the truth or is caught uttering a lie. He *omits* mention of the dead. However, not so in his letter to Markham: 'I must admit I was weak and indecisive and maybe I was not stronger because it was the thought of my wife that made me make the final decision in that moment when he [Amundsen] arrived to seek my answer (in September 1907).'

Undeniably, this admission portrayed Nansen in a tragic light, interpreting his human need as weakness. To his compatriot he was not prepared to expose his human side or his real motive. On the contrary, Fridtjof Nansen consciously and emphatically pushed the entire burden onto the shoulders of Roald Amundsen.

The conquest of the South Pole was 'a natural outcome of my entire experience and polar development; compared to our toil in the drift ice it appeared to me like an enticing fairy story.' Here the master demonstrated to his successor that the Pole was conquered using *his* methods. He also echoed Johansen's opinion on his return that 90° South was as nothing compared to 86° North.

The Professor responded to Roald Amundsen on behalf of the nation. The letter from Polhøgda, the exercise in retrospective self-analysis, might have been written by an ageing Ibsen. It was a crushing, but not unfeeling, document – an attempt to guide the younger successor. In any case the Professor closed by assuring him that he 'out of genuine friendship wants to prevent you, as the result of a gloomy mood, doing things that you later and too late might regret.'

The day after Amundsen received the letter a telegram was dispatched from America: 'Everything OK writing'.

The letter arrived: 'It is possible I deserve the hard rebuke you give me. From anyone else and I would decidedly have fought back. You I owe so much, yes, so much more than I realised, that I meekly bow my head and accept your words.'

Nevertheless, Amundsen could not entirely resist insisting on the importance of the seemingly trivial. 'It appears to me that so many large undertakings fail, because the trifles have been overlooked. As minor as it can appear in our circumstance, whether Helmer Hanssen is promoted to customs officer or not – whether Wisting gets a lighthouse keeper's job, as promised, etc. – yet I am worried that these small matters, during the long and monotonous drift through the ice, might grow large and threaten our real work. It is my experience that absolute discipline is necessary during a polar journey.' His argument might have been dubbed far-sighted, but it said a lot about Roald Amundsen's fear of losing authority, about the worry regarding his own crew. Hjalmar Johansen's name was writ large between the lines.

To sum up, his letter was no less humble than the one he sent from Madeira: 'In closing I ask you to forgive me. I will summon all my strength and will in this last phase of the journey too.'

He was slightly cockier to his brother: 'The old man sent a pretty sharp letter, but I gave as good as I got – calmly of course. I'll let you read it later. He too feels rather hurt.'

In the middle of this national showdown Leon received an unexpected and dramatic instruction from America: 'See that you sell Uranienborg and let me be rid of it. It would make me feel considerably freer.'

The question about the house appeared to be closely connected to another domestic problem. The polar explorer had received a letter from his sister-in-law Malfred. It referred to Busken. 'According to this he has obviously been threatening her with suicide. I can respect – in some instances – a man who takes his own life, but not one who only threatens such an act.' The polar explorer is inclined to give in to the pressure and give his brother a house. 'But we must first see if we can get rid of Uranienborg. To go away – as I am about to now – for several years and own two houses is not feasible.'

Uranienborg to Roald Amundsen was not only a place to lodge; to him it represented a national affiliation. He might have bowed his head to Fridtjof Nansen, but to Norway in general he maintained an unbending attitude. 'I will talk to Knudsen when I return but do repeat to him what I said in one of my last letters, that unless every single promise is kept – I'll stop.' To Leon he admitted what he could not frankly tell Nansen. 'I'm really fed up with it all – and my dear compatriots. Promises, promises and more promises – that's all. I would feel freer knowing all ties to Norway were broken. The treatment I have been subjected to since the South Pole journey makes me want to seek American citizenship. You yourself know how much easier my work would be.'

The threat, from Norway's great son, to change to American citizenship, was aimed at Prime Minister Knudsen. It was a threat to register the North West Passage, the South Pole, the North Pole, et al., abroad. Norway was not the pinnacle of Roald Amundsen's universe, as it was for Nansen. What he regarded most highly, if one is to believe his letters, was 'his work'. And what was his work? Not science, not to uncover the laws of nature, as Nansen would have liked to force him to do; his work was to discover the world. For this life's mission Norway was merely a resource, a public purse. When the purse was empty, one was obliged to change nationality. The polar explorer was ready to emigrate to America, driven by poverty.

Roald Amundsen cunningly allowed this rabid move regarding Norway's government to be directed via Leon; that was how he saw their separate roles. Roald's was the uncompromising primitive force, the unyielding determination. Leon might utilise this power, but filtered through his discretion and aptitude for shrewd diplomacy. Thus Roald Amundsen emerged as the strong man, unafraid, yet without sacrificing his civilised appearance. Only towards Nansen had he exposed himself and lost face, twice.

In May, still in Canada, the polar explorer tried to explain matters to Leon: 'The old man was right when he thought I was irritated. Had he known the reason he might not have been surprised. The news about Gustav has really shaken me.'

So, it was not the government's broken promises, but a family matter which had made Roald Amundsen threaten to cancel the expedition – minor obstacles could still derail major expeditions. 'Settling his debts was not enough, he wanted me to buy him some property too, and if not he would go mad or take his own life. Under such circumstances what else was there to do?'

Roald Amundsen had suffered a crisis during the lecture tour of America in the spring of 1913. It was a crisis triggered neither by Hjalmar Johansen's suicide nor by Captain Scott's death. It had nothing to do with guilt. For Nansen's sake, for the sake of Norway, he was obliged to continue northwards. It was a matter of honour – a fate which Scott's death had further sealed.

Roald Amundsen knew all the conditions of his lot; not even Fridtjof Nansen's South Pole plans were news to him. When he all the same took desperate measures to regain his freedom of action, strong forces must have been driving him.

To Nansen he gave as his reasons the government's broken promises. Norway had betrayed him – the Governor, his boys, his backers. The argument was weak and Nansen dismissed it out of hand. As a strategic move aimed at the government, however, it proved to be quite successful. But it is not possible to interpret the ultimatum as pure stratagem; for that it was too desperate.

To Leon he cited increased pressure from his brother Gustav as the psychological reason behind his actions. The thought of yet another suicide in the immediate vicinity was, of course, not appealing. However, there is little to indicate that a guilty conscience was a strong motivating force in Roald Amundsen's psyche.

Some hidden reason must have lurked at the bottom of the 40-year-old polar explorer's crisis, not to say rebellion, in that spring of 1913. Because a rebellion it was – a deluded attempt to sever himself from the North Pole expedition, from

Nansen, from Uranienborg, from his family, from Norway, from the life which lay, like a trap at the end of a tunnel, waiting for him. The polar explorer had reached that crossroads where a mountain of commitments barred his way to the new goal he had discovered. The North Pole was barring his way to happiness.

Ever since Carmenzia disappeared from his life there had been no talk of women between Roald and Leon. Nonetheless, momentous events had taken place since they last sat face to face, and in this department the polar explorer had one confidant only, Herman Gade. He had probably briefed Leon of this new element in Roald's life. But it was still a closed subject, not up for discussion.

Herman Gade was preparing to sail with the newly built transatlantic steamship *Christianiafjord* on her maiden voyage and Roald Amundsen suggested that the two of them return to Europe at the beginning of July. 'But by no means will I sail with the Norwegian line as you will understand I must go to London before returning home. I will have plenty of time on board to talk to you about these matters and listen to your wise advice.'

The polar explorer had urgent need of good advice. In addition to all his visible ties and commitments, he had bound himself 'for eternity' to a woman who was already established in marriage to another man. Then, he was supposed to journey to the North Pole. Fridtjof Nansen had established that, once and for all. Few duties could appear more absurd to a man passionately in love than to prepare for exile in an icebound male community in the Arctic Ocean. She might be bound by the social conventions of marriage; he was caught in a snare that entailed complete separation.

Kiss was the new goal in Roald Amundsen's life and the innermost puzzle in the polar explorer's crisis. She was the unspoken reason behind his actions – more important than the government's broken promises or brother Gustav's blackmail. He wanted to assert his right to live his own life, on his own private terms.

Roald Amundsen had earned honour and fame. He was about to make a fortune. 'The debt of honour' to Gustav he could pay with ready cash; the other commitments he could rid himself of through bellicose ultimatums. But his debt to Fridtjof Nansen, sealed on behalf of Norway and the world, with Hjalmar Johansen's revolver and Captain Scott's death-march, could only be paid with years of his life.

Nothing would cost Roald Amundsen more dear, now, when he had at last glimpsed her, the goddess of bliss, waiting for him by an open window. But Fridtjof Nansen's merciless rebuke had made the polar explorer realise that if he betrayed his 'big promise' he would forever be a man without honour. In Norway as in England he would lose face. The battle for happiness is lost for a man without honour.

All signposts pointed to the icy wastes.

TWENTY-THREE

A Polar Explorer Plays the Mandolin

In the tent where Captain Scott died was found a worn-out shoe, inside the shoe a small cloth bag, in the bag an envelope and in the envelope a letter. The letter remained unread until it reached the addressee: His Majesty King Haakon, The Palace, Christiania.

Roald Amundsen's South Pole letter, dated 17 December 1911, was brought to England on the *Terra Nova* in May 1913. Here it was handed to George V who sent it by post to his brother-in-law and cousin Haakon VII. 'I had completely forgotten about it,' the polar explorer wrote when he was informed that the letter had, at last, reached the recipient.

Tryggve Gran was received in Christiania on 1 June. The young Norwegian lieutenant had been employed as the ski expert on Scott's expedition on Nansen's recommendation. The Norwegian decision to go south put him in an awkward position. With that, Gran lost every chance of being part of the actual Pole party. Skis now came into their own only as crosses over the Captain's grave.

Tryggve Gran and Roald Amundsen's paths would cross many times, on the ground and in the air. Their relationship would fluctuate. When the 24-year-old returned from the Antarctic Amundsen was distant and suspicious; there was no knowing what Captain Scott's flunkey might say. 'I hope you don't turn up to welcome T. Gran,' he wrote to Leon, still from America. 'That would be going too far. He's a bit of an imbecile.'

But Leon turned up. 'Gran arrived from Bergen yesterday and was welcomed by the Board of the Geographical Society headed by Steen, Borchgrevinck, chairman of the Board of Trade and a few others – Borchgrevinck called for three cheers whereupon Steen gave a long speech and yet another three cheers whereupon Gran thanked everyone – it was Sunday evening 10.15 and I cycled in for the occasion to greet him.' There had been 'considerable attendance and jubilation' to greet Captain Scott's hanger-on.

Leon had sent the Royal Geographical Society and the empire's public representatives in Norway condolences. When Lieutenant Gran arrived home he made a journey by bicycle in the service of diplomacy. Besides that, Leon made sure he knew what the lieutenant actually had to report. That trusted individual, Sverre Hassel, was assigned to pay Gran a visit during his stay in Christiania. Towards the end of June Leon received the confidential report about what had really gone on behind enemy lines in the Antarctic. 'He was very polite and forthcoming. There had been no ill-feeling with the English regarding the competition. Those who trusted more in dogs than ponies expected that we would get to the Pole first, the others sided with Scott. He assumed that Scott personally was rather downhearted about the situation, but he never said anything. And of course the automobiles were complete shit.' Commenting to his brother, Leon concluded that the bad feeling towards the Norwegian did not originate in Scott's camp, but had originated with 'Curzon, Keltie & Co. who were the instigators of the jealousy'.

What killed Captain Scott and his four brave comrades – cold, hunger or disappointment? Officially this discussion did not concern Roald Amundsen. But in a letter to Leon he nevertheless gave his interpretation.

In America the polar explorer was kept updated concerning preparations for the approaching expedition. Among other things he was informed of the discovery of several boxes of contaminated pemmican, supplied by the Danish tinned food company J.D. Beauvais. The Norwegian expedition's expert on nutrition, Professor Torup, ordered a thorough investigation, as Scott had used food-stuffs from the same company. Later Leon reported that he had decided to wind up deliveries.

Roald Amundsen's comments were sensational. 'I'm pleased you are rid of Beauvais. It was their pemmican which finished Scott off. But on that subject we must hold our tongue.'

At the turn of the month June/July Roald Amundsen left the United States after six months' criss-crossing the 'nerve-racking' country and giving more than 160 lectures. He had made $40,000 or about 150,000 crowns and felt that it was 'better than nothing'. But neither the manager nor Don Pedro, who received the money for the expedition's fitting out in Buenos Aires, were especially pleased. They were of the opinion that it was the promoter, Lee Keedick, who had made a pretty penny. It appeared that the combined income from the South Pole expedition would only be half as much as the income Nansen achieved after the first *Fram* expedition. Nansen's English book rights had apparently made him rich.

At home in Norway the government had at last reached the stage in the agenda where they decided to grant the South Pole conqueror an annuity of 6,000 crowns. He was initially offered a professorship, similar to Nansen in his time. But after some deliberation he declined; in part he felt a notch too un-academic; in part he feared the loss of freedom it might entail. The entire crew too received a 'national award', a once only pay-out of 4,000 crowns. In that connection the leader of the first *Fram* expedition had advised the manager: 'Regarding the money payments the old man thinks the money must be banked and used in the shape of annuity otherwise it is his experience, and I agree with him, that the money goes on drinking sprees in no time.' After another round of negotiations, Hjalmar Johansen's widow and children were included in the honorary pay-out. Besides, Leon made a last ditch attempt to save Johansen's *Fram* watch and gold chain from being sold at auction. The family must surely hang on to one memento.

On 10 July Roald Amundsen booked in to the Savoy Hotel in London. His travelling companion, Herman Gade, continued home via Hamburg. It was the first time the South Pole conqueror had visited London since the death of Captain Scott. But this was no visit of condolence. It was private.

After six months' separation Roald Amundsen stood again before the object of his dreams. He needed no sextant to find her at 28 Amhurst Park, Stamford Hill. The great volume of his voice to reach her on phone number 2127 was superfluous. He had arrived; at his goal.

The polar explorer remained in London for ten days. The rest of the summer he was forced to devote to the study of oceanography. In Bergen, in spite of his lack of experience, he was offered the position of joint director at the as yet embryonic marine research institute. The proposal was flattering but of no interest to him. Unfortunately, instead he took it upon himself to ask Don Pedro if he would contribute a small sum towards the planned institution.

The way in which Roald Amundsen dissociated himself completely from this enforced field of activity was confirmed in his begging letter. This is how to go about getting no for an answer: 'I hereby permit myself to ask you whether you might contribute towards a marine research institute in Bergen – and then I draw a deep breath. It has taken me two months to formulate this request; it has worried me so much. Unfortunately, I promise rashly and must pay for it later.' The polar explorer saw no reason for marine research drawing money from the patron's account and Don Pedro agreed. He intended his means to be associated with Roald Amundsen's rich crop of achievements, not with commonplace institutes on land or sea.

Only after his homecoming and a settling of accounts with former Prime Minister Bratli can the polar explorer draw a line under the matter of broken promises. 'Everything will now be arranged by Knudsen,' he wrote to Leon. 'Few realise how much this affair has meant to me. I am sure you understand how the relationship between the boys and me is strengthened when they know that they have a job to come home to.'

During the autumn of 1913 a marked movement of troops took place in what was still called the third *Fram* expedition. The expedition's principal leader, and his manager, alias the brothers Amundsen, were in Uranienborg in the Bunnefjord. Meanwhile the captain and crew had travelled back to South America to set the boat in motion yet again.

In 1912 the idea had been mooted to let the *Fram* sail through the Panama Canal, possibly as the very first ship to do so. Not only would it save a huge amount of distance en route to the Bering Strait but it would also be a publicity coup. Roald Amundsen was immediately enthusiastic and gambled everything to make it happen. The finishing touches of this never-ending undertaking, which the building of the canal represented, were in the hands of an American company. In the United States John A. Gade worked tirelessly to obtain the authorities' blessing. The plan was for the two conquerors of the two Poles, Amundsen and Peary (no one spoke about Cook any more) to sail though the canal aboard the famous polar ship, possibly in the wake of an American warship.

Fram arrived in Colon, at the Panama Canal's approach, on 3 October 1913. In the temporary absence of Thorvald Nilsen the ship was navigated by Lieutenant Christian Doxrud. The lieutenant had been bitten by the flying bug and was now considered 'leader of the expedition's flying corps'. The journey from Buenos Aires had not been all plain sailing he reported back. 'I must admit it was the most difficult command I have experienced, as when all the boys came aboard in Baires, they were more or less spoilt by all the festivities and the honours, and then I, a complete outsider, was set to lead them.' It was not easy to take command of Roald Amundsen's laurel-wreath-plastered crew: 'they really all wanted to be captain.'

In Colon Thorvald Nilsen took on the honourable task as the most prominent of *Fram*'s many skippers. All was set for the big leap from the Atlantic to the Pacific. There was just one drawback. The Panama Canal was not ready. The polar ship hung around waiting for the green light for two months.

Eventually, a pessimistic telegram from Captain Nilsen dated 10 December forced them to revise plans. 'It's looking bad for departure 1914,' Leon wrote. 'We need to act,' Roald answered. He had left the Bunnefjord and was in Berlin. The Panama Canal was abandoned.*

The entire unsuccessful operation triggered off massive frustration on board the *Fram*. 'The whole crew are cursing the Americans, Goethals and all, who are connected to the canal,' Nilsen wrote later. Colonel Goethals was 'king of the canal zone' and responsible for all the delaying tactics. Amundsen referred to him simply as 'a thug'.

---

* The first ships were let through late in 1914.

The polar ship set out on its laborious return along the coast of South America. The plan was now to tow the broad-beamed vessel, using a high-speed tug, from the Straits of Magellan at the southern tip of the continent up to San Francisco on the West Coast. There the Governor would board and the victualling be completed. Then off, earliest possible late summer of 1914, to the Bering Strait by Alaska's north tip and at last to set out for the polar basin. A circumnavigation; interminable!

While *Fram* was still waiting around in Colon Roald Amundsen set out on yet another lecture tour. In Europe, a few important assembly rooms remained, which he had previously been unable to visit. On 14 November he started in Kiel and worked his way south towards metropolises such as Vienna and Budapest.

Before leaving, he instructed Leon to purchase Uranienborg's neighbouring property Rødsten. Rather than sell his home by the Bunnefjord, the polar explorer expanded his property. Allegedly Leon persuaded him to concentrate on Uranienborg as a permanent base. With the new property came a villa for the manager and his wife and children. In addition, there were servants' quarters for the unfailing nanny Betty and the less permanent maidservants. The properties were paradise in summer but completely out of the way in winter. The polar explorer had visited the place in sunshine. He speculates, instructs and departs.

While the Panama Canal lay like a half-finished swamp, the activities at Bunnefjord during the autumn were irreproachable. The houses were repaired, wells dug, pipes laid, telephone lines erected. On 26 November the polar explorer received a report: 'On the occasion of the Queen's birthday the houses are decked in flags and there will be a glass and cigars for the workers; apparently they are not royalists but I'll anyhow tell them the reason for the glass – I imagine they'll accept.'

After one month the first part of the tour was over, 44,000 crowns in the kitty. What now, big man? Off to South America to take command of your ship? Or home to supervise the victualling? What about a trip to Bergen to study oceanography's tribulations? For an expedition leader there are a thousand things to do. What is the most pressing need for a man who is about to spend seven years in the eternal ice?

Sunday evening 14 December 1913 Captain Amundsen booked in to the Savoy in London. A week later he wrote his brother, his wife Aline, their children and Betty a Christmas card. 'I am celebrating a quiet Christmas, all on my own but am with you in spirit and take part in the celebrations.' The last was a white and well-intentioned Christmas lie. Roald Amundsen's thoughts were in the same town as he was himself. 'Well, here I am,' he wrote to Herman Gade the same day, 'and am as happy as anyone could possibly be.'

Such was the status of the third Fram expedition, Christmas 1913: the manager, as always, at his post; the polar ship, under Lieutenant Nilsen's command, somewhere in the Caribbean, en route on its never-ending journey to the south. And the Governor himself, divorced from it all, in his tails, staring across the white damask tablecloth at his lonely table in the Savoy. His thoughts are neither at home nor on board the Fram; he is playing the mandolin under a window in Stamford Hill.

On 3 January the polar explorer forced himself to act. He packed his bags and moved on to fashionable Biarritz. The newly appointed Knight of the Order of Saint Olav, Don Perutcho – finally – was about to marry a French noblewoman. Lending lustre to the Christophersen family is a wise move.

The lecture tour went on. The South Pole conqueror appeared to flourish in the Old World. 'Last lecture in Vienna was my biggest success,' he wrote home. 'Two thousand festively dressed people in the most beautiful surroundings I have ever seen, mad jubilations. An evening to remember.' Whether he travelled through icy wastes or civilised habitats, the demand for quality must be maintained. 'Staying at the Adlon,' he reported from Berlin, 'a wonderful hotel, the best here, since the Kaiserhof started going downhill.'

The polar explorer knew how to value a luxurious bathroom above all; a modern bathroom with twentieth-century fixtures and fittings, just like an aeroplane; indispensable to a modern man. He took a bath every day, not only during tours, but at home too. In Uranienborg he had installed a bath which could run both fresh and salt water. From distinguished continental resorts he instructed those at home. 'Don't install an ugly basin.' Soon the fitting-out was completed; water closet, bath, wash-stand – and a bidet. 'Make sure the little fountain in the bathroom has access to hot and cold water.' The details are all-important.

On 8 February, during his Berlin stay, Roald Amundsen was himself the host of a dinner-party, which during the evening they christened the 'Antarctic Conference'. One of the guests at the Adlon was Captain Scott's former second-in-command, Captain Edward Evans. As with Shackleton, Amundsen had established good relations with Evans; Evans had not been on particularly good terms with his deceased boss. The captain had already offered the Norwegian use of the expedition offices when in London. After the Berlin dinner he sent Amundsen a set of exquisite waistcoat buttons as further proof of his friendship. The other guest had been the leader of the *Deutschland* expedition (the Germans were in the Antarctic at more or less the same time as *Terra Nova* and *Fram*), Wilhelm Filchner, discoverer of Prince Regent Luitpold's Coast. During the winter the Bavarian officer was actually hired by the forthcoming Norwegian expedition, to join the aerodynamics department which was in a constant state of expansion.

Roald Amundsen delighted in this cosy meeting between the three superpowers of the Antarctic stage. Not only owing to the wine, the food, the conversation, but, as he wrote to Leon, 'It looks so good.' The polar explorer had a talent for viewing himself from the outside.

On 18 February he was to have boarded the passenger boat *Olympic* for the passage to America. Thereby, in principle, he would be on his way to the north, direction Bering Strait. The passage is postponed until the end of April. Instead, Roald Amundsen travelled to London. Where else? He did not want to miss the blossom in the imperial capital, this last spring before the icy wastes. After ten or twelve days he left the city by the Thames and made a last round through Europe, to Paris and Vienna. Was he alone or had he borrowed the goddess of bliss?

At last, round about 17 March 1914, the polar explorer was expected home to a country still in the grip of winter to inspect his property before departure. 'Should I not spend the first night at the Grand Hotel?' he wrote to Leon. 'If the snow conditions are good we can ski home.' About time he skied a bit.

TWENTY-FOUR

Black Animals

Montevideo, 25 March, 1914

Beck died 18 March, brain fever
Able seaman Skaane appendicitis hospital
Must berth and take on oil
Stock fish thrown over board

Nilsen

The news from *Fram* was all bad. Three to four months had elapsed since abandoning the Panama Canal and the polar ship was no further south than the coast of Uruguay; a long way to go to the Straits of Magellan, not to mention Frisco town.

What now, Roald?

What now, Leon?

Well, a response. 'Await orders. Best wishes, Amundsen.' Norway's pride, the Viking ship, the royal yacht, the flagship *Fram* had turned into an ill-fated vessel. It had been constructed to tackle snow and ice, but had been dawdling around the tropics for two years. The ship was off to the North Pole, but getting nowhere.

Fram had been invaded by rats already in Buenos Aires – rats by the hundred. Cockroaches followed, then moths, mould and rot. Not to mention 'the black animals', called 'fish flies'. Skipper Nilsen talked about them in a long letter which followed the depressing telegram:

The last days in Colon we noticed a lot of worms in the hold, about 1cm long, and black. Thought they came from the fish. At the same time the fish started to stink and it was virtually impossible to stay on board. On further inspection it transpired that the worms had developed inside the fish, possibly or more likely probably the worms' germ had been in the fish from Norway, although I cannot be sure. The 2 thousand kilos of coffee were taken up and put in the workroom. The worms developed into a sort of fly with a hard shell. When we trod on them it was like cracking a nut. Later the black animals invaded our cabins. In the end it got so bad that I decided on first opportunity to throw the fish overboard. I was loath to do it in the Gulf or the busy Straits of Florida, so we waited until we got further out. To make sure no one knew where the bundles came from the address which was painted on one side was cut off, but on one of the bundles only. The fact is they were black with animals and to get most of them away the bundles had to be thrown away whole. Anyhow, they sank immediately. The fish was all eaten away, only skin and bone left.

The fish stock was not the only expensive provisions to be jettisoned; a couple of hundred kilogrammes of potatoes and at least the same amount of tinned food – lamb stew, cod roe, and crème caramel – all went overboard. The choice of food suffered, the ship suffered, and most of all the crew suffered. 'This trip is ruining our relationships,' Skipper Nilsen wrote. 'We are all bad-tempered and everyone must be treated with kid gloves. Even Stubberud. Since Christiania, when he and Rønne went for a booze-up and they became bosom buddies, he has changed completely and I think R is a bad influence on S. In Buenos Aires for example they went on a three-day bender without even setting foot on board. But it will take too long to tell you everything I have heard about them all. Actually, most about Doxrud.'

One thing was temper, another thing was health. The hospital visits in South America had been many and expensive. Able seaman Skaane, who had come down with appendicitis, had been hired in Buenos Aires and was an unknown quantity to the brothers Amundsen. The real tragedy was Andreas Beck, the huge bear of an ice-pilot from Tromsø, who was to have been one of the key personnel in the forthcoming North Pole expedition.

He fell ill at the beginning of March. But how was he to be treated? There had been no doctor on board the *Fram* since Dr Svendsen shot himself on the second *Fram* expediton. 'It is a puzzle to us what Beck is suffering from,' Nilsen noted in his diary on 17 March. 'Initially I thought it was nicotine, then mental derangement, then brain fever. He has never been in pain, his pulse is normal, temperature normal. All we know is that he "sees double" and see only that he is failing.' Nor did Wisting know what to do, in spite of having been promoted to medicine man, dentist and tinsmith.

It was all over on the 18th. 'Beck died five minutes before eleven this morning. Wisting and I were with him. It went so quickly we could not get hold of the others. He never uttered a word and his death was easy; a last breath and it was all over.'

The next day the big body made the same journey as the potatoes, the tinned food and the fish stock. It was wrapped in a flag. The engine was turned off and it was calm. Captain Nilsen said the Lord's Prayer. The *Fram* crew sang: 'How far, how near is my end'. The ice-pilot was lowered into the sea at 33° South.

On 25 March the ship reached Montevideo. The engine needed oil, the propeller a refit, and, above all, the bottom needed a scrape. The polar ship was so tropically overgrown that it virtually stood still in the water. By the time spring was over the ship ought to have arrived in San Francisco. The polar explorer had booked tickets on the *Olympic* for 29 April. Masses of equipment was en route to the West Coast; the aeroplane had been bought long ago.

Thorvald Nilsen stepped ashore and sent his depressing telegram. Beck is dead, fish stock overboard, must berth, etc.

Now what?

By 26 March the decision had already been taken. The brothers telegraphed their faithful assistant, the Norwegian Consul in San Francisco, Henry Lund: 'Expedition postponed 1915'. Yet another postponement. The journey, which should have gone north in 1909, had now been delayed for a total of six years. The ship must be re-routed, the provisions returned, sold or forwarded. What a mess!

'It was my solemn duty, as they say,' Roald Amundsen wrote a few years later, 'to give orders to clean the vessel and return home as soon as possible. Now there was no other solution but through the North East Passage.' *Fram* was ordered home to Horten. Again the old man of honour, Don Pedro, forked out tens of thousands of dollars to ready the ship for its passage home. Luckily Roald – or, in other words, Leon – had remembered to send a birthday telegram, like he remembered old Consul Lund's golden wedding in Frisco. It is the small things that count, even in the diplomacy of polar research.

Not only had the schedule broken down, the route had too. After all the tropical troubles, Roald Amundsen gave up the idea of sailing round South America and into the Polar Basin via the backdoor. Now, like Nansen, he was obliged to sail the *Fram* wholly or partially through the North East Passage – the laborious route round the coast of Siberia.

The third *Fram* expedition was back at its starting point. When the ship arrived in Horten in midsummer 1914 all the expedition crew were once again together on Norwegian soil. If one were to accept Roald Amundsen's explanation that the South Pole journey had been an economic necessity in order to realise the North Pole expedition, then it must all be summed up in two words: complete fiasco. Five years had been lost. The ship was run down, the equipment and crew in total dissolution. In spite of the polar explorer having pocketed considerable sums, the lost investments and enormous running costs were as extensive. Thanks to Don Pedro, however, the majority of his personal capital was intact.

What had been won these five years since the first postponement of the expedition?

The South Pole.

That was worth the price for Roald Amundsen. The economic excuses had never been anything other than a smoke screen. Therefore it is not possible to write it all off as bad business. But what had started out so brilliantly ended so lamentably – why? Had the polar explorer lost his grip?

Roald Amundsen had left the *Fram* in Hobart in March 1912. Since then the ship had been left to its own devices. Maybe all the catastrophes were unavoidable, programmed like the grubs in the fish stocks. Or maybe it had something to do with the Captain abandoning ship, letting go of the reins. All Roald Amundsen's triumphs were decidedly wilful. Did he really *want* to go north?

Not really. Not like that anyhow. During the last years the polar explorer had avoided two geographic points: *Fram* and Norway – ship and base. Otherwise he had been everywhere. He had chased money, happiness and the new-fangled liberating device which would lift him up over *Fram*, over the Arctic Ocean and over Nansen: the aeroplane. It was as if the fate of the polar ship did not affect him. Maybe the postponements were a relief – costly, but welcome to a man who did not really want to leave civilisation – who was not ready for the ice.

On his return home Roald Amundsen lived partly at the Grand Hotel and partly at Uranienborg. On 26 March, the same day as the 'heavy' decision was taken on the further fate of the expedition, the polar explorer was busy trying to get hold of Kiss Bennett's sister Gudrun on the telephone. He was making plans for a dinner in the bosom of the family. A little celebration maybe?

'The future of polar exploration lies in the air and I am cheeky enough to claim that honour for myself as I was the first serious polar researcher who realised this and who practically demonstrated this method's potential.' Thus Roald Amundsen's self-congratulatory words read in his *My Life as a Polar Explorer*. At last, towards the end of his life, he had demonstrated his own solution and could proudly consign Nansen's dogs, skis and sledges to the museum showcases.

Roald Amundsen was not the first flying polar explorer. Engineer Andrée's tragic balloon trip to the North Pole took place in 1897, even before young Amundsen had joined his first polar expedition as an apprentice. But when he is 'cheeky' enough to make such an assertion, he emphasises *serious*. Who is more 'serious', the balloon pioneer Andrée or the flying visionary Amundsen? The question is unanswered. The point is that in his book the author needed to consign the engineer to the ranks of the foolhardy and frivolous to enable him to cash in on the *air* as being *his* way, this in spite of the fact that on several occasions he had expressed great admiration for his flying colleague. It was so important for Roald Amundsen to rid himself of Fridtjof Nansen's borrowed plumes – to make it known that he was a pioneer, an initiator on a par with his compatriot.

Fridtjof Nansen, too, had reached the conclusion that the future of polar research was from the air as well as the sea. But for the Professor 'the air' was for the purpose of meteorological observations, just like the ocean was a scientific area of research. To his successor all elements were subordinate to the only area that interested him: geography.

Roald Amundsen had arrived late in the world. Time was fast running out for anyone who wanted to stamp their name on the map. Anyone wanting to discover needed to go up high, hence the crow's nest. Less than ten years after Engineer Andrée's disappearing act, technical developments around aviation started to shoot ahead.

The breakthrough came in 1909 when the Frenchman Blériot crossed the English Channel. That summer Roald Amundsen experimented with his man-bearing kites. In this phase of the aeroplane's development all planes looked, more or less, like motorised dragons. The idea of the dragon was primarily to scout out ice conditions for the purpose of manoeuvre. But the higher the elevations and greater the radii the better suited were the flying contraptions as instruments in the explorer's real activity – to spy out new land.

Add to that a factor that turned Roald Amundsen's eyes skyward. Blériot's sensational flight made it all plain: pilots were the heroes of the future.

The polar explorer's first move following the expedition's temporary breakdown was to order the sale of the two sea-planes he had bought in San Francisco. At this time planes needed to be transported by ship. It would be an expensive affair to get them to Norway; they were anyhow probably no longer on a par with the latest technology.

Together with his old kite expert, Captain Einar Sem-Jacobsen, the polar explorer set out for Europe to buy new equipment. On 4 May they visited the expedition's German member in Berlin. That spring Dr Filchner bought himself a pilot's jump suit and took flying lessons in preparation for the forthcoming journey.

The two continued to France, foremost among the flying nations. Here the expedition bought a Farman aeroplane, price 20,000 francs. Having visited Maxim's and spent a few days in Paris Roald Amundsen took leave of the pilot, whom he instructed to transport the plane back north. The polar explorer headed in another direction, possibly over the Channel.

At home again time had come to learn something about the art of flying. Roald Amundsen had his skipper's certificate; now he wanted to be the first Norwegian civilian to get a pilot's licence. Sem-Jacobsen would be his teacher. The exams were taken on 11 June at Gardermoen and he passed – with flying colours! The pupil, who in all had had twenty hours of instruction, only crashed once. The King sent a greeting's telegram.

Earlier in the year Tryggve Gran, Captain Scott's skiing expert, had gained his Air Force pilot's licence. On 30 July 1914, the 25-year-old set out on a breakneck deed of daring: he flew across the North Sea, from Scotland to Jæren in southern Norway in 4 hours 10 minutes. Attached by a cord around his neck the lieutenant carried a piece of pioneering airmail, addressed to Queen Maud of Norway.

As if by a miracle the skiing pilot Gran reached Norwegian territory before the tank went dry and the First World War broke out. That same day Europe started to mobilise. Two days later war was declared; the world war was suddenly a reality. The period of peaceful expeditions was over.

On 3 August, in a letter to the Norwegian government, the 42-year-old Roald Amundsen wrote: 'I hereby permit myself to offer the Norwegian Army my aeroplane – Maurice Farman 1914 – as a gift, unconditionally. I would at the same time like to express my wish to be attached to the Army Air Corps as a pilot with the rank of *private soldier*. Yours sincerely, Roald Amundsen.'

That same day a telegram arrived from Berlin. The expedition's other pilot, Wilhelm Filchner, wished to be excused, 'for the duration of the war'.

In the spring the government had granted 200,000 crowns for the purpose of re-starting the third *Fram* expedition. Roald Amundsen calculated the costs at 400,000 and pledged the remainder. On 27 August he renounced the amount. Prime Minister Knudsen answered: 'I can understand that this must be a huge sacrifice for you that you now bestow on your native country and I think the general public will know how to appreciate it.'

The majority of the crew were called up. *Fram* had arrived in Horten midway between the shots in Sarajevo and the final declarations of war, and was entrusted to Oscar Wisting for unloading. Roald Amundsen was quoted in a newspaper as saying that the expedition had been cancelled owing to the difficult times.

'What are your plans for the future?'

'I have none. For the moment I am living at Svartskog,' the polar explorer answered. He was not optimistic about his chances of flying; not for some time anyhow. In the meantime Norway remained neutral; in the meantime Amundsen was a private citizen. Free.

Saved by the, very large, bell.

TWENTY-FIVE

The Royal Yacht

After the outbreak of war Roald Amundsen entered an unusually peaceful period, unlike any other in his turbulent life. The world, which had been his boundless playground, had, in the twinkling of an eye, been turned into a theatre of war; the peaceful scientific campaigns would run into military front lines and political barriers. Sir Ernest Shackleton managed to slip off to the South Pole on his second Antarctic expedition; every other voyage of discovery would be an elusive one.

As a private soldier of an army air corps in a neutral country the former polar explorer was to all intents and purposes unemployed. He folded his arms and let his capital do the work. In the United States he had $25,000 which Herman's brother, John Gade, had invested with considerable profit. In the sea-faring nation of Norway the war developed into a gilt-edged story for anyone who knew how to exploit the situation. Roald Amundsen had plenty of crowns to invest and, just as important, he had Leon to invest them for him.

The brothers Amundsen had, owing to the forces of history, landed back in shipping, the family's traditional profession. In their childhood home at Hvidsten a cannonball stood on a plinth. It originated from the Crimean War, the war which made their father a well-to-do man. Now the new global war turned his two youngest sons into rich men. To the explorer only one worthy goal remained: happiness; only one territory which could occupy a man's entire energy: a woman; just one place in the world: London.

Like his relationship with Sigg Castberg, his alliance with Kiss Bennett had the appearance of an unspoken agreement – to all intents and purposes proper, but deep down unsatisfactory, to the polar explorer at least. Roald Amundsen was a no-compromise man. He could shove things in front of him, he could repress and conceal. But sooner or later his tendency was to push everything to the extreme, to a definite all or nothing.

Behind him: the landlady and her fatal zinc bucket in Amsterdam; in addition: the dissolved Castberg marriage. He might not have been the guilty party, but he was the catalyst. He arrived as an intruder, a conqueror. Or, was he, possibly, the conquered?

There was no shortage of marriageable women for a man like Roald Amundsen, if that was what he wanted. But the polar explorer needed something less simple; he needed resistance. He shunned a prize which was there for the taking. Happiness must be had at a price. Love demands a victim.

For the first time since his return from the South Pole the polar explorer celebrated Christmas in Norway. But he left the country in the New Year. Roald Amundsen and Kiss Bennett were to meet a lot in the times to come. He travelled to London; she came to Norway. In Christiania she booked into a hotel in the wooded hills that surrounded the town. She visited her older sister Gudrun who was married to the German businessman Robert Maus. But she was also a frequent visitor at the polar explorer's remote residence at Svartskog. In a way the relationship had found its equilibrium. But the South Pole conqueror was no tightrope walker.

In the autumn of 1915 Roald Amundsen travelled to London, this time for a specific purpose. To a question from his brother Tonni, Leon answered that 'Roald is in London from whence they will probably arrive sometime'. 'They will' probably? Will he at last effect an abduction, push things to the limit and demand action? Later Leon received a letter from London. It appeared less resolute. 'Should I not return home, please deal with my shipping stocks as if they were yours.'

All correspondence between Norway and the warring Britain was controlled and censored. In order to protect his private life against intrusion the polar explorer asked his brother to go through all letters that were sent on to London. Roald Amundsen set up his own security checks. Nothing of an intimate nature must leak out. One person he called 'K'. Leon never talked about her during this period, other than indirectly.

For anyone speculating, the war developed into an economic business. 'How is business?' he asked Leon at Christmas time. 'I do not believe peace will come so it might be a good idea to keep some of the shares.' At this point Roald Amundsen had taken a clear stand in the war: 'Germany surely has long ago lost any right-thinking person's sympathy'.

It appeared that the polar explorer's own feelings had shifted this first year of war. 'Ask Roald if he still supports the Germans,' a family letter asked. Certainly Amundsen, since his student days in Hamburg, regarded Germany and the Germans with considerable fellow feeling. While the representatives of Empire were shouting their hurrahs for the dogs, the Kaiser, according to diplomatic channels, read his South Pole book with the greatest interest.

Roald Amundsen himself had hired Germany's leading polar explorer for his forthcoming expedition. The newly qualified pilot Wilhelm Filchner was still hoping to travel north. During the spring of 1915 he wrote optimistically from the battlefields: 'By the autumn I am sure it'll all be over and victory ours, as you cannot imagine with what heroism and trust in God our people fight.'

Wilhelm Filchner spent some time in Norway during the war. As the head of a German naval office in Bergen he became involved in a spy scandal and was forced to flee the country in a hurry. According to Filchner's memoirs, this blocked a peace initiative which was being brokered at Lysaker in November 1916 with himself and Nansen as liaisons between British and German authorities. A year down the line Nansen regretted that he had not 'had a go'.

If he had not been so before, the polar explorer now became immune against any German sympathy during his stays in London. His antipathy towards the Empire was deep-seated, but England was, if not his, then at least *her* second native country. Kiss Bennett's older brother Niels Gudde, who lived in England in between battles, had exchanged Indian polo for active service in the cavalry. If one lived in London it was necessary to take sides. The war days were characterised by bloody news, the nights by hysterical worship of life.

Nevertheless, it was not really the historic drama which occupied Roald Amundsen during these years, but rather a private drama with its human repurcussions. During the autumn of 1915 the polar explorer was alone with the object of his choice. But her husband and sons arrived home before Christmas; 'so she is terribly cut up', he confided frankly to Aline and Leon.

The 22 January 1916 was the date the polar explorer has pencilled in as the one on which he would go underground. Before Christmas he wrote to Leon: 'Let no one know of my whereabouts.' The plan was ready. The 'abduction' *would* take place in some shape or form. Leon received his last power of attorney just before the bridal procession disappeared. 'When I leave here in a short time, I will not be contactable, and you must act for me in every affair, please,' Roald wrote on 18 January.

But letters continued to arrive from London in February too. 'Money seems particularly round in this country and has an ability to roll away. Please be kind enough and send 1,000 [crowns] to Hambro; that should be enough for the time being.' On 18 February a letter arrived from London containing seven Indian war stamps and the news that the elderly Baron Wedel Jarlsberg had got married for the second time.

A month later Leon wrote to Tonni that 'Roald is expected home next week.' Tonni's answer was decisive: 'Is he alone or is his wife with him?' On 22 March Leon replied: 'Roald is home and is very well.'

Rather than 'the wife' Roald Amundsen arrived home with a resolve. He wanted to resume his work. The North Pole was next. Roald Amundsen had taken Kiss Bennett to the brink of decision – made her face the options. She had failed or, rather, she had chosen to stay in London. The bridal abduction had been founded on an illusion.

We must assume he set her a time limit: round the North Pole and back. He assumes time is on his side; the sons are growing up, the husband ageing. In the meantime the polar explorer's star would be in the ascendant. What about Sigg Castberg? She too said no until he returned from the ice. Then she stood on the shore, welcomed him with open arms, while clutching the divorce papers.

Roald Amundsen journeyed home and declared that he would honour his old promise to Nansen and to the nation. He was off to the North Pole. The princess awaits him beyond, his pearl of great price.

Two days after his return Roald Amundsen wrote optimistically to Herman Gade, who had now moved back to Chicago, that he hoped to leave civilisation behind him as early as the summer of 1917. 'Here the quarrelling and wrangling is such that I will find it a relief to turn my back on it all. The timing is perfect. Personally I have never felt healthier or in better form than just now. On top of that, by advantageous investment, I have increased my capital in such a manner that I am completely independent and can pay for all myself. Can you imagine the satisfaction of that? Hardly – as you have never seen things from the beggar's point of view.'

Early in 1916 the polar explorer sold off a major part of his shipping shares; Leon chose to keep his back, but soon established that the time to sell was 'advantageous'. Amundsen had doubled his capital and still had shares with Leon and Gade. The polar explorer can afford to build his own ship.

In the autumn of 1914 the naval shipyard in Horten had estimated that repairs to *Fram* would amount to 100,000 crowns. The same request two years later showed that the rot had spread. Even Roald Amundsen called the nation's former glory a 'wreck'. But when he chose to build a new ship, rather than gamble on 'the old lady', the decision was nevertheless based on more than financial calculations.

Fram belonged to the state. That was an advantage, but it implied dependence on government and Parliament. Anyhow, historically and morally, it was still Fridtjof Nansen's ship. It was certainly not abhorrent to the polar explorer to free himself from this ship of the past. In keeping with his nature Roald Amundsen decided to order his own ship – item: one polar ship from shipbuilder Chr. Jensen in Asker.

At last things were moving. During the summer he was in London again, in the autumn he had misgivings about the schedule; he needed another year. In any case, the financial independence seemed to be coming to an end. 'I'll go to the Prime Minister and ask what I might expect from there,' he wrote to

Leon. Before Christmas he travelled to America to arrange the victualling with Herman Gade.

During the war years Leon left Svartskog. He moved to the south coast and bought the property Fredly outside Arendal. During these overheated times the manager too had become a well-to-do man. The polar explorer addressed him now, with absolute legitimacy, 'ship-owner' Amundsen. From the south coast Leon asked Tonni to inform him of his brother's last plans before departing for America. He could relate that Roald wanted to sell the property in Bunnefjord as he was at this moment furnishing a flat in the fashionable Thomas Heftye's Street. Kiss Bennett's sister, Gudrun Maus, lived close by with her family. At this strategic point the polar explorer wanted to establish his new base. The oldest brother ended his report with 'I hope he gets round the world and back via London.' Tonni too has realised what was the expedition's real goal.

But the property sale was not effected this time either. Not least the tax implications caused Leon misgivings. The polar explorer had once, referring to his work for the good of the fatherland, achieved permanent tax exemption in his home municipality of Oppegård. A corresponding guarantee was not necessarily forthcoming in the socialist-dominated capital. According to Leon, 'considerable sums' were involved. Neither Fredly nor the new flat became permanent dwellings for the brothers Amundsen.

Having celebrated Christmas with the Gade family in Chicago and concluded his business in New York, the polar explorer arrived in London at the beginning of February 1917. He was back in Norway after one month; it was no longer a joke to cross the North Sea, dodging U-boat periscopes.

In the meantime, at home in the peaceful Bunnefjord, dramatic happenings were taking place. The *Fram* crew member Jørgen Stubberud had tried to take his own life. Leon reported that the former South Pole man had gone 'incurably mad; sad but understandable'. It was the same comment as when Johansen shot himself in Solli Park. He cannot have been completely incurable, however; he recovered from his troubles and would live the longest of any of Framheim's nine inhabitants, until he was nearly a hundred.

The polar explorer and his brother, the ship-owner, both believed that it would only be a matter of time before Norway was drawn into the war against Germany. Not least Leon, with his strong ties to France,was keen that Norway should play an active part. They were both in the awkward position of profiting from the misery of war. It could be interpreted as double standards, but also as an expression of gnawing despair, when Leon in March put pen to paper and formulated an appeal for 'a memorial to our naval heroes'. This is the only time Leon Amundsen took a public initiative, on his own, and not on the polar explorer's behalf. 'The matter must be set in motion immediately, while money is forthcoming.' To the editor of Norway's *Trade and Shipping Times* he wrote: 'It ought to be the country's largest monument, placed in the best spot somewhere by the sea.'

But the polar explorer too was about to engage actively in the historic events. He was planning a tour – not to benefit his own wallet, but for the benefit of the defence of the realm. And if that were not enough, the Army Air Corps pilot private was getting ready for action. It might only be a matter of time before the German Reich's zeppelins dropped their bombs over his native country. On 13 March he wrote to Leon: 'Should really have resumed flying manoeuvres this week in preparation for the zeppelins; but owing to snowy weather all exercises have been postponed, so I will have to wait until my return. Hope the "Zeppis" will stay away until then, although I have a feeling it's touch and go.'

Roald Amundsen's tour on behalf of the country's defence constituted an exception from what had become the polar explorer's norm – to concentrate exclusively on his own line of work. While Fridtjof Nansen left polar research for an increasingly scientific, political and humanitarian field of activity, Roald Amundsen turned the other way – towards an increasingly narrow specialisation, a concentration on himself, his own world. He did not want to play the Nansen role more than was strictly necessary.

The popular speaker Roald Amundsen toured the northern Norwegian skerries for all of six weeks. Attendance was good but it can hardly be called a revelation. According to the *Nordlys* (*Northern Lights*) journalist the 'halls were packed'. But there was not much to report. 'He just wanted to remind us about the great world crisis going on in Europe and why it was important for us to maintain a solid defence and to remain neutral. He said socialists were without a native country and wanted no defence. I doubt whether his talk took root among the audience. I have a feeling the masses left feeling rather put out at having heard nothing new.'

The news was a bit better from Vesterålen. It had been reported that the polar explorer had ordered no less than 200kg of goats' cheese for his North Pole expedition. 'Thereby our famous compatriot killed two birds with one stone: he has ordered a considerable amount of Raftsund cheese and put the local population in a better mood. In Bø, which lies exposed to U-boats, to be on the safe side, they founded a defence society.'

When he returned the zeppelins had not yet attacked the capital. Thus the polar explorer's war efforts were limited to the north Norwegian village halls, besides the Christiania stock exchange – for the time being.

Before he travelled north Roald Amundsen had applied to the government to reimburse him with the 200,000 crowns that he declined in 1914, as the expedition, according to the newspapers 'turned out a lot more costly than expected.' He could trust Prime Minister 'Gunnar'. Within fourteen days the money was safely in the polar explorer's account.

Right up to the day of the launch speculation was rife as to the name of the new boat. The papers plumped for *Betty*, after the immortal nanny who apparently still survived in an annex at Uranienborg. His last ship bore the age-old Norse female name *Gjøa*, but it was christened long before the polar explorer took over the ownership. And which woman, other than Betty, was part of Roald Amundsen's life?

Of course, like Fridtjof Nansen, he might have chosen a word or a motto, like *Fram*, 'Forwards'. But were he to choose a motto it would have to be *First*. That was a bad idea, however, as the North Pole had already been discovered and *Fram* had already made the voyage through the ice. The polar explorer had a better idea. On 2 June he received a reply from the palace. 'The Queen gives her gracious consent. Haakon R.' The name was to be *Maud* – feminine and national all at once. The vessel was as broad as the Queen was slender.

The launch took place early in the morning on 7 June 1917. The polar ship was christened, not in decadent champagne, but in its rightful element – ice. 'The launch was perfect and a wonderful celebration,' the polar explorer noted in his diary, full of optimism on behalf of the ship and the future.

Together with Herman Gade, Roald Amundsen had arranged victualling in America. The plan was to load the ship in San Francisco. So, in spite of the war, he had resurrected the old route, through the Panama Canal, along the West Coast to the Bering Strait. The rejected diplomat Herman Gade had not laboured in vain. Through his best friend in Christiania at least one diplomatic channel was open for Gade – via the polar explorer direct to the Prime Minister. 'I will talk to G.K. in the near future and will whisper all you wish in his ear.'

But like so many times before: departure is postponed, plans revised. On 10 July Roald Amundsen wrote to his friend in Chicago. 'I had hoped to get over already in the autumn and then over to S. Frisco but it cannot be done. I must try to start from here and straight north next summer – 1918.' That meant that five years' worth of provisions needed to be transported to Norway – through the U-boat war.

In its determined fight against Great Britain Germany had earlier in the year declared an unrestricted U-boat war. That led to the sinking of a large number of Norwegian merchant ships and a corresponding loss of life. In April the United States had joined the war and at the end of October 1917 Roald Amundsen took his single-handed campaign to the Kaiser's legation in Christiania.

'As a Norwegian seaman I hereby hand back my German decorations as a personal protest against German murder of peaceful Norwegian seamen.' With this declaration the private pilot-recruit and simple sailor thumped the imperial decorations on the table of the German minister. The decorations had been bestowed by Wilhelm II in person, at a solemn audience in the Berlin Residence, following the conquest of the North West Passage.

Roald Amundsen did not share Nansen's superior attitude towards decorations; that they were an unattractive manifestation of human weakness. To him decorations represented real value. As a motivating force, as a commodity, that type of metal ware had proven its full worth in the arena in which he operated. To give a decoration back was no easy act of protest for Roald Amundsen. His colleague Sverdrup followed suit a few days later. Fridtjof Nansen was the government's representative in Washington; his decorations were in some drawer or other at Polhøgda. They lay there, untouched, until the bloodbath was over.

The Norwegian's diplomatic break with the Kaiser was taken up and commented upon, not just in Norway but all over the warring world, including Germany. In the stream of good wishes a letter arrived from Trondheim: 'Receive my sincere and warm recognition of your free and manly conduct in returning the German decorations.' The letter was signed lawyer and reserve officer Trygve Gudde. The pilot-recruit had no doubt been successful on several fronts.

But the campaign was not over. Roald Amundsen's appetite was whetted. He turned to his friend John A. Gade, who during the war served as American naval attaché to Scandinavia, and asked if he could possibly clear away the formalities in order that the polar explorer might serve in the Royal Navy. Compatriots like the pilot Tryggve Gran and the 'brother-in-law' Niels Gudde were already fighting in British uniform; why was *he* being kept out, he, whose physique was superior to all of theirs?

John Gade applied to the admiral in charge and received the answer that of course they would arrange sightseeing to the fronts in order that Mr Amundsen might form an opinion of the situation. Following the episode with the decorations it had become obvious that the polar explorer could be more advantageously put to use in the propaganda war than as cannon fodder on the battlefield.

Roald Amundsen made a 'very interesting tour of the three fronts'. In a letter to Leon the warrior told of 'extremely happy times' with old friends in Paris. What he did not mention was that, during his stay at the Hotel Meurice, as guest of the French government, he received a young American in audience. The humble American served at the Air Force HQ in the French capital, but his greatest wish was to follow the Norwegian on his Arctic journey. Unfortunately, Amundsen saw no possibility of fulfilling this exotic wish.

Later the two would meet at another hotel in another country, but in this manner did Lincoln Ellsworth for the first time knock on the door of Roald Amundsen's fabulous life story.

In the middle of February the explorer booked in to the Ritz Hotel in the war-capital London. The beginning of March saw him in the United States where he toured the northwestern states to recruit Norwegian-American farmers to the trenches. According to John Gade the results were 'astonishing'.

All winter work had gone on in America to obtain export permission for the *Maud* expedition's victualling and equipping. Here Fridtjof Nansen, who was in Washington to secure Norway's food supplies, rendered his young colleague a last favour. In cooperation with, among others, the brothers Gade he succeeded in securing an agreement with the authorities which allowed the material, contrary to rigorous war restrictions, to be sent out of the country to arrive in Norway during the spring. At the end of April the polar explorer too arrived home from the propaganda-fields in the northwest.

What a 'serious' researcher like Roald Amundsen was doing that last year before embarking on a scientific journey estimated to last maybe five years might appear quite extraordinary. For the first years of the war he played the role of the soigné, well-healed, roving gentleman. A few years earlier he would have turned his back on 'all and everything'. But then, as departure loomed, he was increasingly concerned about doing his bit in war-torn Europe; first as an airman in the newly established hero's role of war pilot. Then he wanted to enlist and wear the uniform of a British officer. His heroic shenanigans smacked of a middle-aged man's melodrama and unrealism. Which battle was he actually fighting? One thing is sure: it was no longer the epoch of the civilian, not in London anyhow.

During the spring of 1917 the newspapers reported that Sergeant Herland had been named as the North Pole expedition's pilot: 'Thus he and Amundsen will be the two who make the push to the Pole.' The sergeant had already drawn notice to himself with an exceedingly daring flight from Kongsvinger to Lillestrøm. But by the next year there was no more talk of a plane on board the *Maud*. The great idea had been put on ice.

Kaiser Wilhelm's zeppelins might at any moment appear with their fatal loads. When all is said and done this might not be the moment to take sparse aeroplane material out of the country. As long as the war lasted a plane's proper place was over the skies of Europe. The real arena of heroic deeds was there, in the limelight of the Air Force.

Any aerobatics over the icy wastes would appear untimely. If one person risked life and limb it would make no impression at all in the light of the enormous casualty lists the public was fed every single day.

What happened on board *Maud* was not all that important. The main issue was his absence. He would be missed. During his absence *she* would make up her mind.

Woo him back from the ice's embrace.

TWENTY-SIX

In the Embrace of the Ice

On 24 June 1918 *Maud* left Christiania, at the close of Old Europe's *anciens régimes*. Within a few weeks Queen Maud's cousin, the Tsar of Russia, had been executed with his entire family somewhere in remote Siberia. The trenches ran like tightly packed blood vessels throughout Central Europe. It was only a question of time before two more empires would crumble.

Maud hinted at something big and full of promise. Twenty-five years had passed since *Fram* had headed out of the Bernadotte kingdom of Norway. It had been a voyage of hope and independence; its goal, Norway's freedom. The *Maud* expedition was a pale re-release but nevertheless an amusing jubilee-performance. In theory this was still the third *Fram* expedition.

The ship itself was altered; *Maud* was a shorter version of Nansen and Colin Archer's original construction. The plan and the route were entirely of Nansen's devising, although Roald Amundsen would approach the ice further east and thereby arrive on a more northerly course. While *Fram*'s drift had started west of the New Siberian Islands, *Maud* would sail further east, to Bennett Island. Not only would this route bring him closer to the North Pole, the only one of its objectives the *Fram* expedition had not realised; it would also take him into unexplored territory between the Pole and Alaska. The polar explorer declared to a newspaper that 'it is undeniably possible that there is solid land in there somewhere.'

Maud was a research vessel, but had something of the pleasure yacht about her, elegantly fitted out with a single cabin for every crew member; there were nine of them. Only a few weeks before departure Amundsen had appointed the *Gjøa* and *Fram* veteran, Helmer Hanssen, as skipper. Oscar Wisting was the first officer, Sundbeck the Swede first engineer. The fourth *Fram* veteran was the not quite so young but just as dexterous Martin Rønne. Four were new: Tessem, Knudsen, Tønnesen and – last but not least – the geo-physician Dr Harald Sverdrup, the expedition's only real scientist.

The ninth member joined the expedition when it arrived in Tromsø on 14 July. Roald Amundsen never spent more time than necessary on his polar ships. This time he took the costal steamer. So what was the Governor's role on board? On his first expedition he was both skipper and leader of the scientific work. On *Maud* both these tasks had been delegated. Nevertheless, his own responsibility was two-pronged. He was an explorer. Earlier he had led the push to the magnetic North Pole and the South Pole; now he would lead the attack on the North Pole – when the time came. Besides, he was on a private mission too.

Roald Amundsen's cabin was a monastic cell fitted out like a cupid's den. The wall over the berth was covered in a large silk hanging; white embroidered gulls soaring over a blood-red sky. 'Friends had done up my cabin,' he wrote in the *North East Passage*, 'and it was so beautifully done that I blushed and lowered my eyes the first time I saw it. You would have thought I was on my honeymoon.' On the wall over the desk were two poems in English, reproduced in embroidered letters.

> The stars are with the voyager
> Wherever he may sail
> The moon is constant to her time
> The sun will never fail.
> But follow, follow round the world
> The green earth and the sea
> So love is with the lover's heart
> Wherever he may be.

Oh yes, he was on his honeymoon. The bride was present in his heart, in his red cabin and in the ship which he had painted – shining white. The journey had two geographic goals: the North Pole and London.

Maud steamed out of Tromsø on 16 July, on Roald Amundsen's forty-seventh birthday. Two days later the expedition waved farewell to a festive Vardø. Having left the Norwegian coast Amundsen was sincerely afraid that the research vessel would be 'sunk by German pirates'. But they soon reached peaceful waters, beyond the reach of the Kaiser.

From Khabarovo, east of Novaya Zemlya, the expedition sent post home, one month after having left Norway. The Governor hired a tenth man, a 21-year-old Russian-Norwegian who would assist engineer Sundbeck. 'His name is Olonkin,' the polar explorer wrote home to the manager. There was no hurry to inform anyone of his Christian name. Next bulletin arrived a few weeks later from Dickinson Island. Telegrams were sent too, but the station was not able to receive signals *from* Norway.

A year passed. A disastrous year.

Maud passed Cape Chelyuskin, Asia's northernmost point on 9 September, twenty-five years to the day after *Fram* had passed that way. So far so good, the ship was on course. But soon she was caught by the ice and was forced to seek shelter for the winter. 'The nook we chose,' the polar explorer wrote to Leon, 'or rather the only ice-free lead [channel], was a tiny notch on the north coast of the Chelyuskin Peninsula, 21 nautical miles from the north cape. This nook we christened Maudhavn.'

Having been icebound for a year they prepared to dispatch post from *Maud*. The postal departure brought forebodings of internal dissolution. Roald Amundsen wrote to Leon: 'I am sending Tessem home under the pretext of carrying the post. The real reason is that he has a bad head and suffers long periods of melancholy.'

As Tessem's companion the Governor pinpointed another problematic case which he was keen to rid himself of, Emanuel Tønnesen. 'The Tønnesen case is different. I am dismissing him for negligence and rudeness, which the attached communication, an extract from the diary, will prove. I ask you to keep this communication in case he decides to make trouble on his return and in that case use it all. If he behaves well, then let him be. He is a young, silly boy, who needs a few more years until he is fit for anything.'

The big row with young Tønnesen erupted towards the end of June 1919. With its roots in a few discarded lumps of coal, a furious bickering had developed between the Governor and the disrespectful 26-year-old. In the meantime, before the letter to Leon had been completed, Tønnesen had returned to favour. 'He is at heart a good boy and I am loath to lose him.' In spite of Tønnesen having sinned against the first commandment on board, Thou shalt not show insubordination towards the Governor, he remained a harmless young boy, devoid of any feelings for authority. When, in addition, he appeared to repent of his sins, the Governor could afford to temper justice with mercy. In no way was Tønnesen a rebel in the Johansen mould.

So who would accompany Tessem southwards? The Governor had already pencilled in Paul Knudsen. When he broached the question at the dinner table and Knudsen volunteered, the matter was settled. In the middle of September the two left Maudhavn and made their way south to the nearest telegraph station. They were both experienced hunters, took six dogs with them and were well equipped. Notwithstanding all the safety precautions, their departure from *Maud* was the start of a tragedy and a mystery which would cause Roald Amundsen a lot of worry.

The letter to Leon was accompanied by the first part of a manuscript for the book which was later called *The North East Passage*. The polar explorer's 'most urgent wish' is to instruct Leon how the income from the book is to be invested in order that the brothers and Betty are financially secure: 'This is a gift I donate to them in my lifetime and has nothing to do with my will. Make sure that the two items are kept separate.'

In so doing, the polar explorer makes it clear that he made his will before departure. As it favours neither the brothers nor the nanny an outsider must be the beneficiary. 'All income from the book I want you to put in your name,' he writes to Leon, 'in order that that sum will not have anything to do with what I leave.'

Roald Amundsen had already started to fear that he would not survive the *Maud* expedition. He was suffering from a guilty conscience; those nearest to him could not all support themselves, while his will, allegedly, was written as a gesture to benefit someone who was already abundantly provided for. In addition: 'Should I not survive, do what you can for Hanssen & Wisting. I would also like to reward Rønne & Sundbeck, but especially the first two.' The polar explorer is not preparing for the expedition's downfall, but for his own, private death.

The same postal dispatch contained a letter from Roald Amundsen to his physician, Dr Roll in Christiana. It contained a case history full of drama and starts immediately following arrival in Maudhavn. 'On 30 September 1918, I fell from the rail down onto the ice and broke my right upper arm in at least two places. Firstly just over the elbow joint and secondly just under the shoulder joint. Wisting, who has had considerable instruction in the treatment of such cases, bandaged me. With the exception of 14 days of severe cramp in the surrounding muscles, it all went well. Five weeks later – I was supposed to have worn the bandage for another week – I got caught up with a polar bear on the ice and fell flat on my face. I managed to get away from its claws and got on board.' The bear was, at the very last moment, distracted by 'Jacob' the dog and shot by 'Dr' Wisting.

Yet a third near-death occurrence in the first six months aboard *Maud* was added to the case history, this time from the buried magnetic observatory. 'There was no ventilation. We obtained light and heat from a 100 Luxlampe (petroleum). After a time during observations I noticed that I was short of breath. I never paid any attention to this until 10 December when I suddenly felt I needed to pay heed. My breathing was shallow and my pulse was racing, not under 150. I had to stop working and run out into the open air. My legs would not carry me but I managed to get over to the vessel, about 200 metres away.'

Roald Amundsen thought he might have been fallen victim to poisoning. During the winter heart, breathing and pulse troubled him. 'Can you find out about this? Might the broken arm, the encounter with the bear and the choking affair have detrimentally affected my heart? Personally, I fear that might be the case, but am trying to persuade myself that it is all nerves.' In conclusion the polar explorer admitted to his doctor that he was suffering from insomnia. 'Otherwise all is well here in the prison; food, drink, light and fuel for many years.' In other words, he lacked for nothing, bar happiness.

Dr Roll was prevented from diagnosing his patient; for the time being he would have to leave that to his local colleague, tinsmith Wisting. Later the polar explorer would take advice about his Siberian illness from several doctors. Something was wrong with the polar explorer's heart. But what?

Roald Amundsen revisited the problem in *My Life as a Polar Explorer*. Here he added a new dimension to the 'encounter with a bear'. 'It has always been told me that when a person stands face to face with certain death – as I did when I lay under the bear – that his whole life passes in front of his mind's eye. I never thought of anything so serious or important, lying there and waiting to be struck down. I lay there and wondered how many hairpins were swept up off the pavements of Regent Street in London on a Monday morning. The significance of this pathetic thought in this, one of the most dangerous moments of my life, I leave to the psychologist to decide, but this personal experience regarding mortal mind's extraordinary characteristics under stress has never ceased to interest me.'

'What would Freud have said?' Doctor Otto Kratter from Florø asked this question as soon as he had read Amundsen's autobiography. On 31 January 1928, he received an answer from Vienna.

Honourable colleague,

Your quotation is really very interesting. Amundsen's extraordinary thought at the moment of death must have some explanation. Unfortunately it would be necessary to ask the brave polar explorer what his associations are. Without that all one can say is that the thought shows that Amundsen had given up all hope of rescue and sees his life as valueless. How the detachment has expressed itself in this form would be interesting to ascertain by analysing him. Yours very sincerely,

Freud.

Doctor Kratter, who himself practised psychoanalysis, tried many years later to unravel the problem based on available biographical information. In vain he looked for the key which connected the imperial capital to hairpins – female adornments, lost props.

It was a wounded Roald Amundsen who emerged from the first wintering by the Siberian coast. The proud polar explorer was reduced to a travelling convalescent. He had already given up plans to leave the ship like Nansen once did. Before departure preparations had been made to establish depots at Cape Columbia on the north tip of Greenland. The plan was to complete a sledge-expedition over the North Pole to Greenland. Suspecting nothing, Leon worked in Christiania, to position the supplies. Their old ally Godfred Hansen had been appointed to carry out the assignment. As yet he knew nothing of *Maud*'s pathetic progress nor that the polar explorer's cabin had been transformed into a sick-bay.

Roald Amundsen was battered but not broken. Deep down he was restless. He actually envied Tessem and Knudsen the day they left. 'I long to go south and hear news,' he had written in the letter to Leon.

Halfway through September *Maud* succeeded in breaking loose from the ice and continuing eastwards. But ere the month was out the expedition was forced to seek new winter quarters. As it was impossible to sail north, the ship moored next to Aion Island, between the New Siberian Islands and the Bering Strait. Dejection spread; it was unavoidable. Is this an expedition to the North Pole or banishment to Siberia?

'Have today dismissed Rønne and Tønnesen and told them they can go home,' the Governor wrote in his diary on 26 September. They both got a piece of his mind. 'Rønne is an agitator, who makes mischief behind one's back. Tønnesen is a stupid little boy who cannot bear that one is nice to him without behaving in a disrespectful and anti-social manner. It is important to rid oneself of all harmful elements before we leave this world for good.'

Martin Rønne had already several times appeared obviously drunk. During dark hours the sail-maker was gripped by an uncontrollable urge to drink spirits from a coffee cup, for like *Fram* on the trip south *Maud* was carrying abundant supplies of alcohol. But now as then rationing was strictly enforced. Even such fellows as Lindstrøm and Johansen had had to adjust to the Governor's tyranny of temperance. Nevertheless, it was the *agitator* Rønne and not the *alcoholic* Rønne who was dismissed.

On 1 December 1919 Wisting and Hanssen set out on the long journey to Nome by the Bering Strait. A new postal dispatch is en route from *Maud*; Tønnesen will be taken home to where he belongs – civilisation. Rønne is allowed to stay; he is restored to favour. Anyhow, he would never have survived the trip.

On 4 December 1919, messages of peace reached the Norwegian colony. A year after the German capitulation a roving Russian gave Amundsen the latest news of world events. The next day he wrote in his diary: 'We have celebrated and flown the flags on the occasion of the Kaiser's flight. Hopefully his scoundrel of a son – the ghastly crown prince – has followed his father into exile.' The polar explorer's hatred was uncompromising and he extended it to the next generation. A few months later unconfirmed information reached him regarding the arch-enemy's fate. 'There are rumours, so I am told, that Wilhelm, the German murderer, has been confined to a desert island, like Napoleon in his time. Too lenient a punishment for that monster.' Unfortunately, at that very moment, the Kaiser was safe and sound in a castle in the middle of civilised Holland. It was the polar explorer who found himself on a 'desert island'. How unfair the world could be for someone who knew better.

The cuisine was not what it was on board *Maud*. For want of Lindstrøm the Governor wanted to 'hire a yellow or black cook. The coloured are better fitted for that work than us white. Now we have no permanent cook and that's a bore,' he wrote in a serial letter to Leon. Rønne, the jack of all trades, was useless. As no one else felt at home in the galley, the Governor decided to try his hand. He took pride in his new profession and quickly outdid the Lindstrømian hot cakes with his own brand of breakfast roll. 'Governor and cook sounds funny,' he noted with some satisfaction in the New Year, 'but does after all represent the two most important jobs on a journey such as this.' It does not bode well for scientific yields.

But the Governor had in no way shelved the scientific work. At the end of May 1920 he adopted a tiny polar bear cub and christened it 'Marie'. Who was Marie? Maybe a childhood sweet-heart from Hvidsten or Christiania – or was that the name of the Belgian woman? Was her name Marie? Roald Amundsen never named something without a reason. He was a dreamer, but no poet.

With the bear cub the Hagenbeck animal experiments could resume. The Governor single-handedly took charge of the training. It was necessary to win the animal's trust. His diary: 'The relationship me/Marie is getting better every day.' But unfortunately, after a month he came into contact with the bear's paw and was forced to give up the beast. 'Chloroformed "Marie" to death this morning.' Not to say thereby that Hagenbeck's theories had been disproved. 'In the experienced hands of an animal trainer it might have become well-behaved, but I had to give it up,' he concluded humbly.

After more than six months, on 14 June 1920, Hanssen and Wisting returned to *Maud*. The journey had been difficult, but they had rid themselves of Tønnesen and brought a telegram to the Governor from Leon. They had not quite reached Nome in Alaska, but the telegrams were sent from Anadyr via the Bering Sea.

Only now was it clear to Roald Amundsen that Tessem and Knudsen had not returned to Norway. When Hanssen for some reason did not answer Leon's telegraphic question regarding the two, the Governor sat down and wrote: 'Very soon after the expedition had left Norway Tessem started suffering from ill humour. It was so bad that just before Christmas I had to reprimand him and ask for an explanation. He said then that he did not feel he was strong enough for this journey. I asked if he wanted to go home. To that he answered that there was nothing he would rather. I considered the journey from Maudhavn to the telegraph station at Dickson and from there on home to be without danger – owing to the many depots Sverdrup put out in 1915. *Solely as an excuse for this return I thought of the necessity of sending post home.* He needed of course a companion and Knudsen was the most obvious choice as the one who had accompanied Sverdrup on his depot journey.'

In his letter to Leon the polar explorer put forward the first of many theories as to why the two had not yet returned to Norway or to the telegraph station on Dickson Island. It was based on 'a solid stone dwelling' the two had built near Maudhavn where he thought they quite simply had wintered in order to hunt polar bear. In that case there was no mercy: 'Should they have undertaken such a dereliction of duty they must get no recognition. In that case you must destroy my letter to the King asking for Order of Merit for the two.' The Governor felt sorry for the families 'who must be so worried', but he had no doubt that the two bear hunters would turn up.

On the other hand, young Tønnesen had clawed his way back to civilisation via Nome. He saw no reason for returning to his native country for the time being. But to Norwegian authorities in New York he leaked confidential information about the state of the *Maud* expedition which was telegraphed back to Norway. Among other things he talked about the 'meeting with the bear' and the Governor's illness: 'Amundsen aged a lot not allowed to use spirits coffee tea tobacco mood apparently always rock-bottom'. The general state of things was not much better: 'Relationship crew not good all like Amundsen not Helmer Hanssen'.

Even aboard *Maud* Tønnesen had maintained that it was the skipper and the first officer, Wisting, not the Governor, who had wanted to get rid of him. This did not entirely tally as far as Amundsen was concerned, but the statement indicated that Skipper Hanssen's position on board was not a bed of roses. Maybe the Governor continued to favour his comrade from the proud exploits of the South Pole and the North West Passage.

TWENTY-SEVEN

Ring-billed Gulls

The Arctic Ocean explorer Helmer Hanssen never quite understood what business he was on when one day at the end of March 1920 he reached Anadyr on the uttermost edge of infinite Siberia. Anadyr could hardly be associated with either the Kaiser or the Bolsheviks; it lay beyond all state control. But it was nevertheless in this world. Anadyr had a telegraph station. Helmer Hanssen, the messenger of love, was there.

In addition to press and business telegrams a private message was sent to Leon Amundsen from Roald: 'Inform elizabeth our arrival in nome alaska end july this year all well love signed roald amundsen'.

Even before Hanssen and Wisting's departure from *Maud* on 1 December 1919, the Governor had decided to stop by Nome before again tackling the Arctic Ocean. On arrival in Anadyr, eighteen months had elapsed since the last contact with the outside world. That is a long time for a bridegroom without a bride.

Connection between Anadyr and the rest of the world was complicated in the extreme. It took ten days for Helmer Hanssen to receive an answer from Leon Amundsen in Christiania. Tessem and Knudsen had not reached Norway. But the telegram contained more news. In words which Helmer Hanssen was not qualified to decipher, the telegram related the last decisive news about Kristine Elisabeth Bennett.

This was the message with which Helmer Hanssen returned to *Maud*. On 25 June, ten days after Wisting and Hanssen's return, the Governor raised the question, for the first time, regarding who wanted to leave the expedition on arrival in Nome. To Leon he wrote: 'A few days ago I told the boys that legally I was of course within my rights to keep them on board and make them accompany the expedition when it departed Nome. But morally I decided that I did not have the right. I therefore chose to go by the unwritten law and let them choose freely between staying or going ashore.'

The Governor immediately noted the result in his diary: 'Hanssen said right away that he wished to leave in Nome. He has not felt well, is tired and weary, and I understand him well. Rønne too will want to go home. He is too old anyhow. The others have not yet decided.'

The tone is compassionate, although Hanssen's weakened condition is a bit of a surprise. A week later the Governor, in a comprehensive letter to the manager, gave an altogether different version of the skipper's departure. 'I have been dissatisfied with H for a long time. He has behaved badly. He does not give a damn about my advice and often answers me back in front of everyone. I made a big mistake, when I made him skipper on board. It went to his head and at the same time he was not qualified for the job. I recently had a long talk with him and made it clear that he *had* to take his leave. If not I would dismiss him. This hurt us both. But the continuation of this expedition must be according to experiences gained and feelings thrown overboard. He has made himself unpopular with everyone on board and if we are to have peace he must go.'

The meeting with the crew was purely for the sake of appearances. It must be realised that Amundsen's expedition diaries are private only to a certain extent; they were above all written as the basis for what would become the official account. In a letter to the old *Gjøa* crew member Peder Ristvedt one year later, Amundsen's comments on the skipper's dismissal were entirely in line with his letter to Leon: 'Well, as you know, I lost Hanssen. It was my fault Ristvedt. I thought I might be able to do something for my old travel companion, by making him skipper of *Maud*. I wish I had never done it.'

Roald Amundsen was probably right: it had been a mistake to promote a hunter from the Arctic Ocean to captain of the scientific research ship *Maud*. The mistake was made because Amundsen valued one quality above all others: loyalty. Helmer had accompanied his leader through the North West Passage and to the South Pole; he was zealous and hard-working and had shown more humility than anyone else. But six years had elapsed between *Fram*'s homecoming and *Maud*'s departure – six years of splendour and glory – and even the most sophisticated subject could turn cocky from so much homage.

An honest representation of Skipper Hanssen's dismissal would put an intolerable strain on both the *Maud* expedition and Amundsen personally. Helmer Hanssen himself, whose entire reputation was based on his cooperation with Roald Amundsen, had nothing to gain either. So, the skipper walked the plank voluntarily.

With his generous offer of liberty Roald Amundsen had rid himself of two men he anyhow would have dismissed. 'Rønne has deteriorated a lot and is suffering from rheumatism so I am sending the two of them home from Nome,' he wrote to Leon.

But then, on 4 July, the unexpected happens. The diary: 'Sbeck has given his notice. "He's homesick". Deserter, that's what he is.' Knut Sundbeck, the

engineer who had once saved *Fram*'s engine, and who at the start of the voyage
Amundsen considered 'a genius', on a par with Lindstrøm himself, asked to be
released. To Leon: 'Yesterday Sbeck came crying to me and said he wanted to
go home. "He was disheartened." I never expected this. He knows himself he
is irreplaceable – most of all in Nome. I am treating his departure as a cowardly
flight. I would not even think of preventing him from leaving.' This was the
unexpected price the Governor had to pay for the charade he had enacted about
individual freedom and moral rights.

There was an obvious line of demarcation between the voluntary and
allegedly voluntary departure. Thus any future treatment was also shaded. 'I
will pay for Rønne and Hanssen's homeward passage,' the Governor wrote to
the manager, 'but under no circumstances will I pay for healthy Sbeck. He goes
with all my contempt. He's no man, that's for sure. I don't have a lot of respect
for Hanssen either, as you can see. On the other hand, Rønne is poorly and not
fit to go on. If you can show him some kindness, please do. Do not make any
fuss about the Messrs. return. The quicker they are forgotten and out of mind
the better.'

To escape any more misunderstandings about the notion of freedom and
morals, the Governor turned the question upside down. 'At breakfast this
morning I asked who was willing to follow me out of Nome. Sverdrup, Wisting
and Olonkin answered that they would accompany me under all circumstances,'
he wrote in his diary on 5 June. 'We have achieved nothing yet. We will only
show what we are worth when we depart Nome, but then they all put their tails
between their legs and run. What a disgrace!'

It is not to overstate the case to say that the *Maud* expedition, and its four
remaining members, had fallen apart. In his pithy summing up the Governor
himself gave an explanation. In two years the expedition had done 'nothing'.
That was an exaggeration, certainly as far as Sverdrup was concerned, but still:
none of the goals had been reached. The journey in fact stood at a new beginning,
and as such it was natural for the leader to leave it to the crew's discretion.
Nevertheless, it was conspicuous that in all six men, willingly or not, left the
unhappy ship. And they forsook Roald Amundsen. Only two of the original crew
were left.

Roald Amundsen had not been capable of inspiring his men throughout two long
winters. He had overcome his physical sufferings, but his thoughts were not on
board. The Governor was pulled between two poles. It could not have been easy
for his men to follow him.

Roald Amundsen had never been an easy man to follow. In the past it had
been the Governor who sowed discord and dissatisfaction. On the *Maud* it

appears that he played a more withdrawn role, never taking part in card games but rather sitting silently reading a book in the lounge or in his cabin with the framed poem. But the Governor had never been the unifying, social centre of attraction, either in Gjøahavn or Framheim. That role had been allocated to Adolf Henrik Lindstrøm. 'Send Lindstrøm my best wishes,' Roald wrote to Leon, 'and tell him I've never missed him as much as I do now.' He wrote this with the cook in mind, but Lindstrøm was more than cook. He was the chubby, good-natured stabilising force. He represented well-being on board. He transformed the windswept outposts into cosy little homes; Lindstrøm was the house-mother of polar exploration – easy to ignore, impossible to replace.

A total of only three crew decided to follow the Governor. 'Mark those three, who have decided to follow me under all and every condition and do their duty to the last,' he wrote to Leon in the tones of a general about to commit himself to his last battle. What were the motives of the three?

It was clear-cut for Gannadi Olonkin. The young boy had more or less been rescued out of a Russia starved and ravaged by revolution. Existence on board *Maud* was safe. And every month the expedition manager sent home 200 crowns to his Norwegian mother and Russian father in Murmansk. To young Olonkin, the *Maud* was fate's stroke of good luck – a happy ship. The Governor appreciated the expressionless but willing Russian, although in time he too would show signs of insubordination. Olonkin was actually a telegraph operator but up until then had not succeeded in establishing a wireless connection between *Maud* and the outside world. Amundsen had hired him to assist Sundbeck. Following the chief engineer's 'flight' Olonkin was left holding the baby.

In contrast to Olonkin, Harald Ulrik Sverdrup was initially a man of many talents. His education was first class and he was descended from one of Norway's leading families. As meteorologist and oceanographer he was the expedition's most important man. Or in other words: the expedition's entire scientific profiling rested on his shoulders. When all else failed he had devoted himself to ethnological research among the Chukchen in Siberia. Thus the expedition, so far, was not entirely without scientific results. This work meant that he spent less time on board than anyone else.

The 32-year-old scientist was disappointed at not having been able to utilise his expertise. But he saw it as his duty, as long as he was physically able, to remain at his post. He understood that he really had no alternative. If he left the expedition he would probably forfeit his reputation at home. Dr Sverdrup's work was independent of Roald Amundsen and his position clearly defined. The scientist chose to endow the Governor with absolute power. He was both humble and self-aware; moreover, his intellectual capacity allowed him to view both the expedition and Roald Amundsen from a wider perspective. Even if everything else evolved unsatisfactorily, he would do his best for his own sake and that of science.

Roald Amundsen's portrayal of the third member carried absolute validity. Oscar Wisting followed his general like a brave soldier – if necessary to the end.

And what about the Governor himself? The expedition could look back on two useless years, and possible an infinity of years ahead. Ought he not admit defeat and go ashore? In his long letter to Leon he wrote: 'If only I were well, I would have closed my eyes to all this unpleasantness, but I'm actually the one who should be going home. My heart is not what it was and does not allow me to rush around. I try to overcome it to the best of my ability, but as you know, the cold, lack of sunlight and all the responsibility will soon take their toll.'

This sounds more like a death wish than a go-ahead spirit. There was anyhow not much left of the legendary optimism. The polar explorer's health was a convenient alibi, should he need it. His actual work was to lead the push to the North Pole. This type of 'rushing around' demanded first-class fitness; when it was absent the conclusions were obvious. He 'should be going home'.

Home to what?

'Oh well, honestly I prefer to stay out here rather than return to the unchanged conditions which appear to reign, according to your telegram, in London. Anyhow, I say with the French: *Le vin est tilé, il faut le boire*. I'll just have to fight it out, whatever the results.' Roald Amundsen was no longer able to suppress his self-pity. The honeymoon had been turned into a death-voyage.

What was in the telegram from Leon? What was the message Helmer Hanssen had brought back all the way from Anadyr? It can't have been long-winded, but Leon must have chosen the words – presumably as usual – with precision and discretion. Enough to clarify the polar explorer's further journey into the ice.

That the 'conditions in London were unchanged', cannot be taken in a literal sense. On the contrary, conditions *had* changed, and for the worse, as far as Roald Amundsen was concerned, for the better for Mrs Bennett. Leon's informer in London was the omnipresent diplomat, Herman Gade.

Following *Maud*'s departure the polar explorer's unceasing efforts on behalf of his best friend had at last borne fruit. Herman Gade had been appointed Norwegian Minister in Rio de Janeiro. That was probably not the place-name the polar explorer had whispered into the Prime Minister's ear, but it was a start. Herman Gade had a title, a job and a uniform of which he was worthy. That is not to say that the enterprising man was weather-bound and sat around waiting for the next carnival to happen. In the New Year of 1920 he was in London.

'Many thanks for your kind letter from London and its content which of course is of special interest,' Roald Amundsen wrote to Herman Gade; 'I hope you had a later opportunity to meet the person concerned and that I might expect to hear more from you again.' The letter is dated 9 February 1920. Two months later the conclusion was passed on via Anadyr. What sort of information 'of special interest' could the diplomat impart even before he had met 'the person concerned'?

It was clear for all to see. Charles Peto Bennett had presented his wife with a new house. The house in question was a huge villa, a manor house surrounded by a large estate near Cobham in picturesque Surrey. The house was called Leigh Court. It had a tennis court and formal gardens but lay close to the centre of Empire and the world. A dream house for a dream woman.

This had more the character of renewed commitment than of an early break-up. From a marital point of view it all pointed towards 'unchanged conditions in London'. So much Leon could hint at via Anadyr.

He was imprisoned; the polar explorer and his poisoned lungs, and weakened heart, with a shortened arm that had been broken in two places, a back and a bottom showing long scars from a bear's claw. He was imprisoned; the bridegroom in his lonely bridal suite watching the white seagulls flapping over a red background – struck down by a telegram from Anadyr.

> So love is with the lover's heart
> Wherever he may be.

In the letter he sent his brother from Nome dated 5 August 1920, more than two years after his departure, Roald Amundsen wrote the following admission to his brother: 'I must tell you that before I departed from home I left Uranienborg to Kiss.' Leon Amundsen must have received this very belated message with astonished disbelief. In his brother's absence he administered both properties by the Bunnefjord. Besides, the properties made up a considerable part of Roald Amundsen's and therefore the *Maud* expedition's capital.

It is the thought that counts. 'I did it to make sure she had a home,' the polar explorer justified his generosity. The truth is that he had gambled all on the wheel of fortune – his years, his ship, his men . . . and his house. By giving away his home the polar explorer had cut off his line of retreat. As Nansen had once proclaimed: the west coast or death, so Amundsen now found himself in a cleft stick: the goddess of bliss or eternal exile. Thus he had acted and thus he must have felt it.

Had Roald Amundsen, in this game of happiness and tangible values, sacrificed his old nanny and his impoverished relatives for the benefit of an enormously rich lady?

He cannot mention one to Leon without immediately, for his own conscience's sake, mentioning the other. 'If I make enough money out of the book, I would like Betty to have 150 crowns a month. I would also like to help Malfr. & Gust.' All that remained for the nearest and dearest was the book.

The polar explorer had no doubt that the book would have more success than the actual journey. Bad luck that he could give such little time to his poetic talents: 'My job as cook has unfortunately prevented me from continuing my scribbling, but I am sending off my diaries, and you might get a clever chap, like Vilhelm Krag, to deal with it.' If only Tessem and Knudsen would appear soon with the missing chapters, 'which I am sure they will', the manuscript would, with a bit of poetic licence, reach 200,000 words.

Once again the wayward, semi-romantic author Vilhelm Krag is charged with salvaging the polar explorer's marathon of words.

A bird cried over the desolate sea, far from land.

When the literary raw material at last left Nome it was insured for no less than 300,000 crowns, roughly estimated at 1 crown per word; 100,000 for photographs and maps. Surely this was enough to safeguard Betty's old age and Gustav's future? With his book *The South Pole* the polar explorer had set records in the publishing world too. But there was just one drawback with the North East Passage: it had already been discovered. It was old hat. Everyone knew it ended at the Bering Strait.

The most sensational thing about the manuscript Roald Amundsen sent home was the dedication. His first book had been dedicated to 'Minister Dr Fridtjof Nansen'. The second one was dedicated to 'The brave little band, who on that evening in Funchal Roads, promised to stand by me in the battle for the South Pole'. On an otherwise empty page in his third book, *The North East Passage*, was the following inscription:

> To *the birthday child*.
> Maudhavn, Chelyuskin, 10 February 1919.
> Roald Amundsen

Into the chronicle of a national journey's place of honour the polar explorer inserts what looks like a cryptic message. With the stroke of a pen he changed the expedition's official report into a private birthday gift. A riddle for the people of

Norway, a party game for the world. Whose birthday, where, when and what was the connection with the North East Passage?

The very few in on the secret immediately understood that the solution could be found in London. The 10 February 1919 was the day Kristine Elisabeth Bennett celebrated her thirty-third birthday.

To put it mildly, the dedication was a strange move from a polar explorer who later would consider himself 'serious'. But it was in keeping with earlier expeditions. The *Gjøa* expedition was based on Fridtjof Nansen's prestige and support. The attack on the South Pole depended on the ship's loyal crew. The journey in *Maud* had its foundation in the battle for Kiss Bennett's heart.

The dedication was part of this battle. He gave her his all before he left. Now he gave her a place in history. Maybe he gave her the opportunity to stand forth, acknowledge the date, show her true colours and declare her great love for him. With a dedication he expected would be broadcast in every language, the polar explorer had pushed the relationship to the brink, and aimed his sword directly at the timber merchant's breast.

The book's preface, reproduced in Roald Amundsen's handwriting, was also dated 10 February 1919. One can safely interpret it as a speech to the birthday girl, as an untiring suitor's greetings from the barren coasts. 'Not with a shining victory behind us, which in its richness can afford to draw the veil of oblivion over the medal's reverse side and allow its polished face to appear; but with the infinitely long way towards the goal ahead of us, enveloped in the future's impenetrable cover. What lies beyond? Without doubt, victory and defeat, sorrow and joy, hope and disappointment.'

The mandolin player's long-suffering realism – 'yet broods the polar night' – is replaced by growing hope: 'But in the south we perceive a faint blush, as on the cheek of a young maiden, increasing in strength day by day. We know what it is. It is the sun, jubilant brandishing its torch, higher and higher, to bring life and light to the world. Welcome, blessed day. We have had our fill of night.' In truth, unfamiliar words from a man of action.

Roald Amundsen's direction is clear to him, even as he was dreaming his lyrical dreams. He had not lost the 'infinitely long way' from his sights. The goal was just not, as so many times previously, a geographic point. The goal was the real light. It was a state of mind, the day, happiness, love. It was not to be found in the cold, in the centre of the polar basin, but in the warmth, in the glow of thirty-three lights, with her. The goal was the birthday child.

The last few days before the approach to Nome Roald Amundsen was busy distributing the expedition's material yields. First of all the mother country: 'The mammoth-teeth and the extensive bird collection are a personal gift to the Norwegian state. They have not been collected by the expedition but bought by me and as such are my property.' Public transactions are often characterised as gifts, although the line of demarcation between expedition leader and private citizen is not always obvious.

A huge consignment was prepared; more than fifty crates. Among them forty polar bear pelts, sacks full of brown bear, white and arctic fox pelts, besides masses of handicrafts, worked on during the endless winters on board *Maud*.

'I would like all the furs, essentially the bear and fox furs, to be at Kiss's disposal.' There was talk of considerable sums; the management thereof was elaborated in the next letter to Leon. 'Make sure all the furs are well stored with a furrier, please, until such time as Kiss makes any decision.' Just like the house; at her disposal, full power of attorney, only the *decision* is lacking.

The polar explorer's pride was the bird collection which he had amassed that last spring, ten cases, plus one: 'In the bird collection there are 18 good specimens of the extremely rare ring-billed gull: *Larus rossi* and also 9 of the virtually unknown tundra gull: *Larus sabinii*. The value of these 27 birds alone cannot be ascertained. Real connoisseurs will probably find that they alone will pay for the expedition. It would not surprise me.' It will probably surprise the manager even more. Nevertheless, the gift from the polar explorer to the Norwegian state was truly a magnanimous one, too magnanimous.

'Apart from the already mentioned 18 – official ring-billed gulls – I am also sending a case with 20 of the same. The case is marked with no. 100. Take them out and hide them away immediately.' The line between donations to the state and feathers for a strictly private nest was a sensitive one.

'I have written to Kiss and told her how she is to use them. I want her to get the best people in London to make 2 fans from their marvellous plumage. One is for her, the other I would like you to present to the Queen in memory of *Maud*'s voyage through the North East Passage. I would like you at the same time to inform her from which birds the feathers have been taken.'

Twenty birds equals two fans, one for each queen. They can hide behind the ring-billed gull, the shy Queen Maud, the secret Queen Elisabeth.

As more pieces in the puzzle reveal the full picture, so much more does the journey with *Maud* appear the journey of a dreamer, like a ship launched on illusions. On departure from Norway Roald Amundsen had thrown the mandolin away and gambled all on happiness. Sure of reaching his goal and winning his bride, he had set out on an anticipated honeymoon. Not only had he given his 'future wife' a home, but out there in the icebound wilds he had worked unceasingly to secure her material existence.

Are we dealing with a fearless lover who has the courage to gamble all for love on a grand scale? Or is it all a pathetic expression of a confused man's diminishing sense of reality – testimony to a clouded mind?

On one point Roald Amundsen was clearly about to lose his grip on reality, most obviously regarding his expectation of income. The income from the book, which normally would be part of the expedition's earnings, was donated to a sort of family trust, with a completely unrealistic hope of numbers sold. The bartered gulls might have been worth twenty to thirty crowns each, or maybe 50,000, who knows? Wishful thinking seems to compensate for a rather traumatic reality.

As far as happiness was concerned the illusions had been badly shaken. The telegram from London put things in their place; where they belonged, in London. However, he still clung to a *decision* which he would not admit to himself had been made long ago.

Roald Amundsen did not give up. He was back at the beginning – in his hunt for the North Pole and the Goddess. His heart was damaged, his men had left him, but he continued on the only course he knew. The polar explorer returned to the icy wilds; he wanted to 'battle it out'.

He sends a flight of gulls home. And he deposits fifty polar bear pelts at her feet.

TWENTY-EIGHT

Kakonita Amundsen

'As I moored the ship,' Roald Amundsen wrote in his diary after having passed the Bering Strait, 'I succeeded in uniting the North East Passage with the North West Passage from 1906 and so for the first time completed the circumnavigation of the Arctic Ocean. In this era of records it might be significant.'

This was a poor consolation at the end of an unsuccessful North Pole expedition, an attempt to give meaning to the meaningless. The discovery of the North West Passage was in itself of no practical value. But as an achievement, as an expression of bravery, it was indisputable. *Gjøa* was first, while Nordenskiöld's *Vega* had travelled the North East Passage more than forty years before Amundsen. A thing can only be discovered once. *Maud* was apparently number three.

When the Norwegian had succeeded in uniting the two Passages, this link-up was by virtue of his person. The ships and the journeys were separate; Roald Amundsen was the same, the only human to have circumnavigated the Arctic Ocean, of course, if we forget Helmer Hanssen. He was a record on his own.

Having passed the Straits which not only separated two continents but also two ideologies, the Governor arrived in Nome in Alaska on 29 July 1920, on board a tug. He dispatched his telegrams without much fuss. A few days later *Maud* arrived and anchored up in the shallows outside Nome.

The stop-over in civilisation was short. To save time Amundsen gave his local assistant, the Norwegian-born goldmine-owner Jafet Lindberg, who would be handling the shipping of the expedition goods, the task of reporting to the manager. The same Lindberg also took charge of the three signed-off crew members. It was clear that the Governor had not presented them in the most flattering light. 'Everyone here felt that the men who left the Captain were shirking their duty,' Lindberg wrote.

Roald Amundsen had now decided that he could ill afford to pay for their homeward journey. The opinion in Nome was that under no circumstances would it be 'fair' to pay their retreat. Consequently Lindberg had to employ them, which proved difficult as 'no one could use these three men, since they were considered traitors, if not wimps.' The sole solution was to employ them in the mines. But the only one who would put up with gold-digging was the 50-year-old skipper Hanssen. In the end the three managed to contact Norwegian authorities, and after an agonising month as dishonourable citizens of Nome they set out on the long journey home via Seattle and ultimately the *Hellig Olav* over the Atlantic.

In a letter of complaint to the expedition Lawyer Alexander Nansen, the rheumatic Martin Rønne described the stay in the gold-mining town as follows:

As you know we landed in Nome without a cent in our pockets only referred to Lindberg who was going to employ us in the mines to work for our return and the wages to our families stopped and no help in Nome from someone who called themselves Norwegian Consul, a private man helped us with telegrams home and answer and help came after 23 days, when I stepped ashore from Maud suffering from sciatica and refused to work in the mines as I could not possibly manage such work and stand in water all day and walked around from the 8th of August to the 8th of September I had no other solution but to sell my clothes in order to live and Sundbæk had to do the same. Hanssen was in the mines a few days until his clothes and shoes were worn out.

In truth, a sorry signing-off for the former South Pole heroes.

Before the infamous three disappeared, Lindberg had received supplementary information about the Tessem–Knudsen mystery. 'From what I understand, not only from the Captain, but from those who left him there, these two men had good reasons for not wanting to return home just now.' Yet another veiled hint at culpable affairs among the crew on board the unhappy ship *Maud*.

During his short stay in Nome Roald Amundsen accommodated himself in Lindberg's house. The host, who was also party to Tønnesen's disheartening tale when he had passed through Nome, was astonished to meet an energetic polar explorer, completely on a par with the Amundsen who had arrived in town fourteen years earlier having sailed through the North West Passage. Lindberg's doctor too, following a thorough examination, could confirm that the polar explorer was in 'perfect' condition, physically and mentally. Either Dr tinsmith Wisting's treatment was unusually effective, or the patient's ailments really were subject to nerves, as he himself insinuated in the letter to Dr Roll.

The polar explorer's revived spirits and renewed vigour when in the presence of civilisation must be interpreted as a result of the strong fluctuations in Roald

Amundsen's temperament. However much time he spent in isolation and solitude, he was nevertheless drawn to human intercourse. At last he was out of the depression's stagnation; the time had arrived to implement his plans: a new start and a new optimism.

Everything happened quickly in Nome. After only ten days *Maud* left the tiny Alaskan community surrounded by a handful of local vessels who bade them farewell. Amundsen did not even wait for post and supplies. No less than twenty-one cases and postbags were en route from Seattle to Nome, but the polar explorer had no time to lose. The most important provisions had been bought locally and the telegraph had transmitted the most delicate communications to the outside world. That must be enough. It's now or never; time to get away before the ice freezes over in the Bering Strait.

Besides, Captain Amundsen travelled with an irresponsibly small crew, and was obviously nervous that obstacles might have been put in his way. 'There was quite a lot of trouble, because there were only four of us, but it was the only way to get off,' he wrote to Leon one week later from East Cape by the Bering Strait. Even a thoughtful man like Dr Sverdrup seemed to have had his reservations. 'I am not entirely without anxiety for the future,' he wrote to his colleague, Professor Wilhelm Bjerknes. 'We are so few, and rather a motley lot.'

The Governor saw no reason for concern, in spite of obituaries lurking everywhere in these waters. 'Just tell them at home not to worry about us 4,' he admonished Leon. 'All is well. But of course things may go wrong and in that case tell the Norwegian government from me not to forget the 3 stalwart boys who stood by me.'

The only new crew the Governor signed on in Nome was the middle-aged Eskimo woman Mary, or 'Marry', according to the Governor's phonetic spelling. Luckily a separate tariff applied to locals, otherwise signing on new crew would have been too expensive. Mary's job was to cook and keep the ship in order. Incidentally, Helmer Hanssen had met her before departure and recognised 'Tuttsi' from his immodest wintering by Herschel Island fourteen years earlier. 'Well, good luck,' was the departing skipper's laconic comment.

In 1941, Helmer Hanssen, who lived until 1956, wrote his memoirs *Wrestling with Ice – Eighteen Years with Roald Amundsen*, which had been published in English a few years earlier under the more splendid title *Voyages of a Modern Viking*. In keeping with polar-literature traditions Hanssen chose to view the ups and downs of fate from a grand perspective. He felt no need to call the Governor or himself to account twenty years after his personal shipwreck as skipper of the *Maud*. It was a period filled with light and happy memories – a happy adventure from start to finish.

The day after leaving Alaska the polar ship was stopped by ice. Having been icebound at East Cape they proceeded at a snail's pace, but only managed a few miles further along the Siberian coast. *Maud* was soon squashed up against land near Cape Serdsje Kamen. They were, inevitably, embarking upon their third winter in the ice. Three winters, that was the time it had taken *Fram* to accomplish her proud traverse of the Arctic Ocean. That was the time it had taken *Gjøa* to traverse the North West Passage. After three years *Maud* had reached – nowhere.

They were again in Chukchi territory and associated with locals and commercial travellers. Otherwise spirits were kept up by simple means. The New Year of 1921 began with the popular sport from Framheim: 'Darts-throwing this evening with prizes; very successful,' the Captain noted in his diary. 'Everyone happy.'

It was time for the small occasions and the lesser mortals in the life of the great hero. Even before the New Year was a week old the very smallest participant in the polar explorer's biography made its entry on board *Maud*.

Apart from the Eskimo woman Mary, alias Tuttsi, who after a while suffered from serious mental problems and was taken off to relatives on land, the Governor signed on several natives to do odd jobs on board. One of them was a young man called Kakot. One pitch-black night he brought a tiny bundle to the ship.

On 4 January the Governor wrote: 'I have treated Kakonetta – Kakot's little four-year-old daughter. Lay her stark naked on the dining table, washed her with permanganate. Her whole body is covered in eczema – large sores.' The sick, dirty and hungry Chukchi child had no mother. It was allowed to live with its father on board the ship.

After a few weeks the bundle started to exhibit a personality. There was no land to discover, no important observations to tackle. The polar explorer's diary was full of the ups and downs of life. 'She is a funny little girl – terribly ugly – terribly naughty, but absolutely hilarious. We vie with each other to spoil her. She goes everywhere and is incredibly useful with her four years. Her whole body is washed every evening. When that is done and her hair has been combed she comes out to the galley to show off to "grandpa".' Kakonita has discovered the key word.

The polar explorer was in the throes of melting. After years spent in darkness and cold, after years among polar bears and rough men, where the female element had been reduced to a framed poem on a cabin wall, a child suddenly emerged from the cold and called him 'grandpa'.

At the end of February Kakot left to find a new wife. When the courtship appeared to be bearing fruit the Governor drew his own conclusions. 'I have on this occasion adopted Kakonita. I am fond of her and do not want to see her in the hands of a step-mother. I am working continuously on her rash. I rub her with flour morning and evening and it is looking good.' The polar explorer powders and kneads and puts all his energy into the new job. And he was rewarded. 'Kakonita, my little foster child is devoted to me,' he wrote at the end of March. 'I think she loves her grand-daddy.'

Kakot's new marriage was a passing affair, but there was no doubt about Kakonita's status as the polar explorer's foster child. Even in Gjøahavn he had been busying himself with the idea of adopting an Eskimo child. But the adoption of Kakonita was no well-founded or experimental act: it was an emotional reaction, a personal alliance. Kakonita toddled straight into the polar explorer's frost-bitten heart. One quiet day in March he wrote: 'I am here alone without a single person to talk to – except for little Kakonita. She understands me better than the others.' The 4-year-old filled an empty place in the ageing man's inner being.

Conditions were different with the second Chukchi girl Roald Amundsen adopted. She was virtually 'requisitioned' in order that Kakonita would have a 'colleague' by her side when entering her new life in civilisation. For some time the expedition had been in contact with the trader Charlie Carpendale from East Cape. He was an Australian, but married to a native woman. The Governor's trusted man Oscar Wisting visited him one day in April. This day would be a pivotal day for one of the girls in the family of nine.

Amundsen wrote on 19 April: 'This afternoon at about 4 Wisting arrived back from East Cape with one of Carpendale's daughters. She is a thoroughly sweet girl, quiet and calm and very pretty. About 10 years old. It is my intention to send her home with Kakonita and educate them both. The rascal little Nita has taken over completely, but it appears to be going well. The older girl is very calm and no doubt will go along with Kakonita.'

The younger girl was closest to the polar explorer, which is clear from the fact that he gave her his family name, Kakonita Amundsen. The older girl already has a civilised surname, but the Christian name needed to be adjusted: 'I have called little Miss Carpendale – she is actually quite big for her age – Camilla. This is as close as I can come to her Chukchi name. Translated her name means "little cunt". That might be OK; however, my friends might feel slightly uneasy when I introduce her.'

A few weeks later the Governor announced a 'third foster daughter. She is about 12 and a servant with our friend Tenak. She is typically Chukchi to look at, a bit more Japanese blood than Chinese.' This last mixture quickly disappears from the polar explorer's rapidly accelerating family chronicle.

Roald Amundsen admired primitive peoples, their lifestyle and abilities. Nevertheless, they were subject to a different set of standards from the inhabitants of civilisation. He might be tender and devoted, but he was at the same time the omnipotent ruler, master of life and death, a conqueror after the old school. The Governor had introduced capital punishment in Gjøahavn, at least as a threat. A note from the *Maud* diary shows that he would not flinch from the ultimate solution either 'if necessary'.

It was extraordinary how Roald Amundsen, during this last and apparently most hopeless winter on board *Maud*, built up a go-ahead spirit. The ship was totally icebound but in human terms he appeared to move out of stagnation. He overcame his physical problems. He had rid himself of the major part of his crew and thereby the disruptive elements on board. Once Sverdrup and Wisting had set out on a sledge journey which lasted most of the winter he was in fact the only Norwegian on board. Intercourse with the subservient nomads suited his sociable power-hungry nature; the confidence gave his feelings free rein.

In a way he achieved a sense of an inner stability with regard to his relationship with Kiss. He had dispatched his birthday present, morning gift and allowance. For the moment he could do no more. He would have to leave the rest to the published word, the plucked birds and tanned bears. Instead of nerve-wracking brooding in his cabin he washed and powdered a real live little girl on the dining table. And if the 48-year-old was no bridegroom, then at least he was a grandfather.

When Roald Amundsen had departed on board the royal yacht *Maud* his primary purpose had been *to return* – 'via London'. It was taken for granted that it would be via the North Pole. The ship's construction, the course across the sea, all were tested and feasible. He himself was polar exploration's chief player – the man who always succeeded. The fruits were there to gather in. Three dark years had taught him how high they were hanging. It was necessary to fight to reach them.

The North Pole was, according to the poet Bjørnstjerne Bjørnson, the 'jewel in the crown'. This was the jewel he must bring back and fasten on her breast. It was the only thing outstanding. The introverted romantic lets go; the athlete awakens.

His thoughts started to circle around new plans. He decided on a strategic withdrawal to Seattle, where the ship could undergo the necessary overhaul. He would apply to the government for more money. If successful he wanted 'two aeroplanes and experienced pilots, preferably an officer of the Norwegian Navy'. On 27 April the plan was ready. 'Never have we been keener to get under way than now.'

It was in the air. As soon as the world war was over in November 1918, both the British and Americans were planning aerial expeditions to the North Pole. But no one was closer to the goal than Roald Amundsen. His pilot's licence was in his pocket, he had *Maud*, which from being an outdistanced polar ship could be transformed into a cutting-edge aircraft carrier.

The polar explorer could hardly wait for the ice to let go its grip. He decided to leave the ship. Only one thing held him back: Kakonita.

On 25 May that problem too had been resolved. 'I have actually decided to take my little lambkin with me. I am very fond of her and she of me, so we would miss each other if we separate.' Of course Camilla had to come along too. So saying Roald Amundsen set off in a sledge with his two foster-daughters along the coast to East Cape. From there he hitched a ride on the whaler *Herman* through the Bering Strait to Nome. The vessel was actually en route in the opposite direction, but the skipper, from Sandefjord, gladly left off whaling to satisfy his great compatriot's wishes.

On 17 June the polar explorer was again ensconced in the gold-mining town of Nome. He dispatched a press release about *Maud*'s latest fiasco. And: 'Telegraph the government immediately requesting assistance – 300,000 crowns.'

On one of the last days in June 1921 the harassed but determined North Pole explorer Roald Amundsen boarded SS *Victoria*, the only ship which serviced the stretch Nome–Seattle, and then only in summer. The tall man was accompanied by two little figures. In spite of being partly or wholly descended from Siberian nomadic peoples, from henceforth they were known all over the world as Amundsen's 'Two Eskimo Girls'.

They were all three about to enter a harrowing phase of their lives. For the two little ones their world would be turned upside down; for the polar explorer it would whirl round and round. He had wasted three years; from now on there was not a minute to be lost.

Part Four: In Pursuit of the North Pole

TWENTY-NINE

The Flying Dutchman

'Rather than dwell on the past I might as well jump over into business concerning the future.' Thus wrote Roald Amundsen to Leon from SS *Victoria*. He added: 'I am assuming you will once again stand by me.'

Leon Amundsen was no longer a paper-boat millionaire. Following the collapse of the stock exchange he had fallen from the dizzy heights, albeit still standing on his feet and still worth 200,000 to 300,000 crowns. He, and especially his wife Aline, had been tempted to move back to France with their four children, but as so often before the family once again settled by the Bunnefjord. With regard to the two oldest brothers, Tonni and Busken, nothing had changed: a continuous production of new illusions culminating in lost hopes, dismissals, old debts and more cries for help.

Throughout the three years Leon had managed the *Maud* expedition's local business. That included information, finance and personnel. Although he immediately stopped payment of wages when told to do so, the manager did not share the Governor's condemnatory attitude towards the signed-off troops. In a letter to Gade he noted that 'it is quite understandable, as anyhow for married men [it] is a long time to be away from home.'

The paterfamilias Leon was sensitive to the human side of lengthy separations. An educated man like Dr Sverdrup found it natural to thank the business manager for this: 'In all letters from home I have been told how painstakingly you have kept those nearest to me informed about the expedition prior to their reading thereof in the newspaper and how you have placed manuscripts, photographs, etc. at their disposal. They have all appreciated this enormously.'

In the letter from SS *Victoria* the polar explorer issued instructions for what must be considered a new expedition, or at least a new start. 'I need a list as soon as possible regarding tinned food for ten men for four years'; moreover: 'five tonnes clip-fish (dog-food), twenty goats' cheeses, twenty Roquefort and twenty mature brown cheeses, 500 bottles juice', not to forget a telegraph station and '2 aeroplanes'. Crew required included an engineer and a pilot. 'Otherwise I'll use only natives.' All must be ready for departure from Seattle in the spring of 1922.

To top it all he ordered 'dispatch' of Mrs Wisting. 'I promised Wisting this, as a small thank-you.' It might not have been the romance of the century, but the jack of all trades from Horten might well have suffered a fit of romantic fervour after three years in the Arctic Ocean.

On the other hand the polar explorer gave notice that 'a few other things' will be sent home. 'My two little girls will cause the most stir.' He outlined a plan for the children's future. First Camilla, whom he estimated to be 12 years old. 'I would like her to be educated in such a way that, when she returns home in five years, she will be capable of helping her compatriots up there. What is needed above all is cleanliness and the understanding thereof. She is clever and will grasp it quickly. The other one, Kakonita, is "my own little girl". Don't get me wrong, her father gave her to me.' It would be different for her. 'A sweeter little girl you cannot find in this world. I consider she is mine completely, so she must always be at home.'

The actual foster-parents will turn out to be Leon and his wife Aline, as of course he will not be home for many years. 'Nita loves grand-daddy,' he wrote, 'but she will get over it when she no longer sees me.' The polar explorer has learnt from experience.

SS *Victoria* arrived in Seattle on the afternoon of 2 July 1921. The town was a centre of trade and communication in a state of rapid expansion. It was surrounded by beautiful countryside, next to the Pacific Ocean and close to the Canadian border. The town had 300,000 inhabitants and contrasted starkly with what the polar explorer had experienced of windblown settlements during the past three years. In this jungle of civilisation he established his base for the next year, far removed from old fixed points. His only companions were two children descended from a Siberian nomadic people. The polar explorer telegraphed Leon and asked him to dispatch a suitcase with clothes.

On arrival in Seattle Roald Amundsen brought his *Maud* diary to a close. But first he recorded eight telegrams from Europe. Five were business communications, of which one was from *Aftenposten*'s editor, and one from Prime Minister Blehr. Besides: '2 telegrams from K, one from G & R'. The two last initials stand for Gudrun and Robert Maus. We know the K; it was the only time it made an appearance in the course of three meticulous books, covering three long years. An expedition diary was no safe place for a traveller's intimate thoughts.

What was Roald Amundsen's actual intention in respect of the temporary withdrawal to Seattle? 'It is not desire which forces me to return to the ice, but duty.' Thus he wrote to Leon and added: 'Nansen is no doubt right in his theory regarding the currents; it's a matter of finding the correct place of entry.' After three dark years and total exhaustion of funds, was he still driven by his old promise to the Professor? Or could he not abide the thought that *Maud* had completely failed where Nansen and *Fram* reaped their greatest triumphs?

After three weeks in Seattle Roald Amundsen wrote to Trygve Gudde in Trondheim. This letter did not even mention Nansen's theories; to Kiss Bennett's brother he can reveal far more of his mind's whirlpool: 'Here I am again, a counterpart to the Flying Dutchman, doomed to lifelong travels in the Arctic Ocean. I should really be feeling depressed but don't – as things stand. The point is that there is nothing for me at home. So I might as well spend a few more years in the ice, far removed from foxtrot and fisticuffs.'

The polar explorer's history was the history of a homeless person. He could return home; the sitting rooms and bedrooms were empty and waiting. But mentally his home was the ice. It was not duty that was driving Roald Amundsen, but rather restlessness. He was a man without an anchor, a drifting ship, the Flying Dutchman.

The approaching journey was also a way of maintaining self-respect – a chivalrous act. Not for him to upset the idyll at Leigh Court. 'I have had many messages from K,' he concluded his letter to Gudde. 'I cannot tell you how happy I am to know she is in beautiful surroundings in the country. She says her boys have grown and are well. Thank God. She has suffered a lot in life, now she has happiness.'

The ring-billed gulls never arrived in London. When Leon informed him of practical complications, new instructions arrived from Seattle: 'If fans impossible divide into two. Give one to the Queen and hang the other one up in Uranienborg, preferably under glass.' They would hang there, love's winged messengers, stuffed, under glass, in Uranienborg's empty rooms. They are there today – a few strange birds in a glass case, in Roald Amundsen's museum.

Roald Amundsen quickly made new acquaintances in Seattle. The famous Norwegian had no problems in gaining an entrée into the large Scandinavian colony. He was immediately received by the well-to-do business man Einar Beyer from Bergen who offered him 'his own large, splendid and beautifully situated house'.

After ten days in Seattle all doors were open to the homeless Arctic Ocean explorer. Generous friends and new colleagues offered their services: 'Am seeing a lot of Hammer, a Dane.' This is the first time that name is mentioned.

Later on Leon received a more detailed description of his brother's new, intimate supporter, the broad-shouldered, probably 33-year-old shipbroker Haakon H. Hammer, 'son of Commander Hammer of the Danish Navy and married to a German lady, Baroness "Pumpernickel". He has stood by me in everything here; given me my own comfortable little office with an assistant and entire office personnel. He has been outstanding and must get a St Olav [order of] when he gets home. He has saved me and will save me from many expenses. He is the head of a firm here called: the Universal Shipping & Trading Co. He is my friend, secretary, advisor, etc.'

The polar explorer requested that some of the facts regarding his new 'agent' be passed on to the newspapers back home. All supporters of the national hero in foreign ports were entitled to publicity and the admiration of the man in the street – besides St Olav. 'Hammer himself is one of Seattle's most respected citizens. He has mighty influence in the world of business as well as in the social world. R. A. could not find a better or cleverer advisor and assistant.' Roald Amundsen had found his saviour; the *Maud* expedition its deliverer. The parallel to Dr Cook was ever more striking.

The polar explorer emerged from years among simple nomadic people, and was completely blinded by the wonders of the business community: 'I simply do not know what I would have done without him. The Norwegians are kind enough but seem to lack many of Hammer's qualities. Besides, he is a thoroughly educated man.' Icing on the cake was his friendship with the two Danish Princes, Aage and Axel, who turned up in Seattle during a visit to the United States.

His luck was about to change. On 19 July he received a message that Parliament had granted him up to 500,000 crowns for the *Maud* expedition's further fitting out. Ere summer was over the polar ship arrived in Seattle under its own steam. Time had come for long overdue repairs. In a letter to Professor Bjerknes, Sverdrup summed up the scientific results: 'Misfortune followed upon misfortune; two years have been lost.' However, after a year's stay among American academics Sverdrup too regains some of his optimism.

Two days after *Maud* Mrs Wisting arrived, as ordered. They all moved into the Governor's magnificent house. Time was spent on circus visits and automobile excursions. Chauffeurs were the educated Dane and the Governor himself. Two cars were needed for the entire crew including Eskimo children, the housewife from Horten and picnic paraphernalia. As he waited for his aeroplanes the polar explorer bought a car.

While propeller and other important parts were replaced on the ship, the four polar explorers underwent expensive dental treatment; replacement was virtually 100 per cent. 'Have extracted our teeth and replaced with gold', the Governor reported home. 'My mouth looks like a true Klondike man's – unfortunately.' In addition his heart and broken arm were given an overhaul. The arm was an inch shorter. That apart he was unbelievably fit. 'An unusual and extremely interesting case, according to the doctors.'

The Governor was happy to see his loyal men in Seattle, but so much the more irritated when he received a message that the three signed-off men travelled home at the government's expense. 'That Hanssen, Rønne & Sundbeck are refunded – a single penny – is a blow in the face to us 4,' he wrote to Leon. 'To mollycoddle them like that is an outrage. They are deserters and nothing better.' The Governor's stifled hatred of the three was emphasised when he forbade the manager to send them a free copy of the *North East Passage*, an account of which they were all part and in which Helmer Hanssen's sledge-journey diaries to Anadyr constituted an important contribution.

The entire autumn the expedition's domestic representatives were forced to associate with the 'deserters' who themselves felt shoddily treated. But they were no less preoccupied with the Tessem–Knudsen mystery. Earlier in the year a search party was dispatched, without the Governor having much faith that the 'oaf' would achieve anything. If anything, he himself would rather make the trip to Siberia with Wisting to try and solve the 'puzzle'. Moreover, Wisting had a theory which Amundsen thought was 'reasonable', and which he propounded in a letter to Leon. 'Tessem often suffered from black moods. He would tolerate *nothing*. Knudsen was extremely long-suffering but when he got angry he was furious. Wisting thinks that a tragedy has taken place. To me, at the moment that appears the only solution. *Do not talk to anyone about this*.'

During the spring of 1922 a message was received that the search party had found some Norwegian-made objects and the remains of a burnt body in the ashes of a large fire; one had cremated the other. As the body was unidentifiable a memorial stone was erected to both of them. During the summer of 1922 a Russian expedition made another discovery: among other things they found two waterproof post bags, one addressed to Director Bauer at the Magnetic Institute in Washington, the other to Leon Amundsen, Christiania. Latterly they stumbled over a partly eaten body near Dickson Island. On the inside of the man's wedding ring was the inscription: 'Your Pauline'. It was Tessem. The find was made public in the winter of 1923.

To Roald Amundsen the Arctic Ocean set the standard. After Leon had hired the new crew's first pilot he hedged his bets in spite of the 'slave contract' tone being quite obvious: 'You must make it absolutely clear to him that he must – without any whingeing – do all I ask: shift dog-shit and much more in the same vein.'

The fact that the polar explorer had ordered two aeroplanes did not inspire much confidence among the home-grown scientific milieu where the expedition sought financial support. Via a telegram Roald Amundsen had refused to strengthen the scientific participation; he preferred another jack of all trades.

To the polar explorer this particular jack of all trades was about to metamorphose into something of a human ideal – the man who knows everything, does everything – who obeys every order 'without any whingeing'.

The Governor had decided to double the pay to 400 crowns per month for his three faithful men; the newly hired would remain on 200 crowns. 'Curiosity must still be the driving force.' While the Russian and the man from Horten kept things going in Seattle, Sverdrup, the PhD jack of all trades, had established himself at the university in Washington where he soon announced his engagement to an American lady. At last luck was smiling on science.

The polar explorer had originally decided to send his foster-daughters to Europe accompanied by the childless couple shipbroker Hammer and Mrs Baroness, but after much deliberation Mrs Gunner Wisting was assigned the task instead.

In every letter home the polar explorer gave Leon instructions on how to handle the girls: 'You must buy them "outdoor shoes" and their feet must be kept dry, besides they must never be chastised but treated in a loving manner.' He imagined Kakonita and old Betty playing card games at Uranienborg. With regards to Camilla, he had discovered a new talent. 'She is both beautiful and gracious, so dance might be something for her. She loves dancing and thinks of nothing else. I have put their names down for dancing-school. If Camilla is really talented she can continue her education at the Ballet School in Copenhagen.'

Suddenly, just before Christmas, the polar explorer made a decision regarding himself. He wanted to call on 'Sir Alex Mackenzie – the world's most distinguished heart specialist. The examinations here have not been satisfactory,' he wrote to Leon. 'It is possible that Mackenzie can advise me. I think the effect of the long, dark winters will be the worst. He might give me some medicine.' And where must the polar explorer travel to for this excellent advice and wonder-cure for his 'sick heart'? To London, of course.

As the contact had in no way been broken it is reasonable to believe that it was Kiss who had broached the matter of the heart specialist. This was the excuse he needed. In several letters he had asked the continuously roving Gade to visit her at her new 'estate in Surrey, where it is supposedly so delightful'. But why be satisfied with a second-hand account when he can travel and see for himself the unobtainable delights?

With that, a party of four – two children, two grown-ups, to all intents and purposes a whole little family – left Seattle as soon as the Christmas festivities had come to an end. An unusual anecdote attached itself to the *Maud* expedition's Christmas celebrations in Seattle, in connection with Oscar Wisting's Christmas present.

In the book *Roald Amundsen as He Really Was*, the author Odd Arnesen gives a detailed account of how, in absolute secrecy, Amundsen smuggled the longed-for wife from Horten over to Seattle. And then, in best show-biz style, on Christmas Eve itself: 'Suddenly the sliding doors to the dining room are pushed aside, and – Wisting could not believe his own eyes. There was his wife, large as life, standing beside Amundsen. Amundsen smiles good-naturedly, unites the two and enjoys his little triumph. That is how he was.'

Greater still was Mrs Wisting's surprise when she read the story about the Christmas present in a newspaper in the spring of 1922. 'Tell me, can the papers write what they think and what they want?', Elise Wisting asked the manager in a letter. 'The bit about Wisting's Christmas present is a lie from start to finish.'

The story was, as Mrs Wisting quite correctly pointed out, a 'lie', but in its entirety a true product of the polar explorer's style, in both its cosy execution and scenic effects. The newspaper report was accompanied by a well-informed tribute to the loyal Wisting, composed entirely after the Amundsen spirit. The jack of all trades from Horten was to be presented as the national hero's kind-hearted supporter – a worthy heir to the treacherous Helmer Hanssen. In the service of a much larger cause, the wife would have to put up with playing the role as the polar explorer's 'little triumph' in this otherwise sombre year of defeats.

THIRTY

Engelbregt Gravning

On the whole the plan behind the *Maud* expedition remained the same. In principle it was still about the third *Fram* expedition. They were in Seattle for the purpose of being fitted out for a fourth attempt to drift across the Arctic Ocean.

In Christiania Leon Amundsen had engaged the pilots Lieutenant Oskar Omdal and Sergeant Odd Dahl. The Army Air Corps had placed two Sopwith Camels at the expedition's disposal. Together with a telegraph station they would constitute the expedition's new accessories. But none of these new elements represented a new plan. The planes would operate from the ice around the polar ship, primarily for reconnaissance, and this would contribute towards increased public interest in the expedition.

It was after Roald Amundsen's departure from Seattle on 5 January 1922, heading for London, that a new idea took shape; the captain took mental leave of the ship; Roald Amundsen made the final leap from the old to the new era.

When he departed, he left *Maud* in the care of Oscar Wisting and his business in the hands of Haakon H. Hammer.

The polar explorer arrived in New York accompanied by two Eskimo girls (their ethnic transformation was now complete) and a middle-aged lady from Horten. Without knowing any better, one might think they were any old couple who had fallen victim to a whimsical double mutation. But one did know better. The polar explorer's exotic companions created a considerable stir in the sensation-starved town of skyscrapers. 'The interest around the two little ones was enormous,' he wrote later to Don Pedro. 'The North West Passage, the South Pole, and North East Passage cannot measure up to this. Our hotel was besieged all day.'

On 13 January Mrs Wisting and the two igloo-girls boarded the *Stavangerfjord*. 'It was hard to part from the little ones,' Amundsen wrote to Hammer. Or rather: the polar explorer had now tasted enough family life to address his agent and deputy in Seattle as 'Uncle Haakon', just as the little girls did. And as if that were not enough, he expected the shipbroker to sign his letters 'Uncle Haakon'.

As soon as the trio had left the metropolis Roald Amundsen booked into the Ritz-Carlton Hotel – 'my dear old Ritz'. It was time for business. His first visit concerned the audible supplies. 'We went out and paid old Edison a visit yesterday. He is apparently sending the expedition a gramophone and 300 records. We now have three and that should do.' Then it was the turn of the aeroplane.

Roald Amundsen reported to Leon: 'In New York I happened upon an aeroplane which will stay in the air for at least 26 hours. It would be of great significance to get hold of it. It is expensive, 15,000 dollars, but will pay for itself many times over. We will be able to leave the ship already the second year, fly over the Pole, right across unknown landmasses and reach inhabited places.'

The new plan was progressing rapidly. It only remained for Leon to finish off the transaction. 'Mr Henry Woodhouse [President, the Aerial League of America] in New York knows all about it. Telegraph him please and order a "Larsen aeroplane" of the type we agreed upon, if they can be in flying condition by 15 April.'

Rarely had Roald Amundsen attached so much importance to his camouflage as during this return to Europe. Even before his passage, he disguised himself with a new name, fake beard and horn-rimmed spectacles. To rubber stamp his new identity he paid a visit to the Norwegian authorities in Washington. On 19 January, two days before departure, he wrote to 'Uncle Haakon': 'I got my papers in Washington, all in perfect order. Engelbregt Gravning travels as a special envoy of the Norwegian government and he has access everywhere!'

On 30 January 1922 Engelbregt Gravning booked into the Strand Palace Hotel in London. The camouflaged polar explorer arrived in the Empire's capital at about the same time as the news of Sir Ernest Shackleton's death was broadcast. His heart gave out in South Georgia just as he was about to embark upon his third Antarctic expedition. Sir Ernest was buried in Grytviken, in the private chapel of the Norwegian whaler C.A. Larsen.

No newspaper could report Roald Amundsen's heart-felt response to his colleague's death, as the Norwegian, in those days, was not in evidence. There was no South Pole conqueror in America, in Norway or in London. But in a letter addressed to 'Uncle Haakon', dated London 2. 2. 1922, Engelbregt Gravning gave vent to his feelings: 'Sad about Shackleton, how is Wisting?'

It was precisely his heart which had brought the polar explorer to the centre of Empire. Dutifully he paid a few visits to the famous specialist; the doctor composed a long report bristling with diagrams but barely managed to catch the patient's interest. After all, Amundsen had made the diagnosis ages ago. His heart was suffering 'from long, dark winters'. For him, smog-filled London in winter was a town of sunshine and summer. Here was his medicine, a short train trip out in the country.

Oh yes, the manor house Leigh Court certainly outshone his bachelor pad by the Bunnefjord. The imposing three-storey brick pile lay among shady trees at the end of a long drive. The building was English country-house style, all recesses and tall white windows; ivy-clad with a brownish-red façade. Behind the house lawns sloped down in terraces. Kiss was mistress of all she surveyed. While old Bennett wheels and deals and visits his club in London she can take walks through forest and field, property her husband had bought up for miles around. Tea was served from a silver salver on the lawn; every Sunday there was champagne 'after church'. There were enough servants: three in the house, three in the kitchen and three in the garden. In addition a chauffeur, in charge of the master's old, faithful Rolls-Royce.

In addition, after a short trip by train or car through the beautiful Surrey countryside, she can step out into the pulsating, intoxicating air of London. Kiss loved the healthy country life, she loved being the centre of attention, at cafés, dinners, balls. Her cup runneth over; what she did not have could be ordered and delivered to the door.

The timber merchant had truly presented Kiss with a residence worthy of a queen. In such an environment the polar explorer was not king; rather, an interesting and romantic guest – a wandering minstrel, his voice full of passionate but well-tried ballads. His name and glory conferred on the rustic riches an aura of adventure.

The polar explorer was back at the Goddess's window. He had hoped they might travel together back to Norway. Not as polar explorer and wife, but at least as Engelbregt Gravning and the timber merchant's wife – with the utmost discretion. That was supposedly why the camouflage was so important.

On 10 February he wrote to Leon: 'I'm afraid the programme has changed slightly. Kiss is prevented from travelling, so I'll wait until Friday 24 February. Am home Monday 27.' Prevented – she had always been prevented; prevented from leaving her sons, prevented from marrying another man. Maybe it was this 'prevented' which riled and challenged someone who was not otherwise accustomed to accepting obstacles of any kind.

The Norwegian government's 'special envoy' had otherwise not much to occupy him in London. His heart was with the specialist, *Maud* was with Wisting and Hammer, the purchase of planes rested with Leon. He asked himself: has the manager fully understood the importance of the new element? 'As already indicated, they will be more important to the expedition's economic profits than anything else. With them we can actually *all the time* fly to and from *Maud*. You know, it will add a few crowns to the tally if we are the first to fly over the

Pole,' he wrote to Leon. In the same letter he organised his arrival in Christiania. 'Please make sure that I can go directly home to Uranienborg. As already indicated, I will stay in my cabin throughout the crossing and will wear blue glasses on disembarkation.'

The polar explorer's return one Monday in March followed the pattern of the South Pole return. The camouflage had become a habit, a convenience. But it all told the story of a man who was loath to sacrifice his freedom of action by surrendering to the public. In Seattle he had watched another general, the French war hero Marshal Foch, on his triumphal parade through town. 'Poor man,' he wrote to Leon, 'I felt for him. He looked like a caged animal, who has surrendered to fate.'

For a successful general the endless parades were a necessary part of his duty. Roald Amundsen did not want to submit to society's expectations like Ferdinand Foch or – closer to home – Fridtjof Nansen. He was not prepared to take on duties other than the ones he imposed on himself. He avoided capture, he was supreme and independent. In that way he might catch people unawares and dazzle, but in addition he gave the impression of a man who was hiding something.

In a letter to Gudrun and Robert Maus the polar explorer explained his disguise by the fact that he 'wanted to avoid being saddled with the newspapers. Anyhow,' he added, 'I do not want them to know where I came from.' He came from London. And he had something to hide. Like most men who have been visiting a married woman, he had an unaccountable sense of having a guilty conscience.

'The little girls are thriving here in the lovely fresh air and send their very best wishes to Aunt Adelheide and Uncle Haakon,' the polar explorer wrote to his agent in Seattle. For the few weeks at Svartskog he devoted his efforts to playing grandpa to his two Siberian daughters. The situation in Seattle was entirely entrusted to Hammer whom he 'without the smallest hesitation' wants to promote to the expedition's 'managing director'. 'I have come to trust you implicitly and value your wise judgement,' he assured the Danish-Norwegian during his long absence.

While the little girls attended school and mixed with the blond children of Svartskog the polar explorer had plenty of time to ponder his new plans, associated with the far-ranging aeroplanes which Leon had order from New York. The two brothers sit together, isolated by the Bunnefjord; ice covered the fjord and there was still snow on the ground. The hills leading down to the two villas were so steep no one would willingly drive down them in winter. Two formidable St Bernard dogs, carrying the romantic names Romeo and

Juliet, guarded Uranienborg. No one knew that Mr Gravning was sitting by the Bunnefjord and was in fact Roald Amundsen. Only Leon knew his plans for the North Pole. But it reminded one of the South Pole, when the strategy was laid down thirteen years previously. They composed a declaration which was put into an envelope and sealed. Leon took charge of it.

Only on the day of departure, 17 March 1922, could the citizens of Christiania read long interviews with the polar explorer who had been visiting his native country for the first time since the summer of 1918. The crowd of people who came to take their farewell of the SS *Stavangerfjord* was larger than usual. But the national hero was nowhere to be seen; he had already gone on board at nine in the morning.

At half-past ten he received Gudrun and Robert Maus for a private visit in his cabin. He was able to convey greetings from the sister in England. Roald Amundsen's relationship to Kiss Bennett's family in Norway was virtually one of an 'in-law' – friend of the grown-ups and 'kind-hearted' uncle to the children.

Mrs Bennett hardly represented the sort of solution to his brother's private life that Leon would have wished for. His own wife was a strong and principled woman. They would both like to see the polar explorer established with a spouse and children in the neighbouring house by the Bunnefjord.

When the SS *Stavangerfjord* slipped her anchor at midday the crowd glimpsed Roald Amundsen on the bridge. 'He had thrown off his overcoat and received the cheers bare-headed,' wrote the reporter from *Dagbladet*. 'Now everyone recognised the sharp, distinct face. More ovations rose up to him and while the band played "Norway, Thine is Our Devotion" he waved his last farewell to the town.' At last, his native country got a glimpse of its great son.

'Well, that was a nice departure,' he wrote with contented irony to Leon from the ship. 'The polar explorer waves from the bridge's highest elevation and hopeful youth shouts its approval from below. If everything else fits in like that, all will be well.' Once outside Norwegian coastal waters the transatlantic liner made its way between boats of contraband which encircled the country in this time of prohibition, then turned west out over the ocean.

Among the twenty-two names on the first-class passenger list was that of Omdal, Oskar – Christiania. The pilot was in place. Only the wings were missing.

'Everyone here is of the opinion that the Larsen plane is superior to all others for long flights,' Roald Amundsen wrote to Leon after arriving in New York. In addition to his long-distance plane he had, quite surprisingly, acquired another 'delightful aeroplane – new with instruments and wireless delivered in Seattle – by Curtiss. It can stay up for seven hours. Now have one spare so will see if

I can sell it. If not I'll send it home to the Army.' In truth, progress by leaps and bounds. Yesterday's most advanced model is tomorrow fit only for the army rear guard.

Roald Amundsen wanted to fly his large plane, which was really a German Junkers, delivered by the Danish-American dealer Larsen, via four stop-overs, from the East Coast to Seattle. Pilots and mechanics included two Americans; besides Lieutenant Omdal, the very brave passenger Horace Gade (Herman's younger brother) and the Governor himself. The story of this flight soon circulated around the world via newspaper columns.

Roald Amundsen gave his own version in a letter to his brother dated 12 April, having returned safely to the Ritz in New York. The accident happened on the very first day:

> At half past two in the afternoon about 125 miles from Cleveland the engine – the 3rd cylinder – overheated and everything seized up! We were about 6,000 feet in the air. Nothing else to do but glide down looking all the time for a safe place to land. But we were in an unsuitable place for emergency landing. Just a tiny open space. We rapidly circled towards this. It didn't take long. As we brushed the road we took the top off a tree and landed with an awful bump. I think we must have jumped 10 metres in the air again, on the huge rubber tyres and solid springs, and then rushed at 50 miles an hour along the ground, passed between two huge tree-roots and hit in the end a third huge root which resulted in us being thrown into the air, turning a somersault and landing on our heads. If the plane had been less solid we would all have been mincemeat. As it was we got away with a few bumps and bruises. Horace and I are stiff front and back. It might be our age.

With that the middle-aged acrobat was weather-bound in the Ritz, waiting for a new engine. '"Elisabeth" was 100% insured,' he wrote reassuringly to 'Uncle Haakon'.

Elisabeth. Before it crashed the plane had been christened. In his book about Amundsen Odd Arnesen mentions that the plane had been christened at the Curtiss airport with a bottle of champagne. In that case we must assume that both planes were christened at the same time. The 'delightful' little aeroplane was a gift from the manufacturer Curtiss. Nothing was more natural than that two planes shared one woman's name; the other one was called *Kristine*.

To the *Maud* crew, according to Odd Dahl, the Governor insisted that the name written in big letters on the Curtiss plane was the name of an old aunt. The polar explorer had developed great subtlety in the art of pulling wool over people's eyes. None of his men knew anything about Kristine

Elisabeth Bennett. The North Pole explorer was still under the illusion that she would stand forth and claim her place in history the day he brought her the victory jewel.

During his enforced stay in New York the restless explorer happened upon another 'even larger' Junkers plane. Two specimens were sitting in the customs shed. With the difference of $2,000 he bagged one of them as a replacement for the once so 'superior', now totally wrecked, Larsen plane. As indicated: flying was progressing by leaps and bounds. He kept the name; the new Junkers was called *Elisabeth*.

In the end the airman took the train. He no longer had any time to waste.

At last, at the beginning of May Roald Amundsen was back at the expedition base, Seattle. He gathered the new *Maud* crew together. The new engineer Syvertsen was a 'brilliant' man. A certain Eriksen, however, the Governor demanded be 'sent packing' immediately. 'His behaviour towards Wisting shows that he is incompetent.' Wisting set the standard for how a man should behave. From now on not only would the Governor be respected and honoured; the same deference belonged to the most loyal of the loyal, Oscar Wisting.

At the last moment the Governor agreed to take on a scientific assistant to Dr Sverdrup. The Swedish Master of Science, Finn Malmgren, was ordered post haste to Seattle. With that, science was compensated for the flying jacks of all trades. Although, one can never be certain. 'I'll kick him on the spot, if he makes any demands,' the Governor informed the manager.

Following a year spent in academia the newly engaged Dr Sverdrup once again viewed the future cheerfully. He had received instructions regarding the scientific journey from Professor Bjerknes in Christiania. 'Above all "Maud" must provide the temperature of the polar-cap, on the surface and in the air. Hopefully you will be able to make good use of the kites. On the other hand, for obvious reasons, I do not encourage exaggerated use of the aeroplanes for scientific purposes.' The Professor was still at the kite stage. Oh well, the academic circles could potter around doing their own thing. *Maud* was equipped for all and every age.

The skipper Karl Hansen, the pilots Omdal and Dahl arrived in Seattle too. In addition, to the surprise of some, a third pilot turned up. The Governor had hired a Canadian officer in New York. He had already been swapped for a compatriot, a Lieutenant Fullerton. While the whole crew were obliged to put their hands to odd jobs, the Canadian was treated like a guest on board. According to Odd Dahl's memoirs neither he nor Omdal had at this stage any idea of the Governor's actual plans. The man from Horten was the only one who, prior to departure from Seattle, would receive the necessary information.

Including Olonkin, who had been helping Wisting during *Maud*'s victualling, and the anticipated body of Chukchins, the expedition was complete. Or more precisely: one more member would be added. On 26 May the polar explorer reported to the business manager: 'Gave a dinner yesterday for Hammer. Very successful. Informed all the guests of his Knight of St Olav [slightly premature] and "Honorary Member of the Expedition". Presented him with a diploma. He considers that even better than the St Olav.'

The last weeks before departure the expedition got itself into liquidation problems. Together with his saviour and 'Uncle', Haakon H. Hammer, the polar explorer tried to improvise a few lucrative lectures. When that did not succeed there was only one solution – Don Pedro. To be on the safe side, before his departure from Norway, Roald Amundsen had written to his far-off patron and briefed him about the plans regarding the aeroplanes. 'I know this sounds rather fantastic, but I am sure it can be done. We possess, reportedly, the leading role in polar research, at sea and on land. Let us also try to acquire it in the air.'

Just before departure the expedition received, telegraphically, $6,000 from the Argentine. The polar explorer heaved a long sigh of relief. 'He is in truth a friend,' he wrote to Leon. 'God be with him,' wrote Don Pedro.

In the very last days five enormous crates arrived containing the two dismantled and securely packaged planes. They were loaded aboard the already crammed polar ship which was now ready for its fourth attempt at crossing the Arctic Ocean. On Saturday 3 June 1922 *Maud* sailed out from Seattle. A marine band struck up. 'Norway, Thine is Our Devotion' could be heard all over the boat. Captain Wisting was in command. No national hero waved from the bridge.

The Governor left Seattle that same day, but on a different ship. Rather than spend several weeks on board the lurching, overloaded polar ship, he preferred to make the first stage to Nome on board the passenger ship SS *Victoria*. A few more days in a civilised environment wouldn't harm anyone. The long-established steam ship had at its disposal six en suite cabins, of which one was allocated to the gentleman whose title was discoverer of the South Pole, conqueror of the North West Passage and sailor through the North East Passage – now en route to the North Pole.

Roald Amundsen's biographical details will be changed by someone he meets on board SS *Victoria*. It might not be destiny, but it is at least – a woman.

THIRTY-ONE

A Beauty from Alaska

Roald Amundsen lived a life in hiding. He was drawn towards what might be called 'his hidden self'. He mapped some of the world's last unknown territories. But he laid a smokescreen over his own life. He played hide-and-seek with his contemporaries and erased his footprints from history.

The most secretive area of the polar explorer's life was that relating to women. His relationship to the one who would define so many of his options and constitute such an important chapter of his life – Kristine Elisabeth Bennett – was entirely unknown outside his most intimate family circle. The woman who above all and almost invisibly was identified with Roald Amundsen's life was, on the other hand, an unknown American. By complete coincidence she was mentioned in *Aftenposten* in 1941, then by Harald U. Sverdrup in an unpublished biographical sketch dating from the end of the 1940s. She is given more substance in Odd Dahl's memoirs from 1981. Dahl does not mention her by name either, calling her only 'the mysterious Lady'.

Ever since the winterings in *Maud* and the big dream of conquering Kiss had had to be buried in the sepulchre of his heart, Roald Amundsen had thrown himself into more or less manic activity. His human relationships oscillated between unreserved confidences and brusque rejection.

During the final winter aboard *Maud* a need for new emotional attachments was emerging. It started carefully, tested with the polar bear cub Marie, which after a few weeks of increasing affection quickly became the victim of chloroform. He graduated to little Kakonita, to whom he gave his name and, until further notice, life-long allegiance. Immediately after arrival in Seattle he abandoned himself to the exuberant business connection of 'Uncle Haakon'. With the broad Danish-American and his aristocratic Pumpernickel 'Aunt Adelheide' and his two adopted daughters he had in a short period of time created a 'pretend family', a family in which everyone was fond of 'grand-daddy'.

On the other hand, in a most despicable way, he had dissociated himself from several of his most loyal men, his colleagues through hardship and tough years.

He threatened his new men with dismissal even before they had joined up. This unstable element had always been visible in the ambitious explorer's character, but it came increasingly to the fore after his heart's deepfreeze and the collapse of his amorous illusions.

In spite of adversity and altered circumstance, Roald Amundsen held on to Kiss as he held on to the North Pole. These were his two goals, inextricably connected to each other. There was only one Pole left to conquer; on the other hand, there were plenty of women.

The polar explorer probably met Bess Magids for the first time during this trip on board SS *Victoria*. A letter exists where she briefly gives an account of her relationship with Roald Amundsen. It is written to a Norwegian-American couple and dated as late as 7 May 1968. In this letter, the only known document in which she herself confirms the relationship, she mentions the meeting on the journey to Nome on board *Victoria*. Although her most important appearance in Roald Amundsen's life occurs later, we will give here as accurate a picture as possible of 'the mysterious Lady'.

Her name was Bess, she was very beautiful and five feet four inches tall; her hair was short and dark; her eyes have been described as 'chocolate-crème'. Her background, like her life, was colourful and thus not always characterised by exact information.

Bess was born in Winnipeg in Canada, the youngest of a large family. Her full name was Elizabeth Patricia Berger. Her father, a cattle and horse dealer, was born in Strasbourg in Alsace. Her mother was, allegedly, from Kiev. The young beauty married young, so young that, according to what she told her daughters, she had to lie about her age. Her husband was Samuel Magids; she was only sixteen, going on eighteen.

Sam Magids was a Russian-born Jew. He was probably a few years older than her and about to establish himself as a businessman. Together with his brother Boris (born 1891) he built up one of the largest commercial under-takings in Alaska: Magids Brothers. The brothers, who had apparently acquired their start-up capital during the gold rush, ran no less than eight trading stations in areas mainly inhabited by Eskimos and men prospecting for gold. The firm bought and sold its goods in Seattle, Chicago and San Francisco. The Magids couple spent time in New York and travelled to exotic places such as China and Russia.

Bess possessed a strong will and an energetic personality. She knew how to survive in widely different surroundings. Even among Eskimos and gold-miners she knew how to take care of her looks. Shoes and frocks were ordered and tailor-made by the most distinguished suppliers. Nevertheless, she took an active part in running the business and drove her dog team over long distances in Alaska, just like and as well as the brothers Sam and Boris. Besides, she was a passionate poker player, known for her high stakes and calm nerves.

One would assume that this rough princess from Alaska was tailor-made for someone like Roald Amundsen to marry. However, in the summer of 1922, in spite of being a mere 24, she had been married for eight years. Anyhow, his heart was already taken.

The journey along the Canadian and Alaskan coasts took ten to fourteen days – plenty of time for a light flirtation, well, enough even for a closer acquaintance. The polar explorer travelled alone – with a bath. The Arctic Ocean was ahead, Mrs Bennett was far away in a green garden under tall, shady trees, surrounded by family and friends. In his loneliness, here at the back of beyond, was he not permitted to catch the eye of a beautiful little lady with chocolate-brown eyes?

Was she alone? Or with Mr Magids? There is always a Mr somewhere. A Mr Bennett, a Mr Castberg, a gentleman in Antwerp – and a Mr Magids. Does he need *them* just as much as he needs their wives? Does the suitor need a rival, an adversary? Roald Amundsen was no explorer in his relations with women, a scout who came upon uncut diamonds, untrodden territory; he was a conqueror. Maybe erotic excitement lies in jealousy, in the act of defeating one's opponent. But the duel must be chivalrous, a triangle of tolerance. It is the woman who must decide, who must leave one to declare her love for the other. We do not know if he was in Alaska already, or on board *Victoria*: the point is, there *was* a Mr Magids.

On 9 June, while Roald Amundsen enjoyed his new acquaintance and his warm baths, an envelope was opened in Christiania. Officially the polar explorer was on board *Maud* at the head of his men. The parallel to the event twelve years previously was striking, when *Fram* headed south and Leon published the secret plan in Christiania.

The North Pole flight had already been overtaken by events when it was presented to the press. The highly praised Larsen-Junkers had been turned into wreckage and replaced with a larger Junkers plane. Besides, it was announced in Christiania that Roald Amundsen would fly from Point Barrow to Cape Columbia on Greenland, where Godfred Hansen had laid out depots for the *Maud* expedition's sledge journey. After the plan was sealed, the polar explorer vacillated between a landing on Greenland and a landing on Spitsbergen, in a continuous stream of revised directions to Leon. He preferred Spitsbergen, but kept the uncivilised Cape Columbia up his sleeve. It was a considerably shorter route.

Leon Amundsen entered into an agreement with four Christiania newspapers regarding exclusive rights to telegrams from the flight. The editors were obliged to pay out 15,000 crowns. That was 1,000 per hour. The crossing of the polar basin was estimated to take fifteen hours.

The polar explorer underlined in his announcement that this was no 'hazardous undertaking'. Added was the caveat, probably from Leon, that this was just 'an extension' of the original plan; the prerequisites had always been 'the scientific work, not the purely sporting. If the flight is successful there is every probability that Amundsen will later, having "surveyed" the route from the air, sail the same route with *Maud* and carry through the original plan. The flight is a mere means, not the goal.' This last bit is important to remember as it was in his capacity as leader of the scientifically designated *Maud* expedition that Roald Amundsen had received the sum of 700,000 crowns from the Norwegian state.

Following the unveiling in Christiania shipbroker Hammer gave a press conference in Seattle. His information was materially different from the Christiania declaration. The flight was estimated to take twenty-five hours, not fifteen. Names of pilots were Fullerton and Omdal. In Christiania only the Norwegian was mentioned. In addition, in a reassuring letter to the Norwegian people: 'In case we should fall down somewhere we are carrying with us necessary equipment and provisions.' On the other hand, Hammer reported that fuel would be prioritised, above all: 'Apart from the necessary instruments, there will be some sandwiches, a day's ration of food and water, a gun and ammunition. That's the lot.' In conclusion, the expedition's 'managing director' reported that he would travel to Europe in July 'to welcome the airmen'.

As an excuse for this sensational kick-off Roald Amundsen sighed cryptically: 'Developments have caused me to expand the plan.' Several developments had forced the polar explorer into the air. Since the end of the First World War an international scramble to be the first to fly over the North Pole had been in full swing; most of it still in its infancy and with more or less serious players. Ever since the sensational English Channel flight, the public had been witness to new records and distances covered in aviation's magical advance.

Tryggve Gran, Captain Scott's old comrade-in-arms, was one of the current contenders in this pilots' fight for the North Pole. When Roald Amundsen's plan was made public he was in Spitsbergen, charting the possibility of his own North Pole flight. 'History repeats itself, and once again I can record Roald Amundsen en route to the Pole, this time in an aeroplane,' Scott's man wrote in his diary. 'I wonder if lady luck will smile on him this time. I would say no, his plan cannot succeed, he must be driven by despair to undertake such a game of chance.'

It would take quite a breakneck venture for the North Sea pilot Tryggve Gran to feel uneasy. If he were to fly to the North Pole he would not make do with sandwiches and a gun: he would base his entire retreat on dogs and skis. But however it was done, it was hazardous.

But confidence in the conqueror of the South Pole was stronger than common sense. The Army Air Corps immediately sent a representative to Spitsbergen. All clear for landing!

In Nome Roald Amundsen left his ship with woman, bath and white table-cloths, and boarded *Maud*. He had been obliged to wait a few days for the overloaded tub of a ship. They set sail for the Bering Strait.

On 29 June the ship was halted by currents and sought harbour near East Cape. Roald Amundsen received an alarming telegram from Leon, sent via Stavanger Radio. It concerned Hammer. The exact contents of the manager's telegram is unknown, but the polar explorer's reaction was unambiguous. 'Information regarding Hammer is awful. Hope he has not fleeced the expedition.' He told his brother that Wisting had lain awake all night. 'We were all so very fond of them both.' (Mrs Baroness Adelheide included.)

Roald Amundsen immediately telegraphed the Norwegian consul in Seattle to annul Haakon Hammer's power of attorney. 'Hammer telegraphed me and asked for an explanation. I told him that only one person could have power of attorney during my absence and that was you,' the polar explorer reported to Leon.

What the manager in Norway had uncovered regarding the 'managing director' in Seattle was obviously a matter of financial malpractice. Or to put it more brutally: the recipient of the Governor's unlimited power of attorney was a cheat! How had such sensational news suddenly come to light?

Leon Amundsen had been commissioned by his brother to procure an Order of Saint Olav for the expedition's saviour and uncle in Seattle. The polar explorer had already celebrated the anticipated Knight of Saint Olav, but experience should have taught him that the matter had not been brought to a successful conclusion before the order was fastened to the recipient's breast. Probably this was the connection whereby Leon Amundsen had received reports of a certain shadow cast on the emigrated Dane's business reputation.

The polar explorer did not openly confront Hammer and in 1924 he again raised the question regarding a Saint Olav. In spite of later information placing Hammer in a 'considerably more favourable light', the minister concerned, in a letter to the polar explorer, advised him to give up the decoration, as the case might lead to a public attack on the person in America or Denmark and at worst on the Norwegian government. Haakon H. Hammer was definitely not a good investment.

Apart from the expedition's 'honorary member', the governor was on the whole pleased with his crew. True, three of the natives left *Maud* during the East Cape stay, but 'Kakot – Nita's father – will continue with us. He is the most loyal soul I have ever known and would be invaluable at Uranienborg,' he wrote to Leon. It is part of the story that galley boy Kakot – after several attempts – actually escaped from *Maud* and thus never took up the intended position as odd-job man at Uranienborg. 'He was obviously very lonely on board and no doubt longed for his own kind,' Odd Dahl wrote in his memoirs.

'All will go swimmingly,' Roald Amundsen reported before *Maud* left East Cape for Point Barrow, where the planes were to be disembarked. However, the ship was forced to seek yet another harbour pending more favourable ice conditions; this time on the Alaska side, by a tiny spot called Deering in the Kotzebue Sound. This port of refuge was anything but accidental; the trading station in Deering was run by the Magids Brothers. The polar explorer enjoyed his first reunion with the woman from *Victoria* – and her husband. As was his wont, the Governor left the ship. Together with the expedition's guest of honour, Lieutenant Fullerton, he moved on to land.

During the couple of weeks the ship lay at anchor in Deering, the South Pole conqueror celebrated his fiftieth birthday, on 6 July 1922. Film documentation exists of the birthday boy blowing out all fifty candles in one go. But otherwise, however, it was really Mrs Magids who was being celebrated. According to Odd Dahl she was presented with one of the expedition's gramophones, apparently a gift to the crew from the Norwegian Women's Voluntary Red Cross (so, not the one from Edison). But the climax was reached when the Governor decided to hold an air show in honour of the settlement's meagre inhabitants in general and his new girlfriend in particular.

Odd Dahl says it took a whole week to flatten out an air strip. Paddling the dismantled Curtiss plane to land on a raft was an extremely hazardous undertaking; the plane was assembled on land. But nothing made the stars sparkle in a woman's eyes like the sight of the plane in the air. Young Mrs Magids, who was a passionate dog-sledge driver, certainly knew how to value this futuristic gesture in these otherwise backward surroundings.

While *Maud* was still in Deering, Lieutenant Fullerton's guest performance as part of the expedition crew came to a brutal end. Are we to believe that the Canadian Dahl was the victim of deliberate intrigue on the part of his Norwegian rival pilot? 'Omdal was a real ladies' man and he started to make eyes at Amundsen's girlfriend.' When she complained to the Governor, Omdal pinned the blame on Fullerton. With that the Canadian got the push and Omdal was left as the expedition's sole pilot, with the rank of lieutenant. So says Sergeant Dahl.

Roald Amundsen himself gave this account in his diary of the trial: 'The stay in Deering has been agreeable in every way. Nice, helpful people. Unfortunately I have had to dismiss Fullerton. He suddenly showed a new and rather unpleasant side to himself, saying nasty things behind our backs. I can't think what the reason for this was. I have treated him as a friend all along. Maybe that was the reason! His dismissal was according to contract. Wisting, Sverdrup and I presided, judged and sent him packing. Mr & Mrs Magids, our tireless and dear friends, will send him to Nome on the first mail boat.'

At the end of July 1922 *Maud* telegraphed home that the flight had been postponed until the following summer on account of the many delays the ice was causing. The decision might have appeared hasty but owing to increased fog in the northern territories during late summer, May and June were considered the most favourable months. Should the flight attempt fail it would also be advantageous that *Maud* was reassuringly beyond reach. The polar explorer had done with his ship and had no need for a line of retreat back to new winterings on board.

On 28 July the Governor, together with pilot Omdal and Reidar Lund, a photographer from Bio-film, took their leave of *Maud*. The polar ship, under the command of Captain Wisting and with the reconnaissance plane *Kristine* on board, immediately set out for the Arctic Ocean. The smaller group with the large Junkers plane were to be transported to Point Barrow with the American schooner *Holmes*.

'It was a funny feeling to see *Maud* disappear into the fog,' the Governor wrote in his diary on the rain-sodden day of parting. 'We both approach an uncertain future. Not least those of us who will fly. But one thing is certain, if we both succeed, then the biggest polar journey in history is a fact.' In spite of the new setbacks, the optimism was irrepressible. Four years' fiasco might still be turned into an historic triumph!

From *Holmes* the polar explorer wrote to Leon: 'I feel unusually well and especially fit for the *Maud* expedition's trans-Arctic flight!'

THIRTY-TWO

Columbus of the Air

Maudheim was the name Roald Amundsen gave his winter base on the Alaskan coast. The name was a tactical move. It would not be obvious that he had left his ship. On the contrary, the aviation expedition constituted the North Pole sortie's most advanced division, just as the land party had been in its time when it was established at Framheim, the difference being that when the North Pole had been conquered the ship would not be there to pick them up; they would fly back to *Maud* – having first set out on a triumphal progress through civilisation's metropolises – Paris, Vienna, Rome, London.

Rather than Point Barrow, North America's most northerly point, Roald Amundsen had chosen to go ashore a bit further south, at the extremely peaceful Wainwright. The shore was suitable as an airfield; anyhow the 500 inhabitants of Barrow might have turned out to be troublesome.

Here on the windblown, barren coast, slightly north of the 70th latitude, Roald Amundsen built a house. The first month the place had three inhabitants – the Governor, the flying officer and the photographer – up until the time when Lund had exhausted his subject, the hero's idyllic life, and left on the *Holmes*.

'Our work is proceeding apace,' the Governor noted in what would become the new expedition diary. The diary was small and handy and weighed a mere couple of grammes, in anticipation of the impending flight. 'Dining room, kitchen, and 2 bedrooms are finished. Our stove stands in the middle of the kitchen and the dining table between it and the window. It is both practical and cosy. We have plenty of drinking water with masses of tiny animals therein, but when boiled does not harm us.'

In all this rough living Roald Amundsen was surprisingly drawn to the domestic. Not for him the wintering in caves *à la* Nansen and Johansen. The Governor liked things 'both tidy & practical'. Not only does Maudheim have two bedrooms: 'Yesterday O lay impregnated canvas over the floor. Today I hung up blue curtains. We are improving. O & I agree that they will only have good things to say about Norwegians.' The polar explorer took a housewifely pride in his house, in case a stray Eskimo woman should happen by.

The Governor was cook while Omdal was carpenter and the more handy of the two. 'O is absolutely suited to this enterprise: he shows insight, is industrious, conscientious and very pleasant to have around.' The lanky, boyish lieutenant was a man to the Governor's liking. Oskar Omdal was an adventurer and keen on most things, but that was the nature of the mission; but beyond the actual deed he appeared not to have ambitions, neither for leadership nor any special outcome. Odd Dahl, who had accompanied the Curtiss plane aboard *Maud*, would in time show that he was a person of superior qualities. However, for this particular purpose – the most daring of all the ventures – and for his disposition, the Governor had picked the right man when he chose the hard-working, companionable, but far less demanding or deep-thinking Omdal.

And the lieutenant was content with life together with the Governor. 'The Captain cooks and cares for me,' he wrote in a letter to Lund. 'He does not know what good he can do. Tasty cakes and delicacies and a nip to boot. Oh yes, I am in clover.'

The one thing missing in the cosy house in Wainwright was children. But as so often before, Roald Amundsen found a substitute. This time it was the puppy Columbus and the red fox cub Mikkel. 'Mikkel and Columbus are already thick as thieves. They seem to have known each other all their lives. O is in charge of Mikkel and can do what he wants with him. Oh yes, it is lively enough here.' Once bitten, twice shy; the polar explorer knows he must be patient. 'I am very taken with Mikkel but for his part he seems to be taking his time'.

But of course, their first love was *Elisabeth*, which was housed in its own newly constructed hangar. 'He is looking after the aeroplane as he would a child,' the Governor noted. The lieutenant was in charge of daily maintenance; the polar explorer dreamt proud dreams of the future.

Towards the end of November Roald Amundsen left Maudheim. He went north to Point Barrow. He found a native post-carrier and suitable sledge equipment for his onward journey. On 1 December he noted in his diary that he had 'left for Deering with Magids' dog team'. A short week later he had reached the trading post. 'I have lodged in Magids' shop which is now being run by Mr Henry.'

In her short letter, written many years later, Bess Magids claims that she met Roald Amundsen several times in Deering. His own diary seems to indicate that he only dealt with a male manager. Anyhow, after three days he leaves the place. The polar explorer is again equipped with Magids' family dogs and sledging equipment. But it appears another woman is attracting his attention.

Roald Amundsen made for Nome. In his autobiography he refers to this sledge journey as 'the most tiring journey' he had ever undertaken. Having reached the mining town on 14 December, the South Pole day, he sent Leon a sober report: 'A rather tiring trip, but my heart stood up.'

The excuse given for this 1,000-kilometre excursion was the polar explorer's need to hear news from *Maud*, check the time signal and 'gather more stuff for my next book'. Something told him that a fifteen- to twenty-hour flight, however sensational, might appear rather less sensational between the covers of a book. Anyhow, a sledge-journey belonged in every polar book. Of course, civilisation was the magnet. 'Oh yes, it is lively enough here,' he had written in Maudheim, but for a world citizen of Roald Amundsen's restless disposition it must nevertheless have appeared rather empty.

In Nome he was a welcome guest and was immediately comfortably billeted with bathroom and every convenience. Good old Mary looked after him. With regards to Omdal he was not concerned. 'He is brilliantly equipped and will have enjoyed a good winter up there. Our house was the best on the coast.' The polar explorer could not help mentioning to Leon that property developers are ready to take over: 'I imagine they will pay $5,000 which isn't to be sneezed at.'

Roald Amundsen had come to Nome to live the life of Riley. It might be the last chance before the big, definitive wintering in the Arctic Ocean. In a moment of realism he wrote to his friend Herman Gade in beautiful Rio: 'There is a hell of a chance that we will leave our bones up there.' But the gold mining town is 'lively as hell'. To Leon, who was spending the winter in exclusive resorts like Nice and Baden-Baden, he reported extremely boisterous Christmas and New Year celebrations. The 50-year-old, bright as a button, was having the time of his life: 'I took off 10 kilos on the way down and look exceedingly well. Am thin as a rake and feel better than ever.'

Two days after his arrival *Maud*'s new position was announced. 'Excellent. Could not be better,' he noted in his diary. Success is almost a reality. 'Now it's up to Omdal and me.'

Ere Roald Amundsen could risk his life in the big gamble, it would be necessary to tidy up a tangle of sensitive snags. This was probably the most important reason for seeking out the telegraph station in Nome. Nearly a year had elapsed since he last saw Kiss in London. In the meantime he had met the beauty from Alaska. In the wake of the journey with SS *Victoria* he must have sent Kiss a signal, which he, in his loneliness at Maudheim, had had time to regret and which he later described as an unforgivable 'mistake'.

Post between Nome and London took near on seventy days. It was therefore the telegraph which, in its truncated form, was responsible for tidying up the error in the course of fourteen hectic days. After several rounds of prayers, regrets and assurances, the polar explorer could heave a sigh of relief. 'Thank God all is back where it started,' he wrote in his diary of 8 January. 'I have been exiled long enough, and homeless.' The Flying Dutchman was about to land.

On Kiss's thirty-seventh birthday, 10 February 1923, the polar explorer devotedly noted in his diary: 'All my fondest greetings, my best thoughts and most loving wishes to you!'

On 25 January, a mere two days after the last telegram to London, the polar explorer initiated a new campaign of the utmost importance. He sent the following message to Lawyer Gudde in Trondheim: 'Take all measures necessary secure Uranienborg legally for Elizabeth.' For the second time the polar explorer sealed his love by giving her his home, Uranienborg. But this time it was not as a result of riches and abundance; this time he was acting for reasons of financial necessity.

Right in the middle of the emotional tidying up a business telegram had arrived from H.H. Hammer in Seattle. It was ominous.

It was now, in January 1923, that the polar explorer was for the first time forced to acknowledge that financially he was on the verge of ruin. The expedition coffers were empty; the manager was forced to pay wages and running costs out of his own pocket. The debt in Seattle was the most pressing and was estimated at $20,000. Hammer and wife were in Europe during the autumn and met Leon Amundsen. The manager treated the 'managing director' with contempt. Politely, but determinedly, he refused to take on the responsibility of the expedition's debts in America, as the polar explorer had told him that the outlay had already been paid off with money from Don Pedro. For his part, Hammer insisted that all purchases were done with Roald Amundsen's authority and approval, but: 'It was impossible to keep track of exactly what had been bought and how much we owed.' Thus wrote Hammer in an explanatory letter to Leon regarding the hectic period before the expedition left Seattle. He explained to the manager that before *Maud*'s departure he had briefed the polar explorer regarding the mounting expenses; 'but Roald just laughed and brushed it off and said I'd manage them.'

It had always been a principle of the polar explorer to leave his overdrawn accounts in the secure knowledge that yesteryear's figures in the red would be paid with the gilt-edged achievements of the future. In addition, this time he had been dealing with two managers on two continents. For the present the polar explorer felt reasonably safe, at the back of beyond. 'There must have been a spanner in the works, but not possible for me to right it now,' he wrote to Leon.

Roald Amundsen now tried to crawl ashore economically on Leon's side of the Atlantic. He endorsed Leon's scepticism regarding Hammer's integrity.

1. The cradle of the South Pole. While his childhood home in Oslo has long since been torn down, Roald Amundsen's birthplace at the mouth of the River Glomma is still open to visitors today.

2. The polar explorer's father, Jens Ingebrigt Amundsen (1820–86).

3. The polar explorer's mother, Gustava Amundsen, née Sahlquist (1837–93).

4. The legendary nanny, Betty, in 1906 with Leon's daughter on her knee.

Roald and his brothers

5. Jens Ole Antonius (Tonni), Amundsen,
    aged about 15.

6. Gustav Sahlquist (Busken) Amundsen,
    aged about 13.

7. Leon Henry Benham Amundsen,
    aged about 11.

8. Roald Engelbregt Gravning Amundsen,
    aged about 9.

9. The Greenland explorer Eivind Astrup. He died at a young age.

10. Dr Fridtjof Nansen in his study at Polhøgda, surrounded by important documents. The photograph was taken in 1909 and has been reproduced in *The South Pole*.

11. A camping trip in the Antarctic. Roald Amundsen and Frederick Cook put polar exploration into practice. The doctor, wearing a Greenland outfit, stands between Norwegian skis and North American snow shoes. In the background is *Belgica* – the amateurs' ship.

12. Try and guess which Pole I am thinking of! Roald Amundsen (right) and Frederick Cook had this formal photograph taken before going their separate ways after Belgica's return.

13.   The polar explorer's friends in Tromsø, Gudrun and Fritz Zapffe, gave him this picture before his departure in *Gjøa*. Many years later the couple's son, the philosopher Peter Wessel Zapffe, wrote about the rivalry between Scott and Amundsen.

14.   Three brothers and one Dane. This sombre amateur snapshot was taken in the cabin moments before *Gjøa* left home waters. From left to right: Roald, Gustav and Leon Amundsen; dressed for bad weather: Godfred Hansen.

15. Gjøahavn – Gjøa harbour. The large dark spots are humans, the smaller ones are dogs.

16. Roald Amundsen (far left) called this picture 'the first sledge trip'. It would not be the last.

17. The first Christmas in a foreign harbour. Lindstrøm is both cook and Father Christmas. From left to right: Helmer Hanssen, Amundsen, Ristvedt (behind Father Christmas), Wiik (in front of the photograph of Nansen) and Lund. On the cabin wall to the left is a portrait of King Oscar.

18. A martyr to science. Gustav J. Wiik (1878–1906) at 'Magnetic Villa'.

19. 'All for Norway'. Amundsen in front of the cabin's updated decorations, following their return to civilisation.

20. The scrubbed-up *Gjøa* crew await the King following their homecoming. Seated, from left to right: the cook Lindstrøm, Amundsen, Lieutenant Hansen and the blacksmith Ristvedt. Standing at the back: Helmer Hanssen (who only started to write his name with a double s later in life). On the far right is a nameless footman.

21.   A Viking ship with a diesel engine. *Fram*, in Hvalbukta, Whale Bay, was enlarged and rebuilt many times. Together with skis and dogs (left) the ship was the ideal solution to exploration in polar regions.

22.   An interior from an Ibsen drama. Eva and Fridtjof Nansen in front of the fire-place at Polhøgda – Polar Heights.

23.   Two good friends. Herman Gade welcomes Amundsen to Christmas celebrations in Chicago, 1907. Gade, who was married to a grandchild of President Garfield, was among other things mayor of Lake Forest, Illinois.

24. A secret place. The villa Uranienborg, with flag-pole and bath-house, was an isolated idyll. It lies, unseen, at Bålerud in Svartskog, between the fjord and the hills.

25. Polar explorer with a poker face. Photographed by Wilse before *Fram*'s departure from Christiania. From right to left: Skipper Nilsen, Lieutenant Gjertsen, Roald and Leon Amundsen. The crew keep a respectful distance. All are dressed the same, courtesy of the expedition coffers.

26. *Above*: Outpost of empire or inoffensive Native American camp?
The main building at Framheim (Fram Home) is snowed under (left)
while the characteristic tents for dogs and provisions protrude from the
snowdrifts. In the middle is the meteorological station – the expedition's
scientific alibi.

27. *Right*: Don Pedro Christophersen (1845–1930), one of Amundsen's
patrons, was born into modest circumstances in Vestfold on Norway's
south-east coast. By a combination of business acumen and winning first
prize in a lottery he made a fabulous fortune in Argentina.

28. *Below*: The Viking colony celebrates the local national day,
7 June 1911, with gramophone, aquavit and victory cigars. From
left to right: Olav Bjaaland, Sverre Hassel, Oscar Wisting, Helmer
Hanssen, Roald Amundsen, Hjalmar Johansen, Kristian Prestrud. Jørgen
Stubberud's arm is on the far right of the picture, which was taken by the
cook Lindstrøm.

29.   Bareheaded on the South Pole, 90° South, minus 23°C. From left to right: Amundsen, Hanssen, Hassel, Wisting. (Bjaaland took the photograph.)

Amundsen's own pictures from the Pole never saw the light of day. In that connection the photographer A.B. Wilse writes: 'Amundsen himself did not want to learn. He had an ordinary Kodak 6 × 9. "If I take six pictures with different exposures and times, one of them will be serviceable", he said. But he threw away thousands of crowns of income as he had not one single good photo when he returned home. I remember working hard to ensure he had good enough pictures for his lectures from the lousy amateur material he gave me.'

30.   Absolute nadir. Polheim – Polar Home – one month after the dog-sledge drivers left. From left to right: Scott, Wilson, Evans.

31. Members of the Third *Fram* Expedition in Hobart, 18 March 1912. Front row, left to right: Lindstrøm, Stubberud, Karenius Olsen (cook), a reserve (signed on in Argentina). Sitting: Johansen, Prestrud, Amundsen, Nilsen, Gjertsen, Hanssen. At the back: Hassel, Ludvig Hansen, a reserve, Bjaaland, Kristensen, sail-maker Rønne, ice-pilot Beck, Wisting, a reserve and chief engineer Sundbeck. The mood at the prospect of continuing with Amundsen was not very enthusiastic. 'It will be a long and tough journey', Bjaaland writes in his diary, 'and the boys will no doubt taste hardship, if I know the old man.'

32.   *Left*: King Haakon VII of Norway, friend of Fridtjof Nansen and brother-in-law of George V of England. The Danish-born naval officer supported Roald Amundsen throughout his active career. That demanded not only courage but also a certain amount of judgment, and contributed much to promote the newly established kingdom in the eyes of the world.

33.   *Right*: A classical profile under an Edwardian hat. Mrs Bennett in her twenties.

34. Kings of the Poles. From left to right: Captain Roald Amundsen, Sir Ernest Shackleton and Rear Admiral Robert Peary, Philadelphia, 16 January 1913.

35. The two Captains Amundsen. Uranienborg, summer, 1918. Between the brothers Gustav and Roald is Leon's fourteen-year-old son Nicolay.

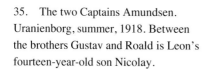

36. The many sided skier and pilot Tryggve Gran (1889–1980) was one of the daring young men who breathed down Roald Amundsen's neck.

37. Launch of the Queen's
yacht *Maud*, 7 June 1917.

38. The brothers Amundsen.
In front: Busken and Leon, at
the back: Tonni and Roald.
Uranienborg, summer, 1918.

39.   The unhappy team.
Maud's crew before departure
from Christiania. From the left,
sitting: Engineer Sundbeck,
Amundsen, Skipper Hanssen,
First Officer Wisting. At the
back: Tessem, Tønnesen,
Dr Sverdrup, Knudsen. Sail-
maker Rønne would join
the ship when they passed
Horten while the St Bernards
would stay behind and guard
Uranienborg.

40.   Scientific experiment or
emotional reorientation? Roald
Amundsen and the polar bear
cub Marie.

41. Champagne in the garden at Leigh Court one summer's day sometime in the 1920s. From the left: the married couple Niels and Eileen Gudde (in England the family name was spelt Gude), Charles Peto Bennett with the couple Astrid and Trygve Gudde. Kiss Bennett is standing at the back on the right.

42. The rhododendron is flowering. This amateur photograph is perhaps the only one showing Kiss Bennett and Roald Amundsen posing together. Most probably the picture dates from one of the last two summers before *Maud*'s departure.

43. A sample of Amundsen's handwriting and spelling. The letter is dated 'Nome 31.7.20' and is addressed to the Norwegian-born mining magnet asking him to take care of the skipper, the engineer and the sail-maker.

44. A child came in from the cold. Kakonita on board *Maud*.

45. Camilla Carpendale, aged 12, in Nome before stepping into the civilised world.

46. Partners in crime. Haakon H. Hammer (left) and Roald Amundsen somewhere in Seattle.

47. From Siberia to New York. Grandpa Amundsen shows off an extraordinary landscape and the press get their picture. Kakonita and Camilla are both dressed in Eskimo-inspired coats and hats.

48. *Above left*: The first stage of a new expedition. Roald Amundsen and Oscar Omdal on board *Stavangerfjord*. The Governor will soon be 50; the lieutenant is 27.

49. *Above right*: The pilot Odd Dahl after his arrival in Seattle and at the start of a long and extraordinary scientific career. Dahl, who was born in Drammen in 1898, died in the spring of 1995, the last to survive of all Roald Amundsen's men.

50. *Left*: *Maud* outside Deering. The crew is engaged in the daring operation of transporting *Kristine*'s fuselage to land. *Elisabeth* lies in an enormous crate on top of the cabin roof.

51. The Junkers aeroplane *Elisabeth* near the weather-beaten Maudhavn. (Roald Amundsen often spelt 'Elizabeth' in the English way – both the plane and the woman from whom it takes its name). Amundsen is on the far left.

52. *Below left*: Closest to the North Pole. Haakon H. Hammer during the Junkers firm's expedition to Spitsbergen. His Danish-American's physique did not correspond with the Norwegians' expectations of a real polar explorer.

53. *Below right*: Wishes of good luck and assurances of admiration. Roald Amundsen received this portrait of Benito Mussolini during the summit meeting in Milan.

54.   Family idyll on the brink of ruin. Herman Gade, the future owner of Uranienborg, surrounded by his two Alices (daughter and wife) and Roald Amundsen with his two gingham-frocked foster children, Camilla and Kakonita.

55.   The aeroplanes are unloaded. The icebreaker *Hobby* has reached Kings Bay with its dangerous and valuable cargo.

56.   Polar explorer or astronaut? N-25's crew: Karl Feucht, Hjalmar Riiser-Larsen and Roald Amundsen.

57.   Useful flags. Lieutenant
Riiser-Larsen communicates
with his colleague Dietrichson
– 87°43′ North.

58.   Amundsen smokes the
victory cigar.

59.   The conquering polar
seaplane. N-25 has ascended
to the Oslo Fjord and makes its
way to the capital, surrounded
by small craft.

60. Back on the winner's rostrum. To the cheers of the Norwegian people an impeccably dressed Roald Amundsen, carrying his South Pole bowler, stands between Leif Dietrichson, who wears a naval uniform, and Lincoln Ellsworth.

61. Polar explorer and artist. Roald Amundsen leaves the National Theatre, Christiania following the premiere of his new lecture.

62.   The airship buildings in Kings Bay. The picture shows the hangar and the mooring mast. In the background is the tiny mining community of Ny-Ålesund. The ski-tracks are of symbolic importance only. (They are en route to the monument commemorating the previous year's flight.)

63.   Hectic days in Rome. Left to right: Rolf Thommessen (dressed like a statesman), Amundsen and Ellsworth. At the back: Mussolini's officers.

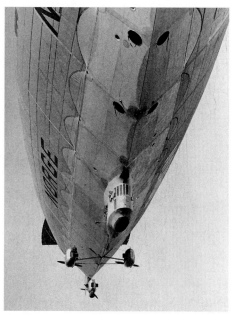

64. *Above left*: The polar
explorer's nephew and secretary
Gustav S. Amundsen ready
for take-off dressed in a tailor-
made pilot's suit and with skis
in readiness for an emergency
landing. Unfortunately, no room
was found on board for the
lieutenant. By way of consolation
Goggen, or Gogo, was allowed to
write a chapter of the expedition
book.

65. *Above right*: A flying theatre
box. Were it not for the cold,
Norge's lead gondola would have
been a comfortable hang-out. But
under the airship there was plenty
of room for acrobatics. Note the
figure by the left engine-gondola.

66. With his hands in his lap.
Roald Amundsen, in Nobile's
armchair, sits patiently looking
for land.

67. Amundsen treats everyone to a grin. The expedition members on board *Victoria*. Standing, left to right: Riiser-Larsen, Ramm, Gottwaldt, Wisting, Omdal, Cecioni (obscured), Malmgren, Storm-Johnsen, Alessandrini (extreme rear), Caratti, Pomella. Seated: Horgen, Amundsen, Ellsworth, Nobile with the polar dog Titina. The picture was taken by the Italian Arduino.

68. Four embittered leaders during the celebrations in Seattle. Riiser-Larsen and Amundsen have exchanged their Alaska costumes for double-breasted suits. Ellsworth has bought a hat, while 'stirrer' Nobile poses in his Italian uniform with Titina on a lead.

69.   Political birthday-party celebrations, 16 July 1926 at Akershus Fortress. The key-note speaker, Nansen, stands between Country Alliance chairman Joakim Lehmkuhl and the birthday boy and guest of honour, 54-year-old Amundsen. The King's Guard keep the other guests at a distance.

70.   'State visit to Japan'. The Conqueror of the Poles is cheered by the Emperor's subjects.

71. Norwegians among the British.
In November 1927 Fridtjof Nansen is
installed as Honorary Chancellor of
St Andrews University. With him are
a gaggle of honorary doctors, among
them Benjamin Vogt (in the doorway),
Professor Bjerknes (left) and the old polar
explorer Otto Sverdrup. At the front are
the University Vice-Chancellor and a
Mrs Low. Within a year Minister Vogt
would appeal to Nansen to save Norway's
honour in Britain.

72.   The distance between a big man
and delusions of grandeur is short. In a
confidential report to the Foreign Office
Minister Vogt writes that 'after all
Amundsen has been through he is now
clearly suffering mentally and consequently one should not take his remarks
too much to heart'. He is shown in a
rickshaw during the visit to Japan.

73. Ready to strike out on his own. Hjalmar Riiser-Larsen and his wife during the *Norge* reception in Bergen. To the left is Captain Gottwaldt.

74. The night-train to Bergen; ready for departure. Roald Amundsen shakes the hand of the Italian Ambassador Count Sennis. To the right is an uneasy-looking Herman Gade.

75. The swan from the south in high northern latitudes. The crew take their places before departure from Tromsø. Leif Dietrichson (second on the left) is about to take the decisive step. Roald Amundsen is already ensconced at the back (far right).

76. The polar explorer's last patron. Fredrik Peterson, third from the right, before *Latham 47*'s departure from Caudebec-en-Caux. Captain Guilbaud is flanked by Peterson's two sons. To the left of the young lady is the secretary Emil Petersen.

77. Bess Magids, shown with her only child, the woman who thought she would be Roald Amundsen's wife. This amateur photograph was taken about seven years after she left Norway.

78.   The goddess of happiness wearing the polar explorer's furs. Kiss Bennett (left) at Leigh Court in 1933 with her brother Niels, his wife and two daughters.

79.   Norway remembers Amundsen. Oslo's Main Street, Karl Johan's Gate, 14 December 1928 at midday.

'You have no doubt behaved correctly by not getting involved with him.' At the same time he had every reason to evade a revealing confrontation: 'Hammer is probably partly responsible for the deficit, although I cannot prove it. But one must not forget that he has saved, many times over, those sums for the expedition.' The polar explorer is squirming; deep down he knew where the responsibility lay.

The fact that in next to no time the expedition had expanded from being a traditional journey by ship to becoming an extensive expedition by plane, with its own base, meant that every calculation of cost had spiralled out of control. Roald Amundsen had devised a new plan, financed with means from the old plan, yet without cancelling anything. That would cost him dear.

And when Roald Amundsen asked Lawyer Gudde to legally secure Uranienborg for Kiss, this means that he was safeguarding his house against his possible bankruptcy, but also and just as pertinently, against his possible demise. Should he not survive the flight, his home by the Bunnefjord would not fall into the hands of his creditors, but would go to his lawful heir – Kiss.

'Thank you for fixing Uranienborg so quickly,' Roald Amundsen wrote later to Trygve Gudde. 'It was all above board, as it had been made over already four years ago.' Aided by the power of attorney from 1918 the lawyer had issued a title deed on Uranienborg. To avoid any publicity being attached to Kiss Bennett's name the property was put in Niels Gudde's name. The oldest brother had at this time established himself as timber merchant in Manila where he also acted as Norwegian consul.

On 14 March Roald Amundsen took another extreme measure, this time regarding the second property by the Bunnefjord. Diary: 'Telegraphed Nansen today [the lawyer] and asked him to sell Rødsten in order that I can keep the creditors at bay for a time.' His creditors, through a bank in Nome, had begun breathing down his neck. 'Apparently they were going to arrest me,' he wrote to Leon. 'In business Americans are cold as ice.'

Lawyer Nansen immediately got in touch with Leon Amundsen, who was in Nice, for further guidance. However, Leon asked the lawyer to await developments as 'the sale of Rødsten will cover but a fraction'. Only two things could save the polar explorer now: either further public funds or a shining heroic deed. The diary betrayed that the polar explorer pinned his faith on the latter alternative: 'Should we succeed in flying right over I'll pull it off.'

Otherwise the wintering in Nome showed no sign of depression. The polar explorer got stuck into the local dog-sledge racing. He was a regular 'starter' for the ladies' class and kept going until the party was over sometime in the early hours.

His stay in the gold-mining town had been more than rich in impressions, although not all material equally suited for the intended book. He had even had signs of life from his foster-daughters at home in Uranienborg. They spent the winter out there with two elderly serving girls. Camilla could assure him that they are both 'clever and good little girls', who were working hard at school. While they were waiting for 'Grand-daddy', they were visited by another man. 'The clergyman was here and christened us and now we are Christians.'

On 13 April 1923 Roald Amundsen's whip cracks over his eleven dogs and he sets off for Wainwright. Only a miracle could save him now.

Scarcely one month later, on 9 May, the sledge expedition noted its arrival at Maudheim. 'It was good to meet Omdal and know that all was in order. *Elizabeth* is securely fastened under the snow. Ready to go.'

The most sensational long-distance flight under extreme climatic conditions over vast unknown territory was fixed for 20 June 1923. The first test-flight following the assembly of the plane took place just two days after the polar explorer's arrival in Wainwright. The real red-letter day in the expedition's history would be 11 May.

In the presence of the South Pole conqueror and a handful of locals, Pilot Officer Omdal succeeded in lifting the ski-plane *Elisabeth* off from Alaska's frozen beaches and made for the cloud cover. Measured against the expertise of the day that was no mean feat; the plane had arrived in Wainwright the preceding summer in three huge crates, had survived an Arctic winter and was assembled *in situ* without assistance of professionals or a workshop. *Elisabeth* could fly!

The lieutenant circled over the 'hamlet' of Wainwright. Then the metal bird turned and descended over the sea ice. Here is how Roald Amundsen described the event in his diary:

> He approached the house in a strong descent and nearly brushed it. He landed down on the bay a few metres from where he had taken off. The left ski caught under the plane, which made a half turn and capsized over on to the right wing. No danger to human life. We rushed down. The undercarriage fastened to the left ski was broken. O said that the engine had been working satisfactorily. Tomorrow he will give a written account. I have now little hope of a flight. It all appears to have been patchwork, what they have given us.

Two days after the disastrous test-flight Road Amundsen had the opportunity to send a report to Noorwick with a letter carrier. He added a telegram and a letter to two of the most important people in his life, Kiss and Leon. It took over a month for the business manager, who was now in Dover in England, to receive the telegram with the news that the North Pole flight had been cancelled. In the meantime much has been happening on both sides of the Arctic Ocean.

On 14 May, two days after the letter carrier departed, the polar explorer revised his decision. 'We have decided, in spite of everything, to get away. O is now repairing the undercarriage and trying to strengthen it. When he has completed that he will start on the engine. It *must* work!' Although Roald Amundsen noted his unswerving determination in his little black diary, alone with his thoughts in Maudheim, he gazed out of the window and addressed the world with a decisive question: 'What would you all say if we gave up?'

The snow bunting flapped around the house, and a skein of greylag geese flew across the sky. Why not *Elisabeth* too? After a couple of days the undercarriage had been patched together and the plane made a ski-trip on the ground. 'The prospects for a flight are extremely good.'

Compared with the South Pole expedition, the flying North Pole mission was devoid of safety margins. The plane was compelled to reach one of two goals, Cape Columbia or Svalbard (Spitsbergen), or the world would be the poorer by two human lives. Roald Amundsen took no precautionary measures, either off the Alaskan coast, by northern Greenland or in Svalbard. The polar explorer had concentrated all his efforts on the ascent; the onward journey he would have to leave to fate.

At home in Norway, on the other hand, the question was raised: What if Captain Amundsen and his fearless companion ditch in the Arctic Ocean somewhere and have to continue on skis – should not someone be there to meet them at the ice's edge?

The Norwegian Defence Forces decided to send an expedition to Svalbard with the naval vessel *Farm*, including two reconnaissance aircraft. The manoeuvre would cost 100,000 crowns. But: 'Roald Amundsen is a man of such stature that we cannot sit here idly twiddling our thumbs if anything should befall him,' said the Defence Minister from the Lilliputian land.

However, simultaneously a privately organised safety mission saw the light of day. This took the form of 'Uncle Haakon' who had allied himself with the Junkers factory and organised yet another welcoming committee, consisting of a film-photographer and a spare plane. That the Danish-American Hammer had gone to Spitsbergen with his own long-distance plane and a first-class team aroused Norwegian suspicions. After all, it was considerably shorter to fly North Pole return from Spitsbergen than it was from Alaska. Had the

Danish-American and the German 'Junkers' gone north to grab the Pole before Amundsen? Speculation was rife in Norwegian papers during the summer.

'The point is not to forget the details'; the polar explorer took note and thought it sounded like his own quotation. After all, he was known as a foresighted strategist and master of details. 'One bolt' can be enough to spoil it all, according to the North Sea pilot Tryggve Gran's announcement to a newspaper on the other side of the world.

He had 'forgotten' something, but what? Was it a bolt or a nut? It might not have been a 'detail' but something really large. Was the weight of the fuel too much, the distance too long, the engine too feeble? Maybe it was quite simply impossible to cross the Arctic Ocean in an aeroplane. Had the plane that was equal to the task not yet been constructed? What did it then matter that the bolts were all in place, the skis repaired with splints, the sandwiches buttered? Anyhow, the flag was ready. 'Should have flown the flag today,' the polar explorer wrote on 7 June, 'but I felt sorry for our lovely silk flag in the thick fog that has been surrounding us all day.' Better save it for the North Pole. The weather would certainly be fine there.

The 10 June arrived. Another red-letter day. They were making a test-flight. The report was short: 'During the ascent this morning the drive-shaft between the skis broke again.' It was all over. One question remained: What would the world say?

The next day the lieutenant handed the legendary explorer four buttercups – the first of the year. A small relief. The next day the sky was blue. 'What if we had had decent equipment? But no point thinking about it. But they deserve a sound beating, the guys who made the undercarriage.'

The telegram announcing the first cancellation reached Norway on 19 June. Total anticlimax. The Defence Forces recalled their expedition. Complete frustration. But who was the scapegoat? Was it the publicity-mad Hammer or the other Danish-American, the man called Larsen, who had made over the useless Junkers to the Norwegian? Or might it really be the national hero himself, Roald Amundsen, who had lost his common sense and made fools of an entire world?

The actual day when the polar flight should have taken place, 20 June, the expedition leader woke up to brilliant sunshine and clear skies. Perfect for a flight. 'I could cuss and curse,' he noted in silence. 'I wonder if anyone will help me to fly from Spitsbergen next summer. 100,000 crowns should be sufficient.' The undercarriage might have collapsed; Roald Amundsen's go-ahead spirit had not. A new plan was being hatched. He had already bagged his new base on Spitsbergen. His intuition told him that his credibility as an object of investment had probably reached an all-time low. To compensate for this new insight he jotted down a cost proposal which was totally and utterly unrealistic. Thus is optimism kept alive.

As a first compensation for his crumbling dreams, the polar explorer adopted some more 'foster-children', two chicks which he might teach to fly. But not even this time did he succeed: 'One of the chicks died last night, the other I let out this morning. No success!' he noted in his diary, 'but that's natural for an old bachelor.'

On Roald Amundsen's fifty-first birthday they start dismantling *Elisabeth*. 'Only the skeleton is left on the beach.' That same day *Kristine* was wrecked during a last unsuccessful attempt to fly over the Arctic Ocean.

Maud was frozen in near the New Siberian Islands but would never fulfil the Governor's optimistic expectations of an actual ice-drift. Using the ship as a base, Sergeant Dahl, with South Pole explorer Wisting in the back-seat, had even managed to lift off from the pack ice during a few test-flights. Later Roald Amundsen would sum this up as the first flights 'over the actual drift-ice'. But that summer's day it was over for good and Odd Dahl, in his memoirs, concluded that the plane had been totally unsuitable for Arctic conditions: 'Curtiss Oriole was actually designed for Californian conditions. It was an upholstered and nicely fitted out Sunday plane which would transport film stars from Hollywood to different locations.' In other words, it was as unsuited for the Arctic Ocean as ponies were for the Antarctic.

On 8 August *Holmes* arrived in Maudhavn. Roald Amundsen had decided to telegraph the aeroplane manufacturer Curtiss at the first opportunity to ask 'if he would give us a new plane'; in the meantime the captain of the *Holmes* handed over a bunch of telegrams, including one from Haakon H. Hammer. It confirmed that a Junkers plane was at his disposal ready for a flight 'from here'.

When the telegram was sent, Hammer was still in Norway with his German team. There was speculation whether Hammer himself might hazard the journey to the North Pole. This was determinedly rejected by the Danish-American; 'the only sporting solution' was to place all available material at Amundsen's disposal.

But nor was Hammer's offer graciously accepted in Norway; rather than an honourable gesture it was branded an 'audacious piece of propaganda-humbug on behalf of the German Junkers factory'. In an unusually outspoken piece the Christiania paper *Dagbladet* wrote: 'It all reminds one of the man who talked about committing suicide for such a long time until in the end he could do nothing except hang himself. No sooner has he escaped death in the grip of a polar night than his good friend Mr Hammer urgently invites him on a new fatal flight to the Pole in the very same aeroplane with which the enterprising Seattle ship-owner equipped Amundsen to "safeguard" his life.'

It reminds one of Russian roulette; but when the polar explorer received the telegram and stared at the revolver muzzle, he sensed light at the end of the tunnel: 'I resolved to journey south as quickly as possible and accept the offer.' Thus did Roald Amundsen's diary end; an expedition diary which contained no expedition.

This time he chose to ignore another voice: 'Advise against Hammer's project'. The telegram was from Leon.

THIRTY-THREE

A Criminal Optimist

Roald Amundsen has neither taken off nor landed; he left Maudheim, that outpost of great illusions, in an elated state of mind.

Haakon H. Hammer, who only a year ago had frightened him with staggering debts, now beckoned him with the promise of new planes. The polar explorer and his agent had both lost their sense of reality; two ruined fantasists en route to new altitudes.

On 17 September Roald Amundsen arrived, via Nome, in Seattle. Hammer turned up the next day, from Europe, with the offer of no less that '3 large metal aeroplanes from Junkers in Germany'. However, in a letter to Herman Gade, the polar explorer said that, understandably, he preferred a different class of plane, which would cost $125,000. 'Personally I could never raise such a sum, but Hammer is sure to manage it in a short time. And from what I have seen of him I know he will push it through.'

The man whom all Norway now mistrusted, who was considered a virtual humbug, had in the eyes of the polar explorer gone from being a jack-of-all-trades businessman to superstar financial wizard. The poor lieutenant on the other hand, who eventually also arrived in Seattle with the wreck of a non-negotiable aeroplane, found himself side-lined: 'Omdal is an idiot in so many ways, rather unreliable too,' the polar explorer informed Leon.

In Seattle the two reunited optimists lay new plans for next year's flight over the Pole from Spitsbergen to Alaska. The polar explorer swallowed the 'spanner in the works' and agreed to acknowledge his old debts to the agent. Hammer on his side guaranteed the financing and new profits once the flight was a fact. When they left the town together and headed for the East Coast, via Chicago, Hammer was again the holder of Roald Amundsen's unrestricted power of attorney.

On 29 October 1923 Engelbregt Gravning booked into the Palace Hotel in London. The time had come to lick his wounds.

After a few days with Kiss he travelled to Dover where Leon was living with his family. He brought his brother up to date on the financial developments. Leon insisted that from now on the flight must be separated from the *Maud* expedition.

Engelbregt Gravning travels home via Copenhagen. When he is recognised in the Danish capital he confirms that he is indeed Roald Amundsen and that he is passing through en route from Berlin.

On 9 November 1923 the unmasked Roald Amundsen arrived in Norway by train from abroad. It was the very same cloudless autumn day that General Ludendorff and Corporal Hittler (the world had not yet learned how to spell the name) attempted their amateurish coup in Munich. To the relief of Europe the two gentlemen were soon behind bars.

'The train stopped at Ljan and hey presto I was out,' the polar explorer reported back to Dover. With that he started walking the last kilometres out to Svartskog. The capital's press corps must yet again admit that they were cheated out of Roald Amundsen's arrival in his native land.

The next day Ludendorff's defeat featured on the front pages.

Measured by his own standards Roald Amundsen was a 'deserter'. But he passed no judgement on himself. Rather it was the people who judged. For the very first time the polar explorer was cold-shouldered in his native country. What was left of sympathy was reserved for Wisting and Sverdrup aboard the polar ship *Maud*, circling around the heroic backwaters by the coast of Siberia. Anyone who had believed in the national hero's flying feats felt they had been hoodwinked.

What had gone wrong with the proud tradition of polar exploration? A broken ski or drive-shaft had been sufficient to upset every expectation; expensive back-up expeditions had been mounted to no avail; nothing had been achieved, only this half-baked Dane Hammer and his propaganda-financed Junkers show. All that Fridtjof Nansen, Otto Sverdrup and Amundsen himself had achieved was now debased. A small nation had become the laughing stock of the world.

'Roald Amundsen relaxed about his countrymen's changed attitude' were the headlines of one of the inquisitorial interviews the polar explorer was forced to give after his homecoming.

With Hammer in America and Leon in England, Roald Amundsen found himself isolated at Svartskog. 'I wish you were here,' he wrote to Trygve Gudde in Trondheim. 'Would so appreciate your sensible advice. Can't talk to anyone here. Must manage alone.'

The ranks around the nation's hero were wearing thin. Old Betty was bed-ridden and in a nursing home. 'She is the life and soul of the party and loved by all,' the polar explorer wrote to Leon. The little girls, on the other hand, were fit and well. 'They are both top of their class.'

But if the telegrams from America were to be believed it would not be long before he too could commend himself as top of the class. Hammer reported guarantees for $100,000. 'If this is the case,' Roald wrote optimistically to Leon, 'he must be a genius.' Not only had he secured the actual Pole flight; he had soon organised the back-up. The US Navy promised that 'the large American super zeppelin will come to our rescue. That sounds good!' Dollars and zeppelins flap on wire-less wings, but the real question remains unanswered: genius or charlatan?

A week after his arrival Roald Amundsen obtained an audience with his old supporter at the palace in Christiania. The King and the polar explorer discussed Hammer. The Foreign Office had given the head of state supplementary background material. 'But the King thought as I did,' Roald wrote to the ever-sceptical Leon, 'that one cannot condemn a man for ever, if he has offended once, but only keep one's eyes open.'

But the lone wolf at Svartskog was increasingly won over by the international support Hammer was able to drum up. The expedition's national character was no longer evident. 'I cannot ask my pompous compatriots for help,' he wrote to Dover. 'But I do believe that they will be there when they see the seriousness of it. At the moment they are just laughing.' He wrote it lightly, but the worst thing that could befall Roald Amundsen was to be made to look a fool. His first big goal was to regain gravitas: 'I hope I can transform mockery into dignity.'

On 19 December *Tidens Tegn* made the following announcement: 'The plan has been realised.' Haakon Hammer had come to Christiania and laid his package deal on the table, ensuring American participation and financial support.

The next few days there followed a series of public attacks on Roald Amundsen and his new men. The North Sea pilot Tryggve Gran wrote that the flight to the Pole was based on 'luck, luck and nothing but luck'. Were one to fall down (and one usually did), none of Amundsen's American companions would survive the onward journey on skis through the icy wilds: 'The new men whom Amundsen names in his new plan are not the type of individuals a totally conscientious leader would take with him into the wilderness,' Gran wrote and foresaw rescue expeditions costing 'many thousands'. The chairman of the Norwegian Geographical Society suggested that Amundsen was no longer 'as strong' as he ought to be.

The old Antarctic explorer Carsten Borchgrevink found the moment right to remind everyone of the lack of 'planning' during the third *Fram* expedition, when the world's eyes were focused on Norway: 'It is then not possible to just change direction at the very last moment, like some sort of juvenile. One loses one's dignity thereby and the moral aspect of the matter is not the least important for our nation.'

Fridtjof Nansen, who was asked to comment every time new information regarding *Maud*'s drift was released, wisely excused himself and diplomatically blamed lack of time to study the new plans. The ageing polar explorer looked at his watch; he was busy saving the world.

Dagbladet spoke out and demanded that light be thrown on the 'polar night'. The newspaper pointed out that Roald Amundsen's activities throughout the past few years had been hidden from the public gaze in spite of governmental funds and their importance to the national interest. The newspaper asked relevant questions regarding the previous history of the expedition by plane. Besides, there were several events clouded in obscurity: 'What has been going on on board *Maud* is not known. We do not know the reasons why Tessem and Knudsen left the ship and set out on a dangerous retreat which cost them their lives. We do not know for sure why Captain Helmer Hanssen and the others later left *Maud* in America. Nor do we know for sure why Roald Amundsen himself left *Maud*, abandoned the real expedition and planned a fairy-tale flight instead.'

Faith in Roald Amundsen had been blind. The nation's debt to its famous son had been great. But the score was no longer so obvious. Questions were being asked.

The polar explorer celebrated a cosmopolitan family Christmas at Uranienborg with the little girls, 'Uncle Haakon' and Aunt Adelheide von Pumpernickel. On the fourth day the Hammers took the girls to Copenhagen 'for the time being'. A few days later the polar explorer joined them. In the meantime Omdal guarded the house. The pilot from Maudheim had been unceremoniously demoted to caretaker at Uranienborg.

In Copenhagen Roald Amundsen met representatives of the German Dornier-Wal company. On 7 January he informed Leon that the contract had been signed 'for the construction of two large sea-planes and with them it should be possible to make the journey right across'. Easy. The factory fixed the planes, Hammer the money, the polar explorer contributed with pen and a signature. Bob's your uncle.

The final contract incorporated three sea planes. The expedition was about to take on new dimensions. In addition to Americans it would also include Italian pilots. That was natural as the Dornier planes were built in Pisa. Besides, in addition to Omdal two Norwegian participants had signed on; two lieutenants from the Fleet Air Arm, Hjalmar Riiser-Larsen and Leif Dietrichson. The latter took part in the Army's back-up expedition to Svalbard, while Riiser-Larsen had been in contact with Amundsen already before his stay in Alaska. 'A lot of good advice. Good guy,' the polar explorer noted having read the lieutenant's letter.

On his return to Norway they had met in person. But as both Riiser-Larsen and his friend Dietrichson, as opposed to Omdal, were married men, they had thought twice before committing to the ageing bachelor's new daring venture.

Roald Amundsen and Hammer were now playing for high stakes with a foot in every camp. In January there was an exchange of words between the Norwegian and American Foreign Offices. It was regarding an (as yet hypothetical) territorial dispute. To whom would the explorers' new land belong?

In an interview with an American newspaper Roald Amundsen allegedly said that he would not annex new land for Norway, and certainly not land outside Alaska. He said the opposite to the Norwegian press; that is to say that as a Norwegian he would claim all new territories. This pronouncement made Hammer slightly nervous as he was about to sell the fictitious landmasses to the Americans and had actually already told his American pilot Davidson that of course he could plant his flag on the islands of the Arctic Ocean.

On 22 January Hammer wrote to Amundsen from Copenhagen; the tone was sharper than normal: 'It was my intention when I now travel over there to emphasise this as it awakens national feeling and makes the money fly. Hell, you cannot expect America to pay for the party when you pronounce that any new territories discovered will be Norwegian. I know it is ridiculous to talk about this but our friends on the other side are ridiculous and want to hear that if there is any land then it must belong to America.'

A letter from the Norwegian legation in Washington to the Norwegian Foreign Office stated that Hammer had apparently handed over a written declaration to the American Defence Ministry, on behalf of himself and Amundsen, that the as yet undiscovered continents would fall to America.

On 8 February Norway's Foreign Minister approached the polar explorer in person and asked him to throw light on the situation. Leon, who had now returned from Dover, answered on his behalf and made it clear that he, the polar explorer, had never given such an undertaking. 'It is my understanding that new land can only be annexed by that country under whose flag one is sailing.' In other words, the Norwegian.

The realisation of the expedition might well be down to the Americans, but, nevertheless, starting from Spitsbergen was dependent on the Norwegian authorities' goodwill. This might mean a blow to Hammer's financial machinations, but the Norwegian could not, when the double-dealing was being wound up, 'flag out' the entire enterprise, however little solidarity he felt at the moment with his suspicious and ridiculous compatriots.

Businessman Hammer, whom the American newspapers addressed as 'arctic explorer', was prepared to trade with fictitious territories for what they were worth in the world of illusions. For Roald Amundsen the situation was different; following Peary's discovery it was not really the North Pole which drew him, but rather the large undiscovered regions between the Pole and Alaska. Ever since the planning stages of the *Maud* expedition he had believed that land existed inside this enormous area. This land, small or large, was perhaps the only remaining land worth discovering before the entire globe was definitively mapped. The whole world talked about the North Pole. Not so Roald Amundsen; he talked about the trans-Arctic flight. And he thought about land.

Might history have room for another Columbus?

It was not possible to build the Dornier-Wal sea-planes at the company's factory in Germany owing to the strict restrictions the country had been placed under following the Treaty of Versailles. The plan was to fly the planes from the factory in Pisa home to Norway, whence they would fly, independently and with their Rolls-Royce engines, to Svalbard in June.

Ahead of the planned transfer of the planes the members of the expedition were busy journeying to and fro. On 1 April 1924 Roald Amundsen wrote to Leon from Pisa: 'All is wild enthusiasm here so no problem with credit so far.' Norway and America were not the only countries to have invested national pride in the great undertaking: 'Am off to Rome tomorrow, mostly with the object of advertising. The factory here is intending to make this a big affair, and as they have been so charming I must help them.' From Rome he travelled on to new, equally charming acquaintances: 'Am stopping off today in Milan to visit Mussolini. Am looking forward to that.'

At the end of the month he was back in Norway. Then he was off south with Riiser-Larsen. The polar explorer sent Leon the key to the front door: 'There is a whole bunch of mail on the top veranda. Had not time to answer it.'

In Copenhagen important events were taking place: 'All is well and Uncle Haakon is cajoling a lot more out of people.' On 12 May the polar explorer made a flying visit to Svartskog. This time the little girls were with him; Camilla and Kakonita had not been home since Christmas. In their great hurry 'Grand-daddy' and 'Uncle Haakon' placed the two nomads in a suitable institution in Denmark. Now Aline and Leon had returned, they could take care of them.

It is pointless to reconstruct Haakon H. Hammer's ingenious pecuniary arrangements eighty years after they collapsed. They included everything from newspaper contracts and film and postage stamp rights to various donations; the main point is that when the three costly planes came to be paid for, or at least a deposit paid, on delivery in June 1924, there was absolutely no money in hand.

In the very last stages Hammer himself realised that the expedition was surrounded by charlatans and bankrupt scoundrels on every side, for whom serious agreements were hardly worth the paper they were written on. And in the middle of it all the polar explorer, with his clumsy telegrams, managed to play the strongest cards into the enemy's hands. But, wrote Hammer in a slightly desperate business letter, dated Paris 8 June, should all go down the drain he still had one secret 'trump card' up his sleeve. And, in spite of feeling rather down the day before, there was no reason for pessimism; 'he who endures always wins.' The polar explorer received the letter and sees his own reflection in the mirror.

On the evening of 26 June 1924 Roald Amundsen issued the following momentous statement: 'As it has been impossible to secure sufficient financial backing the expedition will have to be postponed until further notice.' The decision was taken after a conference with Lieutenant Dietrichson who had arrived at Svartskog from Pisa with the latest news. The same day Riiser-Larsen and Omdal, who were in Pisa, were asked to return to their native country. That was that.

'Hammer has not always been a competent businessman,' the polar explorer admitted in a letter to Herman Gade. And then he drew the conclusion: 'Hammer is a thing of the past and power of attorney is back with me.'

In an extraordinary way the former 'genius' continued to flap around the world. In the middle of October the Norwegian legation in Tokyo reported that Hammer and wife had set out on a world cruise. The multifaceted businessman was visiting the imperial city in order to inspect an aeroplane which was being built at Roald Amundsen's expense. The question was whether the Japanese might not consider financing the flight to the Pole.

Roald Amundsen settled his final account with his agent in his autobiography where he branded Hammer a 'criminal optimist'. He washed his hands of him and said, 'I never entertained any suspicion until the spring of 1924.' The truth is that the polar explorer was warned off the businessman by Leon as early as 1922.

Roald Amundsen wanted to believe in Hammer for the simple reason that Hammer believed in him. Having together irresponsibly buried the *Maud* expedition's finances they were reduced to 'flying' out of the quagmire they had made for themselves. Without taking a stand regarding the legal side of Hammer's – to put it mildly – unlucky business transactions, it must be brought home that if the term 'criminal optimist' is an accurate description for one partner, it needs must also apply to the other.

For Roald Amundsen people were more and more shaped according to his own needs. If he needed a saviour, Hammer is it; if he needed a scapegoat, the same man is a scoundrel, just like Omdal could be transformed overnight from ace pilot to clumsy fool. In Roald Amundsen's world there is only one constant star: himself.

THIRTY-FOUR

The Journey to Drøbak

The combination of Roald Amundsen and Haakon Hammer had been as disastrous as the cooperation between the brothers Roald and Leon had been successful. Rather than complement the polar explorer's weaker points, the agent had compounded them. Besides, the fact that the chubby businessman wanted to take part on the ground as 'arctic explorer' had contributed towards giving the expedition the burlesque appearance of a circus.

The businesslike discretion, the delicate diplomacy, the relationship of trust with the authorities, everything that Leon had built up over twenty long years, were now to a large extent compromised – first and foremost owing to Roald Amundsen's own rash and badly founded ideas, secondly to the Danish-American's total lack of insight into the peculiar and extremely complicated sphere of business which polar exploration represented.

Roald Amundsen's sense of reality had failed him. And not for the first time. But he was used to having something to fall back on. The new side-kick lacked all necessary qualifications to fill this role.

In his autobiography the polar explorer declares that he lacked all and any business experience; he had always had to trust others. 'So far this has never caused any difficulty. I did what I was told to do and all went well.' Thus he stresses his own child-like innocence and at the same time pays his brother Leon an equally unambiguous but unconscious compliment.

Roald Amundsen's partnership with Haakon Hammer had placed a heavy burden on his relationship with Leon. He had undermined his own credibility with one hiccup after another. However, it did not only concern the affair around Hammer; the transactions regarding the two properties, Uranienborg and Rødsten, had also alarmed Leon.

It started in 1920 when the polar explorer, two years late, admitted to having given Uranienborg away, in reality also Rødsten. When he left with *Maud* he had been a wealthy man. But after two disastrous years in the ice his financial position was considerably weakened. Leon was the one who always made sure that there was enough money in the *Maud* expedition account for wages and other expenses. From the moment the polar explorer's reserves and public funds were exhausted the manager had covered the amounts out of his own pocket. In time Leon Amundsen was not only his brother's manager, he had also become his most important creditor.

As security for the ever-mounting outlay there were the two properties by the Bunnefjord. *Maud* too represented considerable value, but there was always the possibility that the ship might founder. A polar ship in the pack ice was in principle to be considered like a warship under bombardment.

No wonder, then, that Leon took it badly when his brother willy-nilly arranged to give away or sell one or other of the properties. So uncertain regarding his brother's transactions was Leon that, when the second gift was made in the spring of 1923, Leon contacted Lawyer Gudde in order to clarify which of the properties had been made over to Consul Gudde, in other words to Kiss.

Kiss never laid claim to the properties; on the contrary she advised Roald Amundsen to sell Uranienborg on the open market, something Amundsen was loath to do for fear of his creditors. When the question of value and security was pushed to extremes in the spring of 1924, it was no doubt connected to the fact that not only was the polar explorer playing a hazardous game, but he was also gambling with his own life. Had Roald Amundsen taken off over the Arctic Ocean the probable result would not have been a settlement between the countries regarding who would take possession of new territories, but a quarrel between the creditors. Who would bear the loss when Roald Amundsen had crashed into the sea?

When the properties could not be sold on the open market, the polar explorer agreed to make them over to Leon. But Uranienborg and Rødsten in no way covered the amount due to Leon, which by now was close to 100,000 crowns. For over a year Leon had been preparing an application to the government for a larger loan. When the brothers met at Svartskog in May Leon strongly advised Roald to apply for funds from the State Research Trust. Roald did not agree. Either he was loath to channel more money into an undertaking in which he was no longer interested and which might have jeopardised the flight or, more to the point, he was too proud to beg his ungrateful compatriots for more money.

Leon was now in a precarious position. He was obliged, indefinitely, to continue to pump money into a polar journey with a most uncertain future, without either financial guarantees or the prospect of any relief. Roald, the eternal optimist, was sure that all would be fine if only the planes would take off. Leon did not agree. He was pretty sure that everything would come to grief even before the planes had left Pisa.

The very moment he put his foot down Leon became superfluous in Roald's universe, surplus to requirements. He did not stop being manager, but he stepped down financially. In so doing he joined the rest of the 'treacherous' crew. The Governor had never accepted those sorts of objections or reservations. A jack of all trades was such until he turned traitor.

From this moment a devious and in time far-reaching drama around the two neighbouring properties by the Bunnefjord started to take shape. An important man in this intrigue was Herman Gade, the Kingdom of Norway's representative in Brazil. He had already in 1923, while in Rio, offered his friend financial support to save his home. But the polar explorer had assured him that he was not giving up Uranienborg with a 'sore heart'. 'I am completely resigned to leaving the place,' he wrote in December. However, he 'treasures' his friend's thoughtful offer.

But the strategy behind the poker game was not what it appeared. Roald Amundsen had always leant on others in matters of business. His advisers had been many: Leon, Alexander Nansen, the brothers Gade, Trygve Gudde, Haakon Hammer; the time was ripe for a come-back. Gustav Amundsen, who had been wandering in a shadowy valley ever since the *Gjøa* expedition twenty years previously, was now ready to regain his position as the polar explorer's trusted man.

When Roald Amundsen returned from Alaska the situation regarding the two brothers Tonni and Busken was the same old miserable one. The former dry-milk producer Tonni had not only been hit by ever-recurring financial setbacks; he had also lost his wife and only daughter. During the last years the polar explorer's letters indicated a constant fear that his oldest brother would do away with himself. However, Tonni tottered on, his personal consumption always rising, at the expense of his relatives. When the dry milk petered out his next big idea was chicken farming.

Instability had also been Busken's hallmark. He too lurched from one illusion to the next, without the ability to provide for himself and his family. Gustav Amundsen had, on the whole, lived on the polar explorer's charity, and he had two assets: he believed in Roald and he hated Leon.

When, sometime in May, Leon had made it clear that he was suspending further payments to *Maud*, the change was sudden. On 5 May the polar explorer had, as agreed, written to Trygve Gudde and asked him to transfer the Uranienborg deeds from Niels Gudde to Leon. Twelve days later the lawyer received yet another commission, dated 17 May: 'As you are familiar with the house and contents – more or less – I would like you to be good enough and value the house as low as you think is possible – and return the deed to me.'

It was now the polar explorer's intention to sell the properties which a mere two days ago had been transferred to his brother, and for the lowest sum possible. This was owing to a couple of exceptional circumstances. In the past Roald Amundsen had been used to dealing with the properties irrespective of ownership. Leon had at various periods, often for tax reasons, been the owner of both Uranienborg and Rødsten. Their financial cooperation was mutually advantageous; Leon was the practical one, Roald the highest authority. The polar explorer now decided to sell his brother's properties, as if the old partnership still existed. Leon might have agreed were it not for the fact that Roald insisted on selling at the lowest price. Not on the open market, but under the table, to Herman Gade.

With the collapse in Pisa the following month, all and every imaginary hope of a quick solution to the polar explorer's financial problems were dashed. A new role was waiting: the lone hero's battle against his creditors. 'I must stand against the wolves that are now approaching,' Roald wrote to Herman on 10 July. 'Their numbers are legion and one is greedier than the other. But if you can look them in the eye without blinking, you know, they'll draw back.' Following this picturesque description the polar explorer came to the point: 'With regard to the property here, I know Gustav has written. He did so without my knowledge. He is more nervous and fearful than me. I will always find a roof over my head.' So: Gustav had been acting behind the scenes. The hero feigned ignorance.

Minister Gade took the hint and answered immediately by telegram from Riga. Of course, the polar explorer could still rely on his wealthy friend. Roald got going, via telegraph and post: 'Thank you for your telegram from Riga yesterday and for all your offers of assistance. You certainly have proven to be a good friend, and you must believe I will never forget it. I answered you per telegraph and asked you to deal directly with Lawyer Nansen as I must not feature in this case. If you decide on Uranienborg: it would be a nice little hideout when you are in Norway. I will look after them.'

When Gade offered to buy one or 'also' both properties, it was clear from the outset that the polar explorer would continue to have the place at his disposal. It was conspicuous how the inaccessible backwater by the Bunnefjord was now, as opposed to six months earlier, perceived in a completely different light. 'You cannot imagine how beautiful it is here today. The fjord is smooth and still and the sun is baking down from a clear sky.' However, the most important aspect of the vendor's argument was not the landscape but rather the human element: 'We could spend many happy hours in this snug and comfortable place, when you arrive to rest for a while. Complete and utter rest is what you will find here. One is virtually as isolated as on the Pole.'

The ex-patriot Gade, like Lawyer Gudde, had been kept in the dark regarding the underlying circumstances. That was a common characteristic of the polar explorer's manner; he never exposed every aspect to any one individual. All got a part of his confidence, but from all at least a part was hidden. Little did Gade realise that he had become a pawn in the battle against the most important of all the 'traitors' – Leon was now the big bad 'wolf'.

When at all costs the brother was not to inherit the properties, it was not owing to the 'snug and comfortable place', or the financial situation. Roald Amundsen had always been generous towards his friends and colleagues; he had been equally consistent in his contempt for and pettiness towards those who 'betrayed' him. He begrudged the 'traitors' a free sample of the *North East Passage*, and equally did not want to see his former partner, his brother in wolves' clothing, lord it over the properties by the Bunnefjord.

At the end of July the two brothers collided. On 26 July Gade received the following telegram: 'Can you buy Rødsten immediately. Formalities delaying sale of Uranienborg. Roald.'

The formalities were the inconvenient fact that Leon, after the transfer of the deeds, was the real owner of Uranienborg and did not wish to sell at a loss. For Rødsten no new deeds had been issued and so Leon could delay the sale by protesting, in his capacity as owner, at the low valuation, which he did. A new valuation showed Rødsten to be worth 22,000 crowns.

'What shall I do?' the polar explorer asked in his next letter to Gade. 'Bitter enmity has developed here and has gone so far that his children wander through the yard and look me in the face without greeting me. Huge flocks of strange children run screaming and shouting through here down to the bath-house, just to bother me.' The wolves were everywhere. One could no longer halt them in their tracks by looking them in the eye. 'I have had to put a padlock on the garden gate to stop this unpleasantness and that has helped.'

The polar explorer had landed himself in a typical quarrel between neighbours. He would most willingly have moved to Rio; 'but it would irritate me to leave the battlefield to my honourable brother. He would burst with pride if he managed to drive me away.' If he cannot conquer the North Pole he will have to make do with guarding the fence. 'Thank God I have Gustav, who is an invaluable support. He rushes around all over the place.' Roald Amundsen's jack-of-all-trades brother was experiencing new glory days. 'Rushing around', he worked towards his big goal, the vision of the brothers, the Captains Amundsen, the younger and the older, living in two houses, side by side, by the Bunnefjord. And Leon, the arch-rival, pushed out into the uttermost darkness.

In *My Life as a Polar Explorer* Amundsen refers to his brother's economic 'treachery' by twisting the facts exactly 180 degrees, when he claims that it was

Leon 'who wanted to take steps and sell the house to cover his claims'. In reality it was the polar explorer who wanted to save the properties out of his estate by means of a *pro forma* transfer to Minister Gade.

'All appeared to be in order,' the polar explorer summed up to Gade, 'but I reckoned without my brother Leon.' Through his Lawyer Albert Balchen, who to Roald's irritation proved to be a childhood friend of Herman Gade, Leon had managed to stop the sale of both properties. 'You cannot imagine how unpleasant it is here.'

Two brothers living side by side. According to the deeds each one of them owned the house the other lived in. Via Lawyer Nansen Roald gave notice without it leading anywhere, maybe because he himself lived in a glass-house. Life together was not much more comfortable than it had been at Framheim between the Governor and Hjalmar Johansen after the last words had been uttered. One of them had to leave.

It was probably Gustav who came up with the solution. What if the polar explorer was declared bankrupt? Bankrupt – Roald Amundsen? What a disgrace, what shame. Shame on whom? Shame on the ungrateful people, on the inadequate manager, but not on the national hero; after all, he had never dealt in filthy lucre, had he?

Besides, there was life after bankruptcy. Gustav knew that. He had been through it all before. From the moment Roald was declared bankrupt Leon would have no claim on either Uranienborg or Rødsten. The transfer took place when the polar explorer was insolvent. Everything must fall to the estate.

But who will declare Roald Amundsen bankrupt? No one. Not even Leon. He was the largest creditor, but he knew his brother's financial situation better than anyone. Roald Amundsen had liquidation problems but he was not insolvent. Not if the *Maud* expedition escaped from the ice. Twice the Governor had tried via the telegraph to call the research ship home, but even with a telegraph on board it was no easy matter to dictate to an icebound ship. No one knew when it would reach its goal. The creditors were willing to wait. So was Leon.

If anything was to be done one must do it oneself. On 2 September 1924 Roald Amundsen handed over his estate to Follø Probate Registry to instigate bankruptcy proceedings. The scandal was a reality. The world was shocked.

On 18 September the polar explorer set out on a short but important expedition. He travelled to Drøbak. By his side in the Ford, up the steep hill from Uranienborg, was Gustav Amundsen. At last he was in his element, the man who had been fighting creditors all his life, who had borrowed a few quid here, a hundred there, who had bluffed his way to thousands, and who had had to hide for fear of being beaten up by people from whom he had cheated a few crowns.

The polar explorer knew his brother's record. But what had King Haakon said about Hammer? 'One cannot judge him for always.'

The brothers arrived at the offices of the circuit judge on the dot of half past eleven for the scheduled creditors' meeting. Others present were Einar W. Nansen, who more and more had taken over his father's practice, plus another young lawyer, Leif S. Rode. He had been appointed estate trustee. The future chairman of the Norwegian Ski Federation had been a great admirer of the polar explorer since boyhood. Leon was not present. This was not his expedition.

Lawyer Rode, in spite of his wintry interests, had not quite grasped what he was letting himself in for when he accepted the role of trustee of Roald Amundsen's bankrupt estate. In the future he would administer a major part of Norwegian polar research. In his report he established that the *Maud* expedition had been pursued by 'extraordinary unfortunate ice and current conditions. Herein lay the probable reason for the bankruptcy.'

As the reason for bringing about his own bankruptcy, Roald Amundsen gave a very gentlemanly excuse, namely the one of 'safeguarding the other creditors', in order that no one could accuse him of acting in his brother's interests. The argument not only underlined his own integrity; it had the advantage of affecting his brother.

He expressed himself more openly to Gade: 'Leon precipitated this by not agreeing to cooperate. Now he'll just have to knuckle under.' In a letter to Don Pedro he described the break with his brother in more dignified but no less heroic words: 'Unfortunately, I have to inform you that my brother Leon is no longer my manager, as he withdrew when adversity reared its head. I am thus all alone but twice as strong.'

The Minister in Rio was 'shocked' when he read about the bankruptcy but added that it would 'give rise to serious reflection'. In Buenos Aires too the news was received with consternation. In spite of declining health Don Pedro was filled with 'shame and anger over our compatriots who can push aside all your legitimate demands for support during such adversity'. The Danish newspaper *Politiken* argued that Norway had 'exposed itself, and the world was shaking its head in astonishment.'

In a letter to Minister Gade the polar explorer's Lawyer Alexander Nansen tried to point out that it was incorrect that the 'Norwegian state and the Norwegian nation did nothing to prevent Amundsen's bankruptcy. Amundsen himself refused to appeal to the government or the authorities. He desired the bankruptcy and the information regarding it no doubt took a lot of people by surprise.'

The day after the creditors' meeting in Drøbak the polar explorer was interviewed by *Tidens Tegn*. The audience took place in the sequestered bachelor pad by the Bunnefjord, where the building and contents had been valued to twice 15,000 crowns. 'I am so lonely,' the national hero announced; he had been robbed of all except his 'two strong arms'. But he was not complaining, although 'I would have liked to have kept my two foster daughters, but it was not possible'. The presence of the two little girls was now justified as part of the scientific work: 'That was an experiment too. You see, people in Nome and up there will not admit that the Eskimos are capable of development. It is generally considered that they can only reach a certain level, there and no farther.' As the polar explorer is able to establish that the 'children had learnt so much', his hypothesis must be considered to have been confirmed.

Roald Amundsen informed readers that the foster-daughters left Uranienborg that same day, to spend four months with Mrs Wisting in Horten, 'and then they'll go home.'

Home? Perhaps so for Camilla Carpendale, she returned to a large family a few years earlier than planned, but what about Kakonita Amundsen? Was not Uranienborg her home? The polar explorer had adopted her. Now he dismissed her 'as an experiment', as one of the many casualties of the bankruptcy.

The foster-daughters' existence had been premised on stable conditions in the properties by the Bunnefjord, on the fact that Aline and Leon could take care of their existence. When Roald Amundsen broke with his brother he sacrificed his daughter at the same time.

THIRTY-FIVE

The Millionaire's Son

The same day as the two nomad girls Camilla and Kakonita, the casualties of Roald Amundsen's experiment in family life, were taken away from the bankrupt estate and put on a train to Horten, the polar explorer wrote an important letter. It was addressed to Kiss. In addition, he started a new diary. It was penned in the first person, in the style of a continuous monologue, and was directed at her: 'Sent you a long letter today. You might not like it but I had to be truthful.'

The polar explorer was left high and dry; the flight to the Pole had collapsed, the *Maud* expedition had been called home, although the ship would need yet another year before it broke loose from the ice. His home was sequestrated; Hammer, the genial saviour, had evaporated. And Leon, the solid, personal and businesslike fixed point, the filial safe haven, had been transformed, in the course of a single summer, into his most bitter enemy.

He was not friendless; his rich supporters Herman Gade and Don Pedro Christophersen were at their posts. And jack of all trades Gustav was by his side. He might even have succeeded in provoking one or other of his gloating compatriots to reflection and self-scrutiny.

The administrators had agreed to let him carry out a planned lecture tour in America to try and raise money to pay the *Maud* crew's wages. But they had confiscated his suitcases. He packed in crates. 'I have plenty of luggage as I am packing with Alaska in mind. I am going into exile, my little friend,' he wrote in his diary, addressing himself to Kiss:

The last months' events have caused me always to be unhappy here. I will therefore remain on the other side of the Atlantic, until you call me. And if you do not call me, I will bury my bones over there. As things stand at the moment, I think my house in Wainwright is the best place for me. There I can be a *man* – here, God knows what. There is the healthy, unspoilt outdoor life, which blows strength and power into one. I will wait for you there. If you find I am unworthy of this, then tell me. You are free to do as you like, and I *must* accept that.

Roald Amundsen drew up the balance sheet, as usual, without giving much thought to reality. The end of the line for the banished, the house in Wainwright, belonged to the bankrupt estate and might have been sold ere he reached his remote outpost. To abandon Norway was all-important. He reverted to the role of Flying Dutchman. Only Kiss could call him back to a life among humankind. Destitute and disgraced he put his destiny in her hands. He had nothing to offer her, no polar bear to spread under her feet, no ring-billed gulls in gold-edged arrangements, no enigmatic dedications, no planes bearing her name, no domestic nest by the glassy fjord. To the rich man's wife, all he could offer was himself. Never before had the polar hero's need for Mrs Bennett been more urgent.

The day before his departure Roald Amundsen was contacted by his brother's lawyer Albert Balchen, who made it clear that Leon intended to prove that Uranienborg had been given away as long ago as 1918 and thus could not be included in the bankrupt estate, but on the contrary belonged to him, Leon, following the transfer of a registered deed from Niels Gudde. The danger that Mrs B's name would be drawn into the negotiations was imminent. Roald Amundsen considered it 'blackmail'.

The frightening prospect was, however, shoved to one side to accommodate another incident; he received a letter from London, with an answer to all his questions. A new red-letter day had joined the polar explorer's chronicle: '25 September 1924. It will always be to me the largest most beautiful day of my life. My little girl is mine, mine, mine.' The polar explorer was clutching at straws and they seemed to be intact.

The next day he left Norway. The bankrupt national hero was smuggled out through the back door, to Gothenburg. Gustav accompanied him to Moss. From now on he was alone, but not entirely; he had his diary and his 'wireless', telepathic connection to Kiss. Besides, he had received another letter.

'Oh, you are so wonderful and sweet, like in the olden days.' The polar explorer dreamt a lot about the 'olden days'. That was the time before he placed all his eggs in one basket and demanded that she break away from the marriage, while he waited aboard *Maud* in the Arctic Ocean. Those were the idyllic days during the war in the trenches when he spent months in London and everything was arranged according to her terms. Then she was 'wonderful and sweet'. Later he forced her to show who of the two was the stronger.

Roald Amundsen was the only Norwegian on board *Drottningholm* – 'very comfortable'. The bankrupt victim travelled first class and dined at the captain's table. The letters from Kiss gave him new impetus; the world appeared lighter: 'I walk around chatting to you all day and send you thousands of "wirelesses". Hope your receiver is functioning?' If the *Maud* journey might have been characterised as a honeymoon without a bride, he now appeared more like an old married man off on a business trip. 'The little miniature portrait of you is with me always, on the night table beside the clock you gave me. I have my own pillow with the pillowcases you sewed. I also use all your handkerchiefs. So, as you can see, you are everywhere.' As long as he can trust his 'own little wife' he is 'stronger than ever'.

Roald Amundsen was certainly no broken man. Before long the exiled Norwegian stood on deck to witness *Drottningholm* steaming past *Bergensfjord* with all his compatriots on board. And one day in the dining room something took place which showed that here, in the wider world, his popularity was still intact: 'It was quite touching to hear everyone today. With the exception of one American and one Dane, everyone is Swedish. At lunch the band played Bull's "Seterjentens Søndag" ['The Dairymaid's Sunday']. Usually nobody claps, but when it was over everyone clapped like crazy. A wonderful tribute to me and my country. It was so beautiful and did me a lot of good.' It was a long time since the polar explorer had experienced the beneficial effect of applause.

But of course adoration had its drawbacks. 'The world is full of cunning temptations and, for one without support, so easy to fall for.' Is the polar explorer thinking of another journey by boat? Maybe of a woman he chanced upon en route to Nome a few years ago? All this must be forgotten. In Kiss's shadow even the most beautiful woman was reduced to little more than a disturbing element during a game of deck quoits. 'These females are all mad. I have not given them any encouragement but they all want to be photographed with me and they all want to go to the Pole with me. They bore me. Can you imagine anything more stupid? I couldn't care less about them, thanks to you my wonderful girl.'

Of course Roald Amundsen had not given up his big dream of flying over the Pole. 'The Pole is not yet lost,' he wrote to Don Pedro a few days after the bankruptcy; he was a habitual optimist. 'It is no good giving up, Don Pedro. Anyone who does, has pronounced his own death sentence.'

In principle only one more year had been lost. The cooperation with the three Norwegian pilots would continue. Nor had the contract with Dornier-Wal been broken. At the factory in Pisa they were pleased that Hammer, who according to them 'had frivolously neglected the finances', was now out of the picture. The German managing director had complete confidence in Riiser-Larsen.

Initially the Norwegian lieutenant needed to clarify whether their former ally, Locatelli, wanted to execute a flight to the Pole himself and thereby steal a march on them. Managing Director Schulte-Frohlinde, however, had little doubt that the Italians' polar-enthusiasm would blow over by the following summer, 'especially as the Fascist regime has been kicked hard and Mussolini will probably not last long.' A flight over the North Pole was not every government's priority.

In parallel to his property transactions the polar explorer had made several attempts to raise new funds for the expedition. In the Governor's absence Riiser-Larsen took over further efforts, now in cooperation with the Norwegian Aeronautical Association. Newspaper articles indicated that a new expedition would be subject to a *joint* leadership consisting of the naval lieutenant and the old polar explorer. Besides, a flight under the auspices of the Aeronautical Association would not include Alaska, but be limited to the North Pole. The manufacturers in Pisa found this solution 'very sensible as one must implicitly gather experience in the local area before venturing out on the larger task of flying to Alaska.' Roald Amundsen's big plan was in the process of becoming other people's affairs.

'I was closer to giving up in desperation than at any other time in my 53-year-old life,' he wrote in his memoirs, although on arrival in New York the polar explorer seemed to be exhibiting an especially light frame of mind. He was met by a representative of his promoter, who 'brought me your wonderful letter'. He immediately started preparing articles and lectures aimed at the American market. 'As usual Keedick is my manager and is very pleased with the prospects,' he wrote to Herman Gade. As befitted his position, the South Pole conqueror established himself in the huge, fashionable Waldorf-Astoria Hotel. The only thing that bothered him in the metropolis was the heat.

The turning point came on 8 October – suddenly and marvellously. Roald Amundsen received a delegation of newspaper editors. A little later he was called to the telephone. An American by the name of Lincoln Ellsworth asked for an audience. 'When I heard his voice,' the American wrote in his memoirs many years later, 'I was as excited as a young hunter who has an elk in his sights for the first time.'

Amundsen noted in his diary: 'Later in the afternoon a man arrived called Lincoln Ellsworth, 42 years old, whom I met in Paris during the war. Large, good-looking character. He wanted to join me on the flight. He has 20,000 [dollars] of his own money which he is willing to part with, but he hopes to interest his father who is very rich. Something might come of this.' The polar explorer dared not expect too much. The unassuming, boyish American did not behave like a patron.

None the less, the miracle has happened; a new Don Pedro enters his life.

Five days later they meet again. 'Had lunch with Lincoln Ellsworth today,' he wrote in his diary. 'I told him to collect all the money he could and join me. He is over the moon. His father is allegedly very rich and could easily pay for the whole shebang.'

The polar explorer set out on his lecture tour.

On 26 October he was back in his hotel. A letter from Kiss awaited him. Three days later the unbelievable message arrived: 'Ellsworth has offered me 90,000 dollars, which in real terms means that the flight is virtually a fact. Telegraphed home and asked their opinion.' His courage will not yet allow him to make any new decisions. To what degree could he trust Old Moneybags, old Ellsworth?

James W. Ellsworth was a 75-year-old tall, slender multi-millionaire – a typical capitalist who owned a villa in Florence, a castle in Switzerland and skyscrapers in Chicago. The Ellsworth family moved in the highest circles of American society; their wealth was based principally on coal mines. The relationship between the cold, authoritarian father and his only son was strained. Lincoln had lost his mother at a young age; he was a qualified engineer and had devoted his life to adventure. The old fellow especially disliked his son's pipe-smoking habit.

Roald Amundsen met the once so strong-willed but now considerably impaired James W. Ellsworth for the first time on his farm in Hudson, Ohio. On his return by overnight train to New York he telegraphed Kiss with the news that the money had been secured and the planes ordered. He then sat down and wrote in detail. 'I am writing to you first and secondly to Riiser-Larsen with the order to go ahead with the expedition.' The sequence was important. Kiss had been the polar explorer's motivation and inspiration in everything he had done since his return from the South Pole. Nothing of importance was relayed to Christiania before the woman in London had been informed. 'So I have started once again and this time with a healthier foundation,' he concluded in his diary.

On 9 November the polar explorer met old Ellsworth for the second time, now in New York. The enfeebled father received his athletic son and his son's grey-haired idol in his library. The guest made a quick calculation: 'Paintings worth 75,000 dollars each adorn the walls. Artefacts from 400 BC everywhere. On the floor in one of the rooms a carpet from the 11th century!!'

For the third time the sum is guaranteed. The millionaire makes only one stipulation: his son must stop smoking!

Roald Amundsen and Lincoln Ellsworth's plans were immediately published in American newspapers. However, the new partner is sceptical of the cooperation with the Norwegian Aeronautical Association. The polar explorer had turned to them for assistance when he was at his lowest ebb. Now he informed them that conditions were being reconsidered, but in any case 'Riiser must immediately order the two aeroplanes.'

On 15 November he wrote in his diary: 'It is just wonderful to meet a person who trusts me as much as Ell. does.' The man possessed Wisting's devotion and Don Pedro's wallet; in addition, he shared the polar explorer's conviction that a flight over the uncharted icy wilds carried with it the greatest happiness that could befall a human being.

Ellsworth represented the finances, but Riiser-Larsen the practicalities. Both were essential prerequisites for the polar researcher's blissful come-back. The organisation of a flight under extreme conditions needed specialist skills which the dog-sledge driver and skier had never possessed. Hjalmar Riiser-Larsen, a 34-year-old vigorous flight lieutenant, was just the man Roald Amundsen needed to realise his dreams. Following the recent spate of telegrams he was given immediate leave from his position in the Ministry of Defence and immersed himself in the practical aspects of the Amundsen–Ellsworth polar flight.

'Sixteenth of November; 12th anniversary. A wonderful day. Many excellent memories. Goodnight, and God bless you.' Right in the middle of the hectic preparations the polar explorer celebrates the anniversary. Twelve years have passed since he met his Goddess of Bliss at the Hotel Cecil in London. Since then she has been wooed by his melting mandolin from every corner of the world. Now it won't be long before she sees him take off for the North Pole.

But first yet another round of lectures.

Everywhere he arrived he anxiously expected a letter from London. He read her missives with burning interest, tinged with a certain amount of disquiet. 'A wonderful letter, but my little friend, you are so busy – earls and countesses, dukes and duchesses! You go to balls and dance too?' Not to say that he was in the least bit uncertain of her. 'Your letters make me happy and joyful. I know you are mine for now and ever, all doubt has left me.'

In his thoughts the polar explorer followed Kiss, whom he knew would celebrate Christmas in her native town of Trondheim. He himself returned to his beloved Waldorf-Astoria. 'Arrived at 9 this morning and you should have seen them all. The faces of all, from bell-boy to manager, were beaming. I had to shake hands with everyone. I seem to be loved.'

But unforeseen complications awaited him in New York. 'Ellsworth came immediately. His father has given him a lot of unpleasantness. He is old and moody and difficult to get on with. He is very ill too. He has suddenly decided that the boy must give up the trip. The son has flatly refused and has taken leave of his father and the house for good.'

Old Ellsworth would allow the polar explorer to keep the $80,000, on condition that the son withdrew from the flight. 'That might be tempting for a poor man, but not for me. Only a coward and a traitor would behave like that. Lincoln Ellsworth has given me a leg up and he will always command my friendship. It hurts me to break up a family but I think the circumstances warrant it.'

Roald Amundsen was obliged to give his American creditors notice of bankruptcy but he took this new humiliation in his stride. Young Ellsworth presented him with an overcoat, lined with mink and with an astrakhan collar; 'so now I'm a millionaire too'.

The two friends dined together at the St Regis. But in his thoughts and in his diary the polar explorer quickly left the wintry metropolis. 'Tomorrow I board the train with you and Christmas Eve at 7 in the morning we will step out in Trondheim. Hurrah, we'll celebrate Christmas together, dance round the tree and sing: Holy Night.'

The polar explorer spends Christmas Eve in his hotel room – alone with his dreams. 'Thank you, thank you, my sweetest little wife, for the Christmas present. What a wonderful scarf. I will keep it until we meet. I dare not walk around with such gay colours here.'

In his memoirs *Beyond Horizons* Lincoln Ellsworth describes this period as 'an awful winter', rowing with his sick father who soon bitterly regretted that he had agreed to support the life-threatening journey to the North Pole.

Old Ellsworth fought a fierce battle in an attempt to save his son from the polar explorer's clutches. 'Oh my God what hardships,' Amundsen wrote in his diary on 26 December. 'I was so sure I had Ellsworth on my side, and then he tells me today that he must withdraw if I cannot find a third aeroplane.'

The next day it dawned on the polar explorer that he had completely misjudged Ellsworth, who was clearly trying to meet his father half-way, somewhere, regarding the safety of the expedition: 'All well with Ellsworth today. I have misjudged him and take my words back. His entire life lies in the air.' The son of the millionaire trusted his destiny to the polar explorer.

All the same, some sort of compromise was worked out around the New Year. It appeared that consideration for both old Ellsworth's concerns and the Norwegian Aeronautical Association at home played its part. When it quickly became clear that there was no possibility of raising money for a third plane, Amundsen and Ellsworth relinquished their plan to fly across to Alaska; they agreed to define the journey as a reconnaissance for 'future transpolar flights'. In his memoirs Ellsworth writes that he and Amundsen, in spite of their signatures, entered into a secret pact to 'fly beyond Alaska anyhow, if all went well'.

The total cost of completing the expedition would far surpass the sum Ellsworth could raise. The polar explorer was sure his partners in Norway could generate the balance. In this connection the properties by the Bunnefjord were once again brought into the equation.

In the absence of his friend, Herman Gade made an application to Don Pedro Christophersen and suggested that they two might buy the properties Uranienborg and Rødsten. The trustees were willing to sell back to Roald Amundsen via his friends Gade and Don Pedro, but the principal creditor, Leon, was not. He continued to maintain that the properties belonged to him and decided to take the case to court. For Roald and Leon it was no longer the two houses that were at stake, but their wish to assert their rights.

While the polar explorer was absent Gustav held the fort at Uranienborg while Leon continued to live at Rødsten. 'Last time when I went ashore at Baalerud landing stage,' Busken reported, 'Leon was there too. I used the opportunity to confront him and said very calmly what I wanted to say. I can only say that he cut a very pathetic figure.'

What was on Leon's mind he let his lawyer communicate to the circuit judge. 'The properties in question have been and are still much used by smugglers. And the garden at Uranienborg for instance, when Mr Roald Amundsen is absent, has been used as a depot for cans of spirits, etc. Since Roald Amundsen's departure Mr Leon Amundsen has noticed much activity on the fjord and he fears that the property once again is being used by smugglers.'

After Christmas the polar explorer's new, rich friend made an offer of a permanent place of residence. Lincoln Ellsworth suggested the medieval castle in Lensburg in Switzerland as a suitable place for Roald to spend the rest of his life. According to his diary Amundsen's answer was: 'No, you just wait until you have been to London and I'll show you where I'm going to spend the rest of my life!!'

Never since first setting out with *Maud* had Roald Amundsen felt so secure in the knowledge that Kiss was ready to have him. On New Year's Eve he wrote: '12 years! Sorrow, happiness, bliss, pain, all we have been through to build stronger and more splendidly year by year. Thanks to you, most wonderful of women, we have succeeded. I can never find words for what I owe you. I can only offer you gratitude now. Later, I hope a life of heartfelt love. You know, my little wife, I am with you and you feel it all the time.'

That sounded like a celebration speech after twelve years of married bliss. In reality he was not one single step closer to matrimonial felicity. But over the years so many edifices had crumbled; she was now more than ever necessary to him.

Next day, the first of 1925, he awoke, in his thoughts, with her. 'Good morning my little pussycat and the best of all new years to you. Can you feel my kissie on your forehead? Eyes? Cheeks? Mouth? Breast? – No, I better stop. But a good start to a new year!'

On 5 January the polar explorer set out on a new tour with his box of slides. The reception for the lectures exceeded all expectations and during the tour of America he was able to send home – to the 'lion's jaw' – 27,000 crowns. Throughout this last round, however, he felt a mounting sense of unease. The expedition was under control and the bankruptcy proceeding apace, but the unease was deeper than that. He felt Kiss sliding away. 'Where are you?' he asked early in the New Year.

During the period of a few short weeks the entire relationship, the strong and splendid structure, had started to wobble. Her letters were less frequent; he suspected her of corresponding with another man. After the lecture on 18 January he wrote: 'I do not know if you are mine anymore. For God's sake remove my doubt which is starting to poison my mind. Forgive me.' The last letter received was dated 26 December – no greetings for New Year's Eve.

In Boston he lodged with Herman Gade's younger brother Horace. He received a telegram; Kiss had been ill. 'What on earth is the matter with you? Write immediately. God willing you are well again.' He must leave, still bewildered. 'Your letter may reach me but yet might not.' Three days later, on the 23rd: 'I do not feel well. The secure foundation on which I stood is failing me.' Jealousy grows in him; it is the Canadian businessman, a friend of the family: 'Campbell is in my thoughts a lot. Ten years ago you would never have started corresponding with another man.'

He was back in New York on 27 January. No love letters awaited him at the hotel. In return a snowstorm played havoc with the town. '5th Avenue is transformed into a footpath. Wonderful!'

Rather than the longed-for letter from Kiss, Roald Amundsen received a momentous letter from old Ellsworth. As he himself was too ill, the letter was written by a trusted colleague but signed James W. Ellsworth. The old businessman claimed that Roald Amundsen had on several occasions broken the financial agreement the two had signed at Ellsworth's farm in Ohio. The way in which the polar explorer had handled the business questions had made Ellsworth Snr lose all confidence in the practical implementation of the expedition. The old man wrote that the worry had already completely destroyed his health. He was convinced that his son would lose his life during the flight and, if he held to his resolve, his father would not 'survive the ordeal' either. This was a broken man's last-ditch attempt at saving the life of his only son. The argument was logical, but did not stand a chance. Lincoln Ellsworth had put his life in Roald Amundsen's hands.

A few more days of lunches, dinners and lectures, then on 3 February the polar explorer boarded the ship which would take him back to Europe. A letter arrived as he was about to depart. 'But I do not understand. You ask which boat I will arrive on and I know for sure I have told you five times already.'

It had long been obvious that the polar explorer intended to return via London. The idea of emigrating to Alaska was shelved immediately the Ellsworth dollars hit the table. Mrs Bennett had obviously not felt it necessary to excite the arctic traveller ere he arrived in the imperial capital. She encouraged him when he was elsewhere; the closer he approached the more reserved and withdrawn she seemed. *His* goddess lived in London; *her* knight in shining armour lived, if possible, in a hut by the coast of a distant, windblown Alaska.

On boarding the American ship the polar explorer was informed that the captain wished him to be seated at his right hand at meals. 'That would not have been the case on an English ship.' On the whole he had felt extremely popular in America. And 'when I entered my cabin there was a huge bowl of wonderful roses.' Do not feel too safe, Kiss. 'If men adore you, there are other fish in the sea for your boy-o. Goodnight.'

THIRTY-SIX

Beloved above All in the World

As a child Roald Amundsen had dreamt a Jules Verne dream of an electric ship which would convey him elegantly and painlessly through the ice to the Poles. Fifty years later he was nevertheless taken aback when he realised how far science had advanced; the captain of the modern passenger-ship invited him onto the bridge. 'It was extraordinary to see that no one was at the helm. The course is set with the use of electric power. Strange.'

Roald Amundsen was considered a pioneer of modern polar aviation. His real contribution was limited to the realms of fantasy. He never understood the technique; he understood only how to pretend.

His bathtub with its effective but comprehensible taps was and remained his dearest contraption, even on the Atlantic crossing. 'You cannot believe how excellent my bath is. I can choose between salt and fresh water.'

The polar explorer booked in to a hotel in London. The Bennetts' house Leigh Court was full of Norwegian guests. The polar explorer, who had behaved impeccably during the whole crossing, went on a bender. God knows how he got into bad company. 'The host was a swine.' What sort of women were they? The next day he confessed to Minister Vogt. 'He said I need not worry if anyone had seen us as the women were probably all right. That's a relief. The devil if anyone had seen me in dubious company. That's the last thing I want. I've learnt a lesson.' Luckily Kiss phoned the next day. 'I heard your dear voice at 5 and I feel well.'

Then, a dramatic bulletin from Leigh Court. 'What a shock to hear that you have taken to your bed. Bloody hell, why do you always fall sick whenever we meet?' This type of party game was too sophisticated for the polar explorer. He did not realise that 'illness' was a woman's weapon with which she keeps a man at bay. 'But good God, it is wonderful just to hear your voice on the phone. I hope there might soon be a connection Oslo–London so we can talk more often.'*

---

* Translator's note: Christiania reverted to its old name of Oslo in 1925.

At last the Goddess of Bliss can receive the conqueror of the South Pole. Diary entry, 17 February: 'Wonderful to be with you today. You should have seen my stride and deportment; when I walked around the streets here afterwards. I actually felt like a man once more. The life I lead forces me to see myself as some sort of eunuch, one who never can show his true colours. It is a horrible feeling and depresses me. God knows I long for the day when I will be a complete man and you – a complete woman.'

With this he can fly to the North Pole, maybe even all the way to Alaska.

Roald Amundsen saw Kiss as something approximating a magnetic Pole – a strong power in constant motion. In reality she was more like the geographic Pole; firm and mathematically immovable at Leigh Court. He was the one in motion – between the heights of certainty and the depths of jealousy.

At Marina di Pisa the Governor met his second-in-command, Hjalmar Riiser-Larsen. Together they inspected the sea-planes which were undergoing their final overhaul. The lieutenant was the expert, the polar explorer the fantasist.

On 25 February they set off north by train. The aeroplanes would be shipped over; the only safe method, steamship and steam-locomotive. 'Riiser-Larsen is an unusually nice man to travel with. Quiet and calm. With his 6 foot 4 he towers over everyone and the Italians stare all the time.'

After a thirty-hour train journey the two Norwegians arrived in Berlin on 28 February. This day was to become a turning point in the history of the Weimar Republic. The Republic's first President, the Social Democrat Friedrich Ebert, died: 'The most beautiful weather – on the occasion of the President's death there is a sea of flags, all of them at half mast.'

The two got some business out of the way before the lieutenant continued on to Kiel. The polar explorer dined with the Norwegian Minister and relaxed. He lived at Hotel Kaiserhof, which would soon become Adolf Hitler's local in the capital.

His next meeting with Riiser-Larsen was in Copenhagen. The two were invited out on the town by the Norwegian ship-owner Ivar Christensen. This was the same 'swine' who had enticed the polar explorer to the Savoy in unsavoury female company just a few weeks earlier. When the once bitten twice shy Roald Amundsen declined this time, the ship-owner insinuated that maybe he was not all that keen on women. 'No,' said the polar explorer, standing his ground, 'only one, but I'm damned fond of her.'

At midday on 4 March 1925 the train from the Continent made a quick stop at Kolbotn, south-east of Norway's capital, which, at the turn of the year was once again called by its old name Oslo. The snow was still deep. Three men, a horse and sleigh were waiting; Captain Gustav Amundsen and the local village shopkeeper, plus a journalist who had smelt a rat. The polar explorer jumped off the train. 'R-Larsen continued to Oslo and was caught by the mob – reporters and photographers.'

Unfortunately, no letters were waiting, only an old one forwarded from New York.

On 9 May Roald Amundsen met his partners in Norway's Aeronautical Association. The chairman was the exceedingly industrious Dr Rolf Thommessen, editor-in-chief and owner of *Tidens Tegn*, the country's most modern and go-ahead newspaper. The year Blériot crossed the Channel Thommessen submitted his PhD on 'The Artist in Greek Art'. Since then he had developed a weakness for the science fiction of aviation, coupled with a nostalgic worship of a bygone Norse golden age. The editor-in-chief spent some time as a member of the National Assembly but he had more faith in strong, dynamic men than in the pale subjects in Parliament. In his collaboration with Roald Amundsen he would soon learn that strong men also have their weak sides.

The editor-in-chief was voted in as the business manager of a company which would be responsible for the polar flight; thus there would be no mixing together of the expedition's affairs with the polar explorer's ruined finances. However, with Ellsworth's backing, Roald Amundsen's position as the unchallenged Governor was not in question. Other central figures on the administrative side were Johan Sverre, Norway's representative on the IOC (International Olympic Committee) and the lawyer Arnold Ræstad, recently stepped down from a short period as Norway's Foreign Minister. He too was a pronounced nationalist with a particular penchant for Arctic imperialism.

When Roald Amundsen returned to Svartskog following these encouraging talks, a 'wonderful' letter from London awaited him. The next day, 11 March, the telegraph informed him that the ship with the aeroplanes had left Pisa. The journey has started.

Apart from his pilots and their wives, in the period before departure to the icy wilds, the polar explorer kept company with Gustav and his family and Gudrun and Robert Maus. In addition Kiss Bennett's two sons, Alfred and Peto, arrived by train to spend the last week at Uranienborg. The two boys, in their twenties, were spending the winter working in the offices of timber merchant Westye Egeberg in Oslo. This was not their first visit to Uranienborg but they had no idea of exactly what kind of friendship existed between their fêted young mother and the world-famous explorer. It's a good thing he knew how to cover his tracks: 'When we arrived a big bunch of letters to me were lying on the table. "Oh", said Peto, "post for me." But I had caught a glimpse of the pink envelopes and hey-presto they were all gone as if by magic.'

It says a lot about the second-in-command's efforts when we read how, during the last few days prior to departure, the Governor occupied himself with sawing and repairing the bath-house, walks and quoits. On 24 March Parliament approved a grant of 25,000 crowns in order that the naval vessel *Farm* could be placed at Roald Amundsen's disposal; this time not without some opposition: 87 voted for, 54 against this very modest public support of the North Pole flight. 'It is important to attach Norway's name to Arctic regions', said Prime Minister Mowinckel on behalf of the Cabinet.

'The first four left today,' the polar explorer wrote on 26 March. 'There were huge rejoicings at the station. I wonder how I'll trick them on Tuesday?' Tuesday was the day he would travel north. Was it to be with or without a fake beard and dark glasses?

On Monday 30 March Lincoln Ellsworth arrived in Oslo with *Oscar II*. The unassuming millionaire had but one day to enjoy the Norwegian's hospitality at Svartskog. With Alfred and Peto the two expedition leaders took a walk in the spring forest. Roald Amundsen packed and made 'final arrangements'. He wrote his last will and testament in Tromsø; initially to benefit Gustav and Tonni; later those two irresponsible figures had been crossed out and replaced with 'my sister-in-law Malfred Amundsen'. In contrast to her husband, Malfred Amundsen was a woman of great integrity who was generally respected, not least by her famous brother-in-law. She was on good terms with both Kiss and her sister Gudrun Maus. Should Amundsen disappear it was important for the polar explorer to know that his private effects were in safe hands.

The evening before departure Amundsen and Ellsworth booked in to the Grand Hotel where the Norwegian Aeronautical Association held a gala dinner in their honour. A large number of leading personalities, headed by the Minister for Trade and the old polar giant Otto Sverdrup, took their seats in the Rococo Hall. 'From a hollow in the middle of the large, square banqueting-table the globe emerged, snow-covered in cotton wool and flanked by two aeroplanes, ready for take-off.' According to newspaper reports handsome speeches were given for the departing Arctic travellers. Roald Amundsen thanked everyone and proposed a toast to the two ladies present, Mrs Thommessen and Mrs Ræstad.

They departed from the East Station the next day. The polar explorer had given up trying to lead the public up the garden path. There were several in the party, among them a reporter representing sixty American newspapers. Amundsen and Ellsworth both wore a carnation in their buttonholes; like a groom and his best man they waved farewell from the open train window. Diary entry, 31 March: 'Left at 6.50 this afternoon. Masses of people at the station. I thought I glimpsed you among them.' The polar explorer experienced a happy moment in the centre of publicity. He was at peace with himself.

'We are rattling north and soon it will become serious. I am happy I feel you with me. Then all will work out.'

The next morning the two expedition leaders were met by Trygve Gudde in Trondheim, and served breakfast in the lawyer's home. A conversation in English regarding the flight to the Pole took place, and continued in Norwegian regarding the bankruptcy. Kiss Bennett's brother had been in Oslo and negotiated with the Lawyers Nansen and Rode. He now gave the polar explorer a first-hand report.

With his young wife and daughter Gudde accompanied his two rugged guests to the quay where they boarded the north-bound coastal steamer. Their departure was accompanied by great festivities, a students' choir and speeches. The polar explorer noted that Trondheim had run out of the polar stamps specially issued in aid of the journey. Within an hour, 14,000 stamps, depicting polar bear and aeroplane, were snatched up. Kiss Bennett's native town treated Norway's great son to a jubilant send-off.

On 4 April Amundsen and Ellsworth moved into pharmacist Zapffe's house in Tromsø. 'Ells. is so impressed with all the nice, hospitable people.' While the American went shopping the Norwegian made a phone call to hear what was happening to the expedition. The main body were still a good way further south, in Narvik. The expedition had reached its first critical juncture, unloading and reloading the planes from one ship to the other. They were packed into six enormous crates, plus twenty-one containers of tools and spare parts. The not too spacious arctic vessel *Hobby* had been chartered to carry the precious cargo north. The ship was so precariously overloaded that it was obliged to await the go-ahead from the expedition meteorologists before it set out on the crossing. Only flying appears more hazardous.

Hobby arrived in Tromsø on 8 April. That evening there were more festivities with speeches and a male choir. The forecast was favourable. At five in the morning of 9 April 1925 the boats set out over the ocean – the Navy's transport ship *Farm*, fitted out with bow-cannons, and the low-lying *Hobby*, weighed down with the expedition's mechanical gold. So far there was nothing to show that this was an aeronautical expedition.

The crew's composition was entirely different from those of Amundsen's former *Gjøa*, *Fram* and *Maud* expeditions. It consisted of four important groupings: pilots, mechanics, meteorologists and representatives of the press. The colourful crowd ranged from Dornier-Wal director Schulte-Frohlinde to sail-maker Rønne. The rheumatic *Maud* deserter ate humble pie and was restored to favour. As a specialist he was simply indispensable. Even in 1925 not every craft could be left to the mechanics. As Captain Wisting was icebound in *Maud*,

Martin Rønne became the only one of Amundsen's old boys to be part of the new expedition.

And what about his rivals? Wherever Amundsen laid his plans rivals buzzed in the air. It had long been clear to all that an airship was the ideal craft for a flight over the Polar Sea. But such a flight would demand a huge contraption. The Americans had worked on just such a plan – until the President shoved his oar in and put a stop to it all. It was too expensive, even for a superpower. For the time being the most conspicuous challenge was a British expedition led by a 24-year-old with the Icelandic name of Grettir Algarsson. The young adventurer had allied himself with a couple of Shackleton's old colleagues and was, allegedly, constructing an airship.

While Roald Amundsen travelled north editor Thommessen tried to get as much information as possible out of the challenger. He ordered his correspondent to interview Algarsson. That led to a full-page article in *Tidens Tegn* regarding the British preparations and the leader's theory about the superiority of the Nordic race. The element of competition was important to increase public awareness and thus strengthen the expedition economically. But at the same time Thommessen asked the Norwegian legation in London to report to him privately regarding Algarsson's plans 'and particularly the time of his departure from England'. The editor-in-chief was kept updated by none other than Roald Amundsen's old colleague Kristian Prestrud who was serving at the legation. The lieutenant from Framheim considered, however, that the British plans were 'a pretty loosely supported affair'.

Before long *Farm* and *Hobby* were overtaken by bad weather; the ships encountered high seas and bad visibility. They quickly lost contact. Amundsen and Ellsworth, on board the naval vessel, were in the dark as to *Hobby*'s fate. Would the deck cargo survive, or were the planes already at the bottom of the sea? On 11 April, not far off Bear Island, *Farm* received another, rather unexpected, but no less ominous, telegram.

Kiss has been operated on for appendicitis. The telegram was signed by a mutual friend in England. Roald Amundsen immediately telegraphed home to Gustav. 'How K. Inform me immediately.' Suddenly everything was in a state of flux. *Hobby* and the planes had disappeared in storm and snow squalls. But what did that matter now? 'I have one prayer and one burning wish, that God will hold His hand over my little girl and save her for me.' Without Kiss no wings can take him to the Pole. Everything is founded on her.

On 13 April *Farm* docked in Kings Bay on Spitsbergen, 79° North. Roald Amundsen was frantic, about both Kiss and *Hobby*. 'I have not yet received an answer to my telegram to Gustav and am very uneasy. Am going up to the wireless now and will send another one. You know, you are all I have. You know

I love and worship you. You know, that life without you – even if it must be lived separate from you – is unbearable.'

The next evening Roald Amundsen was standing on the deck of *Farm*, weighed down by anxiety, when a lieutenant walked over and handed him his binoculars. Later he wrote in the diary: 'I took the binoculars and there, out of the ice, *Hobby* appeared, big and fat, carrying its deck cargo. A sigh of relief and a feeling of warm gratitude coursed through me, a warm thank you to the excellent boys, a warm thank you to Him who seems to have a hand in it all.' Soon there was commotion everywhere. The shout '*Hobby* is here!' was followed by the sounds of Hurrah! as the ship slipped up to the quay.

They celebrated and feasted through the night. But only on the afternoon of 15 April did the Governor receive the important message from Oslo: 'Telegram England. All well.' In his diary he thanked God yet again. 'I can start to breathe freely once more.'

During a few hectic spring weeks the little mining community of Ny-Ålesund was entirely taken up with Pole fever; it was like Framheim fifteen years earlier. A world lay between the two events, however, and not just literally. The leap had been taken from skis and dogs to motorised vehicles. The tempo belonged to a new reality. There was no over-wintering for which to make preparations. By 2 May the planes would be mounted and ready for take-off.

Every day Roald Amundsen set his watch by the telegraph station in Ny-Ålesund according to the time signal from the Eiffel Tower in Paris. But if his watch was always correct, he himself was about to lose all sense of time. He represented the same restless spirit as Leiv Eriksson, Columbus, Vasco da Gama, Admiral Franklin. As the last great world explorer he was the expedition's spiritual overlord.

Roald Amundsen was not the driving force in the practical tasks, as he had been at Framheim. From the very first preparations at Marina di Pisa, Riiser-Larsen had worked closely with the Dornier-Wal director. Together with the mechanics they now finished off the lengthy technical procedures. All was dependent on the sea-planes' construction and execution. The polar explorer knew that this was not his line; nor was meteorology. *That* would decide the time of departure. The old skier was not even very familiar with the flight's navigation.

As he and Ellsworth were supposed to function as the flight's navigators, Lieutenants Riiser-Larsen and Dietrichson were forced to set aside badly needed time to instruct their two commanders-in-chief. And if the worst came to the worst (just in case there was a crash), the American needed to learn how to ski. At last the Governor could teach someone something.

It was −10°, the days were clear and it was light around the clock. Surrounding the small cluster of painted wooden houses, white peaks rose skywards. The polar explorer had time to make tracks around this unreal spot, hovering somewhere between the noise of civilisation and complete silence. 'My thoughts are always and ever with you,' he wrote to Kiss in his micro-scopic pencilled letters in the black diary.

One day they tested the engines. Rolls-Royce had sent its own mechanic. The world press was following even the smallest detail with the greatest interest. 'One of the carburettors froze!' the Governor noted. 'Oh well, I have always been suspicious of engines when it's cold.' He had never forgotten Captain Scott's famous motorised sledges.

The two sea-planes were fitted out with, in all, four engines. That gave them four chances. The balloon pioneer Andrée had only had one chance, said Roald Amundsen in an interview: 'a strong storm might have pushed him over.' One chance was good enough reason for one go. The polar explorer's admiration for the Swedish engineer had increased. First he admired Franklin for his martyrdom, then Nansen for his skill and now Andrée for his – why? They had all had courage. But the engineer's fatalism was not for Amundsen. Nor had Salomon August Andrée sought martyrdom, the heroic suffering, battling to conquer; he had given in, to the power of the elements, to God's will. The flight of the balloon *Ørnen* had had a religious dimension. It could only have succeeded if Our Lord had steered the engineer with the winds of His almighty hand.

It was Roald Amundsen's intention to start the flight from Danskeøya, the same place whence *Ørnen* had ascended into the sky towards the North Pole twenty-eight years earlier. Since then no one had seen it.

On one of the last days of April Roald Amundsen summoned Ellsworth and the two pilots Riiser-Larsen and Dietrichson to an important meeting. It took place in the mining company's none too sumptuous director's dwelling, where Amundsen was lodging with Fritz G. Zapffe, the expedition storekeeper. To the assembled 'gentlemen' the Governor submitted his plan, namely that he had not given up his objective of flying all the way to Alaska. On the contrary, it was his intention to continue with one plane, while the others turned back at the Pole.

Of course, it was Amundsen's plane that would continue – Ellsworth would return. The Governor knew that he could count on his former pilot-in-charge Omdal as the mechanic; but he was also dependent on support from one of the two named pilots. The diary: 'RL resisted fiercely, also D. The result was that I had to abandon the plan.'

The flight lieutenants' objection was based on simple calculations of distance and fuel needed; but also the fact that changing the expedition's objective would go against all agreements entered into, not least with the expedition's administrative leadership in the Norwegian Aeronautical Association.

Roald Amundsen was imagining a new Madeira. Yet again he wanted to surprise and hoodwink the world. That was not possible and for the following two reasons: first, he was not the expedition's real leader – he was obliged to give in to the second-in-command; second, he had no fall-back plan. There was no Leon sitting at home ready to implement the new plan. Not only had he handed over the operational and professional control of the expedition, but also the administrative. Without he himself realising it, the Governor's role had changed from that of absolute ruler to constitutional monarch.

He was obliged to give in, but not before firing a last shot across the bows: 'I ask myself so often. Where are the guts? If they are the slightest bit uncertain they pull in their horns. Well, for the moment I will have to give it up; I cannot fly alone. But when we return from the Pole I'll raise the issue again. If they won't agree then I'll take it up with the Norwegian Aeronautical Association.'

These lines proclaim an ageing hero's triumph over future generations. This is more than inflated posturing. His thoughts have certainly returned to the *Belgica*, when, as a 25-year-old second officer, he was more than willing to accompany the ship's commandant into an unknown Antarctic winter. He had not yet made the step into the age of the plane; now the consequences of daring behaviour were far less easy to calculate. As always the polar explorer's diary entry ended with a greeting to Kiss: 'God bless you my girl. Good-night. Where are the real men?'

On 2 May, the day the planes were scheduled to leave, the polar explorer settled his internal balance sheet, addressed to the woman in London: 'You will understand me and understand how I am suffering. Let me first fly to the Pole and back, and then we shall see. One thing gives me peace and makes everything else unimportant: You are well! Little Kiss, you know I love you with all my heart and you know I am working for one thing only, to get you. God help you (and me).'

It would have been natural for Roald Amundsen to have reinstated the two old names *Kristine* and *Elisabeth*, but public attention was probably too intense: a christening ceremony on Spitsbergen would resound around the world. Publicly the planes remained nameless. They were having to make do with the registration numbers N24 and N25. In the polar explorer's heart the planes had anyway long ago been named.

On 3 May the Governor made a note of a telegram from Prime Minister Mowinckel to the effect that he had government approval to take possession of any new land in the name of His Majesty the King of Norway. That was not the telegram he was waiting for: 'If only I had received the smallest note from you all would be wonderful.'

Two days later *Farm* and *Hobby* sailed north to seek out an airfield on Danskeøya. However, it was still cold and the engines were playing up. 'I think this adversity is good for us,' the Governor noted dutifully. 'One learns a lot from it.' On his daily ski trips over the frozen fjord he had discovered a seal with her newborn pups. Every day, while the mechanics and pilots did battle with the engines, he wandered alone or with Ellsworth out to inspect the seal pups – wondering whether they might soon be able to swim.

The farewell telegrams started to pour in, public and private, from Gade, from Gustav, and even from the boys Alfred and Peto. The last postal delivery south was made ready. 'Wrote to you, as always. I long for the post from the south. Is there a word from you? But no. Have you forgotten me?'

The ships returned with bad news from Andrée's old base in Virgohavn. It appeared impossible to set off from Danskeøya; it would have to be Kings Bay. As the temperature rose the engines performed like clockwork. It was now up to the meteorologists to pinpoint the historic moment, based on visibility, wind direction and temperature. The Governor did not mind waiting: 'this might be the last time I have the opportunity.' They had already been informed by telegraph that young Algarsson had given up his polar adventure. 'That suits us, now we can take it easy.'

At home in Norway many believed that the journey would take off on 17 May, Constitution Day. In Ny-Ålesund they amused themselves with an 'Olympic Games' sack-race and pillow fight on the ice. On the 18th the Governor received a warning from the weather diviners that the time was drawing near.

The planes are positioned on the fjord ice, ready for take-off. The petrol tanks are filled. Three nerve-racking days follow.

Diary entry, 19 May: 'At three this afternoon a big flight of migrating birds rose and set off towards the north. I know and feel that you are all nervous, but this is not the case with us at all. We will go to our flight as though we were going to breakfast. When we rise up I personally will be vindicated – the dirty mouths will be silenced. And so farewell beloved above all in the world. When you think of me let it be as in the olden days.'

But the flight is postponed yet again. The meteorologists are undecided; then the weather clears.

On 21 May 1925 Roald Amundsen concluded: 'We leave at 3. Farewell and never forget that your boy will love you with all his soul until his last breath. Send your two wonderful sons my love. I know they will be your great joy in life. Good bye my friend. Roald.'

With these words Roald Amundsen said goodbye to Kiss Bennett.

It was Ascension Day.

THIRTY-SEVEN

In the Kingdom of the Dead

The mountains threw out a loud echo over Kings Bay. With full throttle N25 set off over the ice. The time was 19.40, 21 May 1925. For a moment the sea-plane is hidden by a cloud of snow. Then it lifts off. Roald Amundsen is on board. They set a course for the North Pole.

Three minutes later N24 is airborne and sets off in pursuit.

Something new and untested was about to take place. An historic event at the point of intersection between Jules Verne and Yuri Gagarin. Through air and fog, above a gently curving expanse of ice, at a height of 3,000 metres, at a temperature of −10°, days without nights, a journey into the great void. What would they encounter?

Columbus too had known that at some point or other he would hit land. Amundsen knew that Alaska lay on the other side. But what lay in between? That was the unanswered question.

Like engineer Andrée's crew they were three on board each craft. N25 was piloted by Hjalmar Riiser-Larsen; the Governor was navigator, the mechanic was Karl Feucht from Dornier-Wal. Ever since the New Year it had been agreed that the little mechanic would represent the firm during the flight. The rather bashful Feucht was from Württemberg and according to Norwegian newspapers 'he clearly belonged to the Alpine race'. Director Schulte-Frohlinde had probably chosen Feucht for three reasons: he was a clever mechanic, he was light in weight, and he claimed to be an experienced skier.

N24 was piloted by Leif Dietrichson; the tall naval officer had nine years' flying experience under his belt, just one year less that the even taller Riiser-Larsen. Lincoln Ellsworth was the navigator, newly trained by Dietrichson. Without the American, or rather his father, Roald Amundsen would never have got off the ground, but would have touched rock-bottom, figuratively and literally. For over twelve years Ellsworth had dreamt of finding the continent of which his compatriot Peary allegedly caught a glimpse north of Greenland – the as yet undiscovered Crocker Land. Luckily the American was humble. On N24 Dietrichson was entrusted with planting the flag and taking possession of the land.

The third man was Oskar Omdal. He was the youngest member of the crew but the one who had worked the longest for the Governor. By virtue of his unpaid salary Omdal was not only N24's mechanic, he was also Roald Amundsen's creditor.

The aeroplanes were built of the ultra-modern material Duralumin; the crew, however, were wearing traditional polar clothing. The men sat in the open air behind glass screens; the navigator at the front. If necessary the mechanic could climb into the engine gondola which was suspended in line with the wings over the fuselage. The sea-plane was, of course, capable of landing on water as well as on snow and ice.

Both planes were over-laden by about half a tonne. Among other things they were carrying complete polar equipment in the case of a retreat over the ice: sledges, skis and canvas boats. The planes were of German construction, assembled in Italy with Rolls-Royce engines; the skis were Norwegian. During the loading of supplies Riiser-Larsen had rejected the offer of six pairs of skis made from imported hickory wood and had instead demanded Norwegian ash. He wrote to the Governor: 'Ideally, in order that all the equipment is Norwegian through and through.'

After eight hours in the air the planes should have been over the North Pole itself. N25 decided to go down in order to make precise observations. One of the unanswered questions, maybe the most important, was whether there were any suitable landing places inside the polar basin. The planes were dependent on either open water or level ice floes that were adequately extensive.

Hjalmar Riiser-Larsen spotted a small open channel where he put the plane down. They landed by the skin of their teeth, without the plane sustaining damage from the ice which piled up on both sides of the channel. Excitedly they started to calculate the latitude. It took a while before they knew exactly where they were. They are not on the North Pole.

They had landed in the Kingdom of the Dead.

After a few days in the pack ice Roald Amundsen stepped onto the wing of N25. He placed the field-glasses to his eyes and saw what Captain Scott had seen through *his* field-glasses when he stood by the South Pole: he saw the Norwegian flag.

As a result of landing in the very narrow channel N25 sat, immovably wedged, between the ice cliffs. Three men cannot move it, not even a Norwegian giant, an international legend and a German mechanic. As soon as the reality of the situation became apparent Riiser-Larsen started to prepare the sledge. Without reinforcements there was only one solution: walk to the nearest coast, to Cape Columbia on North Greenland. They had provisions for one month; that was their deadline. But one question remained. Where was N24?

The answer lay between the ice-hummocks a few kilometres away. N24 had faithfully kept pace with N25 during the descent. Having landed, the crew worked out that they were 87°43′ North. So, not the North Pole. That was disappointing.

Having ascertained their position they too had an urgent question. Where was N25? Dietrichson thought Amundsen might have taken off again for the Pole on his own. 'That would be like him,' he added.

N24 was easily manoeuvrable but the sea-plane leaked; it had been damaged already at take-off, and one engine was malfunctioning. Besides, the pilot had gone snow-blind. All they could do, having done all they could, was to hoist the flag.

This is the flag Amundsen spotted through his field-glasses on 23 May. In spite of the short distance, Nansen and Johansen could not have been more elated when they happened upon Jackson on Franz Josef Land than Amundsen was at that moment, catching sight of life in the wilderness. The lieutenant had soon re-established contact by semaphoring through the spyglass lenses. After yet another day, they realised that the planes were not stationary; on the contrary, they were moving towards each other at a rate of knots. Had not Fridtjof Nansen already confirmed that the pack ice was in constant motion? But what a coincidence that the two parties were not moving *away* from each other!

Luck, old polar explorer, haphazard luck or ice-cold calculations? Ask Roald Amundsen the very day he acknowledged the planes' movement and he will answer: There is no luck; what cannot be explained within the arena of human calculations has only an explanation which lies *outside*. That is not luck, that is Providence.

The parties agreed, via their silent communications, to gather strength and try and coax N25 into the air. (Later N24 was thoroughly inspected and found to be, all things considered, beyond repair.) Only a few hundred metres separated them but it was exceedingly difficult to pick their way forwards. Drift ice is a fickle substance. It towers in the air or is thin as paper, hard as rock or soft as wool; insurmountable barriers alternate with open water.

On 26 May Ellsworth, Dietrichson and Omdal set off after several unsuccessful attempts. They each carried a load of 40kg and wore skis with loose bindings as they were obliged to manoeuvre over thin ice. To off-set the rucksacks' force of gravity they all carried Tethys lifejackets, picked up from the costal steamer on their way north. The Governor and Riiser-Larsen met them half-way. It was soon clear that even such a short trip could embrace harrowing drama and shining feats.

'Just as we reached them we heard the most awful yell and I suspected the worst,' Roald Amundsen wrote that evening in his expedition diary. 'They had fallen into the water, but how many? They had disappeared behind an ice hummock. The situation was a nightmare of the very worst sort.' At this moment the expedition's future hung by the thinnest of threads. First Dietrichson disappeared through the ice, then Omdal. They both grabbed the ice's edge but the polar current was pulling in the opposite direction. At the same time the cold gripped them. The skis disappeared into the watery abyss. That alone was serious as the expedition did not allow for spare skis. But one pair remained, Ellsworth's.

Carefully, carefully the American pushed his Norwegian-made ash skis forwards to Dietrichson. The lieutenant grabbed them eagerly and was hauled up onto safer ice. Next Ellsworth turned to Omdal who was at the point of fainting away. The same current which had once pushed the polar ship *Fram* across the polar sea was about to receive its unresisting victim. But at the very final moment of consciousness the ski proved to be the weakened mechanic's last resort. In the age of the aeroplane, Norwegian wood had been equal to the task.

Lincoln Ellsworth, when he presented the Governor with two soaked subjects, did not know then that he had saved two human lives, but two which between them would live for only another five and a half years. Their dip through the ice at Latitude 87° North was a sign of things to come for the two lieutenants.

At last the parties were united. Everything was now geared towards getting N25 into the air. They decide to limit the daily rations and give themselves a deadline: 15 June. If nothing had happened by then a new plan would have to be worked out – whether to continue the battle to take off or set out on a short-cut to Greenland. With the remaining rations the real question was: Would they die en route – walking, or on the spot – standing?

Ellsworth wrote in his memoirs that Amundsen had aged during the few days they had been apart. And that in spite of the 'terrible yoke' he had shaken off when they lifted off from Spitsbergen. In the final account the polar explorer writes that he had already been rehabilitated. 'If we fell down right there, the stamp of sincerity could never again be erased.' The situation was in truth deadly serious. The Governor might have thrown off the 'contemptuous disdain' he had so long felt, but he was now stuck with the heavy moral responsibility for the safety of the men who had accompanied him on this basically very egocentric journey.

Roald Amundsen was the only one of the six who understood snow as an element. With his sum total of frost-bitten, fatiguing experiences he was the right man to lead a handful of men in such remote conditions as these. The sky, the fog, the ice – all ran together in an endless existence, devoid of night.

The Governor, quickly and skilfully, divided existence into clearly matched bite-sized portions – work, rest, meals and sleep. He calculated the hours in the same way as he rationed the biscuits and the pemmican. In this manner time was tangible. Eternity was pushed to one side. With this well-tried routine he established grounds for hope.

But the polar explorer could not will his way out of the catastrophe. If he thought that might have been a possibility, he would have packed up and led his men 750 kilometres to Cape Columbia, where his second-in-command Godfred Hansen had laid out a depot during the *Maud* expedition's first year. But the polar explorer knew the ice, and he knew that was not possible. To walk 750 kilometres over unpredictable terrain would involve intolerable exertion. Their only hope lay in the air. 'How near to home we are – a mere 7 hour flight – and yet under the circumstances how far,' he noted in his diary.

Hope was administered by Riiser-Larsen. He was the pilot. The silent giant felt the responsibility resting on his shoulders. Feucht vouched for the engine. Everything was in order; it was just a question of taking off. They had an aeroplane, they lacked an airfield.

This became the big challenge: to create an airfield long enough and level enough to enable a heavy engine like the N25 with fuel and six men on board to lift off. They had knives, ski-sticks, an axe and a few wooden spades. Equipment was a problem, but not the biggest. They were in the embrace of the pack ice, in perpetual motion. Any plan, any construction, was threatened by nature's superpower.

On 29 May the seriousness of their situation suddenly dawned on leader and crew alike. Only then was every plan to continue to the Pole shelved. All that mattered was to return to Spitsbergen. From now on it was all about survival.

They sent a sounding-shot towards the sea floor, following the newly developed echo-principle. Within 5 seconds they were able to establish that the sea-floor was 3,750 metres below them.

The German turned gloomy. He was not prepared for this. All the others had in various ways been connected to the planning, or had at least been dreaming about the Arctic for several years. The mechanic from Württemberg might have welcomed a bit of adventure, but he was no daredevil, let alone a polar explorer. Karl Feucht was at home in a dark noisy hangar, not under the polar sky's eternally bright heavens. Yet he was no coward. Throughout an entire world war he had served as a mechanic in zeppelins over France and England. He knew the horrors of war better than the Norwegian lieutenants and the American engineer. This was a new and unknown battlefield. A cold death had already invaded everything around him. After the day's shift he sat and played endlessly with the biscuit crumbs, apathetically, or, worse, with the tobacco rations. Ellsworth swallowed it, Amundsen was furious.

In *Beyond Horizons* Lincoln Ellsworth writes that they were all about to develop 'polar nerves'. The Governor irritated him. All six now lived in the fuselage. There they existed and slept, around the engine's nooks and crannies, when they were not out and working on the ice. One night a howl from Riiser-Larsen awoke them. The plane was about to be forced down into the abyss, like any old polar ship. Time and again attempts to take off failed. Apathy spread. Work continued.

They set themselves a deadline of 15 June. There was reason to doubt that they would make it. The Governor alone among them had experienced miracles.

On 9 June Riiser-Larsen, with his long legs, paced out what he imagined would make a new point of take-off. It would take ten days to complete. On the short rations they were only capable of enduring eight hours work per day. The Governor's speciality was cutting ice-blocks with a knife mounted on his ski-stick.

On 10 June Roald Amundsen observed a goose flying towards the north-west. 'Does that indicate Crocker Land?' he noted in his diary. There might be an island or a whole continent between them and Greenland. Might that be where the miracle awaited them? But it would be a land without depots; but beyond that, further south, they could hunt. That same day Dietrichson fired at two geese. He missed.

Diary entry, 11 June: 'Started to shovel snow this morning at 9, but at 1 were so tired we had to give up.' They needed to clear 400 metres of deep, heavy snow. Their equipment was wretched; their strength dwindling. They had already made too many failed attempts. That is when Omdal added his important contribution to Roald Amundsen's heroic chronicle. The mechanic was a simple man; he thought with the soles of his feet. 'What if we trod the snow down?'

All next day six men stamp the snow. Luckily no one saw them – it was foggy.

They measured the track once again. It was 100 metres longer than initially thought. 'A good addition,' the Governor noted in his diary. For him personally, this could be translated into an extra three years. Without those extra 100 metres it would be curtains – up here on the ice by the North Pole. They would just have disappeared. Like Andrée and his two colleagues in *Ørnen*. Not a bad finish. Perfect, really.

The addition was not only good; 100 metres might spell different lengths in the lives of six men. For half of them it meant just a postponement:

Dietrichson, Omdal and the Governor all ended their lives in the same ice-cold environment. Ellsworth and Riiser-Larsen on the other hand would enjoy long and adventure-filled lives. They would both fly to the Antarctic; they would both chart new land. The melancholy mechanic would return to his obscure hangars. He might possibly have survived long enough to perish in the big European shipwreck.

Summer arrived. The temperature gauge crept up to zero. Should it tip over, the track would melt and become useless. On the 14th they made two unsuccessful attempts. It was too late in the day; the foundation was not hard enough. They will try again tomorrow.

Dawn, 15 June. Should they not succeed they would have to face up to where they wanted to die. It would be up to the Governor to coordinate the votes.

Riiser-Larsen could not sleep that night. Time and again he climbed out of the fuselage where his colleagues lay in restless sleep. The pilot watched the thermometer, tested the wind direction, walked apprehensively over the ice floe which made up the track, calculated and marked the distances with black pieces of film negative. Everything must tally: number of degrees, number of metres, number of revolutions per second, number of litres of fuel, number of kilos. They had but one card to play. They must stake all in one effort. Equipment, supplies, weapons, skis, boat – they must leave it all behind if the plane was to take off and reach Spitsbergen with the minimum amount of fuel. Fuel meant weight. They had 500 metres to play with.

The fog lifted. Just like the departure from Gjøahavn. Just like the departure from Framheim. The silence was total. The base had no name. It lay beyond the world. Only the pilot's head protruded from the plane; the other five lay down in the fuselage as in a dark common grave. The engines revved. At that moment everything depended on Riiser-Larsen. Luckily, he no longer weighed 100kg. If he decided to take off he must take off; if not the plane would be smashed to pieces against the ice blocks where the track stopped.

They were off, the sea-plane was pulling well. He reached the critical point where he must decide: give all to win all, or stop the engines to save the plane. The speed is on the slow side, but Hjalmar Riiser-Larsen had a good feeling. He decided to chance it.

The Governor's diary: 'We saw nothing where we sat, could only feel the speed by the movements. Suddenly it started to judder, as though it wanted to leave the ground. At last it gave a final jerk and we felt we were airborne. The feeling of release was indescribable.'

It was by the skin of their teeth: 'Only right at the edge of the floe did the plane lift up. If not we would all have been a pile of ruin.' Omdal let out a howl of victory as they took off. This was his second howl. The first one was the howl of death when he fell through the ice. The Governor crawled forward to the pilot and laid a piece of chocolate in his lap, as big as a matchbox. That was his reward.

Nonetheless something has happened which was larger than the pilot's achievement, something which shattered the frame of human calculations. The polar explorer had experienced it before, in dramatic, fateful seconds; ships had been salvaged, human lives saved; time had touched eternity. They had spent twenty-five days in a white-washed floating mirage. They had spotted the head of one seal, seen one razor-billed auk, three geese; otherwise all around them had been lifeless. Only the cold had been substantial.

Conquered by this merciless existence the polar explorer turned to a higher power: 'I think I have prayed to God for help a thousand times these weeks, and things have turned out in such a way that I am certain beyond a shadow of a doubt that He stretched out His hand to us.'

THIRTY-EIGHT

The Resurrection

An entire world had been gazing towards the foggy north. The first week they said: They'll come back. They need a few extra days to complete the scientific investigations. Roald Amundsen is always thorough. Look how long he spent at the South Pole.

When fourteen days had passed *Farm* and *Hobby* were to begin patrolling along the ice north of Svalbard. After three weeks all hope had faded that the expedition would return by air. Cape Columbia was the only remaining option; they were en route to Greenland, on skis. There was no one to meet them there; the time for a search party had arrived. Plans were laid in Norway, in Europe and in the States. The slimmer the hope, the more plans.

The world was in for a surprise.

The flight from the Kingdom of the Dead took 8 hours 35 minutes. The tension had been unbearable. They could not land but *had* to reach land before the tank ran empty. Dietrichson's paramount job was that of navigator. When they spotted land the plane was forced down owing to steering problems. By now there was open sea under the plane and they were able to navigate the remaining 25 kilometres on water, albeit choppy water, to North Cape, on the tip of Nordaustlandet.

No sooner had the six stepped ashore than the whaling vessel *Sjøliv* came chugging in to the wilderness. '15 June will always be for me a holy day and I thank God who guided us so well,' Roald Amundsen wrote in his diary when the last link in the chain of miraculous circumstances had been forged.

N25 was made fast in the Franklin Straits while *Sjøliv* abandoned any pretence at hunting and made for Kings Bay with its precious cargo. 'As we passed Virgohavn we hoisted all our flags and little *Sjøliv* was fully dressed,' the polar explorer wrote in his final account. 'We wanted to honour the memory of the man who first tried to conquer the polar sea by air – Salomon August Andrée. Were there any men in the whole world who had more right than us six to celebrate his memory as we looked towards the spot from where he in 1897 made his daring journey? I think not. We lowered our flags and pressed on.'

When the young Roald Amundsen chose the North West Passage for his first journey it was to complete the work his childhood idol Sir John Franklin had started. The exploits of his old age were dedicated to engineer Andrée; now his odyssey was being wound up. The Englishman and the Swede had both tempted fate; both met death. Is that what Roald Amundsen wanted to overcome and conquer? In that case this time he had come very close to achieving his goal.

It was one in the morning on the night of 18 June 1925. A nondescript whaler came alongside the quay in Kings Bay harbour. The expedition ship *Hobby* and the warship *Heimdal*, together with two reconnaissance planes, were tied up ready to go; the ships had steam on as they were preparing to leave for the north that very night. A handful of inquisitive miners had gathered by the quay. Sauntering down to the harbour were the remaining members of Roald Amundsen's expedition and the officers from *Heimdal*. They had been sitting together in the director's house, discussing the prospects. The agenda had consisted of one item only during the last weeks. They fought against doubt for a long time, trying to kindle new hope. Now hope had left them altogether.

Six bearded men stood in the bows of the whaler which was gliding towards land. They waved, but no one heeded them. They were concentrating on the two ships and the two aeroplanes which were off to search. There had been no plane in Kings Bay since. . . . Suddenly someone recognised Roald Amundsen. Shouts reverberated in every direction. Amundsen has returned! He has risen from the dead.

A miracle had taken place; no one could believe their eyes. Everyone had to touch and feel them. It *was* them all right. They had returned.

But they had returned from another world.

Outside the director's dwelling cigars were handed round. Store keeper Zapffe had kept them in readiness. There were six in the case, one for each. They smoked the victory cigar, just like Roald Amundsen and his men had done at the South Pole. Photographs were taken. But when the pictures were developed they looked nothing like the ones taken with Olav Bjaaland's camera fourteen years earlier; they were more like the ones taken on the same spot with Scott's self-release camera. All six were marked by death. Robert Scott and his men would have looked like that if luck had been with them and they had struggled home to the victory cigars at base-camp Cape Evans. Eyes shone out of the bearded, dirty faces; only the glow of the cigars told the story of the marvellous triumph.

Inside feelings were channelled into one common voice. The crowd of expedition members, naval officers, miners and sailors broke into song. A psalm would have been natural, but the national anthem was on everybody's lips; yet another hurdle for the six exhausted men. 'It was hard to remain dry-eyed,' Roald Amundsen wrote in his diary. Now they can start to talk.

This time Roald Amundsen really had something to talk about. It had been no dance across the ice; it had been a battle for survival on a par with tales of suffering experienced by Franklin, Shackleton and Scott. It was not about rations and daily stages, like the saga of the South Pole. It was not even about the North Pole. (Had they actually been there?) It was above all about a human drama played out beyond the limits of existence, on death's territory. Victory lay not in a mathematical and geographical point but in life itself.

Next day 5,000 words flew around the world. On 19 June front-page copy was pushed aside for this sensational news. Soon hundreds of telegrams ticked in to the station in Ny-Ålesund. That same day, among hundred of others, three women sent the polar explorer their wishes. From Sigg in Oslo: 'Hurrah, congratulations.' Kiss in London: 'Overwhelmed with joy.' And from Bess in Nome: 'Skaal.'

But there was also sad news in among the congratulations. It arrived from Italy. James W. Ellsworth, the man who financed the aeroplanes, had passed away in his Villa Palmieri in Florence on 2 June; just as he had predicted. The price of victory had been paid. Old Ellsworth never saw his son smoke his victory cigar.

The expedition left Kings Bay on 25 June, waved off by a brass band, fireworks and lowered banners. Crew and seaplane were both accommodated on board the spacious coal-steamer *Alber. W. Selmer*.

For the first time since the North West Passage, during a long life of heroism, Roald Amundsen would experience a real homecoming. The triumphal journey southward down the Norwegian coast reminded one of *Fram* and the Viking king Fridtjof Nansen's 'coronation progress' from Tromsø to Christiania during the summer of 1896. His native land was already braced for commemoration; independent Norway's first Prime Minister, Christian Michelsen, had recently passed away and was buried two days before the aviators' entry into the capital.

'This looks merry!' the Governor noted in his diary when news reached him from the south regarding the festivities awaiting him. Having been hailed up the coast, the hero and his company stepped ashore in Horten. The next morning they would fly to Olso, the only time Roald Amundsen returned home in his own craft. *Gjøa* had ended her voyage in a park in San Francisco (the remains were brought home on the polar explorer's hundredth anniversary). *Fram* returned home unheeded and clandestinely. The accident-prone *Maud* had still not reached port in Alaska. But this time Roald Amundsen, conqueror of ice, returned home in his own winged ship, at the head of his men.

'At last the thumping great thing – N25 – appears from the south, droning, accompanied by naval sea-planes,' one newspaper reported on the festive Sunday, 5 July 1925. 'The large bird circles in wide arcs over the town. To it the whole town must resemble a sea of flags and waving handkerchiefs. Just outside Bygdøy, Riiser-Larsen puts his plane down. One propeller revolves slowly and the plane glides carefully forwards between the flotilla of boats. The warships parade their crew and when the plane passes *Tordenskjold* 13 gunshots from the boat and Akershus Fortress are fired, after which *Curacao*'s cannons thunder away with hollow booms.'

The public were as gripped by the noise from the aeroplane engine as they were by the gunshots. The heroes were rowed to the quay in a barge. During the lightning visit to Horten the three lieutenants, on the initiative of Riiser-Larsen, saw their chance to change from civvies into uniform. Thus the polar explorer's private army had acquired an official hue. The second-in-command had effected a military coup with a simple wardrobe trick. It appeared that the Governor did not oppose the Norwegian lieutenants' need to make their mark. His reaction a year later, when an Italian colonel carried out the same circus trick, was quite different.

After speeches and national anthems the triumphal journey proceeded by horse-drawn carriage to the residence of Their Majesties where decorations awaited them. Fifty thousand of their cheering fellow countrymen lined the route and joined in the festivities which followed on in rapid succession. Between lunch at the Grand Hotel and dinner at the Palace, the polar explorer found time to greet the Oslo Labour Party at a huge gathering on Hovedøya. Roald Amundsen was treading in the footsteps of Fridtjof Nansen on this unforgettable summer's day: the Viking king who united the people in an outburst of national fervour. 'The reception was royal,' was the sober entry in his diary.

All this lay well beyond the polar explorer's expectations. The expedition had not even reached its goal; they had merely saved their own lives. The enthusiasm surpassed every calculation. And yet, he had now reached his actual goal. People clasped him to their bosoms; the whole world cheered him. They were not interested in the geographical point. They were not interested in adjusting their atlases; they wanted to feed their fantasies. They desired adventure, deeds, martyrdom – they wanted him.

Roald Amundsen had a sense for the effects of theatre, not for its essence. All his life he had tried to hide from them what the public desired – the human drama. The human drama was what had made Robert Scott the real victor in the battle for the South Pole.

While he had conquered the South Pole with reasonable ease, Roald Amundsen was forced, in his encounter with the North Pole, to acknowledge his own inadequacy. 'We did what we could up there,' he pronounced during the banquet at the Palace: 'and when we could do no more, I said I was not frightened to admit it: we have done what we can, God will have to take over.' The polar explorer had acknowledged his human limitations. He had drawn closer to God.

On 7 July the victor returned at last to his bankrupt estate at Svartskog. 'Down the hill there were about one hundred people carrying flowers. Out on the fjord round a huge Midsummer Eve's bonfire thirty boats were moored, all beautifully decorated.' Only nine months had elapsed since he had left the place, virtually exiled. Now not a day went by without feasting and celebration. Enthusiastic guests banged on the door, and pleasure boats filed past, their burgees lowered.

His nearest and dearest too united around the returned 'in-law'. Trygve Gudde and wife arrived on a visit from Trondheim; Robert Maus came for dinner from town. Kiss's old aunt Caro Astrup wrote from Bygdøy and begged him to visit as she had a 'bad foot'. Kiss herself, who was being visited at Leigh Court by her sister Gudrun following that very inopportune illness, dispatched letters and telegrams to Uranienborg at regular intervals.

Everyone beat a path to his door; he just had to gather them in. Dornier-Wal suggested building a super-plane to enable him to complete the flight from the North Pole to Alaska. 'The wingspan will be 47 metres,' he wrote enthusiastically in his diary. 'Colossal. I need not pay. Will probably accept the offer.' He considered the pros and cons; he could afford to be finicky.

On 20 July he received a telegram from London. 'So you think you'll come in a year. It would be nice if it were true, but I'm not holding my breath.' The diary entry smacked of unusual level-headedness. Was she no longer the only one? 'Have had a stream of visitors today, Americans and others.'

During the weeks after his homecoming Roald Amundsen was fêted by the enormously wealthy French yachtswoman Madame Hériot who was sailing in northern waters in her extravagantly luxurious yacht. 'What on earth can she see in me?' the polar explorer asked himself, becomingly self-effacing. 'Young, beautiful and rich. Surely she can find someone who would suit her better!' Nevertheless, the ageing conqueror was more than willing to meet her, not only at the French legation but at Svartskog and on board the 'wonderful yacht' too. It might not have beeen so odd that Kiss felt her position threatened, sitting as she did in her country retreat, far removed from the centre of events.

Non-stop lunches and dinners at foreign legations; invitations arrived in a steady flow during the hot summer months; at the Grand Hotel and the Royal Summer Retreat, interspersed with refreshing swims in the sea. 'Arrived home this afternoon at 6 and got your two letters from 16th and 17th. Thank you my dear little wife. You say you are ready in one year. What do you mean by that? Are you coming? Let me know.' Again, unaccustomed language. She is repeating her enticing promises; he wants to be told in so many words. Something is brewing at Leigh Court and at Uranienborg.

At the same time important developments were taking place regarding the North Pole. On Saturday 25 July a new character entered the gates of the polar explorer's universe. 'The Italian air ship constructor Nobile arrived in Oslo today and came to see me with R-L. More later.' The polar explorer was in a hurry. The airship will have to wait. A car toots at five. It has been sent by Baron Wedel Jarlsberg to fetch the conquering hero out to Skaugum Manor. The great singer Nellie Melba was giving a performance in his honour. He can choose the piece himself: 'Home sweet home'. 'As long as I live,' his host summed up the evening in his memoirs, 'I will never forget this wonderful voice in the twilight and Amundsen's deep emotion.'

On Tuesday 28 July yet another important visitation crossed the gravel to Uranienborg: 'Nobile, Ræstad, R-L and Omdal arrived this morning. We are discussing plans to go over to airships next year. It will cost about 2 million crowns. Wonderful weather all day.'

Roald Amundsen was about to shelve the Dornier-Wal offer of a super-plane in favour of Colonel Nobile's airship. As far back as April 1924 he and his agent Hammer had met Nobile and test-driven the very latest in hovering construction. In addition, during his tour in America, he had discussed the possibilities with the German zeppelin expert Dr Eckener. Neither his second-in-command Riiser-Larsen nor the Governor doubted that the airship was the ideal craft for the Svalbard–Alaska flight. It looked as if only financial considerations could delay such a flight.

Shortly after his homecoming and even before the meeting with Dornier-Wal, Amundsen had telegraphed Nobile in Italy and invited him to secret talks in Oslo. When the polar explorer fairly quickly appeared to turn down the Germans' favourable super-plane to avail himself of the Italian, it might not have had much to do with the airship's superiority but rather with the timing of the enterprise – a factor to which Roald Amundsen often ascribed more importance than to finance and safety. The super-plane needed to be built; the airship needed only modification. Under pressure the Colonel agreed to try a flight as early as the summer of 1926. One year could be decisive for someone who wanted to discover the world – before it was too late.

At the moment it looked as though Amundsen's most threatening rival was no less a person than Fridtjof Nansen. As early as the spring of 1924 the German commandant Bruns had submitted plans for an internationally composed expedition by airship and led by the Norwegian. Nansen had expressed great faith in airships as the medium for conducting meteorological, oceanographic and geographic research. However, the expedition could set off at the earliest in the summer of 1927 as the airship was not yet built and the saviour of the world was still otherwise occupied.

Nothing would have been more galling for Roald Amundsen than to see the old skier and dog-team driver Fridtjof Nansen in free flight over the polar sea. The air belonged to *him* – to Roald Amundsen. The aeroplane had enabled him to break away from the old master and introduce a new era – his own era – to polar research. Least of all did he relish being caught in Fridtjof Nansen's mighty shadow. The moment Colonel Nobile hesitantly accepted the frantically chosen year 1926, Amundsen no longer feared Nansen's cumbersome international clout.

Roald Amundsen got going on his new book, *Through the Air to 88° North*. He wrote between 2,000 and 3,000 words a day. At the end of the month he could tot up 'about 10,000 words, but I must have 30,000, so on we go'. Soon the lyrically minded Lieutenant Riiser-Larsen moved into the author's home at Svartskog. The Governor wasn't going to do all the spade work on his own.

Wednesday 5 August he journeyed into town on business. He inspected the new slides and decided that the premiere of the new lecture would be held at the National Theatre as early as the following week. He talked to his publisher and obtained an undertaking from the expedition's journalist, Fredrik Ramm, to contribute an extra 15,000 words for the book. Soon the cash would come rolling in.

But something else happened that sunny Wednesday in August. 'Received a telegram from K. She will leave on Saturday.' She is coming! She will be at Svartskog in a few days. In one year she will leave England for good. In truth, he had reached the end of the road. All he needed to do was to open his arms.

'Telegraphed: Circumstances changed. Must advise against travel. Will write later.' He refused to receive Kiss! He advised her against travel. This was a sudden change indeed. Circumstance certainly *have* changed.

What had happened?

Two and a half months had elapsed since Roald Amundsen wrote his farewell greetings to Kiss Bennett and set off for the North Pole: 'Do not forget that your boy will love you with all his soul until his last breath.' Since then he had been given a new lease of life.

In spite of his momentous experiences the polar explorer seemed quickly to settle back into the old relationship's tame manner. But when she started to intimate that a separation was in the offing followed by total reunion, he turned luke-warm. And when she booked her ticket to Norway the polar explorer warned her of a break-up.

He warned her of a break-up. In a letter to Niels Gudde written two years later Roald Amundsen threw light over the relationship's collapse. Consul Gudde, who had been resident in Asia for many years, telegraphed an invitation, presumably to London, which he 'unfortunately' was forced to refuse, 'for reasons that circumstances, since you and I last met and spent so many unforgettable days together, have slowly changed and have now taken on a completely different character.' The telegram from Svartskog precipitated this gradual collapse.

Of course it is more than possible that, all things being equal, not even this time would Kiss have freed herself from the marriage's many moorings. But the polar explorer had already experienced one miracle and when the goddess actually booked a ticket, albeit for a flying visit only, illusions were perilously close to reality.

A pattern emerged; his relationship with Sigrid Castberg. He had begged her on bended knee before he set off for the South Pole. Two years later, while still in the Argentine, she was prepared to meet him half-way. Too late. She was not there when *he* asked her. Later all contact was broken. *She* had initially refused him – and when *he* withdrew, it was out of consideration for her. He chivalrously refused her.

The polar explorer needed her before he left; women were the driving force. She gave flesh and blood to the big trials of strength. But in the hour of triumph she was superfluous. Sigg had embodied the South Pole just as Kiss had been the magnet behind the North Pole. Through long winters the polar explorer had fought to reach his goal. Now the deed was done; he had received satisfaction. Next summer he would sail dry-shod, to Alaska on the wings of triumph.

He had played his mandolin under her window for thirteen years. As she took the first step down the ladder the knight threw the mandolin away and rode off on his white horse.

Following the telegram the polar explorer wrote a letter to London explaining his reasons. The conclusion cannot have been difficult to draw as it was originally hers. At last he was able to accept what formed the basis of her refusal: the commitment to her husband and – above all – consideration for her sons. The question is, who is the wounded party? In his letter to Niels Gudde he wrote: 'I will not bore you with any explanations, as to what constitutes these circumstances, but only say, that I regret them with all my heart.'

Roald Amundsen never reached the North Pole, although from the plane he would have been able to see the whole way. Thus he conquered his two Poles. For each one he had conquered a woman's affection. But in the hour of victory he pulled away. Only then could he do it with his pride intact. In the dual climax of adoration and rejection he found his apotheosis.

Roald Amundsen sought suffering, not happiness. Or rather: he never sought love, he sought compassion.

One person he loved more than anyone else in the world.

Part Five: The Lost Continent

THIRTY-NINE

Thanks to Mussolini

The curtain rose to the sounds of 'Norwegian Rhapsody'. Roald Amundsen stepped in, weather-beaten, erect, and took up his position by the simple decoration, the Norwegian flag. It was 14 August 1925 and the world premiere of the polar explorer's latest lecture tour. Barely a week earlier he had completed his new book (22,000 words). But this is the medium in which he feels most at home – the theatre.

The premiere public wore evening dress. Minister Wedel Jarlsberg, the Baron behind the Treaty of Svalbard, surrounded by the corps diplomatique, sat on the front bench. Behind him the hall was overflowing with Norwegian and foreign dignitaries. The Prime Minister and the Prime Minister designate were seated. One registered that Madame Hériot had not yet left local waters. Immediately before the curtain rose the royal family took their seats in the royal box.

It was half past five at the National Theatre in Norway's capital. The evening's story for that matter was already known to the newspaper-reading public. But the slides were up to date, fresh from the laboratory and the subject matter so miraculous that it needed confirmation from the horse's mouth. Roald Amundsen could once again play out his one and only role: the returned polar explorer, the man who reveals the world, who produces new pictures out of the dark.

Dagbladet's critic confirmed next day that the polar explorer 'delivered his lecture without notes and in a loud, calm voice'. He added that although the university auditorium was normally the place for scientific revelations, the National Theatre had been without a doubt the correct venue for yesterday's performance. 'Ever since Ibsen and Bjørnson no one has excited the Norwegian imagination like Amundsen. His deeds appeal to our creative powers. We all need to be inspired and Roald Amundsen has made us sit up and take note. His thirst for action, for travel, his dreams and longings, have affected us all so much that we feel we have been part of them.' Even the most jaded prima donna would have been pleased with such a review.

The biographer Roland Huntford wrote that Amundsen 'had all the instincts of an artist.' Roald Amundsen was a polar explorer with an artistic bent. Not because, like Fridtjof Nansen and Julius von Payer, he had artistic talent. When measured against copies sold and the material at his disposal to draw from, then his abilities as an author lie many poetic latitudes away from what is considered great literature; and even his meagre descriptive sketches of nature are sufficient to reveal the absence of any literary talent. His creative ability was one-sided – bound up with his achievements.

Without he himself being aware of it, Roald Amundsen was now at the height of his career. He had not conquered the North Pole but he had captivated the human soul. Set against this the flight over the polar sea would prove to be an anti-climax.

No outside circumstance could prevent Roald Amundsen from steadily approaching a stage of internal dissolution. He had broken away from the two people who had stood nearest to him, first Leon, in a rupture bitter and sudden, then Kiss, in a move gradual and chivalrous.

Leon Amundsen had been the absolutely vital shock absorber between the unpredictable polar explorer and his difficult surroundings. The relationship to Kiss Bennett had in many ways been illusory, but nevertheless a fixed point in his life, a lead to follow. They were both independent personalities, rooted in their own existences. More and more the polar explorer would seek out only those who were willing to surrender to him and his ideas.

Two days before the premiere in the National Theatre, news arrived that *Maud* had broken free of the ice north of Siberia. Captain Wisting's vessel had given up the North Pole for good and made for Nome, entirely for the sake of the estate's solvency.

On 22 August Roald Amundsen and Hjalmar Riiser-Larsen travelled to Italy. The polar explorer would have preferred to have discreetly slipped up the gangway, but it was difficult for an aviation hero of his size to travel incognito, even disguised with a fake beard and horn-rimmed spectacles. So, the two were making a visit to the Eternal City and no one doubted that they had their eyes on an airship. In their minds' eye they were already stepping ashore on the north coast of Alaska. What they were now about to plan would be the ultimate journey, the last great feat of exploration.

'Thanks to Mussolini's great interest this was quickly solved and the conditions excellent,' Roald Amundsen summed up the Rome negotiations in a later report. The whole matter was simplified as Benito Mussolini, in the initial phases of establishing himself as a dictator, had himself taken over the attractive post of Air Force Minister. On 1 September 1925 the contract regarding the airship's transfer was signed by the two upright men; the tall Napoleon of the icy wilds and the chubby Roman. All was in place for frictionless cooperation between two like-minded souls.

In the best of moods the polar explorer and the First Lieutenant set out on a well-deserved drive through Rome's beautiful surroundings. The latter filled the back seat, the former had taken a seat beside the chauffeur. At the steering wheel on this sunny late summer's day sat the man who would navigate the airship over the polar sea nine months later: Umberto Nobile. Only Ellsworth was missing; otherwise the entire expedition was present in the Colonel's automobile. Here, on the Roman highways, occurred the initial stages of the trans-Arctic flight.

These kilometres cover more than two pages of the great explorer's autobiography. The salient point is the chauffeur's high speed at the approach to every curve. Rarely have the two tough Norwegians felt nearer to meeting their Maker than in Nobile's Fiat. Not only was the situation life-threatening; the polar explorer found it disturbing: 'his entire behaviour on this trip exposed his tremendous nervousness, eccentric character and lack of quiet judgement.'

Fifty years later the chauffeur stood up for himself when he described what to him was perfectly 'normal' driving. The 90-year-old airship constructor pointed out that he had had a driving licence since 1910 and had only once missed the road and that was in foggy conditions. 'Amundsen noticed that I accelerated owing to the centrifugal force, but what he was not aware of was that I had gradually reduced the speed.' Nobile argues. The two could not even agree on the trip's destination: Amundsen was en route to the seaside resort of Ostia, Nobile to the port of Anzio. The fifty-year long discussion can really only lead to one conclusion: they had been sitting in the same Fiat, but not in the same universe.

The aerial trip was not abandoned subsequent to the test-drive on the highway. But the excursion with the Colonel in the front seat, the Governor in the observation tower and the pilot ousted to the back seat, contained most of the elements that would characterise the forthcoming expedition.

On 9 September the agreement with the Italians was made public at the Annual General Meeting of the Norwegian Aeronautical Association in Oslo. To general approval it was announced that the airship N1 would, during the journey, carry the proud name *Norge*. First Lieutenant Riiser-Larsen briefed the assembly. The immortal polar explorer had, strangely enough, taken to his bed. He calmly told the press 'his illness is only a small indisposition'.

The same day as the newspapers published the plans Roald Amundsen sat down at his desk and formulated a letter to Benjamin Vogt: 'Dear Mr Minister. I am sorry to have to tell you that I cannot come to London as planned. An indisposition of a not very severe nature has caused my doctor to advise absolute rest, until I go to America in October.'

After his return from Svalbard Amundsen had received a letter from the Norwegian colony in London. They wished to celebrate their famous compatriot as they had done after his conquest of the North West Passage and the South Pole. The table was set for a repeat of the fateful feast at the Hotel Cecil, 16 November 1912. That was where, that was when, he had met the lady in red.

Since that memorable day the polar explorer had grasped every opportunity to return to the Empire's capital.

A month had passed since he sent Kiss the decisive telegram. In the meantime he had given his lecture in the National Theatre and signed the contract in Rome regarding the airship which would take him to the culmination of his dreams. Conditions *had* changed. She had always been the one to be struck down by all sorts of illnesses as soon as the suitor knocked on her door. Now he was prepared to sacrifice Europe's homage for an indisposition in the nether regions. Roald Amundsen had really taken his leave of Kiss Bennett.

Of course, the polar explorer was forced to retract his excuse. It was not accepted either in England or elsewhere. A tough polar explorer does not overturn contracts worth thousands, lectures and banquets, meetings with heads of state in several capitals, because one day in September he feels 'a little indisposed'.

The polar explorer jolly well had to set off, as usual accompanied by his second-in-command. Soon the newspapers were reporting huge enthusiasm in town after town. At the end of the 1920s, Roald Amundsen's great achievements were one of the few things a confused Europe could agree on and admire. Among the prominent public in Copenhagen was the representative of the new Soviet Union and the exiled, widowed empress. The tales of the aviators' heroic struggle and miraculous resurrection gripped everyone.

Following the lecture in the Danish capital laurels were placed around the polar explorer's neck. But as the Governor was being garlanded, according to the newspaper reports, spontaneous cries emerged from the overflowing hall: 'Let's see Riiser-Larsen, let's see the pilot, whereupon Riiser-Larsen in all his magnificent might stepped onto the rostrum and accepted his share of the applause.' The public were not without an inkling as to who had been the drama's real hero. Even garlanded with laurels the white-haired dogsledge-driver was in danger of being consigned to the pilot's shadow.

The railway station in Prague, the capital of the new Czechoslovakia, was jam-packed when the two arrived. Jubilation was no less in the retired Emperor's town, Vienna. Everyone was about and the polar explorer was feeling better than ever. He told one of the newspapers that he was not at all tired. 'Rushing from one town to the next – I'm in my absolute element.'

But in Berlin – the capital of mechanic Feucht and President Hindenburg – the reception was ambivalent. He was not popular with the German public, not least owing to his anti-German behaviour during the First World War.

During the lecture in the packed Kroll Opera House on 17 September a considerable number of policemen were deployed in order to forestall any interruptions. National Socialist handbills were handed out but otherwise the lecture proceeded without incident. But in his hotel room the polar hero was directly confronted by his opponents when a retired major pushed his way in to deliver a piece of his mind. On the other hand Foreign Minister Gustav Stresemann delivered a beautifully executed speech in honour of the important guest during the ambassador's dinner at Hotel Adlon.

Later in the autumn Riiser-Larsen was given the none too rewarding task of touring individual German towns. 'So far the halls have been half-empty and consequently it is slightly difficult to talk owing to the, at times, rather strong echo,' he reported home to the Norwegian Aeronautical Association. 'Large-scale counter-propaganda has been organised. They are furious with A regarding the decoration history and with both A and me because we will use an Italian rather than a German airship.'

Roald Amundsen's forthcoming expedition was considered a rival to the planned international airship voyage under Fridtjof Nansen's leadership. The German Dr Hugo Eckener, who a year earlier had crossed the Atlantic in an airship, was now in the process of building a super-zeppelin for this scientific purpose.

Dr Eckner and Dr Nansen had both wanted to encourage Roald Amundsen to join the International Association for the Exploration of the Arctic. But those sorts of academic projects were not to the liking of a man like Amundsen. However, following several requests, he promised to give Fridtjof Nansen his definite answer in the autumn of 1926 – an answer which surprised the ageing Nobel Peace Prize laureate. 'The reason is quite simply the fact that I was kicked out of Germany last year during my lecture tour and therefore I do not wish to have anything to do with that nation or anyone who is in any way even remotely connected to it.'

Ten years had passed since the polar explorer had broken with the German Kaiser. Now he severed relations once more and this time with the entire nation. The first break had been owing to German U-boats attacking Norwegian seamen; the second was based on a few handbills and a loyal major's intrusion into his hotel room. The polar explorer had never been 'kicked out'; on the contrary he had been hailed by the Republic's leading statesmen. Officialdom in Germany had done all in its power to create peace and dignity around his person.

The break with the Weimar Republic indicated a pattern of behaviour and a distorted sense of reality which would come to characterise the last years of the polar explorer's life.

On the afternoon of 26 September 1925 Roald Amundsen arrived at Victoria Station in London. He came from Paris and was accompanied by the aviation hero and his wife. This would be his last entry into the Empire's capital. The stay was short.

That same evening a banquet was held at Hotel Cecil. One hundred and sixty gala-dressed guests were present to hail their two compatriots. Minister Vogt praised the polar explorer who in turn thanked his men. Present was also the former South Pole explorer Kristian Prestrud who was still attached to the legation in London. According to reports he 'spoke animatedly of his old Governor Amundsen and proposed a toast for his comrades.' Following the dinner the party continued in the Norwegian Club where the polar explorer was knighted with the title 'Knight of the Norwegian Bear'.

This was probably the last time the newly dubbed 'knight' spoke to his goddess. They maintained contact, on an entirely pragmatic basis, and he never returned to London. After a few hectic weeks, on 30 September the polar explorer boarded a steamship for America. He left Europe to his two lieutenants. Riiser-Larsen would tour the Continent, Dietrichson Scandinavia and the British Isles.

And while the Norwegians trawl the world Colonel Nobile takes care of the airship *Norge*.

FORTY

The Managing Director

While Roald Amundsen's first expedition might have reminded one of a boy's outing or a pirate's raid, his last expedition was to take the form of an international undertaking. The polar explorer defined the goals and set the timetable. In addition, the entire enterprise was based around his name and prestige. However, the polar explorer was not in charge of the daily running; it could not really be said that he was in charge of anything.

At the same time as Roald Amundsen crossed the Atlantic to New York the first member of the expedition was on his way to Spitsbergen – First Lieutenant Joh. Høver whose job it was to measure out a site for a new gigantic structure in Kings Bay. Later shiploads of materials and prefabricated parts, twenty carpenters and other craftsmen arrived. It all took on the characteristics of new industrial development in the barren mining community.

The hangar which would house the airship *Norge* measured 110 by 34 metres and was 30 metres high. It was constructed of tightly woven wooden scaffolding, stiffened with enormous stays which were anchored to the concrete foundation. There was no roof but the walls would be covered in canvas, as protection from the wind was its main role.

Compared with the prefabricated Framheim, which carpenter Stubberud and ski-maker Bjaaland had erected in the course of a few days on the other side of the globe, here they were dealing with totally different dimensions. The crew needed to winter in Kings Bay as they worked in low temperatures using huge floodlights in the dark of the polar night.

To ensure the airship *Norge*'s safe passage to the uttermost outpost of the world three mooring masts had to be erected on Norwegian soil. Landing places existed for the transport through Europe; but the mountainous country to the north was not cut out for dealing with flying super-whales.

Decisions were made and plans put into effect without any direct involvement from Roald Amundsen. The polar explorer did what he had always done – he toured the world giving lectures. The polar explorer had not changed. Brother Leon had been exchanged – for a complex international expeditionary concern.

Roald Amundsen's forte was to be a superior general on the battlefield or an artist in his fantasy universe. The democractic moves that from time to time he was obliged to stage were no more than for appearances sake. Nevertheless, even at an early stage he had been forced to delegate authority. Numerous persons were accorded wide powers of attorney. But everything must be done according to his spirit. The Governor was loath to give up the last word.

This had changed only during the North Pole flight. His second-in-command had been the driving force during preparations and was the foremost expert in the field. All was performed in the spirit of the Governor by a man in whom he never lost confidence. Besides Lincoln Ellsworth, Hjalmar Riiser-Larsen was the important, happy find in this last phase of the polar explorer's career.

Suddenly all would change.

The man who this time was to become the key expert during preparations and implementation was not automatically the Governor's obedient instrument; Umberto Nobile represented a different culture, a different people, a different flag. In addition to Roald Amunsen and Colonel Nobile, three men enjoyed leadership status. Number one: Rolf Thommessen, chairman of the Norwegian Aeronautical Association, the company responsible for the airship; followed by the hero Riiser-Larsen, who was in no way prepared to give up his position as the Governor's second-in-command; and lastly, the American Ellsworth who had this time bought his place next to Amundsen for $100,000. He represented a valuable contribution, but at the same time a third flag, and, as we shall see, a complicated psychological element.

But not only the leadership of the new expedition proved problematic; the composition of the crew became a source of continuous strife, often with nationalistic overtones. The Governor was already caught up in the first conflicts to do with personnel in the wake of the initial celebratory dinners on the American continent.

With his dollars Lincoln Ellsworth had not only secured himself a formal position, but also a real function. The American had been granted the key position, that of the airship's navigator. This was more than Lieutenant Dietrichson could stomach.

It was Leif Dietrichson who had performed the heroic navigation from death to resurrection on 15 June 1925. Besides, he had been Ellsworth's instructor and did not think that the American was qualified for such a responsible task. The leadership in Oslo informed the Governor. He chose to oppose Dietrichson on the basis of principle. On 17 October he telegraphed from New York. 'It is not possible that he starts to criticise decisions taken in the Norwegian Aeronautical Association meetings. If he does he is useless. Discipline is everything. Nothing works without it.'

Discipline or not, it appears that the board showed a certain amount of sympathy with the lieutenant's arguments: 'What concerns D,' was the answer, 'is that he will be blamed if the navigation fails, but not be accorded the corresponding amount of glory if the navigation is a success.'

But Roald Amundsen, who in New York had been reunited with his wealthy partner, was not proposing to demote the man who at one time had saved his career. 'On the other hand,' he wrote, 'E is willing to withdraw from the position of navigator, if he should, before the expedition's departure, find that he is not up to the job. In all fairness, we can do no more. In any case, Dietrichson's behaviour is incomprehensible. He knows E well enough to know that he would never meddle in his business. He merely wishes in the eyes of the world to have performed more than the other crew members.'

Neither Amundsen nor Ellsworth, who both valued Dietrichson highly, wanted to lose him from the expedition. However, that is exactly what happened. Within the year Leif Dietrichson withdrew from the expedition, ostensibly for family reasons. The power struggle between the two navigators would later have its parallel in a far dirtier struggle, that regarding the airship's command between the two officers Riiser-Larsen and Nobile.

In the middle of the preparations for the *Norge* flight, the *Maud* expedition was at last wound up. The ship was met by police on arrival in Nome on 22 August, later seized and sold to set against the bankruptcy when it docked in Seattle. In truth, not a very glorious homecoming.

During a total of seven years *Maud* had tried to enter the current that crossed the Pole. In vain. Now a new era had caught up with her. The vessel which had been *Fram*'s heir and the pride of its native country was now demoted to the role of asset in a bankrupt estate. The ship that drifted across the ice had been discarded for another – one that sailed across the sky.

From the polar explorer's standpoint the *Maud* expedition had been a complete failure. That was not the only conclusion drawn, however. The scientific leader, Dr Sverdrup, wrote home to Professor Bjerknes: 'From a popular point of view our journey is no doubt a fiasco. Personally, however, I feel in no way dejected, because I believe our scientific results are so varied and so valuable that the expedition will stand in the front line of polar expeditions which have enriched geophysics with new data and new perceptions.' And if one were to think deeply about it, the *Maud* expedition was, after all, a scientific expedition.

The last three years under the command of Wisting and Sverdrup had passed without the shedding of manpower which had characterised the year when the Governor himself was on board. The only such loss happened in July 1923 when engineer Syvertsen died of meningitis, according to Wisting's diagnosis.

On the evening of 4 November 1925 the first three *Maud* chaps arrive in Oslo with the boat from America: the Russian Olonkin, the Swede Malmgren and the Norwegian Karl Hansen. Before stepping ashore the three were sworn to secrecy as the estate might still make some money out of the journey's reports. In light of the aerial expedition's wonderful reception a few months earlier the sea expedition's piecemeal homecoming invited sarcastic comments. *Dagbladet* printed a sharp comment about 'the world-idolised leader and his abandoned crew'.

Captain Wisting was the last to leave the ship. Only after the New Year, having conferred with the Governor in America, did Oscar Wisting arrive home in Norway. On 3 February 1926 a dinner was held in Oslo in honour of the expedition members. Fridtjof Nansen, who had a tendency to absent himself from his colleague's celebrations, was there giving the principal speech for *Maud*'s men. Wars might have ravaged the world, dynasties toppled; the Professor had not forgotten his moral responsibility for this expedition. It was for this scientific journey, nearly twenty years earlier, that he had relinquished his own plans to conquer the South Pole. It was the journey of atonement with *Maud* he had pressurised his younger compatriot to undertake. Now, at last, the expedition's scientific part was brought to a close. The journey of discovery, the daring feat, the sporting element had not yet reached the end of the road – not before the airship *Norge* landed in Alaska.

The old man from the Polar Sea stressed in his speech the scientific results – treasures that 'live by their inner glow and power', in spite of not being embraced by transient 'world acclaim'. He remembered the victims of the research, Tessem, Knudsen and Syvertsen, 'who were lowered into the Polar Sea's cold, lonely grave'. Having remembered the dead the Professor also paid tribute to the expedition leader, who was en route to 'new goals with that indomitable restless energy which we all admire'.

It is the energy which the Professor admired, no longer *the man*. Fridtjof Nansen could choose his words with great precision. And as a contrast to the Polar Sea's noisy circus which was now building up around the airship *Norge*, he ended his speech: 'A toast to *Maud*'s unassuming men!'

Harald U. Sverdrup too had a chance to meet the Governor in America before he crossed the Atlantic for home.

In a note he penned many years later with the idea of a possible screen version of the polar explorer's life, he wrote: 'In November 1925, a few months after our return from the *Maud* expedition, I met Amundsen in New York. He asked if I would have lunch with him in his hotel where he had a surprise for me. The surprise was the lady from Alaska, who was as at ease in the Waldorf-Astoria as she was in a trading post in Alaska.' This lady was Bess Magids.

Sverdrup knew her, like the other *Maud* chaps, from the stay in Deering and described her not only as 'very attractive', but also as the only 'serious affair' among the Governor's female acquaintances. Considering the three years they spent together on board *Maud* it speaks volumes about Roald Amundsen's ability to bottle up his deepest feelings.

Just like jack-in-the-box the Alaskan beauty Bess Magids appeared at a restaurant table at the Waldorf-Astoria. In spite of being married to someone else it appears that the liaison with Bess was far less restrained than the deeply ambitious relationship with Kiss. The two love affairs were played out against widely different backdrops. A milieu frequented by American businessmen and opportunists must have been closer to the polar explorer's heart than the heavily conventional atmosphere of the British upper classes. Among his unprejudiced friends in New York the Norwegian enjoyed a frivolous existence consisting of cocktail parties and poker games. The Magids couple were an obvious part of this circle – when they were not travelling to such exotic places as Alaska, China and Russia.

Amundsen's relationship with this energetic, dark beauty was at this stage obviously conducted in an uncommitted manner. Nevertheless, as contact was so quickly re-established, one must assume that the polar explorer must have had her in mind as he was starting his gradual withdrawal from the goddess at Leigh Court.

The stay in America was not a good time for the polar explorer. 'My lectures here are, interestingly enough, not successful,' he wrote to old money-bags Don Pedro. 'In spite of the huge amount of advertising I often speak to empty halls. Vaudeville seems to be the only thing Americans need at the moment.' The contrast to Europe was striking.

The polar explorer was given further evidence of the enthusiasm at home when the written account saw the light of day. He wrote to Gade: 'The book about the polar flight hit the markets at 8 this morning, 8 October, and 10,000 copies were sold out by 2 this afternoon. That must surely be a record.'

The work was entitled *By Air to 88 Degrees North*. It entailed a certain degree of upwards adjustment from 87°43″. The agreements with the American papers contained a financial clause which depended on the expedition reaching 88 degrees. As a result of the subject's dramatic abundance they agreed to the 88-degree pay out. After what they had been through, the whole world wished them the North Pole.

Roald Amundsen had this time written only one third of the book, but as always the book was under his name. That would become a festering sore as it really was a breach of contract. Not only had Lincoln Ellsworth bought his way into the expedition but also into the authorship. Unfortunately, the autumn's best-seller was published without waiting for the American's contribution.

If an author was missing, the dedication – as always – was carefully considered, this time permeated by the polar explorer's lofty disposition and chivalrousness.

To the two who represent all that is good in Norwegian womanhood – Kirsten Riiser-Larsen and Gunvor Dietrichson – I dedicate this book.

The polar explorer saw no better way of sending his platonic greetings and thank you to the 'Norwegian woman' in England.

In spite of the disappointments in America the North Pole flight could have made good money. Newspaper, book and film contracts and the European lecture tours had fully satisfied financial expectations. The intention was to allow the profits from the 'reconnaissance flight' to finance the forthcoming expedition. But even considerable profit can quickly become loss if no one is intent on saving. 'The expedition members and administration should have seen this and immediately restricted all outgoings,' the accountant writes. 'This has unfortunately not been done and instead of building up reasonable reserves the company per 31.12.25 [31 December 1925] has a debt of 60,000 crowns and without any assets to mention is in effect per 31.12.25 *completely insolvent.*'

Even a limited company is dependent on the individual's responsibility. The accountant found special reason to emphasise the pilot hero's contribution: 'Mr R-L's outlay during travels to lectures is large, very large.' But then he was a large man.

Roald Amundsen discontinued his tour one month earlier than planned, on 1 February. In spite of pushing through an almost frantic timetable for the forthcoming trans-polar flight he saw no reason for going home following his work in the States; on the contrary, he took a month's holiday in the days before the launch. He did not leave America before the first week of March. The last part was spent in New York where he cultivated his new hobby – mixing cocktails – in relaxed company among admiring businessmen and light-hearted American women. Among them the Magids couple.

A contributing factor to the polar explorer's absence might have been the less than pleasant goings-on at home in Norway. On 18 February Leon Amundsen's lawyer Albert Balchen submitted his last plea to the Oslo court. These were his closing words:

Lastly I would like to point out that before I appeal this case at the High Court I want to make it clear that I will not make use of certain proofs regarding Gudde's power of attorney and deed of conveyance of Uranienbrog to Consul Gudde. On this occasion Leon has explicitly asked me to draw attention to the fact that if the case is brought before the High Court he intends to make use of these proofs in their entirety, as this information more than any other will throw light over the whole dispute between the brothers regarding the origin of the enmity between them.

Thus Leon called attention to the fact that he had not submitted all the evidence in the case; at the same time he brought pressure to bear on his brother. Most noteworthy is how he associated 'Gudde's power of attorney' with 'the origin of the enmity'.

As his brother and business manager Leon had based his relationship with Roald on two fundamental elements: financial security of the properties and – most important of all – complete honesty between the two. These two conditions were damaged by the secret power of attorney given to Lawyer Gudde in 1918. That was the first time Roald pulled the wool over Leon's eyes; the second was in his double-dealing with Haakon Hammer; and the third was when he wanted to sell the property to Herman Gade.

On 12 March 1927 the polar explorer arrived in Southampton from America. Six months had passed since he last visited England. That time the stay lasted three days; now he stayed for one day only, without leaving the port. But he was welcomed by his two friends Alfred and Peto. The Bennett brothers were always *au fait* with the whereabouts of the polar explorer. On departure next day he wrote a letter: 'Dear Kiss, just two words. Have just seen your boys and I have to say how fond I am of them. You certainly have something to live for. A warm and sincere thanks for the telegram from you and Peto [the elder]. Yours sincerely, Roald.'

This letter, which may be the only one still in existence from Roald Amundsen to Kiss Bennett, clearly demonstrated the relationship's new character. She, who only a few years ago was all and everything in his life, now has her sons 'to live for'. The relationship to the polar explorer had moved to a phase where even the husband is included with a telegraphic signature.

But she remained the goddess, the bright 'spot of existence', in which the polar explorer sailed on through the world, enveloped in an 'awful darkness'.

FORTY-ONE

Norwegians in Rome

On the afternoon of 16 March 1926 the chairman of the Norwegian Aeronautical Club, Dr Thommessen, was off to Rome to take charge of the airship *Norge* on behalf of the expedition and, indeed, the nation. However, he had been told by a journalist from *Tidens Tegn* that Roald Amundsen would arrive in Oslo that same day. A meeting was hastily arranged in the offices of the editor-in-chief. Lincoln Ellsworth had already been in town for a couple of days and thus Thommessen would be able to clarify the most pressing questions with the two leaders before his all-important trip to Rome.

Throughout the winter Amundsen and Ellsworth had distanced themselves from the administrative discussions and strategic planning. The Governor considered himself to be above it all: 'For me the purpose is to reach the goal,' he had written to Thommessen in February, 'so everything else will have to play second fiddle with that in mind.'

However, during a five-day trip to Oslo in January Umberto Nobile had raised a number of complex problems in a meeting with the Aeronautical Association. During these meetings Amundsen and Ellsworth had given Hjalmar Riiser-Larsen, who had introduced the airship constructor to the unfamiliar medium of snow, their proxy. Later the Norwegian wrote that the Colonel, on his first encounter with snow, had 'continually fallen down and had to be helped to his feet. From that day on he was visibly more nervous about the outcome of the expedition.'

The difficult questions all concerned Italy's honour and the Colonel's own status during the journey. What name would the expedition take? How visible would be the Italian flag? What would be the composition of the crew? What privileges were due to the leader? In every question lay the seeds of conflict, and without the presence of the entire leadership it was not easy to find a solution.

These were the problems which were aired in Rolf Thommessen's office. 'Thereafter we parted in total accord,' the editor wrote in a later statement. The next moment he was on the train south.

For some time now the flow of information from the Norwegian ambassador in Rome to the Foreign Office had made it clear that the whole matter of Italy's participation in the polar flight was considered a political issue and thus subject to the highest state authority. In Norway the airship *Norge* was regarded as being Amundsen's private affair. It did not follow, though, that this was not a national concern; Roald Amundsen had long given up all claim to privacy.

The Italian regime's part in the affair grew in line with their realisation of the potential propaganda value. In a later estimate Thommessen calculated Italy's contribution to the expedition to run to 840,000 crowns. The Norwegian contribution, including both public and private receipts, totalled about 600,000 and the American contribution, in other words Ellsworth's contribution, came to 570,000. As long as Mussolini's gifts were accepted, it was not unreasonable that the Italian participation be recognised as at least equal to that of the American.

But if the Kingdom of Norway was for the moment administered by a lack-lustre parliamentary government, Roald Amundsen's compatriots considered themselves masters of polar exploration. Neither honour nor glory was to be shared cheaply. The scene was set for a national confrontation, between the blackshirts in the south and the fair-skinned men from the northernmost reaches of Europe.

Norway's most uncompromising negotiator had been Hjalmar Riiser-Larsen. Unlike Dr Thommessen, who was in charge of the administration, Amundsen's second-in-command had nothing to gain by giving in to the Italians. The giant, who had qualified as an airship pilot in England, was uncomfortable in the shadow of the delicate Italians; his greatest ambition was to take over himself as leader of the airship *Norge*.

The Norwegian participants, bar the Governor, had travelled to Rome during the winter for essential training in manoeuvring an airship; they felt rather out of their depth in the huge airship hangar at Ciampino Airport.

Colonel Nobile had determined that there would be no more than sixteen members, of whom five would come from his own specially trained crew. Faced with these acrobats of the air the Norwegians felt themselves sidelined. Why retrain the Norwegian skiers when the Italians were already total masters of the art of flying?

Dissatisfaction with Nobile's leadership spread quickly among the semi-employed Norwegians. More than once they were tempted to board the train for the north and leave the airship to its own devices.

Hjalmar Riiser-Larsen's alternative plan involved head-on confrontation. On 13 March, the Norwegian second-in-command wrote a confidential letter to the leadership at home in Oslo. 'The worst consequence of refusing to give in to

Italian demands is, according to Nobile, that the Italian government will forbid their people to take part. I have anticipated this and have therefore organised a sufficient number of Norwegians at each landing stage on the flight to England at which point the Norwegian crew can be complemented with Englishmen.'

Riiser-Larsen had arranged for the expedition to fly via the British Isles on its way north, and had insisted on as large a Norwegian contingent as possible. He had also made sure there was an abundance of crew loyal to Amundsen in place on Spitsbergen. He thought there might even be a possibility that the Italians, given the right circumstances, could be sent home from Kings Bay, leaving the Norwegians to complete the flight to Alaska on their own.

The deterioration in the relationship between the Norwegians and Italians had its root in language difficulties. Colonel Nobile actually tried to rectify the situation. He had engaged an interpreter at the Rome factory to translate newspapers and technical material. The young Danish-Norwegian student Lise Lindbæk who had deputised at the Norwegian legation had guided the Norwegian boys during their stay in Rome; might she also facilitate communications between the nations?

Half-way through February a head-shaking Riiser-Larsen reported to Dr Thommessen: 'A few days ago Nobile insinuated that he wanted his private secretary Miss Lindbæk to accompany the crew to Spitsbergen as an interpreter. I pretended not to understand, to avoid telling him how laughable the idea was.' The Norwegians not only thought the move absurdly comical; it was probably a ploy to infiltrate their ranks: 'Omdal told me he had heard the same thing; she would be there to inform on us.'

Lise Lindbæk never got to Spitsbergen, but she nevertheless continued to work for Nobile. The young lady, who later became well known for her anti-fascist reporting in her memoirs *Brennende Jord* (*Burning Earth*), painted a very flattering picture of her Italian superior. 'I immediately felt strong empathy for my boss and there was never any reason to change this view. He was forty and very attractive; virtually a classical beauty, a clean, noble face with soulful, brown eyes under a high clear forehead.' Young Lindbæk had an eye for the male form.

The female interpreter painted a clear picture of Director Nobile's strong position among the four hundred staff. 'We all knew that Nobile was no Fascist and that he had many enemies in the Air Force Ministry.'

When Rolf Thommessen, together with Major Sverre, arrived in Rome on 19 March, he quickly noted that the 'Norwegian crew was very agitated'. Dr Thommessen, who was on good terms with Nobile, had travelled south in a spirit of reconciliation, something that did not suit the second-in-command's strategy.

Great was Thommessen's surprise when a few days later yet two more important characters turned up in the Italian capital: 'none less than Amundsen and Ellsworth. They had probably been contacted by telegraph by Riiser-Larsen and left Oslo immediately.' As the month of March drew to a close, the days were rich in scheming showdowns and private and national initiatives. Nobile's domestic problems aside, inter-Italian rivalry and the excited Norwegian rank and file, one was left with five leaders all defending more or less legitimate interests.

Rolf Thommessen, who later gave an account of the conflicts 'for use in the Court of Arbitration', allegedly did his best. The editor was certainly a nationalist but, equally, he was sympathetic towards the new dynamic Italy and took pride in ensuring that the two nations could cooperate on a common project. For Roald Amundsen it was not all that easy to rise above personal and national differences. Ellsworth had the most difficult task. He got himself into difficult situations as a result of what Thommessen termed 'a morbid disposition' and an 'extreme dependence on Amundsen'.

In his 'account' Thommessen stressed the American's psychology: 'As everyone who is acquainted with Ellsworth will know, he is a very quiet and unassuming and humble man, but it is a fact that this sort of person is easily hurt, that they store up and recall impressions that others might have forgotten about long ago. This is very true of Ellsworth. His lack of assertiveness meant that he often felt overshadowed by others. His feeling for Nobile on this account is universally known: but it is less well known that he harboured the same feelings for Riiser-Larsen.'

The American's jealousy was well established. According to Dr Thommessen, Ellsworth had his own theory on who was behind the veto of his contribution to the last expedition book. 'It was impossible to persuade Ellsworth that it was not down to Riiser-Larsen's scheming, made possible by Amundsen's favouritism of him.'

Against this background it was not surprising that the American showed some sympathy towards Riiser-Larsen's major rival. If we are to believe Thommessen: 'Later the friendship foundered, but in Rome it was obvious that he was more attracted by Nobile's gentle manner than by Riiser-Larsen's more impulsive personality.'

In Rome Ellsworth was inclined to support Nobile's many demands; for example, that his name be included in the expedition's official records and that he would co-author the report. For his part Amundsen inclined more and more towards Riiser-Larsen's uncompromising stance.

A telling episode took place towards the end of their stay in Rome. They had at last reached agreement regarding procedures for decision-making among the four leaders on board the airship should the flight be terminated. After the

Norwegians had reached their hotel, Ellsworth pulled Thommessen to one side
for a private conversation. The American expressed his mistrust of Riiser-Larsen
and declared that he could no longer support the agreement. However, he was too
timid to air his alternative proposal in front of the polar explorer; that task fell
to Thommessen.

'I arranged a formal interview with Amundsen, who reacted angrily to my
errand. He immediately saw through Ellsworth's intention and exclaimed: "He's
on Nobile's side". We discussed the pros and cons for a while then he sent me
off to Ellsworth with a decisive no. However, Ellsworth persisted, and asked me
to return to Amundsen and assure Amundsen of his friendship, that he would
never act against him and that he could therefore safely agree to the proposal. I
once again set out for Amundsen's room, armed with this slightly contradictory
argument and my audience was this time greeted with the most uncontrollable
fury. Amundsen rushed off to Ellsworth's room where he gave him a severe
dressing down and thereafter rushed back to his own room. When I later went to
see Ellsworth I found a broken-hearted man who agreed immediately to accept
the decision if I promised that Riiser-Larsen would have no say in writing the
polar book. I did not quite understand the connection between the two, but to
Ellsworth it was obviously very clear.'

On 29 March 1926 the solemn transfer of the airship was to have taken
place. But before they got that far Lincoln Ellsworth was obliged to extricate
the expedition from an acute crisis; there was no money for insurance. A few
telegraphic manoeuvres enabled the capitalist to lay his hands on $20,000 which
were put at the disposal of the Aeronautical Association, but again according
to Thommessen, there was a certain condition: 'that I gave my word of honour
that Riiser-Larsen would not write the book.' Apparently this was not a problem
as it had been made clear that Colonel Nobile would write the technical part of
the report.

The ceremony outside the hangar in Rome was a glittering occasion,
characterised by nationalistic posturing and fascist enthusiasm for the heroic
project. The dictator of the Roman Empire, Mussolini, gave the keynote speech
on behalf of the happy donors. The popular press's chief editor Thommessen,
dressed for the occasion in statesmanlike suit, responded with a speech of
gratitude. The climax of the event was the exchange of flags. The Italian flag
was lowered and the Norwegian one raised. This honour was bestowed on that
consummate all-rounder Oscar Wisting.

But the christening needed something of a woman's touch. Neither of the two
bachelors Amundsen or Ellsworth had any to hand. Umberto Nobile's beautiful
wife and little daughter were out of the question; so, once again Mrs Riiser-
Larsen did the honours. 'Of course I demanded that not only would the ship carry

the Norwegian flag but that it should also carry my native country's name,' the polar explorer wrote in his memoirs. In the event, things were not so clear-cut. Not only were the Italian colours painted on the fuselage supplementing the flag on the stern, but the original name had not been removed with solvent before the new one was inaugurated in champagne. Thus the airship *Norge* continued to sail under its old name N1. Ironically, the airship was later given the Norwegian registration number 'N1' (Norway's one and only airship) and thus everything should have been hunky-dory. More or less.

While gunner Wisting, Benito Mussolini, Riiser-Larsen's wife and other minor characters pranced about on the world stage the polar explorer himself was an anonymous onlooker in the background. His lack of a role was not because he was being overlooked, but because he was not supposed to have been there at all. Amundsen and Ellsworth had arrived three days earlier and they left the scene the same day the champagne bottle was smashed, although the airship itself only left Ciampino on 10 April.

In many ways Roald Amundsen's role so far had been that of an onlooker. The polar explorer felt he had suffered enough; for once he wanted to arrive in Spitsbergen to a ready-made expedition. Rolf Thommessen wrote about this in retrospect: 'It was extremely regrettable that Amundsen's knowledge of the expedition and of its Italian participants was so limited. Apart from Nobile he knew none of the Italians by name. Since it was important to stress that the leadership was Norwegian, matters would have been greatly improved if the leader had realised that, in the eyes of the men, a famous past mattered little when hard graft was needed.'

On 21 April 1926 the steamship *Knut Skaaluren* arrived in Kings Bay. Roald Amundsen stepped ashore at the head of his retinue. The man who was closest to the polar explorer, apart from the American money man, was storekeeper Fritz G. Zapffe who had been connected to the enterprise since the *Gjøa* days. He had never taken an active part in any of the operations but could pride himself on being the senior of Amundsen's men.

Visible changes had taken place in the prehistoric landscape round Ny-Ålesund since the polar explorer had left it ten months previously. The most conspicuous was the huge airship hangar which loomed large behind the small painted houses. But the arctic traveller was just as fascinated by the sight of a memorial raised to the previous year's heroic flight. The monument had not been long in coming – the speed was impressive.

Four days after arrival Roald Amundsen was woken by the military band from the naval vessel *Heimdal* which had docked at Kings Bay. The preparations were flawless. Norway was not about to leave its favourite son in the lurch this time either. Only the airship was missing; it had a long journey to make. From Rome it had flown to Pulham Market in Norfolk, then to Oslo and on to Leningrad. When it got the all clear from Ny-Ålesund it would continue via Vadsø to Spitsbergen.

On 29 April, while *Norge* was still sitting in the hangar outside Leningrad, another ship docked at Kings Bay. It made fast alongside *Heimdal*; the warship had no intention of moving. It was the American steamer *Chantier*, carrying the aeroplane *Josephine Ford*. On board was Commander Richard E. Byrd. He was contemplating a trip to the North Pole.

The Byrd expedition, if not entirely unexpected, arrived at a most inconvenient time. Neither Amundsen nor Ellsworth was unaware of the American flying officer's plans. Nevertheless, the Norwegian must have felt as Captain Scott had when he was told of his rival's landing at Hvalbukta. Roald Amundsen saw the parallel and made the most of it. He acknowledged, from the first moment, the American's right to compete for the North Pole, thus absolving himself of his own behaviour sixteen years earlier in the battle for another Pole.

Besides: the North Pole was not the prize it used to be. The Norwegian had already established that the only thing of any value lay on the other side, between the Pole and Point Barrow. Flying over a theoretical point counted for little compared with the conquest of a new continent.

The cigar-shaped airship *Norge* glided in over the snow-sparkling Svalbard on the morning of 7 May 1926. The successful journey from distant Rome was a harbinger of future triumph. Carefully and gently it descended and was towed into the huge box.

The Americans got busy. On the night of 9 May Commander Byrd and his pilot Floyd Bennett disappeared north in their Fokker machine, fitted with skis. At four the next day *Josephine Ford* returned – from the North Pole. Roald Amundsen welcomed them with open arms.

In common with many of the Americans' competitive achievements, this one too will have a question mark by it. Even before the end of May one of Amundsen's contacts in Kings Bay wrote that 'it is starting to leak out among the people here that Byrd does not really know where he has been'. Even honest men find it difficult to navigate above the polar sea. Everywhere everything looks the same. It really did not matter where on earth Commander Byrd had been.

While waiting for the airship's ascent, skiing lessons were instituted in Ny-Ålesund. Roald Amundsen had instructed all members of the flight to bring skis with them. Thus the southerners were given three to four days to learn the art which, according to Fridtjof Nansen, requires practice from the age of three or four. The skiing instructor was the lieutenant and 50-kilometre skier Bernt Balchen, one of Riiser-Larsen's specially drafted 'reserve-crew'. Later to become a super-pilot, he had an impossible task on his hands. Tryggve Gran, who in his time had been given an entire winter to teach Captain Scott's men, had to admit that there was something to be said for Nansen's thesis. Balchen's most important task had been to construct new solid skis for the *Josephine Ford*. It was on this Norwegian-produced undercarriage that the Americans had won the flying competition; it appeared that the Norwegians felt greater solidarity with their American competitors than with their Italian partners. 'The poor souls longed for their sunny Naples,' the skiing instructor wrote despairingly in his memoirs.

Colonel Nobile's original intention had been to complete the journey with an all-Italian crew. After the airship's arrival the southern contingent numbered no less than twenty-three. Riiser-Larsen's plans for a coup had become no more realistic since the departure from Rome.

The airship's actual crew was only made clear on the day of departure, 11 May. It was decided on a combination of weight, competence, nationality and obligations, old and new. They numbered sixteen. Nobile got five of his specialists: a rigger, a technician and three mechanics. Meteorologist Finn Malmgren was an obvious choice in spite of Captain Wisting's warnings and his Swedish nationality. Everyone who had sailed in *Maud* had first refusal. Loyalty was a virtue the polar explorer valued above all. Thus Oscar Wisting, veteran of the South Pole and the North East Passage, secured his place at the elevator and the unfailingly reliable Oskar Omdal took responsibility for one of the engines.

But even the best intentions cannot survive some pressures. The radio operator Gannadi Olonkin had sailed with *Maud* since 1918; only Wisting had served longer. The Norwegian-speaking Russian had accompanied *Norge* from Rome and had carried out his work to everyone's satisfaction. Then suddenly, the day after arrival in Kings Bay, he was abruptly asked to step down. A 'minor earache' had been discovered. The Russian could not believe it, no one could. It was not his hearing that did for Olonkin but his nationality. By exchanging the Russian for the Norwegian Fridtjof Storm-Johnsen, who just happened to be 'serving temporarily' with Kings Bay Radio, Roald Amundsen had ensured that his men would no longer be in a minority on board.

Olonkin was known for his sulky moods and poker-faced silences; nevertheless, one of the Italians saw the hitherto stoney mask shed tears. For seven years he had been frozen in on board *Maud*, and now, on the threshold of the last decisive flight, the loyal Russian had been ordered off. All for Norway. Captain Birger Gottwaldt, head of the radio section, was charged with the responsibility of carrying through the 'ethnic cleansing' of his subordinate personnel. Fredrik Ramm, whose nationalistic pride was indisputable, was the press officer. Lieutenant Emil Horgen got the chance to assist the navigator.

At the head of this ingenious blend of skilled competence and national allegiance, the four leaders towered.

Lincoln Ellsworth had no specific function on board. He was there, it seemed, partly as a practical assistant wherever a willing hand was needed and partly as a complicating psychological element, to stir things up. There was the eternal rivalry for Amundsen's favour, Hjalmar Riiser-Larsen, who was ultimately given Ellsworth's dream job: navigating the airship. In addition to this demanding task, the second-in-command was literally waiting in the wings as the airship's captain and possible saviour.

In contrast to the other three the airship's pilot Umberto Nobile was not really a polar explorer; the neat and tidy southern Italian was rather an intellectual. He bore the title colonel, but he was an engineer by education and a director by position. Nobile's daily place of work was behind a desk; to him the airship flight was a theory that needed to be tested.

The airship was a large but manoeuvrable device. To the constructor the entire undertaking rested upon a set of calculations. All components and variables were computed and weighed: distance, temperature, humidity, wind strength, ballast and fuel. Over such huge distances even the smallest inaccuracy on the drawing board could have catastrophic consequences. Umberto Nobile based his entire participation on the fact that the venture would succeed. He was no adventurer, or rather: he left nothing to chance. From a professional point of view, the *Norge* flight was a clear break with the attitude which had characterised all Amundsen's previous aviation expeditions: the attitude of Andrée. Courage and daring were the decisive elements. One set off – and *hoped* to come back. Umberto Nobile knew that if the airship did not stay aloft and reach its goal, then the battle was lost – for him and for Italy.

If the Italian's honour depended upon flying the ship through the air, the Norwegian crew was prepared to lead the expedition back over the ice. That was when, after the descent, the old polar explorer would take over the command. Then the unique qualities of the Northerners would come into their own. Apart from Byrd and Bennett's lightning action, no polar expedition had ever existed that did not touch ice. The Norwegians loaded their airship with skis and polar equipment, convinced that sooner or later the Italians would have to depend on the true polar explorers.

Among those who were left behind when the airship took off, apart from the future super-pilot Bernt Balchen, was Lieutenant Gustav S. Amundsen. The Governor's nephew too was part of the second-in-command's reserve troops. Alongside a handful of compatriots and Italians, all of whom had lived in hope until the very last, when the hawsers were cut and the airship ascended, young Amundsen waved farewell to a place in history. The Colonel's sums were merciless, the number was sixteen.

One single exception was made: Titina – Nobile's dog.

FORTY-TWO

Nobile's Dog

'Under an Italian flag, in the spirit of fascism, *Norge* sails in to the polar sky!' proclaimed the front-page headline of *Il Piccolo* on 11 May 1926. The papers in both Oslo and Rome brought out special editions featuring the expedition's departure.

The Oslo paper *Aftenposten* had sent editor-in-chief Frøis Frøisland to Rome to cover the event through the eyes of Norway's new collaborator. 'Since the outbreak of the world war Italian papers have not sold a single edition in such quantities as they did today; not even during the Blackshirts' march on Rome was there such excitement in the air, such intense interest, such massive patriotic feeling as there was today in Rome.'

The 'Amundsen/Ellsworth/Nobile Transpolar Flight' was an international press occasion of massive dimensions. Newspapers from around the world, with the *New York Times* leading the way, had a financial stake in the enterprise and thus every reason to give it full publicity. But it was about more than just selling copies; for at least two countries this was a political affair.

Mussolini's press at last had a heroic and patriotic news story that it could get its teeth into. At home in Norway the papers were even more fundamentally bound up in the actual event, most importantly via editor-in-chief Thommessen, owner and publisher of *Tidens Tegn* and *Oslo Aftenavis*. But the polar explorer traditionally cooperated with several mouthpieces, not least the conservative *Aftenposten*. It was clear that the two powerful, fiercely nationalistic editors-in-chief Frøisland and Thommessen both intended to milk the *Norge* expedition for all it was worth, not only in terms of copies sold, but also in the political arena.

'*Norge* lifted off at 9.55 a.m. The weather was wonderful. Clear and calm, minus 4.6°, we are 16 on board.' Sober and exact Roald Amundsen started his last expedition diary. The old polar explorer had not forgotten the practice of looking at his watch, measuring the temperature and counting his crew. But when it came to describing the airship he almost resorted to poetry: 'It lifted beautifully and unfolded its wings.'

Wings? An aeroplane has wings, but an airship? Not even poetical ones. A hovering whale or an inflated dinosaur maybe, but not a bird. And yet, it unfolded its wings. Perhaps the only bird was the peacock describing it.

King Haakon and Queen Maud hung in their oval frames in the lead gondola – just as they had on all Roald Amundsen's ships. Many years later the Norwegian king would have his own seagoing vessel bearing the name *Norge*. But the airship *Norge* was itself a royal ship. N1 had been specifically fitted out in order that Italy's monarch, Viktor Emanuel III, might float majestically and view his kingdom from the air. However, during the rebuild most of the trappings of royal luxury had been removed. Only the throne remained.

Colonel Nobile wrote that he had placed a velvet-covered easy chair by one of the side windows, specifically for Amundsen's use; the polar explorer himself claimed he sat on an aluminium water tank; in this case he is probably telling the truth, not so much in terms of the chair, but because of the positioning. The polar explorer never wanted to sit by a side-window; he wanted to sit in front, by the large window which straddled the entire front of the lead gondola.

Roald Amundsen was no less majestic than Viktor Emanuel, Mussolini's puppet. Resolute, the absolute ruler sat with his back to his underlings. He had, by God's grace, spent an entire lifetime roaming the icy wastes. Not once did he doubt his right to rule – a king in search of a kingdom.

Thus far it was all old hat. 'The ice looks pretty much as it did last year,' he wrote conscientiously. 'Everyone is working enthusiastically.' What they were working at did not concern the Governor, as long as all was well. In a later passage he borrowed an image from the animal world: 'In all three engine gondolas mechanics were running around like monkeys.'

The most acrobatic display was out of sight of the Governor; it took place far from the lead gondola when the rigger Alessandrini was obliged to climb through the hatch in the bows to make an external inspection of the vessel. Back and forth he snaked his way along the vessel's rounded back; it was bitterly cold and the airship was travelling at 50 miles per hour. They certainly knew their monkey-tricks, 'these happy sons of the south' as the Governor called them. The cold and the vertical drop were perils to match any facing a dog-team travelling at a brisk pace over Antarctica's crevasses.

Times had changed. *Fram* and *Maud* had been full of dogs and the decks were hosed down each day, but there was no barking to be heard on board *Norge*, with a single exception.

Nobile's dog scurried hither and thither. While the *Fram* dogs filled page after page in the saga of the South Pole, Titina never really featured in *The First Flight across the Polar Sea*. We are not told what the polar explorer thought, which would suggest a certain degree of generosity, since the presence of Nobile's dog was a breach of the rules. The polar explorer had no time for small dogs. Was it actually a dog at all?

Colonel Nobile claimed that it sneaked on board; it wanted to be with its master. The polar explorer knew how to value loyalty – a dog's noble characteristic, but what use was it? Dogs should either be out in front pulling their master towards his goal, or they should stay behind guarding hearth and home. A lap dog had no place on a polar expedition. It represented a weak link in the undertaking, and betrayed an Achilles heal in the airship's commander. The dog did not depend on the Colonel; rather the Colonel depended on Titina.

However, on further reflection Amundsen came to realise that the animal might serve a useful purpose. He looked at Wisting and remembered Slakteren – The Butcher. Nobile's ornamental dog weighed about 5kg. Wisting knew how to carve up a dog to get the maximum yield. It wouldn't amount to much per person, but they would share and share alike. The moment they hit the ice, he, the Governor, would have power over humans, dogs *and* daily rations.

Dog cutlets are tasty. The jack-of-all-trades is a good cook. He called the dish quite simply 'dog'. The polar explorer glanced at the pointed, dark little head. Its body was smooth and delicate. Was it actually a dog at all?

Time would tell.

At nine that evening *Norge* had crossed 87°30′. In order to stretch his legs the Governor had risen from the water tank and taken a turn at the tiller. Someone slipped him a telegram. It was private, from trustee Rode who said that 'both houses are mine'. The Governor was replaced at the tiller while he wrote a few words on a piece of paper. He handed it to a telegraphist – 'immediately sent Herman a note of thanks'.

These terse jottings in the diary marked the close of a bitter chapter in the polar explorer's life – just a few hours before he reached the North Pole.

The court case between the trustees and Leon Amundsen had ended in a settlement on 19 April. Leon had decided not to appeal, which avoided exposing the sensitive circumstances surrounding his brother's private life. The properties passed to the bankrupt estate which was now free to sell them on to Herman Gade and Don Pedro; this time at the full market value. The telegram to Herman was appropriate because, since the bankruptcy was not yet annulled, the properties were in his name but actually belonged to the polar explorer.

Gliding towards the North Pole Roald Amundsen does not reveal his thoughts. But surveying the icy wilds he knows that the last bonds to his brother are broken. Once upon a time the two had carried through a magical masterpiece; they had led the world up the garden path and turned north into south. The price was high, however. He had to conquer the North Pole on his own.

At that moment too the last bond between Kiss Bennett and Roald Amundsen was severed. The polar explorer was at last released from his moorings, a free man, floating in a ship lighter than air. It was named after Norway, but he himself was still the Flying Dutchman.

Something else happened before the North Pole was reached: 'Midnight, 88°30″, Ellsworth's birthday, 46 years old. We toasted him in tea.' In his restless pursuit of adventure it was a characteristically meagre if expensive birthday celebration for the boyish American bachelor. He married seven years later, on an impulse. According to his memoirs he saw very little of his beautiful wife.

Soon all attention was focused on Riiser-Larsen's tall figure; he was standing by a side window with a sextant in his hands. While the ship's commander was dressed in a wolfskin coat, the navigator sported plus fours and a peaked cap. The air in the gondola was sufficiently below zero to freeze the hot water in the thermos flask but the giant did not feel the cold. In order to defrost some food he had thrust the rissole into his trouser-pockets. As soon as Riiser-Larsen had confirmed 90 degrees the airship descended and the engine was turned off. Silence fell as the ship hung in the air.

The Governor's diary: 'It is 2.20 in the afternoon. Break out the flags. The Norwegian billowed beautifully. The pole went straight into the snow. The ice was broken up into small floes. We were 200 metres, minus 11. The fog lifted as we arrived at the pole which enabled us to make the necessary observations.'

By the time he wrote his book the flag ceremony had been embellished: 'The beautiful, padded Norwegian silk flag whistled down; a cross-bar fixed to a long aluminium pole, like a standard, which gave it excellent steering. It landed perfectly, bored into the ice and in the light breeze the Norwegian colours unfolded.'

The polar explorer, who this time included Ellsworth in the description and therefore wrote in the third person, continued: 'At that moment Amundsen turned round and grabbed Wisting's hand. Nothing was said, it was not necessary. The same two hands planted the Norwegian flag on the South Pole 14 December 1911.' At that moment the captain of the doomed ship *Maud* was rewarded for his loyalty.

Of equal importance was that, with this gesture, Amundsen laid to rest the accusation that he had excluded Hjalmar Johansen from the South Pole party because he did not want anyone else but himself to achieve both feats – north and south. Wordlessly he demonstrated his generosity and welcomed the stocky man from Horten up on to his own high plane. They were the two – the only two – who had conquered both Poles.

Compared with the momentous handshake that bound the two Poles forever to Norway the American's flag ceremony was altogether more peculiar and personal: 'When will a man again plant the flag of his native country on the Pole on his birthday?'

The Italian flag is mentioned only briefly. However, the Italian colours are castigated in the polar explorer's memoirs. Here he revealed that, following the solemn and silent Norwegian occasion, and the 'indescribable feeling' of throwing down the Star and Stripes, he could not control his laughter during the Italian ceremony.

Nobile's flag had gone last, but it was bigger than the others and was followed by a few smaller flags and pennants. In the eyes of the Governor, in the Colonel's hands the airship was turned into some kind of 'heavenly circus wagon'. Such a pompous display did not find favour with the expedition's supreme commander. 'That a grown man and an officer at that had so little imagination that he judged such a moment more by the size of its symbols than by the depth of feeling, struck me as so conceited that I laughed out loud.'

From this point all directions led south. The polar explorer took up his permanent post in front of the panorama window. Now the voyage started in earnest. The North Pole was not the goal, more the start of the secret part of the trans-Arctic flight. It was this area of the earth's surface, between the Pole and Alaska, which Roald Amundsen wanted to discover. Here the absolute monarch would claim his land.

This was the last significant piece of the earth's surface undiscovered by mankind, an expanse approximately twice as long as the one they had hitherto sailed. While Spitsbergen lay up towards the 80th latitude, Alaska's coast, on the opposite side, meandered along the 70th latitude. No ship had ever measured depths in this huge ocean. A whole continent might lie between the Pole and America.

A few hours after *Norge* had passed over the polar point, radio transmission was lost. However, news had reached the world that the flags had been planted on the earth's northernmost point. Fifty-five radio telegrams had been exchanged between the airship and Svalbard Radio – 1,583 words. But as the airship crossed the frontier into the unknown, absolute silence set in. The ship had broken loose from the airwaves and disappeared.

The polar explorer had always been a man of few words and Nobile noticed that he never complained of the silence. Later the Italian insinuated that Amundsen had deliberately caused the loss of the radio connection. He even suggested that the change-over from Olonkin, who had kept the radio going all the way from Rome to Spitsbergen, to the completely unknown Storm-Johnsen, might have had something to do with it.

Whatever the cause, loss of contact clearly came at a convenient time. Roald Amundsen had never been keen on keeping the outside world up to date. He had been uneasy at the way *Maud*'s newsworthiness had gradually haemorrhaged through its radio-transmitter. At the same time he had been impressed by the effect of the previous year's complete disappearance. Radio contact weakened the drama, the element of surprise. The emotional ebb and flow, the relief, the jubilation, the reward, vanished with the constant trivial drips over the ether. The wireless connection was in itself a mystery, a lightning conductor for the actual event. The explorer travelled away *to return home*.

Mankind had inhabited this planet for thousands of years and yet part of it still lay shrouded in darkness. One man was on the threshold of looking into the unknown, from above. The other fifteen were there merely to make it possible. His sole responsibility was to observe; to be the first to see this world.

To whom can one compare Roald Amundsen at this moment? To Napoleon, astride his horse, at the head of his army on the icy Russian tundra? To Columbus or Leiv Eriksson in their ships on the high seas? The polar explorer did have something in common with the adventurers and conquerors of history, but at the same time there was something very different and surreal about the world's last great discovery. It took place from the seated position, in a chair and in the course of a couple of hours. The only things that moved were the eyes. The conqueror's only weapons were a notebook and a pair of binoculars.

There was no horse, no ship's bridge, no dog-team over which to crack a whip; he was not even behind the joystick of a plane. He made his discovery from the stalls, from, as it were, a box in the theatre. It was an opening night staged in the real world.

'Just saw 3 gulls flying over a floe?' he noted in his diary at 3.45 a.m. The question mark indicates – land. Where there is life there is land. But there was no land and no life for several more latitudes until he spotted bear spoors. Although the polar bear can travel long distances, where there is seal there is bear . . .

Slowly, as the hours ticked by, it dawned on the polar explorer: there was nothing. An endless expanse of nothing. No new America, no new Greenland, no Iceland, not as much as a new Franz Josef Land, not even an Isle of Man. There would be no Roald Amundsen Land.

The polar explorer could give his binoculars a rest. There was nothing but ice. He had discovered that there was nothing to discover.

Ever since he first planned the journey in *Fram*, through the Bering Strait and north, over twenty years previously, Roald Amundsen had dreamt of taming this part of the world's surface. The extent of his destitution is evident in the book

The First Flight across the Polar Sea, where the stretch from the North Pole to Alaska takes up barely a page and a half.

The airship threatened to ice up, but apart from that the problems only surfaced after arrival in Alaska where weather conditions were difficult. The crew were exhausted after three days with little sleep and only frozen food to eat. There was a very jittery atmosphere – even the polar dog Titina was restless. Where and how would the airship put down? In spite of strong gusts of wind they decided to land on the ice outside the small town of Teller, between Deering and Nome. It was the morning of 14 May, European time.

Here, at last, in the final phase of the expedition, the polar explorer experienced 'the miracle'. Once again he stepped out from behind the scenes. He who can divide the ocean and still the storm. 'As we were descending strong, fiery gusts of wind hit us from land; suddenly and without any warning it was calm and stayed thus during the entire landing,' the polar explorer wrote in his account.

For want of earthly profits the flight was elevated to a divine plane. The polar explorer 'bared his head' for the ship's skipper, but somewhere there is a larger tiller, a deeper rudder, a higher power. 'Give honour where honour is due. Let us agree to give [this to] Him, who on many occasions on this journey quite evidently held His hand over us and saved us. Let us not battle for supremacy among ourselves. Without God's help we are all so insignificantly small.'

FORTY-THREE

Nationalists at the Ramparts

The disappearance of *Norge* was a godsend for the world press. On 13 May 1926, the very same day it happened, the whole world was informed that the airship *Norge* had passed over the North Pole. But already next day the accurate radio announcements were exchanged for front-page headlines based on editorial guesswork. And, on Saturday 15 May, the world was still ignorant about *Norge*'s true fate. Only during the evening did the longed-for announcement of the landing in Alaska reach civilisation.

In its special edition, on Monday 17 May, Norway's National Day, *Aftenposten* reported how the news had been received in the capitals Oslo and Rome. The first report was from the Grand Hotel: 'Saturday evening the Hall of Mirrors was crammed with dancers and chatting couples. Suddenly engineer Alf Bryn, the Aeronautical Association's secretary, jumped up onto the music stand, called for silence and read out the telegram announcing that *Norge* had landed in Teller. Great jubilation.' Afterwards the three countries' national anthems were played, but that was not all. 'Shortly thereafter Lieutenant Colonel Sverre called for silence, and gave a short speech praising *Norge*'s men and their achievements. And, the Lieutenant Colonel ended, "I know of no one more deserving of a toast than Mrs Riiser-Larsen who is sitting over there".'

This rather impulsive Nordic celebration appears without doubt rather modest compared to what, simultaneously, took place in the Italian capital: 'One hundred thousand people had gathered in the Piazza Colonna, where a tiny Norwegian flag and a large Italian and American flag floated in the wind. All traffic on the Corso was halted and adjoining roads were jam packed with enthusiastic people shouting: Long live Italy and Norway! The Norwegian flag was planted outside Mussolini's window accompanied by a noisy show of emotion. All night the crowds milled about. People studied the special editions and cheered the Norwegian, Italian and American flags outside Mussolini's windows.'

On this intoxicating evening, with general rejoicing throughout an illuminated and flag-festooned Rome, Mussolini received *Aftenposten*'s editor-in-chief.

The dictator sent the following message to his sister nation in the north; he announced: 'The brilliant success of the polar expedition has filled me with joy and pride in my role as an Italian and as Prime Minister. Invincible Italian courage has united with unshakeable Norwegian will and the Latin's ingenious inventiveness with Nordic disciplined creativity. These two different temperaments have complemented each other in a wonderful way. An immortal feat has been accomplished and one of the great prizes after which mankind has long striven has been won under our united banners. It is not necessary to underline the great importance in every way of this journey, but this our joint triumph will never be forgotten. By it the old, traditional friendship between Norway and Italy will be further strengthened and deepened.'

On 29 May *Aftenposten* published a front-page interview with Benito Mussolini. The dictator's portrait was placed inside a laurel wreath under the headline 'FROM THE NEW ITALY'. The Norwegian people were presented with a man of action. The interview started: 'The Happy conclusion to the North Pole expedition' and developed seamlessly into a broad rehearsal of Il Duce's other political programmes. Mussolini is a man devoid of empty phrases; he is the experienced fighter pilot and a fearless motorist. Four years ago he conquered Rome; now he marches towards Oslo.

At the very moment 'Italy's creator' caused a stir at the breakfast tables of the Norwegian bourgeoisie, the promising brotherhood had long since broken down on Alaska's exposed coasts. The two very dissimilar national temperaments had already grown into an irreconcilable hostility which developed at a speed worthy of the new age.

Later that summer an American commentator hit the nail on the head when he wrote: 'When the polar explorers landed in Teller there was honour and glory enough to go round, but if this quarrel continues there will be neither honour nor glory for anyone.'

To reproduce this fast-spreading affair of dirty linen in all its intriguing nuances and numerous national and personal facets is no longer possible or desirable. The background to the conflict was, however, quite simple. Before departure from Rome Ellsworth and Amundsen were obliged to accept Nobile as the third leader of the expedition. Consequently the Italian flag (including accessories) was literally dropped over the Pole. The leadership of the Norwegian Aeronautical Association had realised that the Italian share of the enterprise was so comprehensive that this concession was unavoidable.

Roald Amundsen, however, considered the agreement a formality of limited duration, a sleight of hand for the purpose of getting the airship north. Independent of all and any understanding he behaved in the only way he knew how – that of absolute Governor. In the polar explorer's universe there was no room for the self-centred Italian. 'This salaried airship commander on a Norwegian ship, which belongs to an American and myself, will not be allowed to seize an honour which is not rightly his,' he wrote later in his memoirs.

The problem was, however, that the honour was *exactly* Nobile's – to a degree which the polar explorer could not have imagined beforehand and later would not admit. Rolf Thommessen would express this succinctly in his judicial statement: 'What caused the strife was nothing more than the sensitive and difficult relationship which will always be present between an incompetent leader and a competent commander which came to a head owing to the success of the expedition.' In the margin of this conclusion the polar explorer had added: 'That was aimed at me!'

As a geographical expedition the *Norge* journey had been, measured in square miles covered, considerable, on a par with the important discoveries in the history of mankind. But by establishing that all that existed between the Pole and Alaska was water, the results, which might have been a turning point in the earth's geography, represented an anti-climax. The journey seen from the point of view of flight had not only been a huge success – with 171 hours flying hours from Rome, of which 72 were over the actual Polar Sea – it had exceeded all expectations. As a work of art within communications the airship *Norge* heralded a new era.

The polar explorer's leadership ability had not been tested once during the journey. Not even as an explorer was he able to express himself, let alone as the expedition's heroic Governor on the ice. Roald Amundsen was left to fight Nobile in an imaginary situation, as in the following, from his memoirs: 'Furiously exasperated I reminded him in no uncertain terms of the pitiful sight he would make if *Norge* had been forced down, and pointed out how meaningless his demands regarding real leadership would be under such conditions.'

The day following the arrival in Teller the polar explorer set out on a journey to Nome with a dog team. He was accompanied by Ellsworth and his two most loyal men, Wisting and Omdal. This is how he wanted to arrive in the gold-mining town and end a career which had started twenty years previously when *Gjøa* cast anchor in Nome Roads. He left without even saying goodbye to the Italian.

Nobile arrived in Nome by boat some time later and in time the entire expedition crew was gathered. The airship was left on the ice outside Teller, a virtual wreck. Demounted the *Norge* was a pitiful sight, more like the skeleton of a beached whale. It was of no interest whether or not it represented any value; Roald Amundsen attached no importance to the vessels of yesteryear.

The arrival in Nome was a cold shower. A mere handful of souls were on their feet to greet the great explorer. They had expected to see an airship come sailing in over town, not just an old polar explorer in a dog-sledge. In any case, Roald Amundsen himself, in spite of his new moustache, was not all that sensational. It was far more exciting when a real airship commander came to town a few days later – and, in the words of the dog-team driver himself, made a 'gloating entrance'.

The expedition had signed a comprehensive agreement with the *New York Times*. In spite of jeopardising contracts worth up to 400,000 crowns Roald Amundsen was in no hurry to meet his obligations. According to the agreement he was to deliver an enormous amount of words, presumably based on topographic descriptions of new land areas and other sensational finds. Unfortunately, there was not much to write about; they had seen signs of bear, otherwise little else.

The articles which were eventually telegraphed from Nome were written by journalist Ramm and signed by Amundsen and Ellsworth. Nobile immediately protested against the omission of his name. In Oslo the administrative management frantically tried to defuse the situation. But the Governor was increasingly unshakeable in his conviction that the Aeronautical Association were playing into the Italians' hands. 'We were at this moment so bloody fed up with the whole thing that we felt like telling Thommessen and his gang to take a running jump,' are his later comments on the continuous stream of demands from so-called authoritative quarters.

In order to maintain his commanding position and his nation's interest, and to publish the Italian version, Nobile orchestrated his own press coverage. On account of the open split the weeks in Nome were painful for all parties. At the end of the stay Riiser-Larsen telegraphed home to Thommessen: 'Every joy at the expedition's success spoilt for us all and no one wants anything but to leave and if possible forget it all. Sorry to say that A's last will be a bitter memory.'

At last the longed-for steamer *Victoria* arrived and on 16 June the expedition set off south. The polar explorer bade farewell to the town, which had been such an important geographical point throughout his career, with little regret.

In the book which he was about to start he called Nome to account; the place where he, the world-renowned explorer, was outshone by a subordinate Mediterranean. Amundsen here made use of a device which he refined in later memoirs. He quite simply deleted Nobile from the story. The name of the town is not even worthy of mention; it is a stain on the 'beautiful wonderland – Alaska'. Inhabited by 'a modern, narrow-minded, grasping individual'.

In order to explain the moral decline of the inhabitants of this unmentionable place, the polar explorer turned to psychology and analysed the human being, isolated by weather and winter: 'We know of course from experience how an isolated life attacks the healthy mind's ability to think sensibly. The effect of even one year is noticeable in some individuals. What happens with so many when they live, year in, year out, pent up in this atmosphere? Without they themselves realising it their brains shrivel up into nothing and it is easy to see what the outcome will be when these mentally vulnerable individuals start to judge people and conditions with the tiny brain which is left, as though it were in full vigour.' The polar explorer rounds off his analysis by establishing that 'they are not few in number, the mentally ill patients from Alaska who year after year fill the mental asylums of the States'.

Not long after his return to Norway Roald Amundsen apparently received a letter, posted in Nome, which throws light on his relationship with the local population; but from a different perspective and based on someone other than himself. The letter was written by trader Charles Carpendale, Camilla's father. The occasion was the unexpected return of the two 'Eskimo girls', which had taken place a year and a half earlier.

Kakonita and Camilla had been dispatched across the Atlantic by Gustav Amundsen, alone, on a Norwegian boat. For Camilla Carpendale this was not too problematic as she could return to her family. But what about little Kakonita Amundsen?

'Grand-daddy' had not made any arrangements for his foster-daughter's continued existence. Initially Kakonita was foisted upon the Carpendale family at East Cape, who, with their huge family, had no pressing need of yet another mouth to feed. But what to do? Send her back to her biological father? 'Kakot has no home & is nothing more than a thug and is considered as such by the other natives,' Carpendale wrote of the man who had once given Amundsen his daughter.

Following an unusually severe winter on the coast of Siberia the Carpendale family decided to break away from the native population and travel south to more civilised regions. 'It would have broken little Nita's heart if she had been left behind; she feared Kakot, could not and would not talk to him and owing to the prevalent conditions I would not have left a dog behind. The little girl is the best I have ever met and is loved by all who meet her: What would you like us to do with her?'

The paterfamilias confronted the polar explorer with his responsibility and ended the letter with a reference to Nome: 'People say you have changed; but I like to remember the Amundsen I knew from East Cape and will never believe, unless you actually tell me so, having taught little Nita the white man's way of eating, etc., that you really meant that I should send her back. . . .'

Irrespective of how the polar explorer responded to this letter, in the end little Miss Amundsen moved with the Carpendale family to Seattle where she later married and had a family. If Kakonita every represented an experiment, it is difficult to conclude that the result ever profited her foster-father.

On board *Victoria* the crew members were photographed, together and in groups, but not one word was exchanged between the Norwegian and Italian leaders for the entire ten to twelve days they were together on the ship. In Seattle everything was prepared for a large reception: a flotilla of boats, crowds on the quay and planes overhead – all to honour the heroic airship crew. But here, in the rush of excitement, the big catastrophe took place.

Colonel Nobile and two of his colleagues appeared on the gangway dressed in 'brilliant uniforms'. This in turn led to a formidable snub as a sweet little flower-girl who was standing on the quay failed to notice the drab polar explorer, he who towered above all polar explorers, and handed the town's welcome bouquet to a casual officer with a funny little dog at his feet.

Both in the book about the expedition and in his later memoirs Roald Amundsen launched a scathing attack on the Italian's uniform: 'This was no less than fraud.' First of all, because Nobile had brought with him a spare, heavy-duty, change of clothing while the Norwegians had shivered their way to the north inadequately clothed. The argument is refuted many years later, with Nobile's clarification that the Italians had worn their uniforms inside their outer garments throughout the journey. For those of the crew who had been with the airship to southerly climes this was not news.

Furthermore, 'our anger was increased by his vulgar behaviour and bad taste, in stark contrast to his comrades on the expedition'. In reality the three gold-buttoned Italians were an accurate replay of the three uniformed lieutenants who had appeared just as suddenly following last year's expedition. It was, after all, their right to represent their native country, just as the lieutenants had wished to indicate their connection to the Norwegian Navy. Actually, from the Italians' point of view this was not a civilian expedition; according to the contract with the Air Force Minister, Mr Mussolini, an 'officer' was to be placed at the expedition's disposal and the Italian members were to 'be considered as being in the service of the Italian government'.

It is not difficult to ascertain that Roald Amundsen's hatred of uniforms was determined by nationality. The Governor clearly distinguished between lieutenants from his native country and soldiers from an, in time, exceedingly hostile army.

During the celebrations in Seattle the polar explorer, however, made a half-hearted attempt to mend bridges with the Colonel. Not by conceding anything, but, according to Nobile, rather by blaming Ellsworth for their disagreements. But not even the American's contribution could prevent the total breakdown.

At the fiftieth anniversary of the momentous journey, with the events in their proper prospective, Umberto Nobile summed up what happened thereafter. 'Norwegians and Italians left Seattle separately and were celebrated by their respective immigrant colonies as they continued eastwards through the USA. Our long journey, which had been well organised by our Embassy in Washington, and by the various consulates, on orders from Mussolini, was a series of long, noisy engagements. Mussolini used the occasion to make political capital among the USA's ten million Italians. Then the inevitable happened, namely that both Italians and Norwegians emphasised their own importance in connection with the successful voyage, often by detracting from the others' contribution. In this way in time the split became deep-rooted on both sides.'

Irrespective of how the leadership of the trans-Arctic flight was organised, there is no doubt that Roald Amundsen was the enterprise's real head. But when a brilliant triumph in the course of a couple of weeks had been turned into a total disaster and moral defeat for all concerned, not much can be said for Roald Amundsen as Governor. Roald Amundsen had attained many if not all his goals. That would not have been possible without an ability to lead. But only if certain conditions were present. In spite of his increasingly frequent fits of rage, on the whole Amundsen was considered a quiet leader not given to the grand gesture. However, he demanded total submission; he lacked the ability to meet an opponent half-way. Only someone who licked his boots could be restored to favour.

Like Captain Johansen, Colonel Nobile was a proud and ambitious character. Hjalmar Johansen had been Nansen's man, Umberto Nobile was the subordinate of Mussolini. None of them was able to capitulate unreservedly to Roald Amundsen.

The Norwegians' return was in sharp contrast to the damp and cold airship flight; no method of communication could compete with the railway where high-speed luxury was concerned. Roald Amundsen and his team crossed the American continent on board two reserved carriages coupled to a Pullman. The polar explorer could indulge in his morning bath while speeding along at 100 kilometres per hour.

On 5 July the triumphal progress culminated in New York. 'When the pilots arrived at Grand Central Station, bands and a thousand unending ovations greeted them,' *Aftenposten*'s correspondent wrote. 'The short stay precluded a more formal reception. The pilots drove through town in a flag-adorned and police-escorted cortège to the *Bergensfjord*. They caused a sensation everywhere.' The steamship awaits, the polar explorer is in a hurry. He wants to get home.

Since their arrival in Teller speculation had been rife as to the crew's future plans. Mussolini had already proclaimed that Italy was to build a new airship for use in polar regions. Ellsworth and Riiser-Larsen played around with new ideas, but the Governor had made his intentions clear: it was all over. He indicated his future occupation as inoffensive rock-climbing, or maybe, salmon-fishing. In a telegraphic interview on board *Bergensfjord* he nevertheless made a momentous addition to this life of leisure. 'But the fact that I consider my life of exploration over does not mean that I am going to hibernate. I will always be ready, should anyone, north or south, need to be rescued.'

On 12 July the Norwegian heroes, including Malmgren, were given an overwhelming reception in Bergen. Each and every one of them was raised aloft by local strong men and carried ashore on gilded chairs. The nine polar explorers were similarly dressed in double-breasted suits. Deftly, Amundsen had ordered by telegraph from Nome tailor-made suits which were waiting when they arrived in Seattle. Amundsen's troop was thus uniformed, but in civvies. Among the festive crowd were also the heroes' wives. Roald Amundsen was welcomed by his brother Gustav and Minister Gade. The Hotel Norge had been cleared to accommodate them.

On 15 July the expedition members sailed into Norway's capital on board another Norwegian American Line ship. *Aftenposten* reported: 'On the dot of half-past three yesterday afternoon *Stavangerfjord*'s mighty hull glided into Honnørbryggen quay. A mass of small flag-bedecked boats formed a guard of honour on each side of the ship. High above three Army Air Corps planes circled, their wings glinting in the sun. Thousands of expectant spectators surrounded the harbour and crowded into Tordenskjold's Plass and the roads around the quay. Around Oslo Municipality's grandstand festive flags snapped in the wind. White, blue and red dominated the quay. Stately tall pedestals carrying large urns from which smoke and steam rose were divided into shining white and blue sections. It appeared cool and fresh in the summer's heat and reminded one of snow and ice, sky and sea. From the quay to the grandstand a broad, red carpet was laid down and along this stood ladies carrying red roses for the returned polar explorers.'

In spite of the reception in Bergen, which, being broadcast, was quite epoch-making, the capital too laid on a sterling official reception. The steamships hooted in competition with the bands. Following the deputy-mayor and Speaker of Parliament Hambro's welcoming speeches, the polar explorer stepped forward in front of his countrymen. 'By coincidence, under his arm, he was carrying the flag which had been flying from the airship during its entire journey,' Riiser-Larsen wrote later, with the well-calculated vagueness which characterised the bulk of the heroic pilot's history writing. The photographs show that it is the second-in-command himself who carried the rolled-up flag under his arm. It was no coincidence that the props were in place; as usual the polar explorer had full control of the scenic effects.

The stage management was simple but effective. Before rising to speak Roald Amundsen exchanged the bunch of roses he had been carrying for the flag, handed to him by his props manager. *Aftenposten*: 'I have been asked so many times what it is that drives me. It has been this. [Amundsen unfurls the Norwegian flag.] The flag is worn and torn but I can assure you, it is *clean*! God has held His hand over it, over the entire Norwegian nation. Long live Norway!'

It was a magical moment. The polar explorer, the nine weather-beaten men, all fought an heroic fight against the tears that threatened to overcome them. For some the dam burst. Jubilation reached a climax. The carriages drove up. The triumphal cavalcade continued through town – to the palace.

When the newly appointed General Nobile made *his* entry into a flag-festooned Rome on 3 August a vicious press-war had broken out between Nobile and Ellsworth in American newspapers. The battle for the laurels was in full swing. Mussolini stepped right into the war of words in his welcome address from the balcony of the Chigi Palace: 'I must therefore make it clear once and for all – and I wish my voice had the power and strength of thunder – that although we, with our customary Roman sense of justice, acknowledge the merits of those of your colleagues of other nationalities, it is you to whom the honour and glory must go. You, an Italian, made the plans for the airship; you, an Italian, together with other Italians, guided the airship to its outstanding goal.'

Compared with the powerful political embrace to which Nobile was subject, Roald Amundsen's celebrations were child's play. And yet, the same pride beat in the speaker's breast and it was the same breath of nationalism that animated the two countries' banners.

FORTY-FOUR

Literary Suicide

In a figurative sense too Roald Amundsen's last expedition had been one huge balloon, pumped up by American dollars, unashamed Norwegian nationalism and ready-to-burst fascist ambitions. The combination was explosive. It was probably no one's fault that it all unravelled; least of all Roald Amundsen's.

From the moment the airship landed and his life's work was at an end everything started to come undone. The polar explorer was increasingly less accountable for his actions; not to say, inflammable.

'He is angry with God and everyone at one moment and in the next moment in a good mood. His mood changes quicker than wind and weather,' the manager of the Norwegian Aeronautical Association Skjoldborg wrote, having visited the polar explorer that summer. 'He is always irritated and does not know why.'

On 29 July Amundsen and Ellsworth had broken away from the Aeronautical Association. The break was kept a secret but the situation was precarious as they were dependent on Amundsen to make up lost money. Even before his return from America the polar explorer had made it clear that he did not intend to give any lectures. As this involved a breach of contract he was forced to reconsider. In the end most of the lecture work was carried out by Riiser-Larsen.

During a few summer's days at Svartskog Roald Amundsen composed his contribution to the year's polar book. It was shorter than ever, only 11,000 words, and written as 'we' rather than 'I' as Amundsen was also representing his co-author Ellsworth. *The First Flight across the Polar Sea* was nevertheless a big book as a further five authors contributed. The chapters which, according to the contract, should have been written by Nobile, were written by Amundsen's nephew Gustav Jnr and by the ubiquitous Hjalmar Riiser-Larsen. Another defeat for Ellsworth.

Large parts of this fifth and final volume about Roald Amundsen's explorations are controversial, written with the intention of emphasising Norway's contribution in general and Amundsen's leadership qualities in particular. The second-in-command ends his chapter with a parting salutation bordering on a funeral panegyric: 'Thank you, thank you from us all, Roald'. In spite of including chapters about navigation, meteorology and radio communications, the tome appears incomplete, having omitted any reference to the airship's constructor. It was translated into about ten languages but never achieved the same success as the previous year's ode to the heroes.

The gigantic airship expedition increasingly appeared a let-down compared with the previous year's humble, but sterling operation. Fritz G. Zapffe had been part of both: 'It is sad about the uproar as it was all so wonderfully done. Those black gypsies should never have been allowed to join in,' the chemist complained in a letter to the polar explorer. The crew had been decorated with the order of St Olav, but still, Norway had not done enough: 'Not even a memorial medal like the *Fram*-medal, while even Titina gets her gold medal. We remain in the shadow, but thank God, the radiance can never wear off you, even if all of Italy consisted of those sorts of generals.'

Roald Amundsen might have resigned as a polar explorer but his authorship was not yet over. He still had one more volume up his sleeve: the memoirs. The background for the only one of his books not based on an expedition was quite special. The memoirs were written to order for his American publishers Doubleday, Page & Company; the contract was signed on 24 February 1926, during the polar explorer's stay in New York.

A lady by the name of Anice Page Cooper was Roald Amundsen's close contact at the publishing house. She belonged to the same New York social circle as Sam and Bess Magids. After his return he received a letter from Mrs Cooper in which she reminded him of his contractual obligations with the following tactful words: 'I hope you are soon planning a visit to New York. The book is waiting to be written and we might light up the literary scene with a few cosy poker-games.'

For the first time ever following an expedition, Roald Amundsen desisted from all and every visit to Europe. This time he made straight for America.

On 26 November 1926 he set off with Herman Gade. The Rio Ambassador was en route to Washington on a special assignment; the polar explorer was going to write his memoirs and thereafter lecture.

When he set foot on the other side of the Atlantic a great surprise was in store: America had already been discovered, by Nobile! The Italian, following Amundsen's breach of contract and consequently freed from his obligations, had been given free rein to tour the Old and the New Worlds with his Italian version of the *Norge* journey. The Norwegian reacted immediately by having his own (and Ellsworth's) name struck off the membership list of the Norwegian Aeronautical Association. Amundsen still considered Mussolini and Nobile's Italy a subdivision of the airship expedition's shipping company. Consequently, the break was public and a new round of dirty-linen washing began.

On 4 December the Aeronautical Association's board responded by making public all charges against Norway's national hero. The article was given wide publicity in Norwegian and American newspapers. At home the polar explorer's lawyer Einar W. Nansen tried to contest all charges. 'Nonsense,' is the principal character's only comment. Beyond that he referred interested parties to his memoirs where he promised that 'the whole truth' would see the light of day.

When Roald Amundsen signed the contract regarding his memoirs, before the *Norge* flight, he no doubt had a different version in mind, rather than the quick and merciless brew he now threw together in his author's den, financed by the publishing house, in the Waldorf-Astoria. Following a blessed Christmas holiday he wrote to his lawyer in Norway: 'My memoirs are finished. Bloody hell – they are nasty.'

In January the polar explorer mounted a hectic campaign to ensure that his friend and landlord, Herman Gade, was appointed to the post of Norwegian Ambassador to Washington. In this connection a series of telegraphic rockets were fired off from the Waldorf-Astoria, with urgent requests to, among others, the King, the speaker of Parliament and editor-in-chief Frøisland, who was more than happy to engage *Aftenposten* in Gade's battle.

During that winter and spring Roald Amundsen once again traipsed around America. The fees received were transferred to his own account with Lawyer Nansen as he did not trust the money to the Aeronautical Association. Owing to the same mistrust and not absolutely according to the rules, he secured for himself a copy of the expedition film. Income from the book was likewise placed in the lawyer's account. The polar explorer wanted control of his own finances. To gain access to the income and pay the expedition's creditors, the Aeronautical Association was forced in the end to take the case to arbitration.

On 9 June Roald Amundsen left Vancouver on the *Empress of Asia*. He was off on a three-week tour of Japan. In the densely populated and booming little island-kingdom the polar explorer was welcomed and honoured as if he were a head of state. He gave in all ten lectures, including one for the imperial family. Mussolini's later comrade in arms, the young Hirohito, succeeded that year to the divine imperial throne, having previously ruled the country as regent. The giant of the north did not, however, allow himself to be blinded by the imperial god or the other inhabitants of the palace. 'They are nice, ordinary people and it all went well,' he wrote to Gade. The conqueror of two Poles was weighted down by jubilation, honours and gifts. There was really only one thing during the 'state-visit' which fell short of his expectations: 'The little Japanese women are not what I expected, plump and not very inviting!'

When the polar explorer left the Empire of the Rising Sun for Vladivostok on 15 July he was not only laden with precious gifts; he left behind a people full of admiration. 'Wherever he went he always repeated that his achievements were not for his fame or interest, but always for his beloved country, Norway,' wrote one Japanese commentator after the exalted guest had left the country. 'He claims that patriotism will prevent mankind from acting badly and emphasised the worth, in exalted words, of national spirit.' The praise was rounded off by a thought-provoking comparison of the Norwegian polar explorer to the Japanese war hero: 'The Norwegian love of Captain Amundsen is as great as our veneration of Admiral Togo.'

Roald Amundsen had turned into a commercial traveller in national sentiment. He was not himself aware of the dynamite in his luggage. It would soon be clear to most people that national spirit did not prevent mankind from acting badly.

In the wake of the airship flight he stretched the national element to its breaking point. Not only had he christened his Italian airship *Norge*, but his last book was dedicated to 'The Norwegian Flag'. This nationalistic display was, ultimately, Amundsen marking his own territory. In the fight against Italy Amundsen and Norway were synonymous. To Roald Amundsen nationalism was a means. The empire was his goal – *his own* empire.

The polar explorer did not linger during the railway expedition through the Soviet Union. In Moscow he was well looked after by Nansen's assistant, Vidkun Quisling, the man who would later found Norway's own nationalist party.

On 6 August he was back at Svartskog. Immediately telegrams from the palace and the couple at Leigh Court arrived. The lines of communication to Kiss were not severed, but the points of contact were: New York, Tokyo, Moscow – all roads avoid London.

My Life as a Polar Explorer was published on 23 September 1927. The story had already been serialised in the American monthly magazine *World's Work*. With this book Roald Amundsen was made bankrupt yet again; this time, however, morally. The book would prove to be more of a suicide bid than an autobiography.

The author's international prestige was still so high that newspapers in many countries reported and accepted his accusations and revelations without question. But many reacted with disbelief, and disappointment.

Morgenbladet, the newspaper which had hailed the polar explorer at many cross-roads, stressed that self-willed hauteur such as Roald Amundsen's 'must be measured with a different measuring-rod to the one we use on normal people. Without this self-will he would not have achieved what he did. He is made in the same mould as many of history's big characters.' But the paper added: 'If a man such as he is reckless in action so much more must he be careful in words. Amundsen knew this and he tried hard to charm us, until the events of the last years overtook him. His comrades, who put heroic deeds above minor considerations, enthusiastically followed him over icy wilds, north and south, while the entire world bourgeoisie is astonished because the great polar explorer lacks some of our virtues.' *Morgenbladet*'s conclusion was indicative of posterity's judgement: 'this book might be small, but the man is nevertheless big.' A sharp divide was drawn between petty controversy and great deeds.

If one were to believe the subject matter, half the polar explorer's life consisted of a confrontation with Umberto Nobile and the treasonous gentlemen of the Aeronautical Association. But the book also attacked several others by name; some of the most sensational attacks concerned his own brother; his intimate and closest partner throughout twenty years was branded a traitor.

That in the end Leon Amundsen accepted defeat rather than expose his brother in a court of law was used against him in a public denunciation. The mortally offended polar explorer ended with a psychological dig: 'I have often wondered what it is that changed this man's character?' It was important to emphasise that the break was not 'hereditary', nothing that affected the family. 'My mother and father were the best and most honourable people in the world.'

In earlier chapters of *My Life as a Polar Explorer* Leon was mentioned merely as 'escort' and 'secretary'; nevertheless the memoirs show clearly how dependent Roald Amundsen had been on his brother.

In 1981, the last survivor of all the Governor's men, Odd Dahl, defended the forgotten brother. Dahl had served them both: 'In my work with Leon Amundsen I got the impression that he was a sensible man who, besides administering his brother's expeditions, also ran his wine and silk agency with great skill. I see no other reason but that in this case Roald Amundsen went far too far, beyond all the limits of decency.'

Alone among Roald Amundsen's books, *My Life as a Polar Explorer* was dedicated to no one. He had been through them all: teachers, friends, women, native land. One name remained. It was embossed in gold letters on the book's spine, written in the skies, over the stars, the moon and the world.

FORTY-FIVE

Break with the World

'I cannot say that I am entirely enthusiastic,' Harald U. Sverdrup wrote regarding the autobiography in a letter to publishing company Gyldendal's director Harald Grieg. Later Sverdrup wrote the postscript in the 'Souvenir Edition' of the polar explorer's works. *My Life as a Polar Explorer* was not included in this edition. That was *not* how one wanted to remember one's great compatriot. Sverdrup would end his postscript by reminding everyone that it was Amundsen's own tales which 'give us the best and truest picture of his personality'. The autobiography was and became a threat to this synthesis.

Dr Sverdrup, who had been appointed professor in Bergen, met Roald Amundsen as he was passing through and could inform the publishers that he was in 'the best of moods'.

On 7 October 1927 Roald Amundsen had left Svartskog, heavily laden with suitcases. Once again he was setting out on a long foreign journey, initially touring the United States for five months, then planning to continue to the South American continent for yet another lecture tour.

There remained many nations who wished to pay homage to the man who had conquered two Poles, but they were shrinking in number. Italy had been erased from the map and the polar explorer had broken with Germany twice. The turn had come for England and America. In his autobiography Roald Amundsen had picked a fight with the mighty Geographical Societies of both countries.

Without being able to entirely prove it, the polar explorer insinuated that the National Geographical Society of America had 'on several occasions' treated him 'with a confused lack of consideration'. The most 'embarrassing' instance was during the winter of 1926, when Amundsen had visited Frederick A. Cook, who was resident in a prison near Fort Leavenworth. In spite of having first lost the North Pole and then being found guilty of some sort of financial swindle, Amundsen never gave up admiring his old teacher from *Belgica*. After the prison visit he was quoted by the press as uttering some words in Dr Cook's defence regarding the old dispute with Admiral Peary. This had brought him into conflict with the Society, which had long since proclaimed Admiral Peary as the

North Pole's only true conqueror. In his memoirs the author claims that he was 'completely misunderstood'; easy to understand as his remarks in the Cook–Peary conflict are, to put it mildly, ambiguous.

More serious was his conflict with the Royal Geographical Society in London. In his autobiography Amundsen describes the, now deceased, Lord Curzon's call for 'three times three hurrah for the dogs', with great bitterness. In the light of this and other unforgettable slanders, he saw it as his right to assert that 'on the whole the British do not like to lose.'

The accusations that the land of fair play was inhabited by 'bad losers', as the English version put it, caused a storm of protest in England. The Society found nowhere in their minutes, orally or in writing, the documentation of the 'hurrah for the dogs', and called for an apology. If that was not forthcoming the Norwegian polar explorer would have to retire as honorary member of the Royal Society; which was also the outcome. After several inquiries from the Society, Gustav Amundsen wrote on behalf of his uncle: 'Captain Amundsen asks me to inform you that he considers self-respect his dearest possession and would never exchange it even for the great honour of being an honorary member of your Society.' Thus the Norwegian polar explorer had uttered his last word in his battle with the British Empire.

While this conflict was raging Roald Amundsen was en route to New York where in the middle of October he was warmly welcomed by the representative of his publishers, Anice Page Cooper. (It would take a few more months ere the publishers had to admit that *My Life as a Polar Explorer* would never make the best-seller list in America.)

Roald Amundsen resumed his professional and social activities in the metropolis. But he never set out on his long tour. Suddenly, on 25 October, he changed course. Instead of turning up for a dinner in the Explorers' Club he turned up on the quay, a few minutes before the departure of *Bergensfjord*. He bought a ticket and stepped on board.

The world was flabbergasted. The polar explorer's movements were reported in the press more or less like a head of state on a foreign visit. What made him, contrary to his programme and without giving any explanation, break off his stay in America was the subject of considerable speculation on both sides of the Atlantic.

Roald Amundsen's departure was perceived as a definitive leave-taking. 'We have little hope of ever seeing you here again,' the *New York Times* editor John Finley wrote in a personal letter.

Roald Amundsen had quarrelled with at least three American institutions: the National Geographical Society, the Explorers' Club in New York and his promoter of many years, Lee Keedick.

In an American newspaper a small notice appeared under the headline: 'All for love?' It alluded to rumours of a love affair being the cause of the polar explorer's extraordinary disappearance.

According to a letter about Roald Amundsen, written by Herman Gade in the late autumn of 1927, 'a new and decisive factor entered his life'. At the time the polar explorer put America behind him he was entering a new and intense phase in the, until now, uncommitted relationship to the Alaskan beauty Bess Magids.

It might appear topsy-turvy that Roald Amundsen returned to Europe for the sake of an American woman. But not necessarily: Magids Brothers traded all over the world. We might assume that during his stay in New York the polar explorer had received signals from the other side of the world. These enticing tones must have been so irresistible that he turned on his heels. He broke his five-month contract with America; it suited him on all counts. We know for certain that the next meeting with Bess Magids was in Europe.

On arrival in Norway Roald Amundsen refused to answer questions. Later he issued a communiqué where he blamed his promoter. He was back at Svartskog on 7 November, exactly one month after having left, carrying his America suitcases.

'I see you are still a man full of surprises,' his faithful armour bearer Zapffe wrote after his return. 'I see that the English bulldog is still trying to pick a fight.' What the chemist did not know was that it was neither businessmen nor English bulldogs that threatened: Roald Amundsen was about to become his own worst enemy.

In December the affair around Roald Amundsen's 'dog' quarrel with the English reached its climax. Ever since Norwegian independence in 1905, England had been the superpower with which Norway felt the closest affinity. The conflict was causing such a serious strain on relations that the Norwegian Minister in London, Benjamin Vogt, saw no way out other than to ask his famous predecessor in the post, Fridtjof Nansen, for help.

In a letter dated 17 December he wrote: 'It is not easy to measure the damage Amundsen has caused us by calling the English "bad losers". As you no doubt know better than me, he could not have touched a more sensitive spot. I remember my time in Kristiansand, when the director of Eks mental asylum told me how, the quarrelsome mentally ill, knew, with exquisite wickedness, how to torment the doctors or relatives who visited them, and when I now see how Amundsen talks about "bad losers" and in America about Cook and Peary, I have to ask myself whether our wonderful compatriot has been mentally broken by these super-human efforts. Of all the Norwegian polar explorers you and

Sverdrup are the only ones who have come out of it unscathed. Prestrud shot himself – as far as I understand without any reason to do so, and Scott-Hansen has become rather strange. Of course, we cannot say all this in public, but it might be appropriate to remind people of the super-human exertions Amundsen has subjected himself to.'

Minister Vogt suggested appointing legal guardians for the polar explorer. The ruler of Poles was no longer predictable and must be deprived of his power to commit slander. Only polar research's highest moral authority, Fridtjof Nansen, had the authority to do that. A generation earlier, during Norway's hour of destiny, through a personal campaign conducted in the English press, he had saved his native country's prestige during its conflict with Sweden. He had also saved Roald Amundsen's reputation when he pursued Scott to the south. Now the minister asked him to save Norway from Amundsen.

Five days later Fridtjof Nansen wrote to Vogt: 'Like you I think he is suffering from some sort of mental confusion, a sort of clinical nervous disability which has in fact been evident in many ways.'

Next the Professor mentioned previous circumstances, and here – certainly with more frankness than anywhere else – he commented on Amundsen's behaviour during the scramble for the South Pole. 'It was no doubt unfortunate that he did not at that time make his intentions clear. Had he done so everything would have been interpreted in a different light, but apparently he has no sense of that at all, on the contrary he seems to think it was a great coup. Oh well, I suppose I cannot comment on the moral aspect, but the fact is that one does not behave like that, if it is not necessary. And certainly one does not benefit one's country. But he is making matters worse with his behaviour now. It appears he has a mania for kicking the superpowers. In America he has picked a quarrel too by his inexplicable behaviour.'

Although Nansen 'agrees' with Minister Vogt, he sees no possibility, via the press, to save Norway's lost face; 'it would be difficult to do anything now,' he ends his letter.

Certainly Britain was a superpower, but in the battle for the South Pole, the country was nevertheless the losing party. If the English on this or that occasion had been ever so arrogant, the victor, with his 'bad loser', had kicked an opponent who was down. Five British bodies were still somewhere in the Antarctic, frozen.

What Roald Amundsen, with his one-man campaign against Great Britain, appeared not to understand, was that he was morally completely dependent on his compatriots' support, most of all Nansen's. Characteristic is a letter written at the same time by Carsten Borchgrevink, the Norwegian who had led the British Antarctic expedition on the *Southern Cross*; he pointed out the moral line of demarcation between the gentlemen Amundsen and Scott. It was not the element of competition that had upset the British, but rather the Norwegian's *concealment*. 'He made a fool of them. This is a sad fact. It would have been unthinkable for Scott to have behaved in such a manner towards Amundsen and the Norwegians.'

The conquest of the South Pole was a question of honour. That is a composite concept which includes victory, but also morality. By attacking the losing party Roald Amundsen was on the verge of losing his own and his country's great triumph. Honour is not something you grab, rather something you are given.

On 15 November Lawyer Nansen was informed by Gustav Amundsen that he would no longer be employed as the polar explorer's lawyer.

The lines of communication between Norway's two great sons had been severed for ever. But in contrast to his colleague, Fridtjof Nansen had enough ice-free channels around his person. His political career at home could only be described as a failure, but no Norwegian could measure up to him where international influence was concerned. Through his humanitarian work and contribution to the League of Nations Fridtjof Nansen's person was a moral landmark, visible far beyond Norway's borders.

Fridtjof Nansen wrote a letter marked 'private and confidential'; he knew the message would be known, not only to the recipient, but in time to societies the world over and wherever Roald Amundsen's name had any meaning. He wrote to the Vice President of the Royal Geographical Society, Hugh Robert Mill, who already, naturally, had turned to Nansen. This was the man who on behalf of the Society in London had demanded Amundsen's apologies and a retraction. If one were to consider the battle for the South Pole as a national conflict between Norway and England, then Nansen, with this letter, sent a decisive message to the enemy's camp, in effect a message of peace. A sacrifice is required; it is a good thing that the peace-offering is identical to the troublemaker.

Nansen wrote: 'I too am concerned about the Amundsen affair and I am afraid it might cause damage in all respects. I do of course not blame RGS in any way and I think its stand perfectly natural; although it would have been desirable that the entire matter had been conducted in private. I do not at all understand Amundsen's behaviour these last years and the only explanation I can find is that something must have gone wrong with him. Things have happened a couple of times before; but it is my impression now that he has completely lost his equilibrium and that he is no longer responsible for his actions. Please take note of that.'

Professor Nansen stressed that he had not seen the person concerned for over a year, but for an oceanographer his medical diagnosis was conspicuously clear: 'I mean that there are several unmistakable signs of mental breakdown. But as long as this is neither known nor acknowledged, Amundsen's behaviour will of course continue to do a lot of harm. I really do not know what to do. You see, England is not the only country he has insulted, but also the Unites States (besides Germany and Italy). His attack on you and the RGS is, however, what concerns me most. Of course I cannot find anything offensive in Curzon's remarks and I am sure they were never meant to be such, on the contrary. But if they were meant to be offensive, so what? A person of sound mind could not possible dwell upon and remember something like that so many years on and then dig it up again, only to make himself look small.'

With this message, addressed to the enemy's headquarters, Roald Amundsen was declared incapable of managing his own affairs. As so often both before and after in the world of psychiatry, a medical diagnosis had been made with a political motive. It had not been possible to examine the patient. 'I do not think it will do much good to talk to him,' Nansen wrote. What was important was not that the diagnosis was 100 per cent correct, but rather that Roald Amundsen would no longer be taken seriously, that his irresponsible and destructive initiatives could no longer harm Norway, the Norway which was the life's work of Fridtjof Nansen and which continued to be identified with his name.

In the course of a single autumn Roald Amundsen had destroyed his life's work. *My Life as a Polar Explorer* had demonstrated how small words can ruin great deeds. Only a miracle could save him. It had happened before; the time when Lincoln Ellsworth had arrived like a messenger from the world of miracles and saved him from financial ruin. This time the bankruptcy was moral; a greater miracle was needed, more than Ellsworth's dollars; a deed bigger than words.

Before the year was out an omen presented itself. The pilots Bernt Balchen and Oskar Omdal had gone to America to try their luck. Where one lieutenant succeeded the other failed.

Omdal got to know a Danish-American by the name of Miss Grayson. This eccentric lady had got it into her head that she wanted to be the first woman to fly across the Atlantic. 'The ladies' man Omdal immediately got himself installed as head pilot on the trip,' Odd Dahl wrote in his memoirs. On 23 December the *Dawn* took off from New York, in spite of meteorological warnings. After a stop in Newfoundland the expedition continued on Christmas Day. Besides the head pilot and the female senior management, there were two more men on board; all disappeared without trace in bad weather somewhere off the coast of Canada. A search party was sent out, but after a few days all hope was abandoned.

Since the time Oskar Omdal, 27 years old, travelled with Roald Amundsen to Maudhavn to fly *Elisabeth* over the Polar Sea, his life had been like a game of Russian roulette. The ageing polar explorer had been criticised by many for having risked the young man's life. Those were unfamiliar notions to Roald Amundsen. He himself had been even younger, happy and of a cheerful disposition, when he accompanied the Belgian commandant into the Antarctic night. 'He was always happy and in a good mood, however dark things might appear.' That is how the Governor remembered his subordinate.

Oskar Omdal had lost his life for the sake of 'a considerable amount of money'. His death was a tragedy, but no martyrdom.

That role was awaiting the Governor.

Part Six: Flight across the Polar Sea

FORTY-SIX

Internal Exile

On 5 December 1927 the police sergeant at Kolbotn received an application regarding ammunition, signed Gustav S. Amundsen, Roald Amundsen's nephew. 'Please permit me to draw your attention to the fact that Roald Amundsen lives alone at Bålerud, for which reason it would be reassuring for him to know that he is in possession of live ammunition for his gun.'

That last winter at Bålerud in Svartskog, or rather at Uranienborg, the polar explorer was maybe not as lonely as his 'private secretary' made out. He might have wanted to set off a shot or two because he needed to guard someone else from intruders or nosey parkers. It was not a good idea to tread too close that winter.

He received a secret visit. Bess Magids, the dog-driver with the chocolate looks, was smuggled out to Svartskog; according to a confidential letter from Herman Gade this took place before the turn of the year. Among the polar explorer's surviving papers is a telegram, signed with three crosses, dated Newcastle, 22 December: 'Arrive berge[n] by venus'. If this cryptic message originated from Bess, she must have arrived from New York and crossed over the North Sea aboard a ship from the Bergen Steamship Company, thence by train across the mountain to Christmas celebrations at Uranienborg.

Bess Magids loved life in the wilds of Alaska; Norway was, however, not a bad alternative. For one reason or another she had broken away from Alaska and exchanged Kotzebuesund for the Bunnefjord. The polar explorer had no doubt promised that her visit would be secret and under his protection. According to Gade she stayed for a couple of months. In any case, she was back in New York at the beginning of March. At that time the polar explorer received a letter from a mutual friend wherein he wrote that Bess told him 'what a lovely home' he had and what a 'glorious time' he had given her.

Bess felt at home at Uranienborg. Roald Amundsen could behave with exceeding gallantry to the opposite sex and he enjoyed keeping house. He prided himself on making sure that the foreign edition of the *New York Times* was available every morning at breakfast for his American guest. When Bess

Magids left Uranienborg, as unnoticed as when she arrived, sometime towards the end of February, she had probably already made up her mind to return as soon as possible.

On 29 March Roald Amundsen noted in his desk-top diary: 'B.28/3'. Bess had replaced Kiss, the Bs have replaced the Ks in his chronicle. He might have received a letter from her on that day. The letter appears one more time, on 18 April, in the sparsely written diary which must be considered to be the polar explorer's last. The same day another entry reads: 'Excavation of cellar started.' The gallant polar explorer could not present his future wife with a winter house without a cellar.

It was not easy to chart the relationship between Bess Magids and her husband. If we are to believe an interview she gave in Alaska towards the end of her life, her husband was already dead by 1927. But according to Herman Gade's letter she returned to the USA to 'finalise the divorce from Magids, which took place in Seattle during the spring of 1928'. According to a survey of Alaskan businesses, Samuel Magids died in 1929.

When she arrived in Uranienborg during the darkest months of the year, Bess must have felt a strong attraction for this famous but in many ways enigmatic polar explorer. Like all Amundsen's women, she was, however, a strong personality whose alternatives were calculated from pragmatic rather than mere emotional impulses. In spite of her young age – she was only 30 – Bess had had plenty of experience. She was accustomed to a life of luxury but knew too that life could be a fight for survival. Bess Magids was a skilled poker player. She chose to stake everything on one hand.

And Roald Amundsen, 55, bitter, resentful and finished as a polar explorer, had he at last found the goddess of happiness, the woman who gambled all and meets him half-way with open arms? The following chapter of this love story would unfold a few months later – not in the shape of another rendezvous, but as a last flight.

On 5 February General Nobile arrived in Oslo. He was preparing for his next expedition. With an airship more or less like *Norge* but with a completely different name, in fact *Italia*, the General was planning to make three flights to search the still considerable unexplored areas around the polar basin, with Spitsbergen as a base. The dream of new land was not yet relinquished, not in the expansive Italy. Umberto Nobile was still riding high on a nationalistic wave.

The Italians had bought access to the mooring masts and the hangar in Kings Bay; besides they had paid a tidy sum for the wrecked airship in Teller. Consequently the General was well received in Oslo. Personalities like Adolf Hoel, Tryggve Gran and Otto Sverdrup gave good advice to the southerner who was now setting out on his own. On his return to Italy he met Fridtjof Nansen in Berlin. The General intended to add a scientific dimension to his expedition, a fact which appealed to the Professor. Norwegians on the whole were known as civilised human beings.

One day during the Oslo visit the polar explorer at Svartskog saw the front page of a newspaper where his arch-enemy Number One, Nobile, was photographed during a dinner with his arch-enemy Number Two, Thommessen, and – his own second-in-command – Hjalmar Riiser-Larsen!

Of all betrayals, this was the worst.

In his memoirs Roald Amundsen had virtually proclaimed the airship's *actual* pilot and saviour to have been his second-in-command. Riiser-Larsen had responded by writing an 'Addendum', where he added factual ammunition to the Governor's accusations of the hopelessness of the Italians. And then, of all things, he dines with the enemy in the Italian Embassy and even permits himself to be photographed with them. This, to the polar explorer, was the utmost insult; to Riiser-Larsen it was the most natural thing in the world.

For one thing, the newly appointed General Nobile had not read the book with the afore-mentioned addendum; for another, the equally newly appointed Captain Riiser-Larsen treated the Italian with the same professional courtesy as the rest of the Norwegian polar milieu. And besides, Riiser-Larsen had done with his time as second-in-command; he had ambitions of his own, like expedition leader and probably even as a politician. The barely 40-year-old captain could not afford to build his future career on the Governor's old enmities.

Roald Amundsen could not grasp that. To him a subordinate was a subordinate; a Wisting was a Wisting, whether his name was Riiser-Larsen or not. The pilot hero had constituted the skilled component of Amundsen's last phase as a polar explorer. He had been at the same time Amundsen's man and the man of the future. When he turned elsewhere the Governor felt left out, deserted.

In this deeply offended state of mind Roald Amundsen promoted his second-in-command. 'He is top of the list of those who betrayed me,' he confided in his closest lieutenant – Gustav.

Isolated in Uranienborg, the frozen Bunnefjord outside his windows, Roald Amundsen felt increasing bitterness towards his own people. Was not this evil, the little people's ingratitude to the one big hero, not actually a national characteristic? The chemist Zapffe had mentioned something like that in a letter. 'It is so sad that one of the worst characteristics of Norwegians is their inability to recognise others' ability, and the greater it is the more envious they become; these people who sit in the corner and criticise. Awful.' 'Zapfo' was one of the few wise men. Together they had toyed with the idea of the polar explorer moving to the magnificent landscape up north, far away from everything miserable and narrow-minded.

Another man void of deceit was Oscar Wisting, 'one of the best men who ever lived in this world,' Amundsen wrote in his memoirs. Wisting was one of the very few who knew that the lady from Deering was due on a visit. 'Maybe you are alone now,' he wrote at the beginning of February, 'if not do send her my love.'

Tonni, the disastrous brother, had died a year earlier. The family circle had shrunk to Captain Gustav and Lieutenant Gustav and their spouses; none of them lived at Svartskog in the winter. The national hero's honorary stipend had been increased to 1,000 crowns per month, enough to live on for one and all. The honorary residence was still in Gade's name.

It is interesting that in a letter Gade questioned how the relationship between the polar explorer and 'the highest authority', the King, 'had developed recently'. This question is completely relevant. The polar explorer's repeated attacks on the world's great powers, and above all on England, Queen Maud's native country, cannot have been advantageous to His Majesty. Ever since his accession King Haakon had supported Roald Amundsen's endeavours in every way. The polar explorer had paid him back by bathing the kingdom in his glory. It appears that His Majesty of the Mountain Kingdom and the Monarch of the Poles were bound together in mutual admiration.

But the polar explorer who was closer to the King and Queen than the lone wolf at Svartskog was Fridtjof Nansen, the man who had persuaded the then Danish Prince to accept the crown of Norway. He was Their Majesties closest adviser. This man thought the time ripe to declare to the world that Roald Amundsen was incapable of managing his own affairs. Independent of medical advice, it must be assumed that Norway's King, through Professor Nansen, was fully aware that at Svartskog there lived a mentally deranged man.

For want of other tasks, the polar explorer's mind produced ever more enemies; old contempt grew to new dimensions and took on the form of an all-encompassing hatred. According to Gustav S. Amundsen, who from time to time was at Uranienborg and listened to his uncle's bitter tirades, that winter he formulated a 'missive', a sort of testamentary greeting to his native country, 'wherein he declares that when he dies his name must not at all be used publicly in this country'. His pitiful compatriots were not worthy of adorning themselves with Roald Amundsen's name.

First he broke with the world's superpowers; now his existence at Svartskog had taken on the character of an internal exile.

One beautiful spring day, 24 May 1928, a procession of cars wind their way down to Uranienborg. The Australian-born polar explorer George H. Wilkins and his American pilot Carl B. Eielson arrive at the head of a distinguished Norwegian-American company. Six sea planes circle above the Bunnefjord. Flowers are strewn over the old explorer's lonely villa.

The black limousines below the sky's floral splendour bring messages of celebration, but also of death. The company have come to fetch the polar explorer out of the coldness that surrounded him. Recently he had even had the experience of being appointed to chair the newly founded Norwegian Aero Club. The young men's embraces touched the old man. Apparently his thin white hair shone like a halo. The celebrations at Uranienborg, where he fastened medals on the two men's chests, was the prelude to his last expedition. He was brought out of exile, back into the centre of events, two days before the decisive announcement arrived.

The Governor and jack of all trades Wisting had baked a cake. The marzipan overlay represented the Polar Basin, where a line of icing was drawn from Point Barrow on Alaska's north coast to Spitsbergen on the opposite side. One month ago the two pilots had accomplished the trip which Roald Amundsen and Oskar Omdal had planned five years earlier. Since 1923 flying had progressed by leaps and bounds. In these five years the impossible had become the possible. Oskar Omdal was no longer an optimistic young boy but a dead man, Roald Amundsen a white-haired old pensioner.

There followed a couple of festive days. The old man hailed the young heroes and vice versa. On Whit Sunday *Aftenposten* held a lunch for the two pilots at the Dronning Restaurant outside Oslo. The speeches during lunch concerned the two guests of honour Captain Wilkins and Lieutenant Eielson, but the conversation round the table was mostly about General Nobile.

The Italian expedition had already completed two sorties into Arctic regions from the base in Kings Bay. On 24 May the airship *Italia* reached the North Pole, during its third and last flight. But the following day, in the morning, radio connection was broken and there was speculation as to what might have befallen the airship, which should have been back in Ny-Ålesund a long time ago. During the lunch the host, editor Frøisland, was called to the telephone. A few moments later he imparted the information to Otto Sverdrup and Roald Amundsen, the two Grand Old Men of polar research. The message was from the Norwegian Minister of Defence who invited them to a meeting that afternoon to discuss the situation that had arisen around *Italia*'s disappearance.

'Right away,' was Roald Amundsen's answer. The fact that the national hero delivered this immortal line in English was owing to the fact that the guests of honour were English speakers and that he was seated opposite the American ambassador. But no one present was in doubt of the meaning. 'I agree,' Sverdrup added.

The meeting at the Ministry of Defence was attended, aside from Amundsen and Sverdrup, by Major Isachsen and Hjalmar Riiser-Larsen. Defence Minister Andersen-Rysst was in the chair.

He informed the assembled party that the government that morning had received a communication from the Italian Ambassador in Oslo, Count Senni, regarding the possibility of Norway organising a rescue operation for the airship *Italia*.

Roald Amundsen found himself suddenly in an extraordinary situation. First of all he was asked to help in a rescue operation to save a man whom he in public and to the whole world had declared his worst enemy; second, he was supposed to be cooperating with the person who more than anyone else had disappointed him. The old polar explorer knew how to keep a straight face.

It was not against his principles to save the Italians. He knew the rules of honour and guessed the perspective of such an action. The fight against Nobile had been rough, even dirty, but it was a fight against foreigners. It had hurt him, but had not touched his sorest point. Anyhow, the saviour was always the strongest. If the General really would allow himself to be saved, it would give him the greatest pleasure to receive the honour for taking part in such a noble-minded act.

It was far more difficult for Amundsen to sit at the same table as the traitor Riiser-Larsen than to reach out a hand to his arch-enemy Nobile. All winter he had been brooding about the treachery of his second-in-command. No one had been closer to him these last years than Riiser-Larsen. But now, with the old man's career in decline, Riiser-Larsen had not even bothered to visit Amundsen, not even once. Instead he had dined with his arch-enemies and winked at him and the world from the front pages of a newspaper, impertinent boldness right in the middle of bottomless treachery. He it was who had touched the sorest point in the polar explorer's soul.

Captain Riiser-Larsen must have felt the measured behaviour of his old superior, but he never guessed the Governor's totally changed attitude to his person. The hero pilot had bid a tear-jerking farewell to the Governor in the *First Flight across the Polar Sea*; since then he had had other things to do than pester a difficult and inaccessible pensioner. That the Governor regarded his long-ago paid off second-in-command with hawk's eyes from the banks of the Bunnefjord he could hardly have imagined. Riiser-Larsen was neither a psychologist nor a party animal; he was a man of action.

That evening, round the table in the Royal Foreign Ministry a comprehensive strategy was devised for the rescue of *Italia*. Roald Amundsen correctly referred to Riiser-Larsen as the foremost aviation expert, but there was no disagreement about the fact that the major action must be led by the Governor himself, the most experienced of all polar explorers.

That same evening the two foreign pilots gave lectures in the capital's largest assembly rooms. Amundsen should have been present but Tryggve Gran had stepped in and taken over his duties. Later that evening Minister Gade hosted a private party for Wilkins and Eielson at the Victoria Hotel. In an article written a few months later Tryggve Gran wrote: 'Roald Amundsen arrived and when he was asked about the *Italia* affair he answered more or less as follows: "We decided to wait and see for a couple of days. If anything of importance happens during Whitsun I am to be informed immediately. For practical reasons I will be staying here at the hotel."'

While Roald Amundsen kept vigil together with Herman Gade at the town's best hotel, the Italian Ambassador passed on the Norwegian plan to the Italian government in Rome.

Already the next day Count Senni knocked on Captain Riiser-Larsen's door; Mussolini had given his answer.

Captain Riiser-Larsen wrote in his memoirs thirty years later that he was stunned when told that Mussolini did not wish any major rescue action under Norwegian management. 'I was even more stunned when I realised the reason for this extraordinary decision, namely that one was not prepared to give Roald Amundsen the opportunity to save Nobile following the disagreement after the *Norge* expedition.' And he added (still thirty years later): 'I could not rid myself of the idea that it was preferable for the expedition to suffer a glorious *death*, than a miserable homecoming.'

War and polar exploration can be macabre dramas. Both were dramas about honour. Apparently Mussolini had warned Nobile from defying destiny yet again. The *Italia* expedition had been staged by the country's Geographical Society and the City of Milan. It was now necessary for the dictator to grab the stage management in order to save the remnants of Italy's glory.

Death had transformed defeat into victory for Captain Scott and his men in the tent at the South Pole. Only thus, as the heroic victims of science, could General Nobile and his men return to Italy, its glory unsullied. Il Duce knew how to play his cards, and as a dictator he felt it his right to demand such a sacrifice of the General who had gambled with Italy's name. Probably only two men fully understood the drama which was unfolding on the field of honour; in Mussolini Amundsen found a worthy opponent.

Hjalmar Riiser-Larsen got busy resurrecting his favourite role as the saviour of the air. The Italian government, for the sake of appearances, had agreed to the Norwegians dispatching a reconnaissance plane to Svalbard. Riiser's good friend First Lieutentant Lützow-Holm had already been ordered north. In a lightning talk with the Prime Minister Riiser-Larsen made sure that the Ministry of Defence dispatched yet another plane, as a safety precaution, with him in the pilot's seat. 'We are of the impression that the Captain is working more energetically than ever to enable him to reach the goals and the results intended,' *Tidens Tegn* wrote, obviously impressed by the quick turn of events.

While all this was going on Roald Amundsen was waiting, with Herman Gade, more or less confused, in the salon of the Victoria Hotel. Tryggve Gran wrote in his article from the autumn of 1928: 'My surprise was therefore great when on Tuesday morning I was informed that the Foreign Office had acted *without Roald Amundsen's knowledge.* Captain Riiser-Larsen had been authorised to plan and initiate a rescue mission. It goes without saying that Roald Amundsen felt hurt. He returned to Svartskog in a rather depressed state.'

Now it was the turn of Major Gran to storm into the offices of the Foreign Minister. He wanted an explanation. Why had Roald Amundsen been sidelined? And why were the Army's Fokker planes sitting unused in a hangar at Kjeller?

The Foreign Minister apologised profusely for the fact that Roald Amundsen might have misunderstood the situation. 'The decisions had been made from purely military considerations. If Norway were to mount a rescue operation on a large scale Roald Amundsen would of course lead the enterprise.' But when Tryggve Gran passed on this information the polar explorer was far from satisfied. 'They have acted behind my back,' was his comment. The die was cast, the prize was General Nobile. This time Roald Amundsen's arch opponent was Hjalmar Riiser-Larsen.

FORTY-SEVEN

Knight of the Ice

'Roald Amundsen and Lincoln Ellsworth to Svalbard with German equipment and Lieutenant Dietrichson as pilot'; this could be read in *Aftenposten* on 30 May.

The friends of the polar explorer were shocked. How could he publicly proclaim a plan which lacked any sort of foundation? Was it so all-important to act before Riiser-Larsen had left the mainland? His friends had, according to Gran, envisaged for him a completely different role, 'in the conductor's chair orchestrating all Norwegian and foreign rescue operations, *not* as an observer in an aeroplane'.

Roald Amundsen had made two contacts. One with his former colleague Leif Dietrichson, who had immediately agreed to fly with his old Governor. The lieutenant was about to take up a new position in Canada, but he was not about to say no to an heroic deed at the last moment. Besides, on Whit Sunday Amundsen had already been in telegraphic communication with his old comrade Lincoln Ellsworth. This alliance was even now en route north in the imagination of the polar explorer, and in the columns of *Aftenposten*.

Ellsworth, on his part, had written to Amundsen following his abrupt departure from America: 'I miss you, as I always do, when you are away. I will probably never again experience two such wonderful years as the ones we experienced together.' In the spring he had tried to establish a new base. Why could they not live together in Ellsworth's castle in Switzerland? After all, they agreed on most things. 'I like your taste and your habits better than anyone's and it pains me that destiny is keeping us apart. If you could find a solution we could be together again. I have offered you half of Lenzburg but you do not appear to thrive there. You only need to say the word and I'll open it up for you.'

When the American offered him half a castle, surely he could exchange it for an aeroplane? That is how the polar explorer must have reasoned when Ellsworth placed himself at his disposal for the rescue mission. But he was soon to find out that life in a castle with Amundsen and a mission to rescue Nobile carried two different price tags; a couple of thousand dollars was all Ellsworth and his brother-in-law added to the Italian's rescue pot.

Money was no easier to come by in Germany. Leif Dietrichson had immediately travelled south to negotiate with various private and public authorities regarding an airship. Germany was the only nation capable of producing large engines suited for flying in Arctic regions, but not for less than a guarantee of 200,000 crowns. Converted into German marks Roald Amundsen's name was at a discount.

It was soon clear that the polar explorer had made himself look like a fool. His entire proud rescue mission had ended on the front pages of *Aftenposten*. Not a bad newspaper, but humiliating nevertheless.

On 7 June Hjalmar Riiser-Larsen arrived, by ship, in Kings Bay with an aeroplane in his luggage. That very day the world intercepted for the first time sensational radio signals from General Nobile's stranded expedition north of Svalbard. The Norwegian Captain was the right man in the right place – irrespective of what his old Governor and Italy's dictator might think. All that remained was to gather the laurels from the ice.

Italia's breakdown was exactly the situation for which Roald Amundsen and his Norwegian crew had been prepared during their flight in *Norge*. The airship, with a crew of sixteen, of whom seven had also sailed in *Norge*, had become stranded just north of Nordaustlandet on Svalbard. On touchdown the front gondola had broken away while the balloon had taken off and flown away trailing a tail of smoke. On board the balloon were six men who have never been seen since, among them the rigger Alessandrini and two other crew from *Norge*. A fourth crew member from *Norge* was killed the instant they hit the ice.

Nine men had survived the disaster. Five were walking wounded; three were badly hurt, the last three crew members of the *Norge* expedition. General Nobile and the giant Cecioni had each broken a leg; the Swedish meteorologist Malmgren had crushed an arm. Titina was unhurt, a last meal on four legs. The catastrophe was thus a reality. But not a Norwegian in sight.

The only person with any experience of ice was Finn Malmgren, who in the Polar Sea milieu on board *Maud*, in spite of his indisputable qualifications, had been more or less considered a clown. Luckily, however, most of the expedition's survival gear had fallen onto the ice together with the gondola. After a few days they had succeeded in establishing radio contact with the Italian mother ship *Citta de Milano* in Kings Bay.

The radio signals, which were subsequently published in newspapers all over the world, sounded like enticing siren songs to Norwegian ears. At last, the Italians could be saved! But not only Norwegians set out for the north.

In all, six nations with around fifteen ships and a corresponding number of planes apparently took part in the rescue operation. Nobile's rescue turned, with feverish haste, into a battle between nations and men, and a scramble between newspapers, radio stations and news agencies to be the first to transmit news from the ice-covered archipelago which had suddenly become the centre of events.

Everything that existed of polar expertise was drawn into the sensational affair – Fridtjof Nansen included. In order to quieten his conscience, as he put it, he approached British authorities, via Minister Vogt, to clarify the possibility of a rescue mission with an English airship. When Vogt answered in the negative, Nansen wrote that 'your answer decides the matter'. These enquiries, via diplomatic channels, were Fridtjof Nansen's single attempt to act during the *Italia* fever. He wrote to Vogt that 'the world has become rather hysterical with regards to *Italia*'s disappearance. After all, it has happened before that people have disappeared for long periods in arctic regions without there being much hoo-ha for that reason.'

Fridtjof Nansen had appealed to the world's conscience to save tens of thousands of nameless people fleeing disaster, millions suffering famine. On the other hand, the General on the ice-floe was given limited space in Fridtjof Nansen's restless mind. For his retired colleague, however, matters were rather different: General Nobile's rescue occupied his entire mental powers. Like a caged eagle he butted the walls in Uranienborg.

Of course, Amundsen was closer to it all than his colleague at Polhøgda. Only three years ago he himself had been a captive in the Arctic ice. But in the meantime he had broken with the world. He had in truth disqualified himself from all cooperation long before *Italia*'s accident. It was an illusion that he, following all his raving initiatives, could possibly function as a unifying force. Roald Amundsen was not wanted as Nobile's rescuer. The conclusion was as obvious as it was far from the polar explorer's mindset.

During this time Roald Amundsen received the Italian journalist Guidici. To him he spoke the oft-quoted words regarding his longing for the ice. 'Oh! If you only knew how wonderful it is up there. That is where I want to die and I wish death would come to me in a chivalrous way, that it will find me during the execution of some great deed, quickly and without suffering.'

Right up until 11 June Amundsen pushed hard, but in vain, to get Ellsworth, his brother-in-law and friend to raise $60,000. Besides, now that the Germans were out of the question, he needed a suitable plane. But the Americans no doubt realised that this had nothing to do with saving Nobile, but rather with saving Amundsen's lost face. They would have salvaged that, but not at the price. Had not this very Amundsen turned his back on America?

Actually, Roald Amundsen had other things to think about – closer to home than rushing up to Spitsbergen and an honourable death. On 2, 3, 4 and 10 June he telegraphed Bess Magids in Seattle who was in the process of winding down her former life. After the 10th she boarded a train for the journey across the continent to the East Coast. In New York she would embark on a ship which would take her over the sea to the capital of the mountain kingdom where her groom awaited.

All was in place for the start of a new and last phase of the polar explorer's life. He had broken with everything and everyone and withdrawn from active life. His last years would be spent in well-earned rest and harmony. The young bride was as ordered to, as Gade expressed it, 'take up residence at Uranienborg.'

But was the groom waiting in anticipation of his bride? Not a bit of it. He moved heaven and earth to escape. It appears that Roald Amundsen would rather embrace his worst enemy on an ice-floe north of the 80th latitude than receive the woman who had abandoned everything to be met with open arms when she stepped off the boat from America. It was more than a mystery. It was a flight, headlong flight, away from Uranienborg, from a retired life and from the approaching woman.

He escaped back to the role of hero, the old adventurer, into the limelight. There he is, in the glare of the world's attention, well protected by the knight's armour. More clearly than at any time Roald Amundsen demonstrated that he was a man with an impaired core: he could only exist by virtue of the world's admiration.

In spite of radio communications it proved difficult to pinpoint General Nobile and his men from the air. Neither Riiser-Larsen nor Lützow-Holm were lucky. Ever more rescue operations set sail for the north to try their luck.

At midday on 14 June Roald Amundsen was connected by telephone with Paris. On the line was the rich and influential merchant Fredrik Peterson who via French newspapers has followed his unsuccessful attempts at trying to get north to Spitsbergen; the merchant would like to give his famous compatriot a helping hand.

What sort of plane did he have in mind?

This was exactly the sort of telephone conversation the polar explorer pinned his hopes on when the need was most pressing. He immediately ordered a seaplane, suitable for temperatures around 0°. The merchant said he would see what he could do. 'Well, this was really nice. Many thanks,' the polar explorer concluded the conversation.

France was the only major power with which Roald Amundsen was still on speaking terms. That might have been an oversight, but it no doubt eased the merchant Peterson's further work. Rarely had an expedition been so hastily put together. The merchant immediately got in touch with his French contacts. The negotiations were clinched with a formal approach from the Norwegian Minister in Paris, Baron Wedel Jarlsberg, to France's Naval Minister. Before the day was up merchant Peterson could inform Amundsen that the sea-plane *Latham 47* would be flying north as soon as possible.

On 15 June the people of Norway could open their front pages and read that France had come to Amundsen's rescue. Hectic preparations were initiated at Uranienborg to equip the sea-plane as it was being given an Arctic overhaul at the Latham works in Caudebec-en-Caux, 30 kilometres from Rouen. The sea-plane would be winging its way to Bergen the next day.

In Oslo Roald Amundsen was given a private send-off. The forthcoming expedition was not the only topic of conversation; one other event was imminent. Six years later Herman Gade penned the following declaration: 'The undersigned declares that I, during a farewell party for Roald Amundsen at "Victoria" in the presence of Mrs Amundsen heard him give general power of attorney to Lieutenant Gustav S. Amundsen to receive and to his best ability (including financial) look after Mrs Bess Magids when she in his absence arrived here.' The bride was expected, the groom fled.

At 11 in the evening on 16 June Roald Amundsen turned up at the East Station in Oslo. The night-train to Bergen was ready for departure. It was exactly, to the day, twenty-five years since he had set out on his first independent expedition down the Oslo Fjord in *Gjøa*. Then three of his brothers had bade him farewell, now only one. But a few official representatives were present, among them three Ministers: the Italian and French Ministers in Oslo and the newly abdicated Norwegian Minister in Rio.

Several press photos were taken of this heroic scene which show the excited atmosphere in the departure hall. Herman Gade seems to be the only one who is not taking part in the general enthusiasm. He alone knew the sad fate this performance was covering up. A colleague in the Foreign Ministry wrote in a private letter a few months later that 'After all Gade has in recent times often pronounced that he was a sad man without elaborating further'.

Well, what was he to say? When he returned in April he found his 'best friend', the once so celebrated hero, alone and bitter, wrapped up in his internal exile. He gained some insight into his friend's new and daring plans. 'I am *au fait* with all circumstances regarding R.A. – Mrs Magids,' he wrote later in a letter, 'as Roald showed me the whole correspondence and I myself sent some of his telegrams.' Probably the old friend realised that the polar explorer was getting cold feet regarding the important decision and that he had grasped at the Nobile affair as a last resort.

Roald Amundsen was accompanied by two men who would assist him during his rescue of Nobile. One was the indispensable polar explorer, cake maker, tinsmith and surgeon Captain Oscar Wisting. The other was First Lieutenant Dietrichson. On the platform, by the huge steam locomotive which was gearing up for the long haul over the mountains, all eyes were on the national hero, who, according to *Aftenposten*'s reporter, had little to say, 'but his sharp features exuded determination, a compelling energy which the vocabulary of our language is too poor to interpret'.

However, the Italian minister was obliged, for the sake of appearances, on behalf of his government, to utter a few paltry words for the journey. 'It was an unforgettable moment when the two men met in a strong and heart-felt handshake.' Editor-in-chief Frøisland, also present on the platform, recorded with satisfaction that his two great heroes had been reconciled. In Rome an irritated dictator fretted over such sham goings-on; a representative of Italy having to grin and bear it.

'When the whistle blew Dietrichson and Wisting boarded the train while Amundsen lingered a while, rather indecisively, and those standing closest to him spotted a tear on his weather-beaten cheek. He walked a few yards beside the train, then quickly stepped up, followed by loud hurrahs, which boomed around the large sooty East Station glass roof.'

When the night-train arrived in Bergen the next day the sea-plane was already waiting at Marineholmen. *Latham 47* had arrived the night before after a perfect flight from Normandy. In Bergen the 18 metre-long fuselage was filled with fuel and given another overhaul. A small hole on the port wing-float was repaired.

The crew consisted of four. Captain René Guilbaud was 28 years old and an officer of the Légion d'Honneur. His second-in-command, First Lieutenant Albert de Cuverville, was a decorated war pilot. With the mechanic Brazy and the radio operator Valette the French Navy had put an entire crew at the disposal of the Norwegian polar explorer.

In spite of there already being two pilots on board, Guilbaud yielded to Roald Amundsen's request that Lieutenant Dietrichson be included. He knew about flying over ice and, besides, the Governor felt more comfortable among his own. However, Captain Wisting, who made up the seventh member of the expedition, would have to get on the first north-bound boat. There were no problems getting a passage in those days, when half the world was en route to save Nobile.

Bergen was awash with humanity this summer's day when the close to 56-year-old Roald Amundsen – Napoleon of the ice – was about to set off north to do battle on the field of honour. Since the time of the crusades no commander had ever set out on a more noble-minded campaign. His arms were groaning under the weight of flowers as the sailors rowed him out to the sea-plane – the man who was about to save his arch enemy, a fellow citizen in need. It was eight in the evening.

From Bergen Roald Amundsen sent his last telegram to Bess Magids. She was now in New York, kicking her heels for six days waiting for the ship *Hellig Olav* to take her to the promised land. Why must he leave, now that she is arriving?

Deep down she might have been the one who forced him to do it. There is something familiar in the role Roald Amundsen was about to take on. When he returned from the South Pole he rejected Sigg. When he returned from the flight across the North Pole he let go of Kiss. And this time – were he to return as a hero – Bess would encounter a man clad in armour, strong enough to sacrifice love yet again.

With eyes brimming with devotion the people of Bergen watched the French aeroplane ascend from the fjord and fly north in the pale summer night. A week later the population would gather around another rescue vessel which had refuelled to continue north in the night, the Russian icebreaker *Krassin*. The shouts from the crowds on the quay would be 'Save Amundsen'.

At 6 o'clock the next morning, *Latham 47* landed on deathly calm water outside Tromsø. The two Norwegians ate breakfast and went to bed at their usual haunt with chemist Zapffe; the French were resting nearby in the Grand Hotel. At eleven in the morning the crew started to move; this was not the day for sleep. Everything needed to be prepared for the next stage. The Governor could take it easy; he spent his last hours on land in the company of a pipe and his old friend the chemist.

In a book he published seven years later Fritz G. Zapffe described his last moments with the man he admired so much. There was not much to say about the actual journey; that was outside their control. The conversation turned to other things. 'However, I had an indescribable, unpleasant feeling that something alien lay between us. The open and happy atmosphere which usually characterised our conversations, even when talking about serious matters, this time was absent.' In times to come Zapffe interpreted this as a premonition of death linked to the French sea-plane; they both agreed that a Dornier-Wal would have been more suitable. 'An interminable silence fell over these our last hours together. I even felt slightly embarrassed – as I would in the company of someone ill, to whom one does not quite know what to say.'

This awkwardness was something the chemist was unable to fathom. In spite of the unequivocally magnanimous atmosphere which characterised the entire *Latham* affair, Roald Amundsen himself was suffering inner conflict; he was en route to the General, away from a woman. The first was an heroic deed, the second, more or less a betrayal. He had let her go and thus, for the third and last time, let go of a life of love and coexistence with another human being.

The chemist's intuition did not fail him; he was talking to a 'sick friend'. Before departure the polar explorer gave him his defective lighter. The chemist offered to have it repaired. But the polar explorer declined: 'I'll have no more use for it.' The light had gone out. It would not be lit again.

No aeroplane had yet succeeded in crossing the exposed stretch of sea from north Norway to Spitsbergen. That day, however, a Swedish and a Finnish plane were waiting to fly north. Besides, they were informed that the Italian Major Maddelena, who was on a mission from the town of Milan, was already on Bear Island where his plane was being repaired. It was hotting up for a race.

The obvious plan would have been for the three planes in Tromsø to fly in convoy. That possibility did not interest Amundsen. He wanted to fly alone. There were many en route, only one general to be saved.

During the afternoon the four Frenchmen and the two Norwegians were taken to the sea-plane outside Tromsø harbour. The chemist too accompanied his friend the polar explorer out to this extraordinary cross between a plane and a boat. With a total capacity of 1,000 horsepower and a wingspan of over 25 metres *Latham 47* was no insignificant vessel; painted white, built of wood, with three double sets of wings and covered in canvas, nor was it without grace.

Like a swan of unreal dimensions *Latham 47* regarded its own reflection in the waters outside the Arctic town Tromsø. It is tempting to pretend Knight Lohengrin stepped on board, in the shape of Roald Amundsen. Both script and stage-setting were perfect for a mythical heroic drama. But according to the audience, Zapffe, the leading man had completed his role even before the engine was started: 'I shall not forget the expression on his face, sitting astern, something extraordinary and resigned was over him. It appeared that nothing concerned him and yet it was maybe all about him. He sat quietly just looking at me.'

The hero regarded his last admirer without a word. He had lost all energy. During the preparations, when he was shut out, when obstacles were put in his way, then it had been all about action, the General, the need to get away. Now it was all over. The future lay in the hands of God, and the pilots.

The press photos of *Latham 47* confirm Zapffe's impression of a resigned and forsaken figure. He no longer cared about posing. The knight in his peaked cap on the back of the huge swan waiting to be towed out to the sound where the propellers could start up, was not en route to anything; he had left something behind, already bade his farewell; maybe not to life, but to what life had to offer. He knew he would never reach his life's goal. Now the icy wilds awaited him.

The plane took off at four. Later contradictory reports argued to what extent *Latham 47* struggled to ascend. Opinion was that it was too heavily loaded. Anyhow, *Latham 47* was the only one of the three sea-planes which managed to take off that quiet day. Both the Finnish and the Swedish planes remained in Tromsø for the time being. According to Gunnar Hovdenak, who published his comprehensive account *Roald Amundsen's Last Journey* in 1934, the sea-plane was no heavier than it had been when departing Bergen. But the plane had already flown huge distances and during the haste which impelled the crew equipped with the intelligence of Major Maddelena's advanced position, some safety routines might have been overlooked. However, that does not really sound plausible with such a competent crew and such a dangerous stretch of ocean ahead. OK – the Governor was a marked man who might at this moment leave all in the hands of a higher power; but the practical work was entirely the responsibility of the five experienced, vigorous men in the ages between 26 and 38, men in their prime. None of them was disposed towards gambling with their young lives over the Arctic Ocean.

The forecast had been for changeable weather during the day but still appeared promising. The stretch of water was so exposed that a sea-plane of *Latham 47*'s construction could not expect to land on open water without sustaining considerable damage. This was the plane's weakness: it could land neither on ice nor rough water. Measured against the windswept Arctic Ocean the southern-made sea-plane was no more than an aeroplane with floaters. Boats would need to be of a completely different calibre.

The last radio signal from *Latham 47* was received at 18.45. The radio operator tried in vain to call up Ny-Ålesund to send some telegrams. After a flight of three hours the plane would normally be half-way to Bear Island, which in turn was situated approximately half-way between Tromsø and Kings Bay.

It would take a long time before the world realised that the message concerning the never-dispatched telegrams, on Monday 18 June 1928 at 18.45, was the last sign of life from Roald Amundsen.

At eight in the evening Major Maddelena landed in Kings Bay. The Italian had won the race across the Arctic Ocean. *Latham 47* never landed.

FORTY-EIGHT

The Bride Who Disappeared

Roald Amundsen had disappeared from off the face of the earth. Not for the first time. The polar explorer chose his own ways; he made north south and east west; but one thing was certain: he always returned.

Rescue missions and disappearances proliferated during that heroic summer of 1928. Who was looking for whom? Who had disappeared and who had turned up? Many should have stayed at home; but if anyone knew how to survive in the far north it was Roald Amundsen. If no one else, he at least was in his rightful element.

It took time before the information penetrated consciousness that the journey had gone across open sea and that *Latham 47* was no boat. Gradually the rescue mission for General Nobile shifted towards Captain Amundsen. His party had not been heard of for five days. Who would appear first? Many thought the Norwegian had broken off radio contact and flown straight to the Italians in order single-handedly to lift the General out of the ice's embrace. That would be in character!

In the end a Swede saved Nobile. Captain Lundborg landed in his small Fokker engine on the General's ice-floe on Midsummer Night's Eve, 23 June. In spite of the position constantly changing with the drift of the ice, planes had already reached the shipwrecked Italians with drops of provisions. Landing was the problem; the bold Swede managed, however, to land on the strip the Italians had marked out.

Three of the shipwrecked had already left the camp, among them the Swede Finn Malmgren. That left six men on the floe. Lundborg intended to bring them all to safety in the course of a few hours. Unfortunately, he could only take one at a time as there was already an observer on board.

Two men were hurt: the General and Cecioni. The difference in weight was 40kg in the General's favour. With this in mind and the argument that it would be an advantage to the further operation of the rescue mission that the General was brought ashore, the pilot insisted that Nobile be his first passenger. Following a short consultation the General gave in and allowed himself to be saved. The potential meal, Titina, jumped on board first. Thus Sweden's military power triumphed in the battle for General Nobile's safe return.

When the Fokker aeroplane returned to pick up the next two in line it crashed on the ice. The sole difference in the castaways' situation was that the Italian General and his dog had been exchanged for a Swedish captain and his aeroplane. However, for Nobile this all presaged a small catastrophe: from now on he was known as the General who had allowed himself to be rescued before his crew. This involuntary stain on his record has a rough parallel in what happened when Amundsen threw himself on to the first sledge back to Framheim and saved his own skin before that of his frost-bitten men.

The episode became a notch in the systematic dismantling of Umberto Nobile's reputation. The General's fate had already been sealed. Mussolini turned down any retreat from the field of honour. He did not want to see Italy's heroic General or his dog saved by foreign nations, returning with their tails between their legs.

Not until nineteen days after Nobile had been rescued, on 12 July, did the Russian icebreaker *Krassin* succeed in picking up the remaining crew. En route it rescued the breakaway group that had tried to reach land under its own steam. Of these three one had died: Finn Malmgren. The Swede, who in a fit of self-sacrificing pride and in spite of his damaged arm and impaired condition had set out on this rash journey, now became the object of considerable hero-worship. That the one and only Northerner was to die in an attempt to save his southern colleague provoked tremendous aggression against the *Italia* expedition, not least in the Norwegian press. Finn Malmgren, the hero of *Maud*, *Norge* and *Italia*, is one of the few meteorologists ever to have been allocated his own plinth.

Next the Russians forced their way through the ice to the tent and the stranded aeroplane and picked up the remainder of the exhausted Italians and General Nobile's Swedish saviour.

In a letter written one month later Fridtjof Nansen commented on the chaotic circumstances surrounding the *Italia* tragedy. 'It is my opinion that the press is in many ways responsible for all this. The manner in which they reported, here and in Europe, all sorts of nonsense, was exceedingly regrettable and gave the readers a completely distorted view of the affair. It led to all sorts of rescue missions being sent out lacking any defined plan or organisation instead of waiting for the enterprise which had some chance of success, viz. the large icebreakers.' The Professor's critical comments were specially aimed at the hurried journey in *Latham 47*.

The same day on which General Nobile was rescued, 23 June, Bess Magids boarded the steamship *Hellig Olav* which would take her across the Atlantic to her new home. Following *Latham 47*'s disappearance five days earlier she found herself in a pretty desperate situation. There was still no need for despair; what was five days no-show in the life of a polar explorer? Search operations had hardly started. Getting Nobile to land had taken nearly one month; Amundsen had been missing for nearly four weeks when he disappeared together with Dietrichson three years ago. Gnawing unease was growing inside her, but it was too early to chuck her hand in.

Bess Magids had set out on a course and intended to complete it. Would it not be wonderful to stand on the quay at Uranienborg and welcome the homecoming polar explorer, rejuvenated by his latest escapade, the sun shining in his white hair?

Ten days later, on 2 July, *Hellig Olav* docked in Oslo. No sooner had the gangway been secured than the head clerk of the United Steamship Company, Mr Brauer, stepped on board. He called on Bess Magids and gave her the disheartening message that nothing had been heard of Roald Amundsen since she left New York.

Most probably the head clerk had been instructed by Gustav Amundsen, father or son, who, from considerations of discretion, did not want to be seen among the crowds on the America Quay. When Axel Brauer retired in 1941 he recounted in an interview to *Aftenposten* his special meeting with the polar explorer's fiancée. That was the first time a disbelieving public were told that their national hero had been on the threshold of marriage when he disappeared in *Latham 47*.

Bess Magids wrote forty years later: 'The last time I saw Roald Amundson [sic] was in Oslo, Norway in 1928. I had gone there to marry him. The Italian explorer Umberto Nobile disappeared and Roald set out to find him. He never returned.' Her two stays at Uranienborg turned into one; her return to America and subsequent divorce in Seattle were erased from the story.

In spite of all hope rapidly evaporating the rescue mission was still in full swing when Bess Magids arrived in Oslo. It would take another ten days before all the Italians were picked up by *Krassin* and even longer before the polar explorer's old friend H.H. Hammer declared to a newspaper in Los Angeles that Amundsen would probably turn up: 'He loves drama and enjoys surprise.' It was exactly this view which made it difficult for the world to comprehend that Roald Amundsen had actually disappeared, never to return.

In addition to the many ongoing missions, on 27 June a search and rescue expedition was initiated by the icebreaker *Veslekari*. Via a conglomerate of Oslo newspapers 90,000 crowns were collected in record time and, hey presto, the gentlemen editors were again engaged in polar waters. This, the newspaper readers' own expedition, was put under the command of Tryggve Gran and left Tromsø on 7 July. Hope was kept alive for many weeks to come. But in reality it was all based on the assumption that *Latham 47*, rather than fly, as agreed, towards Kings Bay, had headed straight north-east, towards the ice.

Lieutenant Gustav S. Amundsen took an active part in the organisation of the rescue work, in spite of the fact that he must have known it was all based on illusions. As his secretary the nephew had worked closely with his uncle right up until the time when *Latham 47* took off from Bergen. If Roald Amundsen had indeed intended to change his plans it is inconceivable that his nephew would not have had some sort of inkling. In spite of taking part in the hectic activities, true to the polar explorer's spirit, Lieutenant Amundsen must surely have realised after a very short time that his uncle was already dead.

On 5 July Herman Gade received his missing friend's grieving bride at the Victoria Hotel in Oslo. According to Gade she had been sent there by Lieutenant Amundsen, on behalf of the heirs, to claim the properties Uranienborg and Rødsten. It appears that Gade accepted Bess Magids's moral right as the polar explorer's heir in the sense that she would have been a beneficiary in a probable will. The last, albeit disputed, will from September 1927 favoured the sister-in-law Malfred, but also Tonni's descendants.

It appears that Gade, who was himself a lawyer, was not prepared to discuss the properties as long as Roald Amundsen, to all intents and purposes, was still alive.

When the fiancée was no longer a contender in respect of the properties, it appears that the Gustavs, father and son, decided to buy her out of the whole settlement, not to mention any kinship settlement. Without any legal redress in Norway, and having burnt her bridges at home, Bess found herself in a critical position. But she was born with a will to survive and obviously decided to do whatever was necessary to extricate herself from the situation.

According to Gade, Roald Amundsen had deposited large sums in the shape of jewels, furs and other objects with Kiss's brother, Lawyer Gudde, in Trondheim. Where these 'valuable' objects were to be found, in the floating relationships between the polar explorer and his one-time dream wife, it is impossible to tell. It might have been objects the polar explorer wanted to save from the bankruptcy or presents he intended originally to bestow on Kiss. That he liked spreading his wealth about was obvious from the fact that he had worked up considerable reserves in American securities.

Roald Amundsen's private secretary was well aware of the valuables in Trondheim, as he was of the American bonds, but feared that the treasure chest would not fall to the legitimate heirs. They decided to act while the fiancée was still in the country. According to Gade, Lieutenant Amundsen hid behind Bess Magids in his dealings with 'Lawyer Gudde and a certain lady'.

As his source of information Gade quotes Trygve Gudde who personally showed him the letter containing the blackmail, where 'the two threatened to reveal to the press the entire history of R's relationship to a certain lady if the objects in question were not handed over to them immediately.'

Herman Gade wrote that following this revelation he promptly broke with Lieutenant Amundsen.

During the first weeks in Norway it appears that Bess Magids, with the exception of the visit to Hotel Victoria, spent her time quietly at Uranienborg in the company of Gustav S. Amundsen. But on 12 July, after having hired a safety deposit box and replenishing her wardrobe in Oslo, she set out on a journey.

Bess Magids booked into Høsbjør Tourist Hotel at about the same time as the icebreaker *Krassin* picked up the last Italians from the pack ice. The hotel was situated north of Hamar and was one of the most fashionable in the country, recently taken over by the owner of Hotel Victoria in the capital. No wonder the hard-done-by lady from America felt like indulging in a few days' rest after the hectic atmosphere of rescue attempts that had marked her existence at Uranienborg. She might have some unfinished business to attend to at this remote hotel by the railway line towards Trondheim. Maybe this was where the valuables from Kiss Bennett's brother were handed over to the 'heirs'. Regarding this private settlement Gade writes: 'Allegedly a considerable amount of these objects were settled on Mrs Magids to ensure she kept quiet.'

Bess was back in Oslo by 20 July. On her return to the capital she bought two jewel cases and a wallet. Certain repairs at the jewellers cost her a total of 1,000 crowns.

Under her own name Bess Magids drew 'for Engebret Amundsen' two large amounts in dollars from the Oslo Savings Bank, equal to a return ticket to the United States. In addition she transferred a smaller sum to Magids in Russia. In total, during the twenty days the fiancée's visit lasted, the polar explorer's account was debited to the tune of 8,210 crowns, a staggering amount by today's standards. Of course it is reasonable that the woman who came to share the rest of her life with Roald Amundsen was able to leave the country without immediate financial worries. In addition to the cash she took considerable valuables out of the country. For excess baggage she paid 104 crowns, an astonishing additional expense, and more than half the cost of her ticket to Paris.

For Bess Magids marriage to Roald Amundsen was now a thing of the past. The tiny, energetic beauty never had the honour of being referred to as the South Pole conqueror's consort.

Following the death of Sam Magids she became joint owner of Magids Brothers and resumed the busy trading activities in northern Alaska. In 1931 she married the seven years her junior sports reporter Art Chamberlain. By him she had her only child, a daughter, Patricia, who was born in 1933. After a few years she divorced Chamberlain and married the Alaskan pilot John Cross. But this marriage did not last either.

When her brother-in-law Boris died in 1944 Bess took over the entire trading empire with all its subsidiary activities, among them the continent's northernmost fox farm. In addition, she was politically active and served a period in Alaska's legislative assembly, as a Democrat.

Elizabeth Magids, who in turn used the names Cross and Chamberlain, died in Seattle in 1971. Three years earlier she probably sold the majority of Roald Amundsen's silver objects to the Norwegian-American Olav Lillegraven from Juneau. She concluded the dispatch note, in which she referred to the love story, with this statement: 'These silver objects are of great sentimental value to me; they are of greater historical significance to the world.' In 1976 the Lillegraven couple donated the objects to the Roald Amundsen Museum at Svartskog. Thus the silver circle was completed; the gold ring never materialised.

The summer of 1928 had been the most magical interlude in Bess Magid's magical life. Her entire life reads like fantasy. The beautiful poker-player had gambled on winning the polar explorer's heart. She inevitably lost that prize, but she escaped with considerable sums. For that she lost her place in the history of Roald Amundsen's life.

Bess Magids had two more communications from Uranienborg after she left Paris. The last telegram she received in New York on 31 August 1928. That day a French float had been found drifting in the sea off Tromsø.

FORTY-NINE

The Triumph of Defeat

On 31 August a float was found drifting in the sea near Torsvåg north of Tromsø. It was quickly ascertained that it originated from *Latham 47*. The float was patched exactly as it had been during the sea-plane's overhaul in Bergen. Here was the evidence that Roald Amundsen and his five colleagues had crashed into the sea. Only now was there a gradual running down of the rescue operation. The French naval vessel *Strasbourg*, Norway's *Tordenskjold*, the *Italia* expedition's mother ship *Citta de Milano*, the American Miss Boyd's expedition with *Hobby* with Riiser-Larsen on board, the Russian *Krassin*, *Velsekari*, where Captain Wisting had taken over the command from Gran – all these and a host of other boats, with or without aeroplanes, disappeared from northern waters. From now on the question was not about finding survivors but rather more about wreckage. Whalers and fishing smacks continued to keep watch, and there were many who believed that Roald Amundsen would one day turn up. Or, many asked the question, had he maybe left this unfair world to start a new life in some undefiled and pure Arctic solitude?

On 13 October a petrol tank was found, this time south of Tromsø. The plywood float was a reminder of the solidity of the sea's surface; the petrol tank had another story to tell. An attempt had been made to stop it with a wooden bung, hastily whittled into shape with a knife. Probably once the accident was a fact the crew had made a valiant attempt to substitute an empty petrol tank for the broken wing float. It was alleged that the seaplane's second-in-command had witnessed such a solution successfully applied during an earlier accident.

Eventually it became possible to form a picture of what had happened. It had been ascertained that *Latham 47* had been observed from a fishing smack on its way into a foggy area. The pilot had feared fog from the east and had set a more westerly course towards Spitsbergen. Inside the fog bank, where, with the instruments of the time it would have been difficult to hold a steady course, a strong wind was blowing. The conclusion of the investigating committee, as expressed by Captain Hovdenak, points towards weather as the cause of the accident. 'The critical fog and bad-weather area was such that it was not possible to observe conditions from meteorological stations, and an unavoidable fate has led the seaplane into the accident.'

After *Latham 47* had been forced down onto a rough ocean, the crew would have experienced a ghastly period. It might have been short or it might have been long. One would like to believe that the sea-plane, having lost the float and after an unsuccessful attempt to repair it, quickly keeled over in the high waves and the six would have perished swiftly in the cold water.

Riiser-Larsen, who had personally studied the petrol tank, was not convinced that death came quickly. Kiss Bennett was never in doubt: 'I am sure he died a slow death.'

In Roald Amundsen's universe there were two deciding factors: human calculation and God's will. Time and again, from *Belgica* to the *Norge* expedition, the Almighty had intervened and directed the waves of the sea, the winds from heaven and fog banks. His protection had never failed. This last time He had placed the 'critical fog and bad-weather area' in a place where no human instrument could find it.

It would soon become clear that never had such a timely miracle befallen Roald Amundsen; there was no more for him to gather from the surface of the earth. The polar explorer had achieved martyrdom. At last he could seal his worldly triumphs with an even greater victory: the spiritual victory. Roald Amundsen followed in the footsteps of Sir John Franklin and Sir Robert Scott and took his seat in the heavenly hall of fame. He had given his life to save another's, in the battle to save his enemy.

In connection with the Hall of Memory for fallen Norwegian sailors from the First World War, Roald Amundsen had uttered these words just a few months before his own death at sea: 'They followed the call of their native country and carried out great deeds under Norway's flag – they joyfully sacrificed all, yes, even life.' Roald Amundsen joyfully gave all. Indeed, he had not much to lose when he disappeared beneath the waves during the evening of 18 July 1928. He had everything to gain.

It is said that when Umberto Nobile was being brought ashore in northern Norway, the quay was packed with people but no one would catch the ship's hawser. After his return to Italy he was judged a man without honour by an investigative committee and stripped of his general's rank. Umberto Nobile was forced into exile and only allowed home following the collapse of the fascist regime. He had a heavy cross to bear right up to his death at the age of 93. The Norwegian's martyrdom did not make it easier.

Roald Amundsen had, in this his last confrontation with the world, appropriated the hero's role which Mussolini had kept in readiness for General Nobile. He had staked his all and the gods had been on his side. The triumph was total. With one stroke Roald Amundsen had triumphed over all his enemies. From now on no one could question his moral right.

The Italian Minister in Norway, the man who on behalf of Mussolini had rejected a rescue mission led by Roald Amundsen, was forced to admit defeat publicly. 'A tragic accident has robbed his native country of a man who is loved and honoured by all, but this sad end has given Norway an immortal hero and for Italy Roald Amundsen will forever stand as one of the world's greatest men.'

After her stay in Norway Kiss Bennett returned to London and Leigh Court in the autumn of 1928. In front of her lay a long and unusually eventful life.

Her husband too, Charles Peto Bennett, lived to a ripe old age. Their sons Alfred and Peto both married the Norwegian friends Helle Huitfeldt and Olga Olsen in 1935. On the day of liberation, 8 May 1945, two British sea-planes landed outside Oslo. On board was the Allied Military Commission which was charged with taking over occupied Norway on behalf of the victorious Allies. One of the Commission's four members was Squadron Leader Peto Bennett. The reception Kiss's youngest son received during his entry into a liberated capital exceeded even that accorded to Roald Amundsen when he returned from 88° North twenty years earlier.

Kiss Bennett continued to live a life characterised by large personalities even after the polar explorer's disappearance. Queen Maud's secretary Sir Arthur Ponsonby and his wife were popular guests at Leigh Court, and in time Kiss Bennett was on friendly terms with both Queen Maud and King Haakon. At the end of the 1930s, when the Bennetts had sold Leigh Court and moved back to London, she travelled abroad with the royal couple and when war broke out and King Haakon sought refuge in England, Kiss became one of the exiled King's most intimate friends and supporters. She was among the guests at the last private party at Bygdøy Royal Farm outside Oslo on 28 June 1955. That was the evening the ageing monarch slipped on the bathroom floor and broke his femur.

The last years of his life saw the King, who was of an age with the polar explorer, released from his regency, confined to a wheelchair. Two desolate years in the wilderness, at the end of a proud life's work, after fifty years as Norway's reigning monarch.

Kristine Elisabeth Peto Bennett died as late as 1982, 96 years old, on the exclusive Channel Island of Jersey, a paradise and tax haven where she had bought a house.

Captain Gustav Amundsen the elder died suddenly one winter's day in 1930. His brave wife Malfred survived him by another thirty years. Independent of all family ups and downs she was the one who had stood closest to Roald Amundsen. Herman Gade called her 'an upright and good human being for whom R. had great respect and affection'. It was the sister-in-law who was the beneficiary of the polar explorer's will; it was her son who in reality administered the will of Norway's great hero.

If nothing else, Gustav S. Amundsen was the one who took care of his uncle's memory in the spirit of the polar explorer. One of his earliest initiatives was to encourage Oscar Wisting to write his memoirs. As the man from Horten considered himself 'the world's most stupid person' the Governor's 'governor general' wrote the book for him.

One name which was deleted from Wisting's authorised memoirs was that of Leon Amundsen. In spite of having been his brother's right-hand man and left-hand brain throughout twenty long years of cooperation, he was pushed more and more to the side in the heroic history which was Roald Amundsen. Following his defeat in the court case and the public denunciation in *My Life as a Polar Explorer*, Leon had chosen silence. When Roald Amundsen, with his magnificent death was elevated to sainthood, his brother fell into a corresponding hole.

As he had to give up Rødsten Leon bought an isolated cottage on Nesøya, on the opposite side of the Oslo Fjord. In the winter the family rented various furnished apartments in town; but the polar explorer's brother was increasingly less at home among the seething mass of humanity in town. Leon Amundsen preferred to walk around at nightfall. The summer intervals in the cottage grew in length.

During the autumn of 1934 Leon Amundsen remained in the cottage while the family moved to town; he was suffering from an ulcer and wanted it to heal on its own. When the family returned later in the autumn it was too late. He died in hospital. On South Pole Day, 14 December 1934, a notice could be read in *Morgenbladet*: 'Manager Leon Amundsen passed away in Oslo yesterday. The deceased was the brother of our great explorer Roald Amundsen and for many years acted as his business manager and agent here in Norway.'

The brother died no hero's death, in a snow storm or amid the ocean's spray; not even as an officer confronting a gun. He bled to death from an internal sore. Ultimately, Leon Amundsen too was a victim of the South Pole.

Six months after Leon Amundsen's death Uranienborg was handed over to the Norwegian government to be turned into a hall of memory and museum. Minister Gade was in charge of the handover, in the presence of the King, Prime Minister and President of the Parliament. The polar explorer had no grave; the villa by the Bunnefjord would have to make do as his mausoleum. 'Roald Amundsen is close to the heart of the Norwegian people,' Gade concluded his speech. 'It is therefore right that his home shall belong to the entire people and be preserved in holy memory of him.'

Gade himself was long since established in France. He never got the ministerial post he always desired, but no one could stop the one-time Minister in Rio from buying his castle where he wished. Herman Gade died one winter's day in 1943 in his Château du Mensil, St Denis, on the outskirts of occupied Paris.

FIFTY

Two Minutes' Silence

'One name, one people, one heart today.' Those were *Aftenposten*'s headlines on 14 December 1928. The government had decided to make South Pole Day a national memorial day in honour of Roald Amundsen. From midday until two minutes past twelve everyone, in town and country, would set aside two minutes of their lives for the polar explorer – two minutes in complete silence.

Arrangements were instituted at foreign legations and in Norwegian colonies abroad. But claims that the 'entire world' remembered the Norwegian polar explorer were a considerable exaggeration, even though that too could be read in *Aftenposten*. The Norwegian Minister in London, Benjamin Vogt, sent home the following report: 'A local Norwegian journalist tells me that he tried in vain to get various English newspapers to remember the day. The answer was always: '14 December – South Pole – no we cannot better that'.

Speeches were held in all Norwegian schools, the national anthem was sung and two minutes silence followed. The wireless had devoted the entire day to this special event. In the capital tributes to the polar explorer were broadcast to the crowds from a loud-speaker on the tower of Our Saviour's Church. Led by the King and the Crown Prince officialdom was present at Akershus Fortress, including Fridtjof Nansen, *Fram*'s Captain Sverdrup, *Maud*'s Captain Wisting and the surviving Captain Amundsen.

Aftenposten described the two minutes' silence at the old fortress: 'Everyone rises. The guard of honour lowers the Norwegian flag in front of the bust of Roald Amundsen – a deep, respectful silence sets in, only the sound of the bells can be heard, they resound, resound over the whole country, yes, wherever Norwegians live, sending their waves out into space, how far no one knows.'

The commemorative speech at Akershus was given by the badly cast, corpulent Captain Gottwaldt, the radio chief on board the airship *Norge*. Some might have been surprised at this choice. Normally the heir, the successor in the heroic line of Norwegian polar exploration, Hjalmar Riiser-Larsen, should have ascended the rostrum at such a moment. But Gustav Amundsen and son had bitterly protested against the heroic pilot 'tearfully' standing in front of the world and appealing to feelings of friendship which long ago had ceased to exist.

The predecessor Fridtjof Nansen had delivered his speech earlier that autumn. His rather enigmatic words had been broadcast to every wireless in the country; of course, Nansen's words were Roald Amundsen's real eulogy.

Throughout nearly forty years, ever since returning home from Greenland smothered in laurel wreaths as Norway's first polar hero, when a nameless 17-year-old devoured his presence from some pavement, Fridtjof Nansen's shadow had encircled Roald Amundsen's life and work. In the future the two would be measured against each other time and again. On the whole, the conclusion drawn was that the predecessor was larger than the successor. But in a few hectic phases of his career the younger man had triumphed over the Grand Old Man; the first time when he stole the South Pole; the second time when, in record time, he conquered the North Pole in an airship; and the third time when, by his heroic death, he transformed himself from an eclipsed has-been into a shining saint.

Fridtjof Nansen drew his last breath out in the open, on his veranda, in 1930; his death can hardly be called a sparkling act. By choosing the National Day, 17 May, for his funeral, his compatriots tried to turn it into a unifying event; but the pompous ceremony lacked the symbolic strength that had lifted Roald Amundsen into immortality.

Patriotism had always been polar exploration's strongest motivating force. Roald Amundsen had employed it effectively and unscrupulously. Nansen's life was as heroic; he was a striking example of how impossible it was to get an airship to take off under the banner of international scientific endeavour.

Fridtjof Nansen never mentioned the element of self-sacrifice, of martyrdom even – the attempted rescue of Nobile – in his speech about Roald Amundsen; unaffected by the fact that this was the keynote in the wave of obituaries which washed over the country. The *Latham 47* expedition became the greatest of all the polar explorer's ventures, a journey devoted neither to science nor to patriotism, but rather embarked on in the service of neighbourly love. That was when the 'significant human being Roald Amundsen showed the world the generosity of spirit which in every age will seek its equal', *Aftenposten* wrote. Nansen contented himself with noting that 'when his work was done he returned to the icy wilds, where his life's work lay. He found an unknown grave under the clear sky in the world of ice and the eternal whir of wings throughout space.'

With this interpretation, stripped of all poetry, Roald Amundsen had not set out to save another man's life; on the contrary, he was on the look-out for his own grave. For a man with Fridtjof Nansen's background in international rescue missions, it was not possible to interpret Roald Amundsen's self-centred flight as pioneering work in the service of good.

'He was a man, yes a man.' Fridtjof Nansen's eulogy tilted subtly towards rhetorical insubstantiality. He had no words in his vocabulary for 'the *human being* Roald Amundsen'; he cannot find the moral dimension; he cannot find the appropriate development in the life's work he is supposed to be praising. While he himself had progressed from physical deeds to scientific absorption, Roald Amundsen had in reality taken the opposite road. It had started so encouragingly with water measurements and magnetic observations; it ended in increasingly external acrobatics, less and less absorption.

Fridtjof Nansen's eulogy for Robert Scott and his comrades fifteen years earlier showed a totally different intensity and empathy. The conclusion was the same: they were all men. While Amundsen's manhood was based on physical feats, the essence of Scott's manliness was spiritual. The Englishman's greatest deed in the hour of death was a spiritual achievement. 'Exhausted, finished, he lies there never again to rise, the assurance of death's ice-cold eyes glaring down on him, while he quietly writes his diary.'

Fridtjof Nansen had no problems admitting that writing a diary could be as heroic a human endeavour as making ski tracks over a continent. In his enthusiasm for the Englishman's pencil marks, Nansen was willing to explain away his faulty judgements as expedition leader. What did it matter that Robert Scott led his men straight towards death as long as the *word* was brought alive out of the icy wilds?

It was different with the Norwegian: 'He was a man of deeds, one of those silent men who gets things done.'

Roald Amundsen might not have acknowledged his weak points but he knew his limitations. 'My father used to say to me when I was a little boy: never start what you cannot complete.' He was no universal talent like Fridtjof Nansen, far less a renaissance man; he was a professional Viking. He educated himself, perfected his metier. The furious pace of technology pushed him to the limits of what he could allow himself without breaking with his father's advice.

However, with such a comprehensive life's work no one can accuse Roald Amundsen of lacking versatility; on the contrary, what was lacking in the polar explorer's lifetime was rather an underlying dimension of human development, of maturity. As he passed one milestone after another and offered humanity increased geographic knowledge, he himself moved inexorably towards internal dissolution.

Roald Amundsen's achievements can be articulated in four key places: the North West Passage, the South Pole, the North East Passage, and the North Pole. Together these four constitute polar exploration's classic crown. They were the Arctic traveller's four public highways. Throughout the centuries it was these goals that had grasped the interest of the world.

Towards the end of the nineteenth century it was really only the polar regions that had not yet been mapped. To discover parts of the world was probably the greatest honour that could befall any individual.

The choice of the North West Passage had been made with confident intuition. It had more or less been discovered. All that remained was to execute the endeavour of centuries and navigate the Passage with one and the same boat. That was the case with the South Pole too; one latitude remained and the Pole would be conquered. The plateau had already been conquered by Ernest Shackleton.

To the north more complex geographical questions prevailed, but by now technical advances meant the explorer had very little time to play with. The flight to the Pole in 1925 and the airship expedition in 1926 were both succeeded, immediately, by rival expeditions. But here too, in the nick of time, Roald Amundsen snatched the prize. The North East Passage alone stands out as an 'industrial accident'. It had long since been conquered, but nevertheless complemented the end result for an explorer who had taken all.

The geographical goals he set himself show plainly that Roald Amundsen navigated with the world's outlook in mind. Attention was the shining goal of all his efforts. Thus the skier and dog-sledge handler quickly grew wings when aviation spread and all eyes were on the skies; he reported for duty when research was overshadowed by war and it thus became unbearable to sit idle at Svartskog when the world's eyes were focused on General Nobile's flood-lit ice floe. Roald Amundsen's greatest goal was not to discover the world, but that the world should discover him.

It is conspicuous how consistently he pursued his goal, from his boyhood bedroom to an early old age. Roald Amundsen remained true to his childhood ideal and to the child within. Only thus could he pursue his ideas so single-mindedly, so stubbornly, so fanatically as he did. For a child the errors were small, a part of nature; but translated into the grown man's world they became big. The older the polar explorer, the more he showed signs of the little boy who did big deeds. Ever more breakneck, ever more heart-rending in his appeal for applause, in his longing for admiring looks.

Roald Amundsen never committed himself to married life. But he was his entire life dependent on other human beings. He knew how to bind them to him, how to shove them away. He could make them into objects of idealisation, or victims of aggression. But because he lacked the ability to get into someone else's mind his relationships stayed on the level of the impersonal. That did not necessarily lessen their significance. Roald Amundsen could stand alone, but not outside public attention. A polar explorer without the Norwegian people would have been inconceivable.

'Already before midday, the time for silence, the streets were thronged with people; there were more than on any other day of celebration.' We are back to *Aftenposten* on 14 December.

Not among the prominent guests at Akershus Fortress but down among the people:

> Everyone awaits the solemn moment – at once the bells from Our Saviour, Holy Trinity and all the other churches strike up, the flags are lowered to half mast. That is the signal. All heads are uncovered, the trams stop, the workman in his wagon takes off his cap, labourers pause, remember and are grateful, a silent crowd with one thought. A moving moment; no one heeds the biting wind. The grey-haired, stooping man tears off his fur cap, a tear sneaks onto many a cheek. Silence, complete silence reigns; with greater simplicity, greater dignity we could not have celebrated our polar explorer. The man appears so alive, as large as life at such a moment; his image emerges, the clear-cut, strong-willed, dear face which has defied death so many times.
>
> The moment is over, silence is broken and the crowd continues on its way, carrying the image and name of the man in their hearts.

The many small men who worshipped the one big man is a well-known phenomenon from the Europe of the interwar years. The cult of personality would in turn leave its mark on the Italian, German, and Russian peoples. How could it find fertile soil in a democracy like Norway, in the land of the individual?

When Roald Amundsen set out in *Gjøa* Norway was still a dependency of Sweden. The people who remembered him on that winter's day in 1928 had been independent for less than thirty years. They had won their freedom on a wave of unity, carried on the dream of past glory, a belief in the future and an intense consciousness of being a chosen people with a world mission. When the battle was crowned with victory the people's pride was at its zenith. Every individual appeared to view themselves as having something of Fridtjof Nansen's stature when looking in the mirror. And behind him, Olav Trygvasson, the heroic figure from the sagas of a thousand years earlier. The psychological backlash was inevitable.

The all-encompassing unity evolved into party political disputes; class war and discord left their mark on the country's economy. The reawakened Viking nation soon turned out to be a pretty ordinary country, unfavourably situated at the margins of the world. The time of the sagas and its celebrated empire was shown to be nothing more than a few windswept cliffs, a place where the descendants of Vikings were more than busy looking after themselves.

All except Roald Amundsen. When the heroic era of Fridtjof Nansen had passed it was he who stepped forward from the wings, filled lungs and sail and blew new life into the Norwegian people's proud dreams and dearest illusions. He gave substance to the myths, shattered the country's boundaries and gave it the stature of an indefinite empire.

Bibliography

This biography is based on a number of, until now unused and to a large extent unknown, sources regarding the life and work of Roald Amundsen.

The most obviously important find was Roald and Leon Amundsen's business correspondence which saw the light of day in the 1990s at Fladstad Farm in Rakkestad, Østfold. The correspondence consists of twenty-three copious ring-leaf files and eight exercise books (each of up to 1,000 pages) which had lain untouched in a suitcase in the farm's storehouse. The entire material was generously made available to me by Ole Fladstad, Leon Amundsen's grandson.

The archive covers material collected by Leon Amundsen from 1900 to about 1916. Thus it includes the *Gjøa* expedition and the third *Fram* expedition, incoming and outgoing business correspondence, telegrams, contracts, etc. In the case of Roald Amundsen the line of demarcation between his private and professional life is difficult to draw, and the archive bears witness to this.

The remainder of the archives was in the custody of the Norwegian Polar Institute, which has kindly allowed me access. None of this has ever been used extensively with regard to researching Amundsen's life. The remaining, and considerably smaller part, takes us up to 1924. This includes the archives of Haakon H. Hammer from the period when he was Roald Amundsen's agent.

Following the break between Roald and Leon Amundsen in 1924, business functions were on the whole taken over by trustees of the bankrupt estate or by Norway's Aeronautical Association. The duties of secretary were transferred to his brother Gustav Amundsen and shortly thereafter, in 1925, to his nephew Gustav S. Amundsen. Roald Amundsen's archive, from this last period, was put at the disposal of the manuscript department of Oslo University Library.

The copies of Leon's letters to his brother make up a valuable part of the business archives; they are a contemporary account of everything that affected the polar explorer's professional and personal affairs. The replies to these letters, Roald Amundsen's letters to Leon, are in private hands. Kirsten Amundsen, Egil Behrens and Ole Fladstad have allowed me access to over 300 hitherto unknown letters from Roald to Leon Amundsen written during the period 1893 to 1924.

Occupying a unique position among Roald Amundsen's diaries, which are all lodged at the university library in Oslo, is his private diary which was only made available in 1990 and has thus never before been used for research purposes. The deciphering of this diary was the starting point for the work of this biography.

I would especially like to mention Roald Amundsen's letters to Herman Gade, a collection of more than 100 letters that are of a personal nature. This collection was donated to Harvard University in 1958 by Herman's son Gerhard Gade.

Among published sources there is reason to make particular mention of Roland Huntford's book *Scott and Amundsen*. The extensive research behind this work has been of great value for this biography.

PUBLISHED SOURCES

Books

(Reference books have not been included in this survey unless they were of special significance.)

Amundsen, Roald, *Nordvestpassagen*, Aschehoug, 1907
— —, *Sydpolen*, Jacob Dybwads Forlag, 1912
— —, *Nordostpassagen*, Gyldendalske Boghandel, 1921
— —, *Gjennem luften til 88° nord*, Gyldendal, 1925
— —, *Den første flukt over Polhavet*, Gyldendal, 1926
— —, *Mitt liv som polarforsker*, Gyldendal, 1927
Andresen, Kr. S., *Sarpsborg*, E. Sem, 1914
Arnesen, Odd, *"Norge"-færden bak kulissene*, Tønsbergs Forlag, 1926
— —, *Roald Amundsen som han var*, Gyldendal, 1929
— — and Lundborg, Ejnar, *"Italia"-tragedien på nært hold*, Gyldendal, 1928
Astrup, Eivind, *Blandt Nordpolens naboer*, Aschehoug, 1895
Austbø, Johan, *Olav Bjåland*, Fonna Forlag, 1945
Balchen, Bernt, *Kom Nord med meg*, Gyldendal, 1958
Bomann-Larsen, Tor, *Den evige sne*, Cappelen, 1993
Brennecke, Detlef, *Roald Amundsen*, Rowohlt, 1995
Brox, Karl H., *Eva og Fridtjof Nansen*, Gyldendal, 1991
Conradi, C., *Den Norske Klub i*, London, 1937
Dahl, Odd, *Trollmann og rundbrenner*, Gyldendal, 1981
Ellefsen, Einar and Berset, Odd, *Veslekari*, J.W. Eide
Ellsworth, Lincoln, *Beyond Horizons*, Doubleday, 1938
Filchener, Wilhelm, *Ein Forcherleben*, Eberhard Brockhaus, 1951
Fosheim, Ivar, *Storvilt, is og nytt land*, Aschehoug, 1994
Gade, John G., *All My Born Days*, New York, 1942
Gran, Tryggve, *Hvor sydlyset flammer*, Gyldendalske Boghandel, 1915
— —, *Kampen om Sydpolen*, E.G. Mortensen, 1961
Grieg, Harald, *En forleggers erindringer*, Gyldendal, 1958
Hanssen, Helmer, *Gjennem isbaksen*, Aschehoug, 1941
Hovdenak, Gunnar and Hoel, Adolf, *Roald Amundsens siste ferd*, Gyldendal, 1934
Huntford, Roland, *Scott and Amundsen*, Weidenfeld & Nicolson, 1979
— —, *Roald Amundsens oppdagelsesreiser i bilder*, Grøndahl, 1988
Høyer, Liv Nansen, *Eva og Fridtjof Nansen*, Cappelen, 1954
— —, *Nansen og verden*, Cappelen, 1955
Imbert, Bertrand, *Le Grand Défi des Pôles*, Gallimard, 1987
Lindbæk, Lise, *Brennende jord*, Tiden, 1958
McKee, Alexander, *Ice Crash*, Souvenir Press, 1979
Nansen, Fridtjof, *Paa ski over Grønland*, Aschehoug, 1890
— —, *Fram over Polhavet*, Aschehoug, 1897
— —, *En ferd til Spitsbergen*, Jacob Dybwads Forlag, 1920
— —, *Nansens røst*, Jacob Dybwads Forlag, 1942
— —, *Brev*, Universitetsforlaget, 1961
Nobile, Umberto, *Med "NORGE" over Nordpolen* (trans. Helge Rabben), Cappelen, 1976
Omang, Reidar, *Norsk utenrikstjeneste*, Gyldendal, 1955, 1959
Paulsen, Jon Bøe, *Under sydkorset*, JBP Forlag, 1986
Payer, Julius von, *Die österreich-ungarische Nordpol-Expedition in den Jahren 1872–1874*, Vienna, 1876

Peary, Robert E., *The North Pole*, Hodder & Stoughton, 1910
Riiser-Larsen, Hjalmar, *Femti år for kongen*, Gyldendal, 1957
Sjparo, Dmitrij and Sjumilov, Aleksandr, *En russisk sjømann på "Fram"*, Progress/Falken, 1990
Sundt, Hans, *Innen alt går i glemmeboken*, Tønsberg Aktietrykkeri, 1968
Sverdrup, Harald U., *Tre aar i isen*, Gyldendal, 1926
Veel, Haakon Anker, *Roald Amundsen – Slekt og miljø*, E. Sem, 1962
Wilse, Anders B., *Norske landskap og norske menn*, Tanum, 1943
Wisting, Oscar, *16 år med Roald Amundsen*, Gyldendal, 1930
Zapffe, Fritz G., *Roald Amundsen*, Aschehoug, 1935
Østvedt, Einar, *Hjalmar Johansen – et liv i dåd som endte i tragedie, hvori gjengitt H. Johansens dagbok fra Sydpolferden*, Selskapet for Skiens bys vel, 1978
Aas, Ingebret, *Roald Amundsens stamfedre Borgarsyssel Museum og "Roald Amundsens minne"*, Borgarsyssel Museum, 1941

Articles

Bjaaland, Olav, 'Med Amundsen til Sydpolen, Dagbokblad', *Syn og Segn*, hefte 1, 1975
Gran, Tryggve, 'Roald Amundsens siste flukt', *Hjemmet*, 20 October 1928
Nielson, Haakon B. 'Fest for Amundsen og hans mænd', *Aftenposten*, 23 November 1972
Royal Automobile Club Journal, November–December, 1912
Sverdrup, Harald U. 'Et efterord', *Roald Amundsens oppdagelsereiser*, Gyldendal, 1930
Vaage, Jakob, 'Roald Amundsens første skiturer til fjells', Skiforeningens årbok, *Snø og Ski*, 1954

Newspapers

Material from Norwegian and foreign newspapers has been used including material from the newspaper archives at Oslo Municipal Museum, Norwegian Polar Institute and Drammen Public Library. The following newspapers were examined at Oslo University Library and Drammen Public Library:

Aftenposten, Oslo
Dagbladet, Oslo
Kysten, Christiania
Morgenbladet, Oslo
Nordlys, Tromsø
Tidens Tegn, Oslo

UNPUBLISHED SOURCES

Abbreviations

HL Houghton Library, Harvard University, Cambridge, Mass.
NB Nasjonalbibilioteket, Oslo
NSM Norsk Sjøfarstmuseum, Oslo
RA Riksarkivet, Oslo
SA Statsarkivet, Oslo

Diaries

Roald Amundsen: Belgica, 1897–99 (NB); Travelog, 1899–1900 (NB); Gjøa, 1903–6 (NB); Sledge diary from Gjøa, 1904–6 (NB); the Third Fram Expedition, 1910–12 (NB); Sledge diary from the South Pole, 1911–12 (NB); Maud, 1918–21 (NB); Maudheim, 1922–3 (NB); Private diary, 1924–5 (NB); Expedition diary from the polar flights, 1925, 1926 (NB); Desktop diary, 1928 (NB)
Hassel, Sverre: Diary from the Second Fram Expedition, 1910–12 (NSM); Sledge diary from the South Pole, 1911–12 (NSM)
Nilsen, Thorvald, diary from the Third Fram Expedition, 1910–12 (NSM)
Ristvedt, Peder, diary from Gjøa, 1903–6 (NSM)
Wiik, Gustav J., diary from Gjøa, 1903–6 (NSM)

Letters, telegrams, manuscripts, accounts and other documents

Roald and Leon Amundsen's business archives, *c.* 1900–1916 (private)
Roald and Leon Amundsen's business archives, *c.* 1916–1924 (NB)
Roald Amundsen's letter to Leon (private)
Letters to and from, all concerning Roald Amundsen (NB)

Individual collections of letters from Roald Amundsen to:

Bennett, K.E. (private)
Christophersen, Don Pedro (NB)
Gade, F. Herman (HL)
Gudde, Niels (private)
Gudde, Trygve (private)
Hammer, Haakon H. (NB)
Maus, Gudrun (private)
Nansen, Fridtjof (NB)
Ristvedt, Peder (NSM)
Roll, Jacob (NB)

Amundsen, Leon, letter to Herman Gade (HL)
Aurdal, Lars, letter to Bodil Nævdal (private)
Bennett, K.E., letter to Trygve Gudde (private)
Board of Trustees for R.A.'s house, accounts concerning Mr and Mrs Lillegraven's gift (NB)
Borchgrevink, Carsten, letter to Hugo Mowinckel (private)
Castberg, Leif, papers (private)
Cross, Bess Magids, letter to Rosellen and Olav Lillegraven (NB)
Freud, Sigmund, exchange of letters with Dr Otto Kratter (Bergen University Library)
Gade, F. Herman, letter to Roald Amundsen (HL)
Gade, F. Herman, letter to Albert Balchen (private)
Hammer, Haakon H., archive of Roald Amundsen's polar flight, 1924 (NB)
Johansen, F. Hjalmar, letter and telegram to his wife (private)
Magistrate in Follo, papers concerning Roald Amundsen's bankruptcy (SA)
Magistrate in Follo, papers, accounts, addendums concerning Roald Amundsen's estate, 1936 (SA)
Nansen, Alexander, letter to Fridtjof Nansen (NB)
Nansen, Alexander, papers concerning Roald Amundsen (NB)

Norwegian Aeronautical Association Ltd for Amundsen-Ellsworth's polar flight, 1925, 1926, archives (NB)

Norwegian Legation in London, archives (RA)

Oslo High Court case material concerning case no. 424, Leon Amundsen *v.* Roald Amundsen's bankruptcy (SA)

Police station, duty journal, 1938–9 (SA)

Riiser-Larsen, Hjalmar, papers (RA)

Sverdrup, Harald U., Roald Amundsen, biographical sketches (NB)

Sverdrup, Harald U., letter to and from Vilhelm Bjerknes (NB)

Sverdrup, Harald U., letter to Harald Grieg (Gyldendal)

Zapffe, Fritz G., papers (NB)

The papers in private ownership have been made available by Johan Leon Amundsen, Kirsten Amundsen, Nesøya; Egil Behrens, Porsgrunn; Berit Brynhildsen, Tjøme; Valerie Farnes, Oslo; Ole Fladstad, Rakkestad; Trygve Gudde, Trondheim; Arne Maus and Petter Maus, Nesodden; Bodil Nævdal, Oslo; Torfinn Pettersen, Nittedal.

Oral sources

In my work on this book a large number of people have given me invaluable information. I have had in-depth conversations and interviews with: Kirsten Amundsen and Johan Leon Amundsen, Nesøya; Alfred Bennett, London; Patricia Clark, Fairbanks; Valerie Farnes, Oslo; Helge Ingstad, Oslo; Petter Maus, Nesodden.

Index